WHITE PEOPLE IN SHAKESPEARE

RELATED TITLES

The Arden Research Handbook of Contemporary Shakespeare Criticism
Edited by Evelyn Gajowski
978-1-3503-2750-4

The Arden Research Handbook of Shakespeare and Adaptation
Edited by Diana E. Henderson and Stephen O'Neill
978-1-3501-1030-4

The Arden Research Handbook of Shakespeare and Social Justice
Edited by David Ruiter
978-1-3501-4036-3

British Black and Asian Shakespeareans, 1966–2018
Jami Rogers
978-1-3501-1292-6

Othello: The State of Play
Lena Cowen Orlin
978-1-4081-8456-1

Shakespeare and Postcolonial Theory
Jyotsna G. Singh
978-1-4081-8554-4

WHITE PEOPLE IN SHAKESPEARE

ESSAYS ON RACE, CULTURE, AND THE ELITE

Edited by Arthur L. Little, Jr.

THE ARDEN SHAKESPEARE
LONDON • NEW YORK • OXFORD • NEW DELHI • SYDNEY

THE ARDEN SHAKESPEARE
Bloomsbury Publishing Plc
50 Bedford Square, London, WC1B 3DP, UK
1385 Broadway, New York, NY 10018, USA
29 Earlsfort Terrace, Dublin 2, Ireland

BLOOMSBURY, THE ARDEN SHAKESPEARE and the Arden Shakespeare logo are trademarks of Bloomsbury Publishing Plc

First published in Great Britain 2023
Reprinted in 2023

Copyright © Arthur L. Little, Jr. and contributors, 2023

Arthur L. Little, Jr. and contributors have asserted their right under the Copyright, Designs and Patents Act, 1988, to be identified as the authors of this work.

For legal purposes the Acknowledgements on p. xv constitute an extension of this copyright page.

Cover design: Tjaša Krivec

All rights reserved. No part of this publication may be reproduced or transmitted in any form or by any means, electronic or mechanical, including photocopying, recording, or any information storage or retrieval system, without prior permission in writing from the publishers.

Bloomsbury Publishing Plc does not have any control over, or responsibility for, any third-party websites referred to or in this book. All internet addresses given in this book were correct at the time of going to press. The author and publisher regret any inconvenience caused if addresses have changed or sites have ceased to exist, but can accept no responsibility for any such changes.

A catalogue record for this book is available from the British Library.

Library of Congress Cataloging-in-Publication Data.

Names: Little, Arthur L., editor.
Title: White people in Shakespeare : essays on race, culture and the elite / edited by Arthur L. Little, Jr.
Description: London ; New York : The Arden Shakespeare, 2023. | Includes index.
Identifiers: LCCN 2022026608 | ISBN 9781350285668 (paperback) | ISBN 9781350283640 (hardback) | ISBN 9781350283664 (ebook) | ISBN 9781350283657 (epub) | ISBN 9781350283671
Subjects: LCSH: Shakespeare, William, 1564-1616–Criticism and interpretation. | White people in literature. | English drama–Early modern and Elizabethan, 1500-1600–History and criticism.
Classification: LCC PR2992.W45 W45 2023 | DDC 822.3/3–dc23/eng/20220920
LC record available at https://lccn.loc.gov/2022026608

ISBN: HB: 978-1-3502-8364-0
PB: 978-1-3502-8566-8
ePDF: 978-1-3502-8366-4
eBook: 978-1-3502-8365-7

Typeset by RefineCatch Limited, Bungay, Suffolk
Printed and bound in Great Britain

To find out more about our authors and books visit www.bloomsbury.com and sign up for our newsletters.

To Peter Erickson

CONTENTS

List of Figures   ix
Notes on Contributors   x
Acknowledgements   xv

Introduction: Assembling an Aristocracy of Skin   1
   Arthur L. Little, Jr.

PART ONE: SHAKESPEARE'S WHITE PEOPLE

1   'Two Loves I Have of Comfort and Despair': The Circle of Whiteness in the *Sonnets*   29
   Imtiaz Habib

2   Staging the *Blazon*: Black and White and Red All Over   45
   Evelyn Gajowski

3   Red Blood on White Saints: Affective Piety, Racial Violence, and *Measure for Measure*   65
   Dennis Austin Britton

4   Antonio's White Penis: Category Trading in *The Merchant of Venice*   77
   Ian Smith

5   'Envy Pale of Hew': Whiteness and Division in 'Fair Verona'   91
   Kyle Grady

6   'Shake Thou to Look on't': Shakespearean White Hands   105
   David Sterling Brown

7   'Pales in the Flood': Blood, Soil, and Whiteness in Shakespeare's *Henriad*   121
   Andrew Clark Wagner

8   Disrupting White Genealogies in *Cymbeline*   135
   Joyce MacDonald

9   White Freedom, White Property, and White Tears: Classical Racial Paradigms and the Construction of Whiteness in *Julius Caesar*   151
   Katherine Gillen

10 *Hamlet* and the Education of the White Self 165
    Eric L. De Barros

11 'The Blank of What He Was': Dryden, Newton, and the Discipline
    of Shakespeare's White People 177
    Justin P. Shaw

PART TWO: WHITE PEOPLE'S SHAKESPEARE

12 'I Saw Them in My Visage': Whiteness, Early Modern Race Studies,
    and Me 191
    Margo Hendricks

13 A Theatre Practice against the Unbearable Whiteness of Shakespeare:
    In Conversation 199
    Keith Hamilton Cobb, Anchuli Felicia King, and Robin Alfriend Kello

14 White Lies: In Conversation 211
    Peter Sellars and Ayanna Thompson

15 Can You Be White and Hear This?: The Racial Art of Listening in
    American Moor and *Desdemona* 219
    Kim F. Hall

16 'The Soul of a Great White Poet': Shakespearean Educations and the
    Civil Rights Era 235
    Jason M. Demeter

17 White Anger: Shakespeare's My Meat 253
    Ruben Espinosa

18 The White Shakespearean and Daily Practice 265
    Jean E. Howard

19 No Exeunt: The Urgent Work of Critical Whiteness 277
    Peter Erickson

INDEX 289

FIGURES

1 Storming the Capitol, 6 January 2021.   3
2 Literal graphic representation of the blazon in accordance with the Petrarchan discursive tradition, from Charles Sorel, *The extravagant shepherd: or, The history of the shepherd Lysis: an anti-romance* (London: Printed by T. Newcomb for Thomas Heath, 1654).   49
3 Ira Aldridge in Whiteface as King Lear.   203
4 Illustration by Muriel and Jim Collins from *Exploring Life Through Literature* (Glenview, IL: Scott, Foresman and Co, 1951).   246

NOTES ON CONTRIBUTORS

Dennis Austin Britton is Associate Professor of English at the University of British Columbia, recipient of a National Endowment fellowship, a Shakespeare scholar and an expert in reformation theology and race theory, the author of *Becoming Christian: Race, Reformation, and Early Modern Romance* (2014) and co-editor with Melissa Walter of *Rethinking Shakespeare Source Study: Audiences, Authors, and Digital Technologies* (2018).

David Sterling Brown is Assistant Professor of English at Trinity College. His scholarship has either appeared in or is forthcoming in *Radical Teacher*, *David Bevington Remembered*, *Early Modern Black Diaspora Studies*, *Titus Andronicus: The State of Play*, *Shakespeare and Digital Pedagogy*, *The Hare*, *The Sundial*, *Shakespeare Studies* and *Hamlet: The State of Play*. In addition to being a member of the Arizona Center for Medieval and Renaissance Studies' RaceB4Race conference series Executive Board, he serves on the Shakespeare Association of America's Diversity and Inclusion Committee.

Keith Hamilton Cobb is an actor whose regional theatre credits include such venues as The Actors Theatre of Louisville, The Shakespeare Theatre of Washington DC, and the Denver Theatre Center. He has performed such classical roles as Laertes in *Hamlet*, Tybalt in *Romeo and Juliet*, Tullus Aufidius in *Coriolanus*, Oberon in *A Midsummer Night's Dream*, as well as roles in contemporary dramas such as David Mamet's *Race*, August Wilson's *Jitney*, and Lynn Nottage's *Ruined*. He is the creator of the role of Noah Keefer for the ABC daytime drama, *All My Children*, for which he garnered a Daytime Emmy Award nomination, and is the writer of *American Moor*.

Eric L. De Barros is an Assistant Professor of English at American University of Sharjah in United Arab Emirates. His research centres on the politics of embodied subjectivity in early modern literary and educational texts. He has authored several articles, and his main book project, *Shakespeare and the Pedagogy of Sexual Violence*, endeavours to re-think Shakespeare as a socially and politically responsive educational theorist with much to teach us about the role of education in combatting sexual violence in present-day society.

Jason M. Demeter is an associate Professor in the Department of English and Foreign Languages at Norfolk State University. He specializes in Shakespeare, Renaissance literature, and African-American Literature; his interests are transatlantic and transhistorical, centring on the relationship between canonical Anglophone literature and American constructions of race and national identity. He earned his PhD at George Washington University.

Peter Erickson is the former Professor in Residence at the Alice Kaplan Institute for the Humanities at Northwestern University. His research focuses on both early modern and contemporary race. His titles include *Citing Shakespeare: The Reinterpretation of Race in Contemporary Literature and Art* (2007), *Rewriting Shakespeare, Rewriting Ourselves* (1991), and *Patriarchal Structures in Shakespeare's Drama* (1985), and several edited or co-edited volumes, *Approaches to Teaching Shakespeare's Othello* (2005), *Early Modern Visual Culture: Representation, Race, and Empire in Renaissance England* (2000), *Making Trifles of Terrors* (1997), and *Shakespeare's 'Rough Magic'* (1985).

Ruben Espinosa is an Associate Professor of English at the Arizona State University and the Associate Director of Arizona Center for Medieval and Renaissance Studies. He is the author of *Masculinity and Marian Efficacy in Shakespeare's England* (2011) and co-editor of *Shakespeare and Immigration* (2014), a collection of essays exploring the role of immigrants, exiles, and refugees in Shakespeare's England and work. He has published numerous chapters and articles, including essays in *Shakespeare Quarterly*, *Explorations in Renaissance Culture*, and *Literature Compass*. In 2018, he was elected to the Board of Trustees of the Shakespeare Association of America.

Evelyn Gajowski is a Professor Emerita of English at the University of Nevada at Las Vegas, whose primary scholarship focuses on Shakespeare, gender, and presentism, and is the author of *The Art of Loving: Female Subjectivity and Male Discursive Traditions in Shakespeare's Tragedies* (1992) and the editor of *The Merry Wives of Windsor: New Critical Essays*, with Phyllis Rackin (2015), *Presentism, Gender, and Sexuality in Shakespeare* (2009); and *Re-Visions of Shakespeare: Essays in Honor of Robert Ornstein* (2004). She is also the Series Editor of the Arden Shakespeare and Theory Series (2015–).

Katherine Gillen is an Associate Professor of English at Texas A&M University–San Antonio. She is the author of *Chaste Value: Economic Crisis, Female Chastity, and the Production of Social Difference on Shakespeare's Stage* (2017). Her current work focuses on race in early modern drama and on Shakespeare appropriation, and her monograph in progress is tentatively titled *Race, Rome, and Early Modern Drama: The Whitening of England and the Classical World*.

Kyle Grady is an Assistant Professor of English at the University of California, Irvine. His current book project explores representations of black ascendency, racial mixing, and interracial cooperation in Elizabethan and Jacobean drama, using work from the African American tradition to situate early modern England into a longer historical trajectory of racialized thought. His scholarship has appeared in *Early Modern Culture*, *Pedagogy*, *Shakespeare Studies*, and *Shakespeare Quarterly*.

Imtiaz Habib was a Professor of English at Old Dominion University. He specialized in early modern race and postcolonial studies and is the author of

Shakespeare and Race: Postcolonial Praxis in the Early Modern Period (2000), as well as the groundbreaking and endlessly resourceful *Black Lives in the English Archives, 1500-1677: Imprints of the Invisible* (2008).

Kim F. Hall is the Lucyle Hook Professor of Africana Studies and English at Barnard College and trustee of the Shakespeare Association of America, whose pioneering scholarship has been foundational to the field of Shakespeare and early modern race studies, for which she co-edited a special edition of *Shakespeare Quarterly* on early modern race studies in 2016. In addition to the groundbreaking *Things of Darkness: Economies of Race and Gender in Early Modern England* (1996), she is the author and editor of *'Othello': Texts and Contexts* (2006). She is also the author of the forthcoming *The Sweet Taste of Empire* and *'Othello Was My Grandfather': Shakespeare and Race in the African Diaspora*.

Margo Hendricks is the Professor Emerita of Renaissance and Early Modern English Literature at the University of California, Santa Cruz. A recipient of a number of fellowship and research grants, including American Council of Learned Societies, Stanford Humanities Center, Folger Shakespeare Library, she has written and lectured extensively on the concept of race in pre-1700 English culture and literature. Her publications focus on early modern women, race, Shakespeare, and performance. Her current work in progress is *Heliodorus' Daughters: Women of Color and the Romance Industry*.

Jean E. Howard is the George Delacorte Professor in the Humanities at Columbia University where she teaches early modern literature, Shakespeare, feminist studies, and theatre history. Besides editing six collections of essays, Howard is author of several books, including *The Stage and Social Struggle in Early Modern England* (1994); *Engendering a Nation: A Feminist Account of Shakespeare's English Histories* (1997); *Theater of a City: The Places of London Comedy 1598-1642* (2007); and *Marx and Shakespeare,* co-written with Crystal Bartolovich (2012). She is also a co-editor of *The Norton Shakespeare* and general editor of the Bedford contextual editions of Shakespeare.

Robin Alfriend Kello is a PhD Candidate at the University of California, Los Angeles, where he focuses on Shakespeare, the theatre of migration, and early modern drama in Spanish and English. His other current research interests include bilingual theatre, translation, adaptation and appropriation, prison education, and developments in Shakespeare and Social Justice as dramaturgy and pedagogy.

Anchuli Felicia King is the author of *Keene* (2020). She is a playwright and screenwriter of Thai-Australian descent. As a playwright, King is interested in linguistic hybrids, digital cultures and globalization. Her plays have been produced by the Royal Court Theatre (London), Studio Theatre (Washington, DC), American Shakespeare Center (Staunton, VA), Melbourne Theatre Company (Melbourne), Sydney Theatre Company, National Theatre of Parramatta and Belvoir Theatre (Sydney). Her play *Golden Shield* will make its Off-Broadway debut at Manhattan

Theatre Club in 2021–2022. King is currently a screenwriter on *The Baby*, a dark horror comedy produced by Sister Pictures for HBO/Sky. She is also writing on TV projects in development for AMC, Sister Pictures, BBC Studios, Warner Bros, Netflix, Easy Tiger, Lucky Chap Entertainment, Hoodlum Entertainment and the Australian Broadcasting Corporation.

Arthur L. Little, Jr. is an Associate Professor of English at the University of California, Los Angeles. His work focuses on Shakespeare, early modern race studies, and sexuality and gender studies, and he is the author of *Shakespeare Jungle Fever: National-Imperial Re-Visions of Race, Rape, and Sacrifice* (2000) and the forthcoming *Shakespeare and Race Theory* (Arden/Bloomsbury). He is also working on a book entitled *Black Hamlet: Disciplining Race, Memory, and the Geno-Performative*.

Joyce MacDonald is a Professor of English at the University of Kentucky. Her work focuses on critical race theory and history most especially in the context of sixteenth- and seventeenth-century literature and culture. Her publications include *Women and Race in Early Modern Texts* (2002) and her edited *Race, Ethnicity, and Power in the Renaissance* (1997).

Peter Sellars is a MacArthur Fellow and Distinguished Professor in University of California, Los Angeles Department of World Arts and Cultures/Dance. His work as a theatre director has gained widespread recognition over the past few decades for his transformative stagings of classical and contemporary works. Sellars is also the founding director of the Boethius Institute at University of California, Los Angeles, which invites scholars, activists, and artists to work together to explore radical ways of rethinking communities and complex issues in and through the arts.

Justin P. Shaw is an Assistant Professor of English at Clark University. He researches the intersections of race, emotions, disability, and medicine in early modern literature. Committed to both public and traditional scholarship, his work on race and disability in Shakespeare has appeared in the peer-reviewed journal *Early Theatre* and has been discussed on NPR and podcasts. He regularly gives lectures on race in Shakespeare and has consulted on exhibits for the Michael C. Carlos Museum (Desire & Consumption: The New World in the Age of Shakespeare; First Folio: The Book that Gave Us Shakespeare), and has re-developed the digital humanities project, Shakespeare and the Players.

Ian Smith is a Professor of English at Lafayette College, whose research has been dedicated to Shakespeare, race, and early modern drama, and is the author of *Race and Rhetoric in the Renaissance: Barbarian Errors* (2009) and the forthcoming *Black Shakespeare*.

Ayanna Thompson is a Regents Professor of English at Arizona State University, the Director of the Arizona Center for Medieval & Renaissance Studies, and a recent inductee to the American Academy of Arts and Sciences. She is the author of several books, including *Blackface* (2021), *Passing Strange: Shakespeare, Race, and*

Contemporary America (2011), and *Performing Race and Torture on the Early Modern Stage* (2008). Thompson is also a Shakespeare Scholar in Residence at The Public Theatre in New York and chairs the Council of Scholars at Theatre for a New Audience.

Andrew Clark Wagner is a recent PhD Recipient in English at the University of California, Los Angeles, where he completed a dissertation entitled, 'Racial Prosthesis: Properties of Whiteness in Early Modern English Drama'. His work focuses on critical whiteness studies, early modern race studies, and disability studies, with a particular emphasis on drama and performance.

ACKNOWLEDGEMENTS

This project began in earnest when I crossed paths with a fellow Shakespearean at one of those ballroom dances that only attendees at the Shakespeare Association of America annual meeting know how to pull off with aplomb and hard-to-place irony and asked her how she felt about white people. She wasn't sure. She was white, still is. She's also in this volume and one of the many people to whom this book owes a great debt. My gratitude can only fall short of the debts I owe to all those who have made this book happen, have insisted on it happening when I thought about walking away from it.

First and foremost, I must thank all the contributors here: they entrusted their essays and voices to me and worked with me, sometimes perhaps with a tad more passion on both sides than we were expecting or able to control. But in the end, we've produced this, and I do hope they all think this project does justice to their very real efforts. Even as I thank them all, I must also thank particular individuals whose contributions to this project extend far beyond even the brilliance of their particular essays. I must begin by thanking Peter Erickson to whom this book is dedicated. Peter has been relentless in his demands that I see this project through, and, of course, no one, certainly no white Shakespearean critic, has been as relentless as Peter in demanding we attend to the whiteness in Shakespeare's works and to the whiteness of Shakespeare studies. In this vein, this project owes much to my fellow Black Shakespeareans with whom I've laboured in the field for some time now and whose scholarship really provides the foundation for this project and whatever illumination one may find here: Kim F. Hall, Margo Hendricks, Joyce MacDonald, Ian Smith, and Ayanna Thompson as well as Francesca Royster who took her talents to plough elsewhere. I must give sincere acknowledgement, too, to Patricia Akhimie, Lisa Barksdale-Shaw, Dennis Britton, David Sterling Brown, Keith Hamilton Cobb, Eric L. De Barros, Kyle Grady, Justin P. Shaw, and Reginald Wilburn. Without them, nothing going on in these pages would have been possible. Many of my debts are personal even as they involve many a Shakespearean who has more formally helped me see the contours of this project.

One of the most heartfelt acknowledgements goes to the late Imtiaz Habib (his work and the man) who assured me he heard me even when I thought I didn't have a voice, and I am honoured to publish his last essay here. I miss listening to him, his brilliance, and his righteous anger that somehow always managed to make me believe that this project was a must and that I was the scholar who could make it happen. Much gratitude goes to Jean Howard and Holly Dugan, who worked tirelessly alongside me, as many of the essays collected here went through close readings, suggestions, and editing. They are aware more than most of the challenges this project has faced, and I can't thank them enough for their investments.

I owe a special thank you to others who have been instrumental to its generation, including Celia R. Caputi, Devon Carbado, Farah Karim-Cooper, Lisa Corrin, Karen Cunningham, Ruben Espinosa, Lowell Gallagher, William Germano, the late Hugh Grady, Cheryl I. Harris, Elizabeth Harvey, Sujata Iyengar, Natasha Korda, Erika T. Lin, Beverly Moss, Patricia Parker, David Ruiter, Kathryn Vomero Santos, Jyotsna Singh, Caroline Streeter, Jonathan Strong (and Scoot), Arvind Thomas, Cord Whitaker, Virginia Mason Vaughan, and Michael Witmore. A particular shoutout goes to Evelyn Gajowski who opened herself to my many questions and pleas along the way and was in so many ways a very adept strategist the many times I needed one. Special acknowledgement must be extended here, too, to recent and former graduate students from whom I am learning plenty and whose work will certainly take this and other Shakespeare and early modern conversations to new and exciting places: acknowledgements go to Sarah Bischoff, Dyese Elliott-Newton, Mariam Galarrita, Robin Alfriend Kello, Jonathan Van Niel, and Andrew Clark Wagner. I'm honoured to be a part of their discovery.

Nothing comes to fruition, of course, without real smarts and tenacity working behind the scenes. For this I owe far more than is my right to Andrea Acosta and Rhonda Sharrah for their inestimable assistance as graduate researchers and go-getters. I am grateful to both Andrea and Rhonda for taking on this project and thinking through it with me. I owe an outsized thanks to Andrea who with grace and patience has pushed me to let go of this project and turn it over to those who may wish to read it; this project bears her imprint. My research for the Introduction and my knowing what questions to put to the contributors have been greatly enhanced by University of California, Los Angeles English Department librarians, Lynda Tolly and Hillary Gordon, whose generosity, creativity, and kindness I have been an appreciative recipient.

Very much a part of those who must be thanked here are Mark Dudgeon, Lara Bateman, and Margaret Bartley and their ongoing work with me at The Arden Shakespeare. Their support for this project has been immense and their belief in its importance has been inspiring. Their attentiveness to the details of the essays collected here has been sobering. The Introduction and all the contributions here have greatly benefited from their expertise as well as that of the many anonymous readers, who took their task quite earnestly and made the entire manuscript better for it. My gratitude here extends, too, to those who have taken care of everything from its editing to its design to its distribution.

These are only the beginning of the intellectual debts I've accrued to make this project real. I must also thank those institutions and forums that have provided me with opportunities to engage others about the work going on here, including the Shakespeare Association of America, the Shakespeare Globe Centre in London, The Folger Library, the Shakespeare Institute in Stratford-upon-Avon, RaceB4Race, the University of Oklahoma, the University of Arizona, the University of California at Riverside, the University of Maryland, the University of Chicago, and the Keefe Colloquium in the Public Humanities at Lafayette College, among others. I would also like to acknowledge University of California, Los Angeles Center for 17th and 18th Century Studies as well as University of California, Los Angeles faculty research grants programme for some crucial assistance with this project.

Finally, I must thank all those who have listened to me go on about it at various stages and whose friendships have been, I hope, not too tested by my obsessions with respect to it. As always, I must thank Gary Cestaro (who has also generously brought his own academic expertise to reading a draft of the Introduction) and James Hardeman, without whom so much in my life would be less memorable and certainly less vivid. They are both an intimate part of this project in ways that only they can truly know. I would be remiss not to offer acknowledgements here, too, to my nephews and niece (who are my life), my parents, brother Michael, sister Cassandra, and other kinfolk – because they are foundational to everything I think and feel and the motivation for everything I write.

Introduction

Assembling an Aristocracy of Skin

ARTHUR L. LITTLE, JR.

Noting of the lady . . . I have mark'd / . . . To start into her face, a thousand innocent shames / In angel whiteness beat away those blushes.
    —William Shakespeare, *Much Ado About Nothing* (4.1.157–60)[1]

We have here an aristocracy of skin, with which if a man be covered . . . he possesses the high[est] privilege . . . the most perfect impunity.
    —Frederick Douglass (*London Times*, 18 July 1850)[2]

Fierce fiery warriors . . . drizzled blood upon the Capitol.
    —William Shakespeare, *Julius Caesar* (2.2.19–21)[3]

White People in Shakespeare isn't about a Shakespeare or a long list of Shakespearean characters who just happen to be white;[4] rather, it examines how Shakespeare's poems and plays actively engage in 'white-people-making'[5] and how white people have used Shakespeare to define and bolster their white cultural racial identity, solidarity, and authority. Shakespeare's 'white skin' has been staring us in the face, literally giving shape and depth to the 'human' face for more than 400 years, but relatively little critical attention has been paid to either Shakespeare's role in the making of white people or white people's making, celebrating, and weaponizing a white Shakespeare.[6] Nothing surprises here since Shakespeare is so often taken to be part of the natural order of things, a well-tuned iteration or embodiment of what it means to be us and *us* is almost always naturalized as culturally and racially white and whiteness as the natural hue of existential beingness. The fact of Shakespeare's global, representational power existing almost in tandem with a global white cultural supremacy only rendering more unremarkable or invisible a unique alliance of white people and Shakespeare, should, from a critical white studies stance, have already proven to be a rich site for critical inquiry.[7] But critical white studies, often focused on the provenance, sociology, and psychology of 'real' white people, has often overlooked the importance of representation[8] – of image-making – to the *making* of 'real' white people, which, of course, is a cultural or biopolitical category, not a biological one; and given how uncritically whiteness is delimited as a racial category, and race itself as a post-Enlightenment phenomenon, it's perhaps to be expected that critical white studies has been especially focused on the nineteenth century and later. And in Shakespeare studies, where the existence of race as a viable category for inquiry can still be subjected to overdetermined gatekeeping, a dominant scholarly community clings still to reading whiteness as an aesthetic and moral descriptor devoid of all racial signification. This volume stages an intervention in both Shakespeare and critical whiteness studies and aims to take a closer look at the complex representational construction of a 'white people' in Shakespeare's world and how white people in 'our' world have used Shakespeare in the construction of themselves as white. As many of the diverse scholars and theatre artists here have learned in completing their contributions and helping to get this volume into print, whiteness is a rather elusive construct. Even so, a mere perusal of the chapters delivered here by so many highly regarded and distinguished Shakespearean scholars and artists promises to leave even the casual reader at least aware of Shakespeare's prodigious contributions to the making of a white people and Shakespeare's unique embeddedness in white races and cultures.

SHAKESPEARE'S WHITE CAPITAL

The long history of white people seeking racial affirmation and redress through Shakespeare, especially in the United States, was on full display on the sixteenth of June 2017, when two protestors disrupted a performance of New York's Public's Shakespeare in the Park *Julius Caesar*, objecting to what they saw as similarities being drawn in the production between Shakespeare's Caesar and a recently inaugurated, want-to-be authoritarian United States President Donald J. Trump, who was pushing for America to become an unapologetically white nation. The choice of *Julius Caesar* could not have been coincidental for either the demonstrators or the production with its almost-too-obvious provocation, given how unwaveringly this play has been used to emblematize America's white Shakespearean-Roman inheritance. America's Rome, mediated as it is through Shakespeare's play, literally canonizes a genealogical hagiographic historiography that continues to make 'ancient history into white race history'.[9] The protestors, endlessly praised by conservative media, were pushing back against a democracy whose 'state apparatus' they saw as having gone too far in its push for 'advancing and protecting rights, equality, and justice' of non-whites.[10] They knew this 'public' theatre with *its* elite Shakespeare was on the wrong side of what they understood to be the real American 'racial contract',[11] whose espousal of democratic ideals was supposed to be more lip service than real policy when it came to non-whites. They spoke, too, as resisters in an ongoing cultural war in which liberal or progressive white academic or theatre-cultural elites have been accused of marginalizing, politicizing, or trivializing Shakespeare, of committing acts of racial betrayal – *Et tu, Brute*[12] – by stealing Shakespeare from white people in the name of diversity, equality, and the like.[13] However so, this protest taking place in the refined space of a theatre whose mission focused on cultural diversity, racial inclusion, antiracism, and social justice was a mere prologue to the 'uncanny' and cataclysmic return of a demonstratively white *Julius Caesar* on the sixth of January 2021, at the other end of Trump's presidency.[14]

White nationalists, alt-righters, fascists, everyday anti-Semites, racists, and anti-elites gathered at the United States Capitol to 'stop the steal'[15] of their nation not just

FIGURE 1: Storming of the Capitol, 6 January 2021; Reuters/Leah Millis.

by non-whites but even more indefensibly by a privileged white elite whom they saw as thwarting their Caesar's will and once again selling them out to a public-relations 'democracy' campaign,[16] as it was becoming increasingly evident at the ballot box with the country's changing demographics that the United States could no longer meaningfully represent or sell itself as both a (multi-racial) democracy and a white nation. While it's quite likely very few if any of those assembled at the Capitol on that day thought of Shakespeare or theatre (though variously costumed many of them were), along with the Ides of March, the assassination of Caesar, the Capitol rioting against the Roman senators from which the Roman Republic never really did recover, resonances of a white Shakespeare haunted the insurrection. Such reverberations were inexorable, given how often Shakespeare invoked Rome as a 'touchstone of liberty and freedom'[17] and how habitually in performance, education, and politics America has ventriloquized *Julius Caesar*, as though it were America's white anthem or constitution.[18] For the insurrectionists, i.e., 'the people' rioting in 'the world's greatest democracy', the Capitol (with its ratification of the power of one's vote) was both the real and symbolic house of their white nation (Figure 1),[19] not in spite of the fact that it had been built by enslaved Black people who 'even plac[ed] with their unfree hands the Statue of Freedom atop the Capitol dome',[20] which itself pays architectural homage to a republican Rome for which America is very much indebted to England's Shakespeare. Spiting a 'liberal' white elite, a 'white-toga class',[21] who often acted as though liberty and freedom were their exclusive property, the insurrectionists insisted that their status alone as *white* people meant they also belonged to a racially and culturally elite citizenry, one willed to them (whomever their ancestors) by a white Shakespearean-Roman aristocracy. Emulating Shakespeare's 'fierce fiery warriors', the January-sixth insurrectionists, too, wanted to do more than imagine 'drizzled blood upon the Capitol':[22] five people died and some one hundred and fifty were injured. It was *white* people's Shakespearean theatre on a grand scale.

Notwithstanding, the relationship between Shakespeare and white people in America is most often not manifested as an event but enmeshed in our institutions – supporting the white racial ideologies, phenomena, and epistemologies – through which both Shakespeare and white people so often are jointly interpellated.[23] In this context, white supremacy (white cultural and racial hegemony) isn't 'the aberrant ideology of a few Klansmen but structural and routine, a systematic set of theories and legally sanctioned institutionalized practices deeply embedded in the American polity and endorsed at the highest levels in the land'.[24] Shakespeare's supposedly exemplary whiteness was of the utmost institutional relevance, for example, to the dean of the humanities in America, Ralph Waldo Emerson, who in one work portrays Shakespeare as the cultural and racial 'father of the man in America',[25] before going on in his next book, *English Traits* (1851), to draw on that genealogy and situate himself 'as a full contributor to white race theory' in mid-nineteenth-century America.[26] It was institutionally consequential, too, for Henry Clay Folger, who in 1879, his senior year at Amherst College, heard Emerson deliver a Shakespeare lecture that would eventually lead to the 1932 opening of The Folger Shakespeare Memorial Library (deliberately, just steps away from the Capitol), where Joseph Quincy Adams (a scion of the presidential Adams family), surrounded onstage by the white political, religious, capitalist, and military elite, spoke of Shakespeare as the guardian of America's white elite and of the Folger as an institution that would help protect America's racial identity from the 'menace' of non-northern European immigrants who were 'swarm[ing] into the land like the locust in Egypt'.[27] And while Adams lauded over the Folger as the bulwark of the white elite, he also took additional glee in the fact that with Shakespeare serving as the humanist 'cornerstone' of the institutional emergence of 'compulsory education' in America,[28] the white masses would at least *know* that Shakespeare was truly the property of the white elite and that as long as they accepted this reality, they, the *Herrenvolk*, would be allowed to share in Shakespeare's white capital.[29] And, as underscored by some of the chapters in this volume, the institutional – the seemingly inextricable, culturally and racially embedded – relationship between Shakespeare and white people remains foundational both to the capital of America's Shakespeare institutions, including, most especially perhaps, its colleges and universities.[30]

ASSEMBLING WHITE PEOPLE

The first known recorded use of the term 'white people' appears in Thomas Middleton's lord mayoral pageant, *The Triumphs of Truth* on October 29, 1613, where the Black King refers to all the onlookers – aristocrats, laundresses, and chimney sweepers alike – as 'white people'.[31] Whatever the Black King meant, Middleton's 'white people' was incisively oxymoronic. In early modern England whiteness belonged to the elite, not to the 'people', which as a term in early modern

England most often denoted 'those without special rank or position in society; the mass of the community as distinguished from the nobility or the ruling classes; the populace'.[32] 'People' appears more than two hundred times in Shakespeare, for example, with half of those occurring as 'the people',[33] and when preceded by an adjective rather than a definite article, the adjectives trend toward deprecation – *slippery*, *poor*, *barbarous*, *frosty*, *envious*, *rascal*, *tag-rag*, etc.[34] (This 'people' reverberates no less in Caliban's threat of 'peopl[ing] else / This Isle with Calibans' or a resigned Benedick declaring with ironic vulgarity, 'The world must be peopled'[35]) 'White', whether phenomenologically, sartorially, politically, religiously, etc., most often carried with it a sense of distinction and superiority.[36] Whiteness was, for example, very much emblematised by Queen Elizabeth I's court, creating what Peter Erickson has identified as 'a cult of whiteness',[37] in which Elizabeth's whiteness presumably radiated out to others in the court, especially those closest to her. In England's reformed theology, as Dennis Britton has argued, baptism 'fulfill[ed] the human part of the covenant', and also solidified the relationship between the 'Baptiz'd race' (language he borrows from James I himself) and, especially for the most elite, the whiteness of the soul,[38] a whiteness that could not be claimed by non-Christian or non-elite others. Moreover, the soul's whiteness extended beyond religion and into the realm of humanist doctrine, which for a privileged few, linked their whiteness to the 'light' of knowledge within. 'White *people*' was not a thing.

From the latter sixteenth century and especially through the seventeenth century, whiteness increasingly became a valuable property in itself, a perspective mapped out in detail by CRT scholar Cheryl I. Harris, whose article, 'Whiteness as Property'[39] – an essay very important to critical race and critical white theorists alike – argues that 'it became crucial to be "white", to be identified as white, to have the property of being white. Whiteness was the characteristic, the attribute, the property of free human beings', i.e., of being fully 'human'. As a property, whiteness, white skin, signalled elite status, a distinction from the lower classes 'whose work [would have made] it difficult or impossible for them to stay pale'.[40] More than a contestation between it and blackness, the way whiteness has been habitually read since the nineteenth century, whiteness becomes more visible and legible when read as contestations going on within whiteness itself. As Francesca Royster instructs us in an earlier study of *Titus Andronicus*, if we are to 'better understand the costs of white supremacy', we need to become more astute readers of 'a more complex construction of whiteness . . . that is forever patrolling and disciplining the variations within it'.[41] When Middleton announces the presence of a mass of 'white *people*', he stages something of a riotous act of his own, effectively announcing that early modern theatre had successfully stolen whiteness from the elite world of the court and delivered it to 'the people' in the streets. In brief, 'white people' emerged as a strained category that pointed at once to a white-skinned mass and a white-skinned elite, instituting a tension that persists, whether one speaks of the Capitol insurrection or an unresolved struggle between a white mass who apprehends Shakespeare as universalizing and reifying the superiority of their white identity and a white elite who claims Shakespeare as fundamentally their natural property.

It's fitting that a theatrical piece introduced this crux, since it was early modern English theatre that really transformed the English body into a white racializing assemblage:[42] rather than think of 'white people' as something that was discretely invented or created, as does Gary Taylor,[43] this volume suggests 'white people' signals a still ongoing assembling of complexes, i.e., an assemblage, that we have come to organize singularly through/as *race*. Early modern theatre was a crucial site, one of the most crucial sites in cultural history, for this white racializing assemblage. This fact alone makes it necessary for the chapters collected here to engage individually and collectively in numerous methodologies and theories, something not found in a lot of critical studies of whiteness. The theatre efficiently and affectively performed and instrumentalized the coming together, crisscrossing, clashes, infusions, and confusions, of various modalities and heterogeneous ideas, images, genres, genealogies, terms, elements, *inter alia*, as well as of religion, of philosophy, gender, class, race, geography, history, and so on, to make something (wittingly or otherwise) we can identify as 'white people'. It's fitting, too, because it was early modern theatre that had, over several decades, taught Middleton's 1613 spectators, 'a socially and morally undifferentiated crowd of English men and women',[44] that, indeed, they were 'white people'. The theatre lit onstage English bodies, painted them, and discoursed about them to the point where those looking on could with confidence and pride imagine themselves to be 'white people' whether they stood pressed together in the pit or sat separately in one of the balcony's 'lord's rooms', or, even more visibly, on the stage itself.[45] The stage and the plays performed on it were key to the racializing assemblage of white people and the mass production of them into a singular and privileged race,[46] more often more propagandistic or aspirational, of course, than 'real'.

The discursive and performative possibilities offered by the *habitus* of the theatre itself, especially from the late 1580s and up until the closing of the playhouses in 1642, operated as a virtual manual on how to go about constructing and laying claim to one's embodiment of a racialized whiteness. Ordinary spectators, like ordinary actors, could at least imagine a more self-authorised corporeality, one dramatically bolstered by vocabularies and technologies that expanded the body's presentational possibilities. The stage and its use of language, we could say, turned being English itself into a white event. These imaginative vocabularies with the assistance of various stage technologies, including lighting, could quite literally cast a new light on the freedom and whiteness of the English body. The stage made more real a through-line from the whiteness of divinity and a white interiority (e.g., the enlightened Christian soul) to a white cosmos and ecology (e.g., the moon, stars, snow) and on to one's own ownership of white skin (cosmeticized or no). Robert Weimann has argued that the 'symbolizing potential of theatrical space went hand in hand with the expansive capacity of the sixteenth-century English language for evoking, through representations, relations of gender, class, and ideology'.[47] Race should be added to this list. Virginia Vaughan insists in her study of early modern blackface performance that the putting on of blackface was far less significant than its removal: these moments, she argues, read as 'miraculous' and made whiteness seem all the more 'normative'.[48] One of the things the theatre did, more than any other medium, including the church, was to promulgate and solidify an affinity between a miraculous (celestial) and a normative (cosmetical) whiteness. The Bible, of course, could help out tremendously here as in 1 Corinthians 3:16: 'Know ye not that ye are the Temple of God, and that the Spirit of God dwelleth in you?'[49] More than this, while it's true 'the theater competed with the pulpit for both attendance and moral authority',[50] the theatre can be argued to have repurposed and celebrated the whiteness of divinity by rediscovering and redeploying it in playworlds and on stages that were as physically corporeal as they were secular.[51] Theatre (the stage and the plays) could literally and conceptually 'reconstitute' or 'remake' spectators in its 'own image'.[52] Critical white studies offers frameworks, models, and vocabularies for exploring the contributions such image-making makes to the construction of a racialized white people.

Shakespeare never uses the term 'white people', but he remains quintessentially pivotal to its formative history for a range of theatrical, historical, and contemporary reasons. He was one of the period's most prolific writers and was most especially active when the theatre – not just the Globe – was arguably at its height artistically and culturally. Of course Shakespeare was one of the main reasons why theatre enjoyed such prominence, even though we must still acknowledge a confluence of things, including the growing national importance of London, its commercial growth, the exponential rise in its population from 1550 to 1600, and the rise in its urban delights and blights, as well as the increased stature of the sophisticated urbanite for whom the theatre provided a telling space for carrying out their own corporeal, ideological, and hegemonic performances. While we can argue that 'the birth and meteoric growth of England's commercial theaters'[53] is thoroughly implicated in the *zeitgeist* of the period, we can argue with even more confidence that Shakespeare – whom fellow playwright Ben Jonson would eulogize as the 'Soul of the age' and as 'Sweet Swan of Avon'[54] – would by the end of his career become the embodiment of the *zeitgeist* of the early modern theatre world itself. And with what is now Shakespeare's 'near-mythic' status as the human through whom 'we' are all interpellated,[55] it's difficult to imagine taking a critical account of whiteness not just in the United Kingdom and the United States but globally without accounting for Shakespeare's contributions to the same.

More emphatically, this volume argues that Shakespeare's nearly unparalleled talent for assembling, rescripting, and repurposing the English body *at a minimum* opened up a phenomenological and epistemological space for the transformation of the English body into a 'magical' and 'miraculous' assemblage of whiteness, that is, into a property belonging to an assembly of a 'white people'.[56] If Shakespeare more than any other writer may be said to have stretched and shaped the possibilities of language to give us *us*, the modern human, *the* human, by 'expand[ing] the poetic range of the English language itself',[57] then Shakespeare remains key to any study of the further emergence of a 'white people' in the late sixteenth and early seventeenth century. At a most evidentiary lexical level, for example, the word 'fair' occurs more than nine hundred times in Shakespeare, often in relationship to a woman's skin and beauty,[58] and the word 'white' just under two hundred times, with many of those also referencing the 'natural' beauty of a woman's skin and beauty. Moreover, the lexical and rhetorical wheelhouse of white-people-making extends far beyond these terms, as evidenced quite conspicuously and efficiently in a few lines from Shakespeare's long poem *Venus and Adonis* (1593):

> O what a sight it was, wistly to view
> How she came stealing to the wayward boy!
> To note the fighting conflict of her hue,
> How white and red each other did destroy!
> But now her cheek was pale, and by and by
> It flash'd forth fire, as lightning from the sky.
>
> ... With one fair hand she heaveth up his hat,
> Her other tender hand his fair cheek feels:
> His tend'rer cheek receives her soft hand's print,
> As apt as new-fall'n snow takes any dint.
>
> Oh what a war of looks was then between them!
> ... His eyes saw her eyes, as they had not seen them,
> ... And all this dumb play had his acts made plain
> With tears, which chorus-like her eyes did rain.
>
> Full gently now she takes him by the hand,
> A lily prison'd on a goal of snow,
> Or ivory in an alablaster band:
> So white a friend engirts so white a foe.
> This beauteous combat, wilful and unwilling,
> Show'd like two silver doves that sit a-billing.[59]

Whiteness manifests itself here in a rich assemblage of language, eroticism, exhibitionism, the sensorial, ecological, celestial, the epical, the theatrical, and so on. 'White people' emerge from this scene as universal embodiments of the ecstatic and phenomenal universe they supposedly inhabit. The poeticized, white body increasingly comes to masquerade and operate in the early modern period as a kind of centripetal, universal-determinant force, something noted, too, in the first half of the twentieth century by E. M. W. Tillyard: 'the idea of man summing up the universe in himself had a strong hold on the imagination of the Elizabethans'.[60] More commonly than exceptionally, then, as embodied white subjects, Venus and Adonis emerge from Shakespeare's poem as racialized assemblages, claimants at once to a cosmological, singular, and aesthetic and biopolitical superiority. However, as most of the contributors here demonstrate, it's in Shakespeare's plays and on his stage, where he makes his most indelible contributions to white-people-making, where he does his most 'noting' of 'angel whiteness' (see first epigraph).

CRITICAL RECALIBRATIONS OF EARLY MODERN WHITENESS

White People in Shakespeare returns mostly to familiar plays and poems and advances early modern scholarship that has repeatedly called for a more systematic critique of whiteness in early modern English studies. Early modern critical race scholars, most notably Black and other early modern scholars of colour, have repeatedly voiced a need for a 'recalibrated historical framework, with [an] emphasis on the Renaissance as an originating moment for international cross-cultural encounters, [that would allow] us to ask the question of race, including the question of white identity formation'.[61] Even with a wealth of critical work in the field, studying race – to say nothing about studying whiteness – is met almost reflexively in early modern studies with scepticism and accusations of anachronism. Notwithstanding, scholarship does persist.[62] Peter Erickson has written brilliantly and often, for example, about Elizabeth's 'cult of whiteness' and the early modern period as an 'emergent moment [of] ... white superiority in the making'.[63] Kim F. Hall, arguably the most consequential scholar of early modern whiteness, presses as much in her monumental *Things of Darkness* (1995), where she more than carefully illustrates how a language of whiteness isn't just omnipresent in the early modern period but particular, operating 'very often [as] a sign' of race, class, and gender and that it doesn't exist apart from present-day ideologies of white supremacy.[64] And Ian Smith, working at 'the nexus of language, whiteness, nation', shows how early modern humanism as 'cultural practice' (whether as aim or effect) constructed a racial epistemology premised on white supremacy.[65] These scholars and their scholarship, along with that of so many more, provide both the groundwork and the inspiration for this volume. The recalibration for which Erickson and others (myself included) have advocated, has certainly been underway, but recalibrations of Shakespeare have been more rigorously pursued through performances, adaptations, and non-conventional casting than on the literary-critical side of things.

There are at least four intricately related reasons why critiquing whiteness proves so challenging that are particularly germane to a focus on both Shakespeare's sixteenth- and seventeenth-century England and our late twentieth and early twenty-first century relationship to Shakespeare. First, a rather entrenched belief in our own day that when it comes to whiteness there is literally *nothing* to see or critique. Richard Dyer, like many critical whiteness scholars, has repeatedly pushed back against this view, as he does when following Peggy McIntosh's critical reading of white privilege as 'an invisible weightless knapsack'. He argues that this invisibility 'is part and parcel of the sense that whiteness is nothing in particular, that white culture and identity have, as it were, no content'.[66] Such proclamations are only redoubled in the highly fraught disciplinary context of race as a legitimate subject for early modern studies, where, along with an almost reflexive reading of race as synonymous with Black, any serious discussion of 'white people' predictably degenerates into charges of critical heresy. Such critical distortions hold, for example, even as evidence abounds that English humanists and others were busily and obsessively repurposing geohumoralism (the most concentrated heuristic for articulations of race theory in the early modern period) in order metonymically to figure 'white skin' as 'an invisible badge of inherited superiority' while also insisting on its being 'unrelated to any specific disposition or body type – representative, instead, of 'humanity'.'[67]

Second, a very longstanding, overdetermined conviction that 'the [early modern] English only began to see themselves as 'white' when they discovered 'black' people',[68] as though a racialized whiteness was then, as it's so often taken to be now, without content, only existing as a response to blackness. The fact that early modern English persons' increased real encounters with darker-skinned people, especially those from Sub-Saharan Africa, contributed efficiently and exponentially to the English understanding of themselves as white does not (and should not) in itself infer that English whiteness was predicated on the real or even imaginative presence of darker-skinned or Black people.[69] However so, from the courts to the theatres to the streets, English people can be found competing, if not fighting, over whiteness with each other,[70] whether that whiteness signifies in strictly racial terms is not always relevant to the point.[71] As argued above, remaking the world into a world for a *white elite mass* had less immediately to do with any black–white racial difference than with stabilizing a distinction between those with white-skin pretensions and those who thought of themselves as truly possessing 'white skin' (even if it could only be fully realized figuratively or cosmetically). Distinguishing between those who could truly claim whiteness as a property and those who were to some degree impersonators became a matter of art as much as it did early modern 'science'.

Third, perhaps ironically, the representational success of white-people- *and* white-world-making. Contemporary readers and audiences' affective and epistemological grasp of early modern whiteness is, in fact, quite coloured, that is to say, very much mediated through several centuries of the representational history of white-people- and white-world-making, by which I mean the history of white people representing – picturing, fashioning, and exegeticizing and historicizing about – themselves as white.[72] Dyer, who has taken on this history with adept analysis and rich illustrations, stresses the centrality of 'racial imagery to the organisation of the modern world' and offers a rather cogent history of white people picturing themselves as white, what he calls 'white makings of whiteness'.[73] Notwithstanding, his argument that 'the study of representation ... is one of the prime means by which we have any knowledge of reality'[74] deserves further nuancing, since one of the unique features of white-making is how its over-application of 'imagery' (as a broad term) directs so much of its ideological and mechanical force not toward holding a mirror up to reality but very consciously creating (a) reality, as though the imagining and imaging of white people do a far better and more efficient job of signifying who white people (or people in possession of whiteness) really are. Some of the key technologies of this history can be laid out rather succinctly. It's the white-painted skin that begins to appear in stained-glass cathedral windows of the thirteenth century that could truly get at the whiteness of the souls of saints.[75] It's the humanist text in the sixteenth century that could really reveal and sanctify the light, the whiteness within the intellect,[76] and the language of iridescence, along with cosmetics, lighting, and the fetishizing of the physically-present body on the late sixteenth- and early seventeenth-century stage that could expose the real 'miraculous' whiteness (the racialized embodiment) of the early modern English subject.[77] It's the painstaking chemical processes, gels and lighting involved in black-and-white photography and film in the late nineteenth and in the first-half of the twentieth century that could bring out what was thought to be the true realistic-white-essence of white skin.[78] Reading anachronistically, dominant critical discourse fails to register *the processes of white making through white representation* that early modern English culture went about quite openly and exuberantly. As so many of the chapters in this volume lay out with remarkable acuity, the early modern English created representations of white people and a white world that all too many latch on to in our present-day as the axiological 'ocular proof' of a white supremacy congruent with 'real' nature itself.[79]

And fourth, many white people's conscious or unconscious refusal to acknowledge, let alone let go of, an attachment acknowledge, let alone let go of, an attachment to an always elusive and idealized whiteness that always leaves those cathected to it perpetually mourning its loss, always trapped inside a white melancholia.[80] This melancholia leads most devastatingly to what Robin DiAngelo calls 'white fragility', Carol Anderson 'white rage', and Frederick Douglass the 'brutality' of 'the aristocracy of skin'.[81] (The most elephantine imbroglio, like the proverbial elephant in the room, is the imbrication of whiteness and white supremacy.) White people learning to detach themselves from whiteness remains a rather exigent and existential matter in the United States where, as Toni Morrison writes in a short piece, 'Mourning for Whiteness', shortly after the 2016 presidential election but before Trump's inauguration: 'Unlike any nation in Europe, the United States holds whiteness as the unifying force'; it's how one 'becomes . . . a real authentic American'. She understood that election to be within the purview especially of 'tough white men, who [were] prepared to abandon their humanity' in order to protect what they perceived to be the threat to their whiteness. 'These people', she argued, 'are not so much angry as terrified',[82] as they were still on 6 January 2021. Among its many aims, critical white studies tries to wean white people from a pathological dependency on the symbologies of whiteness. Far too many white people's fancy that whiteness as such can be easily disentangled or distinguished from the vulgarities of white racism only works to impede a broader embrace of critical white studies and its wish not only to get the history 'right' but to dismantle white supremacy and the elite status granted to the people who embrace it and are embraced by it. Critical white studies starts by acknowledging that racism, i.e., a conscious or unconscious adherence to whiteness, is 'not an anomaly, a deviation from the norm. Racism *is* the norm'.[83] From the perspective of the vested interests of this volume, 'letting go of' one's whiteness (even as an academic exercise) would unleash a more robust and collective understanding of why America's 'experience of loss or grieving' has so 'frequently proposed [Shakespeare] as a necessary consolation for this loss'.[84] It would permit, i.e., uncensor, more earnest answers in the academy to a question posed by Marjorie Garber: 'What is it about the humanities in general and Shakespeare in particular that calls up this nostalgia for the certainties of truth and beauty – a nostalgia that, like . . . *all* nostalgias, is really a nostalgia for something that never was?'[85] Whatever the answers, they have much to do with the fetishization of a white Shakespeare by a white humanities – as opposed to a more open encounter with a less overdetermined Shakespeare by a more pluralistic humanities – and with the unmistakable and uncanny authority of a white Shakespeare, say, at the United States Capitol.

The fact that Shakespeare as cultural capital protects whiteness as much as whiteness protects 'Shakespeare' renders all the more difficult the kind of interrogations of whiteness the contributors to this volume have set out to make.[86] When (as in the Introduction's first epigraph), twenty-first century readers and audiences witness Friar Francis making much ado about the 'angel whiteness' of Hero's white skin in Shakespeare's *Much Ado about Nothing* (admittedly, an all-too-ironic title here),[87] centuries of white-making and safeguarding Shakespeare have already sublimated the ideological and mechanical (i.e., poetic) underpinnings that have naturalized and made real the whiteness of white skin and made it synonymous with innocence, upper-classness, the ethereal, and the elite. Can we reject with any seriousness, however, the resonance between Friar Francis and Franz Fanon, beyond the alliterative, when the latter, not necessarily thinking about Shakespeare, wants 'to lay bare little by little' the dire real-world consequences of attributing to whiteness 'the bright look of innocence, the white dove of peace, magical, heavenly light'?[88] The fact that 'Whites are deified' has very real-world consequences:[89] 'O, the more angel she, / And you the blacker devil!'[90]

THE CHAPTERS: SHAKESPEARE'S WHITE PEOPLE

There are countless individual reasons why the scholars and artists in this volume have persisted in their critical efforts to engage this seemingly intractable topic, including our local need for a collective but diverse response to the global rise of white supremacy violence and a need to understand our accountability in the ongoing reproduction of Shakespeare, whose texts and person have been complicit not just in a representational but a 'real' history of white-people-making. Whether focused on Shakespeare's texts or on those persons or entities that have racially weaponized Shakespeare, many of the contributors here contemplate Shakespeare as a site for racial and social justice work and more specifically for antiracist contravention.[91] Even more, they attend to how Shakespeare can serve as costume, as 'racism in drag', a justification for the aestheticizing and humanizing of white supremacy, of culturally warranted discriminations.[92] The scholars and artists assembled here argue that it's urgent we begin to grasp more critically than we do now the histories of white-making that are deeply embedded in our shared 'humanity' and in the elitism of our humanities. For these reasons more than any other, this book's title points its readers quite deliberately not to 'whiteness' (which as a word sounds suspiciously ameliorative) but to 'white people' (signalling a more privileged as well as a more deleterious way of relating to the world), which, as a term, often seems more accusatory and aims here, perhaps counterintuitively, to encourage white readers to resist defensive posturing and instead work towards embracing critical introspection.[93] In order to model critical paths forward for talking about white people in Shakespeare, whether in his texts or in the Shakespeare industry, it's important 'white people' does not read as a neutral descriptor emptied of its cultural and racial grounding in white supremacy.

White People in Shakespeare's bifurcated attention to Shakespeare's white people (Part I) and white people's Shakespeare (Part II) intends to make far more conspicuous both the workings of whiteness in Shakespeare's texts and, while not necessarily inexorably connected (white racial history could have played out differently), the way Shakespeare has been interpellated into white identity. Still, the dyadic structure isn't meant to suggest we think of these parts as engaging in fundamentally different conversations. Many of the contributors here, for example, make evident a need for a broader cross-historical and cross-cultural critical view. Katherine Gillen, for example, exposes and traces a white historiography as she studies *Julius Caesar* by reading back from John Wilkes Booth's invocation of Shakespeare's text just after he assassinates Abraham Lincoln. Eric DeBarros examines white self-fashioning in early modern humanist education by analysing *Hamlet* and suggesting how these early habits of thought are still with us. Andrew Clark Wagner notes, albeit in passing, a connection between Shakespeare's *Henriad* and the Ku Klux Klan, as he close reads the former. The first part moves loosely from skin to desire to lamentation and the second from the theatre to the polity to the university.

The late Imtiaz Habib (Chapter 1) brings the volume full circle even as he opens it, arguing that 'in sonnet, lyric, and stage play, whiteness's triumph must be flawed, not for it to be abandoned but to be iterated again'.[94] Attending to white-skin trafficking in Shakespeare's circle of desire, patronage and loss, his chapter helps us see much more vividly the shift of an elite whiteness from the aristocracy proper to the masses crammed in early modern playhouses. Some of these issues extend to Evelyn Gajowski (Chapter 2), whose study of the blazon extends the poetic focus of Habib's chapter, even though she's especially invested in the encounter between the poetically formal and the stage. While noting the significance of white skin in medieval and religious romance traditions, Gajowski focuses her reading on *Othello* and Elizabeth Cary's *The Tragedy of Mariam*, arguing that the white/red schema of Petrarchan poetry 'collide' with a black/white schema that plays out as a story of martyrdom on the early modern stage. Dennis Britton (Chapter 3), who is also interested in martyrdom, studies Isabella's white skin (*Measure for Measure*) and contextualizes it in a broader discussion of female virgin martyrs, the staining of whose white skin with red blood pushes the Christian witness to 'affective piety', which, Britton argues, cannot be decoupled from the whitening of Jesus in Western art nor from 'the doctrines of white supremacy that justified conquest and slavery'. His argument, that Shakespeare's *Measure for Measure* reassures its audience that they may not be saints but their white skin does have the *unique* capacity for saintliness and martyrdom, suggests one of the ways early modern theatre helped expand whiteness to a more general English audience.

While sexual desire permeates all three of the chapters discussed so far, it's a more pronounced topic in the three chapters that follow, beginning with Ian Smith (Chapter 4) turning his critical gaze to Antonio's 'fair flesh' in *The Merchant of Venice*, i.e., Antonio's penis. Smith's chapter looks closely at 'an alignment of whiteness and heteronormativity' that he sees as 'coincident with commerce, interest and reproduction in the Venetian capitalist economy': Antonio's 'non-reproductive sexuality' has blemished Antonio's whiteness. Reaching for a more theoretical view still, Smith asks whether queer studies have 'fallen prey to category trading that retains a firm investment in white supremacy?' Smith's chapter, like Habib's, emphasizes the importance of 'sexuality and race where whiteness continues to serve as political currency in the social barter of identities' (Smith). Kyle Grady (Chapter 5) insists we cannot separate whiteness as a 'ubiquitous descriptor of beauty' from 'ideologies of racial difference', as he delineates whiteness's saturation of *Romeo and Juliet*'s 'fair Verona'. He insists on reading how whiteness, like the play's pestilence, circulates in the play more as miasma than as bodily marker, leading him finally to tease out a connection between the play and intraracial rioting in Shakespeare's London. David Sterling Brown (Chapter 6) calls attention to the many times Shakespeare makes explicit mention of a 'white hand', especially as an object of desire. Doing so allows Brown to establish a critical context for reading Antony's reference to Shakespeare's Black Cleopatra's 'white hand' in *Antony and Cleopatra*. The interplay between the aesthetic and the erotic and the subtending racial politics of each of them underlie both Habib's and Brown's chapters.

In this volume's only study of any of Shakespeare's history plays,[95] Andrew Clark Wagner (Chapter 7) contextualizes the second tetralogy of the *Henriad* in the 'ever-changing [geographical and figurative] boundaries of English whiteness'. By focusing, too, on the Whiteboys and a 1607 rural uprising, Wagner shows how Shakespeare's historical cast of characters 'mark and unmark at will the boundaries of English identity and soil: defining and redefining "streams of blood" as violent symbols of conquest and seminal fountains of identity'. Also, like Habib and MacDonald (to follow), he stresses how the trope of failure activates the sustainability of a 'cultural legacy of whiteness' (Wagner). Joyce MacDonald (Chapter 8) treats some of the same issues but comes at them through *Cymbeline*, which turns out to be less about 'familial origins of dynasties and nations' than about failure, i.e., 'endings and collapse'. *Cymbeline*, she argues, 'reserves its racial anxiety for the fortunes of British whiteness' by mapping them onto a 'persistent sense of women's innate unworthiness'. She sees the bloodlines of the British elite as toggling between Rome and Briton, between 'competing stories of white origins'. Notwithstanding, Katherine Gillen (Chapter 9) argues that early modern England was still very much attached to the whiteness of its Roman past. In her reading of *Julius Caesar*, she sees England as torn between two competing Roman racial models, a Republican understanding of whiteness as the exclusive property of the patricians and an imperial understanding of whiteness that extends it to common Romans 'in exchange for their submission to the imperial state'. She argues that Caesar's body is subjected to a racialized Christ-like martyrdom (cf. Britton's and Gajowski's chapters in this volume) and that Shakespeare's play 'ultimately deracinates Roman whiteness from its foundation in institutions of slavery and colonialism . . . naturalizing a classicized vision of the white humanist subject' (cf. Demeter's chapter in this volume).

Eric DeBarros (Chapter 10) deliberately moves away from historicism as he insists on reading *Hamlet*'s exploitation of blackness as 'a provocative invitation' to think about the workings of whiteness, of early modern melancholia, in early modern humanist education. He argues that Hamlet turns humanist education into 'a de-moralized technical-bureaucratic' white event, an argument worth considering, too, along with Gillen's and Demeter's chapters. More than offering another reading of *Hamlet*, DeBarros wants us to consider the workings of this technical-bureaucratic paradigm in the mutually supportive projects of humanist education and white supremacy in our own time. Justin P. Shaw (Chapter 11) closes out Part I with his close study of Antony lamenting in John Dryden's *All for Love* (1676) that he has a 'Heart a Prey to Black Despair' (1.1.60–1). (Shaw's chapter resonates quite uncannily with Habib's.) Shaw insists that Dryden, like Isaac Newton and Robert Boyle, sets out in the late seventeenth century to find 'perfect whiteness', arguing that whiteness in Dryden's play 'operates almost entirely through nostalgia and promise'. For Shaw, Dryden, who subtitles his play *The World Well Lost*, aims to rescue the whiteness that Dryden sees as having failed spectacularly in Shakespeare's *Antony and Cleopatra* (cf. Habib, Brown, Wagner, and MacDonald).

THE CHAPTERS: WHITE PEOPLE'S SHAKESPEARE

Part II of this volume opens with Margo Hendricks (Chapter 12) apostrophizing through a series of letters addressed to Shakespeare and others: she begins with some reflections on a Shakespeare conference in Johannesburg, South Africa in 1996, not long after the official end of Apartheid, where the legacy of white supremacy and Shakespeare's whiteness were as palpable at the time as they were anywhere in the world. (It was here where Margo and I really first bonded over the issue of white people in Shakespeare.) Moving from one letter to the next, she recalls conversations, professional interactions, and critical histories and imaginings that have indemnified a 'Shakespearean violence perfected on the bodies of non-white people', our being disappeared. Hendricks, like many of this volume's contributors, seeks to disrupt – perhaps with a little rioting of her own – those who have convinced themselves of white supremacy's innocence (its nothingness) when it is filtered through Shakespeare. Two conversational chapters follow. The first with Keith Hamilton Cobb, Anchuli Felicia King, and Robin Alfriend Kello (Chapter 13), who centre their conversation on Cobb's and King's plays, *American Moor* and *Keene*, respectively. While their plays explore the operations of Shakespearean whiteness within the theatre world and the academy, respectively, the conversation, with Kello, as an activist-scholar interlocutor, pushes beyond these discrete venues and allows all three of them to have a more forthright exchange about racial and social justice and how Shakespeare is so often conscripted to serve white supremacy. They repeatedly return to issues of accountability. Peter Sellars and Ayanna Thompson (Chapter 14) in their conversation weigh in on 'official Shakespeare' and the challenges it imposes on racial and creative diversity in Shakespeare theatres and companies. Like the preceding chapter and the one following theirs, they interrogate how economics, politics and white supremacy circumscribe what it is *practically* possible to do with Shakespeare in American theatre. Kim F. Hall (Chapter 15) homes in on the racialization of sound, as she closely studies Keith Hamilton Cobb's *American Moor* and Toni Morrison and Rokia Traoré's *Desdemona*, plays that are quite attuned to the operations and sounds of whiteness in the Shakespearean theatrical space. Like Habib's chapter, which opens Part I, she, too, is interested in 'the circle of humanity . . . the circle of whiteness'.

Jason M. Demeter (Chapter 16) focuses on the Civil Rights era and the anthologizing and teaching of *Julius Caesar* in public high schools in mid-twentieth-century America, where it was being taught as 'a meditation on democracy as well as an anti-dictatorial polemic', and anchored a system of conscripted education designed to promote a white supremacy genealogy (cf. Wagner, MacDonald and Gillen). Shakespeare's play, Demeter shows, manifested a through-line from the Roman Republic to Elizabethan England to America's founding documents. Ruben Espinosa (Chapter 17) takes a close look at the artistic and political uses to which Boris Johnson in the United Kingdom and Steve Bannon in the United States have put Shakespeare. Both Johnson and Bannon have fashioned themselves as Shakespeare afficionados and as proud, angry white men. One of Espinosa's main texts is Bannon's 1990s rap musical (co-authored with Julia Jones), *The Thing I Am*, an adaptation of *Coriolanus*, set during the 1992 Los Angeles riots, a failed attempt to bolster 'white rage' through the caricaturing of Black people (cf. Hall). It's noteworthy, too, that the mesh here of Shakespeare, whiteness, and racial rioting/protesting appears as well in the chapters of Demeter, Espinosa, Gillen, Grady, Smith, and Wagner.

The final two contributions offer more personal and self-reflective analyses, as they – a white woman and a white man, respectively – contemplate their relationship to Shakespeare and to Shakespeare's implication in whiteness. Jean Howard (Chapter 18), taking note of her privilege as a white Shakespearean at an Ivy League institution, offers some concrete ways such institutions and such practitioners as herself reproduce a white Shakespeare. Howard insists that white Shakespeareans need to push for a Shakespeare who is 'less confined by a white epistemology and less protected by white ignorance'. She argues that there's a need for white scholars to aim institutionally, intellectually, and pedagogically for more 'politically accountable' practices.

Peter Erickson (Chapter 19) closes this volume by demonstrating a direct connection between his scholarship and his anti-racist activism. Erickson, to whom this book is dedicated, is widely recognized as a brilliant and tenacious Shakespeare scholar who has nearly four decades of investment in critical race studies. His chapter begins by sharing details of his autobiography, including his participation in the Civil Rights Movement in the 1960s as an undergraduate at Amherst (Folger's alma mater as well) and living in Haiti as a conscientious objector during the Viet Nam War. He also describes the impact on his formation of numerous Black writers and artists, including the poets June Jordan and Rita Dove, the critic Stuart Hall, author Melvin Dixon and the artist Fred Wilson, who engaged with *Othello* across numerous works. Erickson then pivots to close read three Shakespeare plays through a highly self-aware lens formed by this personal history. His chapter concludes with a call to action, imploring us to acknowledge how systemic racism limits and indeed suppresses understanding of both Shakespeare's work and our capacity to transform the academy. He reminds us that scholarship and activism are not separate entities. His chapter is no nostalgic piece about the past; its sights are set on the future: there is *No Exeunt* for white people who suspect they want more (from) life, something more than whiteness from Shakespeare and something more than whiteness for themselves.

* * *

White People in Shakespeare, which was originally conceived as an inquiry into why some of Shakespeare's characters seem whiter than others of his characters,[96] now belongs to its readers. As the caretaker of the chapters contributed here, I anticipate our collective effort will generate at least a few conversations and, hopefully, a few more studies, and not only in early modern critical white studies or critical race studies but in areas as diverse and interdisciplinary as those things comprising the racializing assemblage of a 'white people'. The relationship between Shakespeare and white people should matter to those who wish to channel Shakespeare's representational power and authority in the direction of racial and social justice as well as those who seek further clarity about the languages and histories we activate and occupy. It's the belief of the contributors here that *as* Shakespeareans (in whatever iteration) we must hold ourselves, our institutions, and each other accountable: as *elite* cultural producers, we must own the fact that our work product doesn't tell how the world is, as much as it haunts, betraying how we truly want the world to look.

NOTES

1. William Shakespeare, 'Much Ado About Nothing', *The Arden Shakespeare Complete Works*, ed. Richard Proudfoot, Ann Thompson and David Scott Kastan (London: The Arden Shakespeare, 2011), 4.1.157–60.
2. Frederick Douglass, *London Times*, 18 July 1850.
3. William Shakespeare, 'Julius Caesar', *The Arden Shakespeare Complete Works*, ed. Richard Proudfoot, Ann Thompson and David Scott Kastan (London: The Arden Shakespeare, 2011), 2.2.19–21.
4. No other premodern Western writer – not Dante, Chaucer, Petrarch, nor Milton, for some pronounced comparisons – has come as close as Shakespeare to being so thoroughly implicated in and identified with white people as well as the whiteness of humanism. In art, perhaps Michelangelo but certainly without the broader cultural and racial reach of Shakespeare.
5. My use of this term is inspired by George Yancy's discussion of 'white-world-making' in his edited *What White Looks Like: African-American Philosophers on the Whiteness Question* (New York: Routledge, 2004), 10–11.
6. For a notable exception, see Caroline F.E. Spurgeon, *Shakespeare's Imagery and What It Tells Us* (Cambridge: Cambridge University Press, 1935), 57–66. Perhaps it goes without saying, of course, no one really has white skin: identifying oneself as white is to engage in cultural and racial signifying. It's worth remembering Richard Dyer's observation and question: 'White people are not literally or symbolically white, yet they are called white. What does this mean?' *White: Essays on Race and Culture* (London: Routledge, 1997), i.
7. With their own cultural and racial particularities and local specificities as much may be said globally for the making of cultural and racial white people both in majority and non-majority white countries, even though that focus reaches beyond the scope of this necessarily more modest project, which can only and earnestly hope to open up the critical possibilities of other such stories. For more about global whiteness, some good places to start are Alastair Bonnett's *White Identities: Historical and International Introduction* (Routledge, 2000); Veronica Watson, Deirdre Howard-Wagner, Lisa Spanierman, eds. *Unveiling Whiteness in the Twenty-First Century: Global Manifestations, Transdisciplinary Interventions* (Lanham, MD: Lexington Books, 2015); Yancy, *What White Looks Like*; and Charles W. Mills, *The Racial Contract* (Ithaca, NY: Cornell University Press, 1997).
8. Film studies has far outpaced literary studies in this area. For a rather comprehensive and brilliant overview of white people creating images of *white* people, see Dyer, *White*, throughout. See also, Nell Painter, *The History of White People* (W.W. Norton, 2010), xi.
9. Painter, *The History of White People*, x.

10. Carol Anderson, *White Rage: The Unspoken Truth of Our Racial Divide* (New York: Bloomsbury, 2017 [2016]), 6, 170–8.

11. The 'racial contract' referenced throughout this Introduction is derived from philosopher Mills, *The Racial Contract*. His full one-sentence definition is too long to include here, but it reads in part: 'The Racial Contract is that set of formal or informal agreements or meta-agreements . . . between the members of one subset of humans . . . designated as 'white', and coextensive . . . with the class of full persons, to categorize the remaining subset of humans as 'nonwhite' and of a different and inferior moral status, subpersons, so that they have a subordinate civil standing in the white or white-ruled polities the whites either already inhabit or establish or in transactions as aliens with these polities, and the moral and juridical rules normally regulating the behavior of whites in their dealings with one another either do not apply at all in dealings with nonwhites or apply only in qualified form', 11. He concludes by saying that 'All whites are *beneficiaries* of the Contract, though some whites are not *signatories* to it', ibid.

12. Shakespeare, *Julius Caesar* (3.1.77).

13. See, for example, Heather Mac Donald, 'The Humanities and Us', *City Journal* (Winter 2014): https://www.city-journal.org/html/humanities-and-us-13635.html. Accessed on 13 December 2021. Consider Mac Donald's title in relationship to the discussion of 'us' in this Introduction's opening paragraph.

14. I am not suggesting these two invents were in any way planned together. Also, my reference here to the 'return' of *Julius Caesar* gestures not to the 2017 event but to the play itself and the history within it. I'm thinking especially here of the 'uncanny' in Marjorie Garber's *Shakespeare's Ghost Writers: Literature as Uncanny Causality* (New York: Routledge, 2010 [1987]), especially her chapter, 'A Rome of One's Own', 69–97, where she argues, 'Like any instated view of a civilization and its artifacts, the idea of Rome is from the first belated, already a nostalgic and edited memory when it first appears', 70.

15. 'Stop the Steal' became a slogan and rallying cry for the insurrectionists, who were initially calling for the vote counting to stop when Trump was temporarily ahead in the vote total. Trying to steal an election by accusing the state of stealing the election required a whole host of theatrics.

16. One such milestone event was the 1954 *Brown v Board of Education* United States Supreme Court decision, which, in the name of equality, was seen by many non-elite whites, who were unable to send *their* children to private schools, as forcing them to attend the same schools as Blacks. While controversial from across the political spectrum, the decision remains a watershed moment in the history of American race relations.

17. See Coppélia Kahn, *Roman Shakespeare: Warriors, Wounds, and Women* (London: Routledge, 1997), 77–9. According to Kahn, Shakespeare invokes Roman liberty and freedom thirty-two times in *Julius Caesar* alone, more frequently than he does anywhere else in his plays.

18. See especially in this volume, the chapters by Katherine Gillen and Jason Demeter.

19. For the insurrectionists, predominantly white men, the Capitol was the site of a last stand, where they could be heard repeatedly claiming the Capitol was 'the people's

house': they presumably meant *white* people's house, since they were also hurling racial, ethnic, and xenophobic epithets at the Capitol police they perceived to be non-white and accusing the Capitol police whom they perceived to be white of being race traitors.

20. Nikole Hannah-Jones, 'Our democracy's founding ideals were false when they were written. Black Americans have fought to make them true', *The 1619 Project*, *The New York Times Magazine*, 14 August 2019, https://www.nytimes.com/interactive/2019/08/14/magazine/black-history-american-democracy.html?mtrref=www.nytimes.com&gwh=0EB3111CA7205E52FB16CB94FA7F4781&gwt=regi&assetType=REGIWALL

21. David A. Reed (Senator from Pennsylvania), writing about his sponsorship of the Immigration Act of 1924, 'America of Melting Pot Comes to End'. *The New York Times*, 27 April 1924, 3. The language he uses, like that used by Madison Grant, overlaps quite well with words and images used by Joseph Quincy Adams in Adams's 1932 Folger Library inaugural address (see note 27 below).

22. William Shakespeare, 'Julius Caesar', *The Arden Shakespeare Complete Works*, ed. Richard Proudfoot, Ann Thompson and David Scott Kastan (London: The Arden Shakespeare, 2011), 2.2.19–21

23. See Michael D. Bristol, *Shakespeare's America, America's Shakespeare* (London: Routledge, 1990), where he discusses Shakespeare as an American institution, where institution 'may be understood as an organization, a structure, or a codification of social practice', one of the 'enduring features of social life', 3; see the entirety of Bristol's introduction, 1–11. There is, of course, a critical story to be told about Shakespeare and global whiteness, but that story is beyond the reach of this particular volume.

24. Charles W. Mills, *Blackness Visible: Essays on Philosophy and Race* (Ithaca, NY: Cornell University Press, 1998), 12.

25. Ralph Waldo Emerson, 'Shakespeare; Or, The Poet', in his *Representative Men* (1850) in *The Works of Ralph Waldo Emerson, Vol. 4, Riverside Edition* (Boston: Houghton, Mifflin and Co, 1897), 201. The word 'father' is as racially indexical for Emerson, I would suggest, as it is for Frederick Douglass. For more about Douglass in this context, see David W. Blight, *Frederick Douglass: Prophet of Freedom* (New York: Simon & Schuster, 2018), 6–7, 13–16, and 746.

26. Painter, *The History of White People*, 183.

27. Joseph Quincy Adams, 'The Folger Shakespeare Memorial dedicated 23 April 1932: Shakespeare and American Culture'. *The Spinning Wheel* Vol. 12, Nos. 9–10 (June–July 1932), 212–13, 229–31; also see in this volume, Jason Demeter's discussion of Adams's speech. Adams's language was no mere flowering of prose but an interpolation of Madison Grant's *The Passing of the Great Race Or, The Racial Basis of European History* (New York: C. Scribner's Sons, 1921 [1916]), a eugenicist study much admired and referenced by American presidents, statesmen, and other elites, in which he wishes to bring 'Americans to the realization the impending menace of the impending Migration of Peoples through unrestrained freedom of entry here' (xxxiii), warning, for example, that 'the man of the old stock was . . . being literally driven off . . . by swarms of [immigrating] Polish Jews', 91.

28. Adams, ibid.
29. In a discussion of nineteenth-century America, David R. Roediger argues, '*Herrenvolk* republicanism had the advantage of reassuring whites in a society in which downward social mobility was a constant fear – one might lose everything but not whiteness', *The Wages of Whiteness*, 60; also see Roediger's discussions of Shakespeare in this context, 117, 126–7. Cf. Kimberlé Crenshaw's observation that 'throughout American history, racism has identified the interests of subordinated whites with those of society's white elite', 112: 'Race, Reform, and Retrenchment: Transformation and Legitimation in Antidiscrimination Law', *Critical Race Theory: The Key Writings that Formed the Movement* (New York: The New Press, 1995): 103–22.
30. See especially the chapters in this volume by Eric De Barros, Keith Hamilton Cobb et al., Kim F. Hall, Peter Sellars and Ayanna Thompson, Jason Demeter, and Jean Howard. Also see Rafael Walker, 'The Next Step in Diversifying the Faculty', *The Chronicle of Higher Education* (28 October 2016), https://www.chronicle.com/article/the-next-step-in-diversifying-the-faculty/, where he surveys the lack of early modern/Shakespeare Black and Latinx English professors at the top twenty PhD-granting programmes; his study could have actually extended to the top sixty, where there are currently (fall 2021) four. See also James Shapiro, *Shakespeare in a Divided America: What His Plays Tell Us about our Past and Future* (New York: Penguin, 2020). For more about the theatrical side of things, see Ayanna Thompson, *Passing Strange: Shakespeare, Race, and Contemporary America* (Oxford: Oxford University Press, 2011).
31. Thomas Middleton, 'The Triumphs of Truth', *Thomas Middleton: The Collected Works*, ed. Gary Taylor and John Lavagnino (Oxford: Oxford University Press, 2007), line 408. This section of the Introduction borrows liberally from my contribution, 'Is it Possible to Read Shakespeare through Critical White Studies?' *The Cambridge Companion to Shakespeare and Race*, ed. Ayanna Thompson (Cambridge: Cambridge University Press, 2021): 268–80.
32. See 'people' in the *Oxford English Dictionary*, II.3.a.
33. In *Coriolanus*, the most telling example, the word *people* appears a staggering seventy-eight times (more than a third of its total usage in Shakespeare) with all but three instances occurring as 'the people'. In those three instances 'people' is preceded by an adjective—'good' in one case and 'common' in the other two. Even the use of 'good' substantiates this reading of people as 'the people' or the 'common people', since the speaker only uses it to patronize and placate *the people* (3.1.281, 2.2.6, 2.3.91, respectively). William Shakespeare, 'Coriolanus,' *The Arden Shakespeare Complete Works*, ed. Richard Proudfoot, Ann Thompson and David Scott Kastan (London: The Arden Shakespeare 2001). These observations hold throughout the Shakespeare canon where 'common people' appears eight times and 'good people' ten.
34. For quick notation: *AC 1.2* (slippery), *2HIV 2.1* (poor), *HV 3.5* (barbarous), *HV 3.5* (frosty), *2HVI 2.4* (envious), *2HVI 4.4* (rascal), *JC 1.2* (tag-rag).
35. 'The Tempest', *The Arden Shakespeare Complete Works*, ed. Richard Proudfoot, Ann Thompson and David Scott Kastan (London: The Arden Shakespeare, 2011), (1.2.351–2); and Shakespeare, *Much Ado about Nothing* (2.3.232–3), respectively.

36. See 'white' in the *Oxford English Dictionary*. While 'white' also carries other connotations, such as 'Abnormally pale or pallid, esp. from illness, or from fear or other emotion' (A.1.4.a), it remains a word 'chiefly with positive connotation' (II.7).
37. Peter Erickson, 'Representations of Blacks and Blackness in the Renaissance'. *Criticism* 35.4 (1993): 499–527, esp. 517.
38. Dennis Austin Britton, *Becoming Christian: Race, Reformation, and Early Modern English Romance* (New York: Fordham University Press, 2014), 35–58.
39. Cheryl I. Harris, 'Whiteness as Property', in *Critical Race Theory: The Key Writings that Formed the Movement* (New York: The New Press, 1995): 276–91, esp. 279. Critical race legal theorists commonly use the acronym CRT (critical race theory).
40. Gary Taylor, *Buying Whiteness: Race, Culture, and Identity from Columbus to Hip-Hop* (New York: Palgrave Macmillan, 2005), 36.
41. Francesca T. Royster, 'White-Limed Walls: Whiteness and Gothic Extremism in Shakespeare's *Titus Andronicus*'. *Shakespeare Quarterly* 51.4 (2000): 432–55, esp. 436.
42. 'Assemblage' is a rather difficult term to define, partly because, as Manuel DeLanda notes in *Assemblage Theory* (Edinburgh: Edinburgh University Press, 2016), its creators, Gilles Deleuze and Félix Guattari, define the concept multiple ways. DeLanda quotes from Deleuze and Claire Parnet's *Dialogues II* (New York: Columbia University Press, 2002), 69: 'What is an assemblage? It is a multiplicity which is made up of many heterogeneous terms and which establishes liaisons, relations between them, across ages, sexes, and reigns – different natures. Thus, the assemblage's only unity is that of a co-functioning: it is a symbiosis, a 'sympathy'. It is never filiations which are important, but alliances, alloys; these are not successions, lines of descent, but contagions, epidemics, the wind', 1. For more about 'assemblage' with regards to race, the reader should check out Alexander G. Weheliye, 'Assemblages: Articulation', in *Habeas Viscus: Racializing Assemblages, Biopolitics, and Black Feminist Theories of the Human* (Durham, NC: Duke University Press, 2014), throughout, but esp. 2–4 and 46–52.
43. See Taylor, *Buying Whiteness*, 125–32, where Taylor discusses Middleton's use of the term 'white people'.
44. Taylor, *Buying Whiteness*, 126.
45. Andrew Gurr, *Playgoing in Shakespeare's London* 3rd edn (Cambridge University Press, 2004), 22.
46. Floyd-Wilson's argument that Robert Burton in *Anatomy of Melancholy* (1621) 'manages to "democratize" the humor [i.e., melancholy] so that it appears everywhere and in everyone' (76), squares with the democratizing of English whiteness we see taking place in the late 1500s and into the early 1600s. It's to be noted, too, that while this democratizing is going on, there is also a rather vigorous and rigorous effort to keep whiteness and melancholia elite (76).
47. Robert Weimann, *Author's Pen and Actor's Voice: Playing and Writing in Shakespeare's Theatre* (Cambridge: Cambridge University Press, 2000), 184. See also the second chapter, 'The Expanding Vocabulary', 10–33, in S.S. Hussey's *The Literary Language of Shakespeare* (London: Longman, 1982).

48. Virginia Mason Vaughan, *Performing Blackness on English Stages, 1500-1800* (Cambridge: Cambridge University Press 2005), 109.
49. *Geneva Bible*. Geneva: William Whittingham, et al., 1560: 77v. *Early English Books Online*.
50. Tanya Pollard, *Shakespeare's Theater: A Sourcebook* (Malden, MA: Blackwell Publishing 2004), xiii.
51. Katharine Eisaman Maus speaks to this point when she insists, 'Inward truth, as it is conceived in the Renaissance, may be an intrinsically or originally theological concept, but not all of the settings in which it becomes important are religious ones': Maus, *Inwardness and Theater in the English Renaissance* (Chicago: University of Chicago Press, 1995), 211.
52. Pollard, *Shakespeare's Theater*, xxi.
53. Pollard, *Shakespeare's Theater*, x.
54. Ben Jonson, 'To the Memory of My Beloved the Author, Mr. William Shakespeare' (1623). Throughout, Jonson's eulogy boasts plenty of white and light imagery (racialized or otherwise).
55. 'near-mythic': Pollard, *Shakespeare's Theater*, x; 'we': for an incisive discussion of this universalizing humanist 'we', see Ian Smith, 'We are Othello: Speaking of Race in Early Modern Studies', *Shakespeare Quarterly* 67.1 (2016): 104–24.
56. 'Magical' is borrowed from Stephen Orgel, 'Marginal Jonson', in *The Politics of the Stuart Court Masque*, eds. David Bevington and Peter Holbrook (Cambridge: Cambridge University Press, 1998), 144–75, where Orgel discusses 'the magical power of Renaissance theatre . . . by persuasion or seduction and says it 'is both a quality of language and a way of establishing oneself, of rising in society, a way for servants . . . to become masters', 144–5 – or, I would add, for the same servants to become white. 'Miraculous' from Vaughan, *Performing Blackness*, 109–10.
57. Pollard, *Shakespeare's Theater*, xxii. The making of the early modern humanist human necessitated not just a focus on the 'man' created (so often the focus of liberal humanism) but those being excluded or having their humanity significantly qualified – those found to be less universal. For further discussion, the reader may see Ian Smith, 'We are Othello', esp. 104–9.
58. Stephen Greenblatt, *Shakespeare's Freedom* (Chicago: Chicago University Press, 2010), 25. Greenblatt puts the number of occurrences around 700; the number I'm using comes from opensourceshakespeare.org. For a groundbreaking discussion of 'fair' as a racializing term, see throughout Kim F. Hall, *Things of Darkness: Economies of Race and Gender in Early Modern England* (Ithaca, NY: Cornell University Press, 1995), especially 'Fair Texts / Dark Ladies: Renaissance Lyric and the Poetics of Color', 62–122.
59. William Shakespeare, 'Venus and Adonis', *The Arden Shakespeare Complete Works*, ed. Richard Proudfoot, Ann Thompson and David Scott Kastan (London: The Arden Shakespeare 2011), lines 343–66.
60. E. M. W. Tillyard, *The Elizabethan World Picture: A Study of the Idea of Order in the Age of Shakespeare, Donne and Milton* (New York: Vintage, 1959), 91.
61. Peter Erickson, '"God For Harry, England, and Saint George": British National Identity and the Emergence of White Self-Fashioning', in *Early Modern Visual Culture:*

Representation, Race, and Empire in Renaissance England, ed. Peter Erickson and Clark Hulse (Philadelphia: University of Pennsylvania Press, 2000): 315–45, esp. 316.

62. For some notable earlier examples, see Kimberly Poitevin, 'Inventing Whiteness: Cosmetics, Race, and Women in Early Modern England', *Journal for Early Modern Cultural Studies* 11.1 (Spring/Summer 2011): 59–89; Francesca T. Royster, 'White-Limed Walls: Whiteness and Gothic Extremism in Shakespeare's *Titus Andronicus*', *Shakespeare Quarterly* 51.4 (Winter 2000): 432–55; Barbara Bowen, 'Aemilia Lanyer and the Invention of White Womanhood', in *Maids and Mistresses, Cousins and Queens: Women's Alliances in Early Modern England*, ed. Susan Frye and Karen Robertson (Oxford: Oxford University Press, 1999): 274–304; Dympna Callaghan, '"Othello was a White Man": Properties of Race on Shakespeare's Stage', in *Shakespeare without Women: Representing Gender and Race on the Renaissance Stage* (London: Routledge, 2000): 75–96; Ania Loomba, *Gender, Race, Renaissance Drama* (Dehli: Oxford University Press, 1992 [1989]); Arthur L. Little, Jr., *Shakespeare Jungle Fever: National-Imperial Re-Visions of Race, Rape, and Sacrifice* (Stanford: Stanford University Press, 2000), 'Re-Historicizing Race, White Melancholia, and the Shakespearean Property', *Shakespeare Quarterly* 67.1 (2016): 84–103, and 'Is It Possible to Read Shakespeare through Critical White Studies?' in *The Cambridge Companion to Shakespeare and Race*, ed. Ayanna Thompson (Cambridge: Cambridge University Press, 2021): 268–80; and Margo Hendricks and Patricia Parker eds, *Women, 'Race', and Writing in the Early Modern Period* (New York: Routledge, 1994), where at least eleven of the essays offer critiques of whiteness even though 'whiteness' remains critically invisible in the volume's index. Also see endnotes for Kim F. Hall, Peter Erickson, and Ian Smith just below for other notable scholars and earlier works calling for early modern whiteness studies.

63. See Peter Erickson's discussion of Elizabeth's court as a 'cult of whiteness': 'Representations of Blacks and Blackness in the Renaissance', *Criticism* 35.4 (1993), 499–528, esp. 517; for the longer quote, see his 'Saint George', 339. In addition to these two texts, see other notable critical white studies by Erickson: 'Seeing White', *Transition* 67 (1997): 166–85; 'Profiles in Whiteness', *Stanford Humanities Review* 3.1 (1993): 98–111; 'The Moment of Race in Renaissance Studies', *Shakespeare Studies* 26 (1998): 27–36; and 'Can We Talk about Race in *Hamlet*?' in *'Hamlet': New Critical Essays*, ed. Arthur Kinney (New York: Routledge, 2002): 207–13. For more Erickson bibliography, see page 286 (notes 4–7, and 15).

64. See *Things of Darkness* throughout, especially chapter 2, 'Fair Texts/Dark Ladies: Renaissance Lyric and the Poetics of Color', 62–122, and the epilogue, 'On "Race", Feminism, and White Supremacy', 254–68. For other notable critiques of whiteness by Hall see 'Beauty and the Beast of Whiteness: Teaching Race and Gender', *Shakespeare Quarterly* 47.4 (1996): 461–75; and '"These Bastard Signs of Fair": Literary Whiteness in Shakespeare's Sonnets', in *Post-Colonial Shakespeares*, ed. Ania Loomba and Martin Orkin (London: Routledge, 1998): 64–83.

65. Smith, *Race and Rhetoric*, 70–1, 97–121, 132, and 135–41. For some other notable works by Smith offering up or calling for a critique of whiteness, see 'We are Othello: Speaking of Race in Early Modern Studies', *Shakespeare Quarterly* 67.1 (2016): 104–24; 'Othello's Black Handkerchief', *Shakespeare Quarterly* 64.1 (2013): 1–25;

'White Skin, Black Masks: Racial Cross-Dressing on the Early Modern Stage', *Renaissance Drama* 32 (2003): 33–67.
66. Dyer, *White*, 9.
67. Mary Floyd-Wilson, *English Ethnicity and Race in Early Modern Drama* (Cambridge: Cambridge University Press, 2003), 18–19, 79. Floyd-Wilson, however, does not see her reading of early modern geohumoralism as advancing a racial phenomenon. Responding to this aspect of Floyd-Wilson's study, Ian Smith writes, 'Ironically, the work's corporal telos aligns itself with later biological speculations on race despite [Floyd-Wilson's] refusal to engage this particular arc of racial ascendancy': *Race and Rhetoric*, 6.
68. Gretchen Gerzina, *Black England: Life Before Emancipation* (London: Allison & Busby, 1999), 5; Gary Taylor makes a similar argument in *Buying Whiteness*, where he says, 'Whiteness was, for the English, an imported idiom', 111, and 103–8.
69. It's important to note that a critical focus on the making of white people and white supremacy in no way displaces any critical discussion of Shakespeare's early modern culture and anti-Blackness. While the histories of white supremacy and anti-Black racism are certainly allied, they are not simply parts of some singular phenomenon: to treat them as such under-reads each of them. For a more extended study of anti-Blackness, see Matthieu Chapman, *Anti-Black Racism in Early Modern English Drama: The Other 'Other'* (New York: Routledge, 2017).
70. For an excellent discussion of competitions over cosmetic whiteness, see Poitevin, 'Inventing Whiteness'.
71. In a discussion, for example, of pre-modern identities in China, Bonnett argues, 'although there were no white racial identities in pre-modern China, there were white identities', *White Identities*, 9.
72. Charles Mills notes that by the early twentieth century, ninety percent of the world was controlled by whites and that the ten percent that wasn't 'had still to operate in a white-ruled world', 120: 'Global White Supremacy', in *White Privilege: Essential Readings on the Other Side of Racism*, ed. Paula S. Rothenberg (New York: Worth Publishers, 2016 [2005]), 119–25. Even though white people may seem to have less of the world in their possession at the present, their global control over the representation of white people is perhaps higher than it has ever been in history.
73. Dyer, *White*, xiii and 1, respectively.
74. Dyer, *White*, xiii.
75. For a cogent and well-illustrated brief history, see Madeline Caviness, 'From the Self-Invention of the Whiteman in the Thirteenth Century to *The Good, the Bad, and the Ugly*', *Different Visions: A Journal of New Perspectives on Medieval Art* 1 (2008), 1–33. Also see Geraldine Heng's chapter, 'Color: Epidermal Race, Fantasmatic Race: Blackness and Africa in the Racial Sensorium', in *The Invention of Race in the European Middle Ages* (Cambridge: Cambridge University Press, 2018), 181–256, esp. 182–4; and Dyer, *White* 66–8.
76. It's a rather available early modern humanist trope. See, for example, early modern theologian Richard Hooker, speaking of natural law and 'the light of [men's] natural

understanding': *Of the Laws of Ecclesiastical Polity* 1.viii.9. (1594). Qtd. in Robin Headlam Wells, *Shakespeare's Humanism* (Cambridge, 2005), 63; also, for just one more example, Philip Sidney, *The Defence of Poesy* (1580/1595) in *Sir Philip Sidney Selected Prose and Poetry*, 2nd edn, ed. Robert Kimbrough (Madison: University of Wisconsin Press, 1983), 102–58, esp. on the 'inward light', 123. (For some of the racialized dimensions of this light, see Sidney on 'the most barbarous and simple Indians', 105.)

77. On cosmetics, see Poitevin, 'Inventing Whiteness'; on early modern stage lighting, R. B. Graves, 'Elizabethan Lighting Effects and the Conventions of Indoor and Outdoor Theatrical Illumination', *Renaissance Drama*. New Series. 12 (1981), 51–69; on the 'miraculous', Vaughan, *Performing Blackness*, esp. 109.

78. Dyer, *White*, 86–94, 97–103, 115–19. Cf. Pecola Breedlove's 'education in the movies' in Toni Morrison, *The Bluest Eye* (New York: Vintage International, 2007 [1970]), 122.

79. Although he's interested in the Black side of this story, Fred Moten has quipped about this reality with critical pithiness and genius: 'whether we are talking about the seventeenth, twentieth, or twenty-first [century] . . . it's not so much that Shakespeare [with his Othello] has given an early articulation of the Negro Problem: it's that, instead, he has given Negroes a problem'. Fred Moten, 'Letting Go of *Othello*', *Paris Review*, 1 November 2019, www.theparisreview.org/blog/2019/11/01/letting-go-of-othello (accessed 19 March 2020).

80. See Arthur L. Little, Jr., 'Re-Historicizing Race, White Melancholia, and the Shakespearean Property'. *Shakespeare Quarterly* 67.1 (2016): 84–103, esp. 92–3; also, Imtiaz Habib's chapter in this volume.

81. See, respectively, Robin DiAngelo, *White Fragility: Why It's So Hard for White People to Talk about Racism* (Boston: Beacon Press, 2018), 2; Anderson, *White Rage*, 3–4; Douglass, *London Times*, 18 July 1850.

82. Toni Morrison, 'Mourning for Whiteness', *The New Yorker*, 21 November 2016, 54.

83. Mills, 'Global White Supremacy', 121, original emphasis, but I have changed the tense from past to present, a change fully supported by Mills' text.

84. Bristol, *Shakespeare's America*, 17.

85. Marjorie Garber, 'Shakespeare as Fetish', *Shakespeare Quarterly*, 41.2 (Summer 1990), 243, original emphasis.

86. See Patricia J. Williams, *The Alchemy of Race and Rights* (Cambridge, MA: Harvard University Press, 1991), 84, on this issue with regards to Shakespeare.

87. *Much Ado about Nothing* (4.1.157–60).

88. Fanon, *Black Skin, White Masks* (Grove Press, 1994 [1967, 1952]), 189. The reader should also see the opening of Hall, *Things of Darkness*, where she challenges 'how modern literary criticism remystifies the appearance of blackness in literary works by insisting that references to race are rooted in European aesthetic tradition rather than in any consciousness of racial difference', 1.

89. Ian Haney López, *White by Law: The Legal Construction of Race* (New York: New York University Press, 2006), 130.

90. William Shakespeare, 'Othello', *The Arden Shakespeare Complete Works*, ed. Richard Proudfoot, Ann Thompson and David Scott Kastan (London: The Arden Shakespeare 2011), 5.2.130–1. It's interesting to note that Emilia, who speaks these lines, deifies Desdemona before she condemns Othello: his blackness comes *after* Desdemona's angelic but unnamed whiteness. Also, see Moten in note #79 above.

91. A good introduction to Shakespeare and social justice is *The Arden Research Handbook of Shakespeare and Social Justice*, ed. David Ruiter (London: Arden Shakespeare, 2021). The reader should see Ruiter's introduction, 'This is Real Life: Shakespeare and Social Justice as a Field of Play'. While the volume has a rich repository of essays, from the perspective of *White People in Shakespeare*, the reader will find most resonant contributions in Part 2 from Jason Demeter, Peter Erickson, and Arthur L. Little, Jr., and in Part 3 from Alfredo Michel Modenessi and Paulina Morales, Malcolm Cocks, and Kevin A. Quarmby.

92. Williams, *The Alchemy of Race and Rights*, 116.

93. For an elaboration of this point, see DiAngelo, *White Fragility*, 2 (and throughout): 'The mere suggestion that being white has meaning often triggers a range of defensive responses . . . anger, fear, and guilt and behaviors such as argumentation, silence, and withdrawal', effectively reinstating 'white equilibrium as they repel the challenge, return our racial comfort, and maintain our dominance within the racial hierarchy'. She calls this 'white fragility'.

94. I have taken a few silent liberties with some of the contributors' quotations so as to avoid an unsightly number of ellipses and such. I have been careful, of course, to not change the integrity of the author's statement, but I do ask the reader to please cite from the contributor's own chapter rather than from my renditions here.

95. I should still note, however, that Joyce MacDonald in her chapter included in this volume does read *Cymbeline* as a hybrid history-romance.

96. My inquiry shares something with Winthrop Jordan observing that 'if Europeans were white, some were whiter than others', 254: *White Over Black: American Attitudes Toward the Negro, 1550-1812* (Chapel Hill: University of North Carolina Press, 1968), but, importantly, the impetus for this question had less to do with ethnic, national, or religious differences per se than with 'the social rather than the biological basis of the Racial Contract': Mills, *The Racial Contract*, 78–82, especially the white racial contract operating within early modern England itself.

PART ONE

Shakespeare's White People

CHAPTER ONE

'Two Loves I Have of Comfort and Despair'

The Circle of Whiteness in the Sonnets

IMTIAZ HABIB

I

The projection of whiteness as a national late Elizabethan aesthetic is a solipsistic dialectic, whose systemic failure is not a *terminus ad quem* but is in fact what fuels its recursive affirmation, so that in sonnet, lyric and stage play, whiteness's triumph must be flawed, not for it to be abandoned but for it to be iterated again. The self-renewing nature of this poetic design enables a virtual cycle that is predicated on an ocular subjectivity whose limits are the mandate for its perpetually recursive cultural life. This is similar to but not identical with the arguments of Carol Neely about the locked movement between engagement and detachment in some particular sonnets of Shakespeare, and of Arthur Little about the solipsism of modern Shakespeare scholarship that cannot escape the 'closed circle' of the desirability of a deracialized and desexualized subject position on the one hand and the undesirability of an assumed whiteness that such a stance would leave intact for the *oeuvre* on the other.[1]

The self-blind eye/I of male whiteness is the narrative agent of the closed system of a failing-reiterating white ruling consciousness in the *Sonnets* that spans the end of the Tudor regime and the beginning of the Stuart one, with a frame of reference that is at once poetically conventional and historically allusive and that is formally acknowledged in the capstone sonnet 'Two loves I have of comfort and despair', towards the cycle's end. The argument of this essay will assume a chronology of the sonnets as follows: 127–154 black woman Sonnets, written as a group by themselves in the late 1580s to early 1590 (i.e. sometime shortly before 1590), as a daring innovation at the peak of a competitive sonnet writing craze; 1–17 procreation sonnets, also written as a group by themselves and circulated in manuscript to compliment Southampton on his 17th birthday, also in the early 1590s (1590–1592) but after the black woman sonnets; 18–126, written at various times between the mid 1590s and 1604–1609 and gradually changed as sonnet fashion and tone changes and to match the Jacobean taste for aristocratic homosociality;[2] the complete work put together with the procreation sonnets and 17–126 at the beginning and the black woman sonnets 127–154 at the end and published, (i) to stop pirated publications by others (such as William Jaggard's *the Passionate Pilgrim*, etc.) and (ii) as something that could be usefully put out at the end of Shakespeare's writing career after the immediate need for aristocratic patronage has passed.[3] Beyond the merely personal, however, this essay keeps in its ambit Thomas Greene's observation more than two decades back that 'an anxiety of cosmic and existential economies' haunts the poems, that 'a terrible fear of cosmic destitution' plagues the 'husbandry of the procreation sonnets'.[4]

The insistent recommendations of the 'procreation sonnets' to a noble fair youth to marry in order to extend his family blood are undergirded by the preeminence of a white maleness that is both the active subject and the preferred object of these recommendations. Well known as thematic structures in the conventional Elizabethan poetry of praise derived from the Pindaric encomium and its well-honed art of praising things popularly known, and appropriated by Erasmus and later pressed into service by Thomas Wilson and Philip Sidney among others during Elizabeth's reign,[5] their rehearsal here echoes the modern critical tradition of such identifications, and highlights the latter's doubling as the exegetical offspring of the former after its decline from the seventeenth century onwards. Yet, if the Tudor convention of complimentary lyrics of preferred breeding has in its demise bred an encomiastic modern critical practice, that circularity is at the heart of the praxis of Tudor epideictic poetry itself.

Formatted by the self-reflexive spectacle of the culture at the top, Elizabethan complimentary poetry is bound by an ocular hold that induces a collective seeing of specific aristocratic figures in the drama of their contemporary lives and focused on the cultural aesthetics of such lives that justify the perpetual upward gaze of those located below. The nature of this required poetic seeing is a parallax vision that alights on one individual and its features, as well as on several, to construct the class that is 'the glass of fashion and the mould of form' for all. The principal signature of this virtual construction is a preferred phenotype whose ideal genotype is the *raison d'etre* of its required celebratory perpetuation.

So, as an Elizabeth fresh on her throne is in William Birch's gushing panegyric in 1564 England's 'lover fair', its 'darling' and 'heir', in her forties she is directly in George Puttneham's 'gift' to her in 1579 an androgynous female model ('A Cesar to her husband, A Kinge to her soone') of immaculate paleness ('A fayrer wight then feirye Queene') that is the perfection of nature ('a thinge verye admirable in nature', 'to be reputed [not] an humane, but rather a diuine perfection'), and is in her sixties pointedly in John Davies's eulogy to her in 1597 the state's 'faire Spring', 'Beautie's Fair character'. Similarly, Henry Morison, in Ben Jonson's public memorial to his death at the age of twenty, is 'A lily of a day' that was 'far fairer in May', 'the plant and flower of light' that 'in small proportions' showed 'just beauties'. Robert Devereaux, the Earl of Essex, in George Peele's painting of him in 1590, is 'well allied and lov'd of the best, / Well-thewed, fair, and frank, and famous by his crest'.[6]

A host of writings about the Earls of Southampton and Pembroke, the two most prominent courtiers in the English court in the 1590s and early 1600s, exhibit the same features. These include the poem *Narcissus* by William Cecil's secretary, John Clapham, in 1591 dedicated to Southampton and calling him, albeit conventionally, 'clarissimo et nobilissimo' (noble and 'illustrious');[7] the poem of the Chaplain of Magdalene College in Oxford, John Sanford, on the occasion of Queen Elizabeth's visit to the university in 1592 accompanied by her courtiers including Southampton, describing him as 'a smooth faced boy whose cheeks had yet the downy promise of Spring', and of 'a lofty line . . . no one more comely';[8] George Peele's *This Honour of the Garter* in 1593 referring fancifully to an ascendancy that the aristocrat had not yet acquired, as 'Southampton's Starre';[9] the commendatory letter to him of the Spanish renegade diplomat and the emissary in London of Henri IV of France, Antonio Perez, in his *Obras [Relations]* in 1593–1594 describing him as 'naturally cute and superb';[10] Thomas Nashe's dedication to Southampton of *The Unfortunate Traveller* in 1593 in which Southampton is 'a dear lover and cherisher . . . [as well] of poets themselves';[11] Barnabe Barnes's commendatory sonnet to Southampton in *Parthenophil to Parthenope* in 1593 describing him as 'sweet', and 'thrice sacred' and praising his 'gracious eyes';[12] Henry Lok's commendatory sonnet to Southampton attached to his religious verses in 1597 in which Southampton is 'most noble, noble every way';[13] Similarly, Pembroke is for the Earl of Oxford 'faire conditioned' and for the Earl of Clarendon universally loved,[14] in Francis Davison's dedication to him of the work *Poetical Rhapsody* unchangingly beautiful and lovely ('For as you were when first your eye I eyed / Such seems your beauty still. . . . [your] outward shape though it most lovely be / Doth in faire Robes / A fairer Soule Attire'),[15] and to John Aubrey, 'handsome, and of an admirable presence'.[16] To Thomas Thorpe, the publisher of Shakespeare's *Sonnets* himself, in the dedication of another work the following year Herbert is 'graceful and sweete'.[17] In Ben Jonson's dedication of his *Epigrams* to Pembroke, Herbert is 'the Great example of Honour, and Virtue', and in epigram 102 in his very name is 'an *Epigram*, on all Mankind', he is an embodiment of the life of the kingdom', so that 'they, that hope to see / The Common-wealth still safe, must study thee'.[18] To slightly appropriate the words of one contributor to the *Oxford Dictionary of National Biography* about the young Earl of Southampton, by their early youths *both* Southampton and Pembroke were not just 'patrons of great [potential] but also 'icons of an androgynous beauty'.[19] Fundamental to that beauty is the root sense of the word 'fair', and the other words that appear in these complimentary pieces such as 'lovely' 'comely', 'graceful', 'sweet', 'noble', etc. that do service for 'fair' and implicitly refer to it. Addresses like the ones cited above confirm what Edith Snook has shown in a variety of early modern English texts of this moment, as the 'establish[ment] of 'fair beauty ideologically as a privileged form of whiteness because skin colour is made to signify class, as well as ethnic difference and because fairness defines the normative, healthy state . . . [and that] elevate fair skin as a form of natural social power'.[20]

Disguised metonymically in the generality of 'faire' in Elizabethan and Jacobean poetic usage, which is the unspokenness of the cultural politics of whiteness as the invisible English norm, whiteness's fluidity as the foundational term of compliment for monarch and courtier, female and male patron alike, makes plausible the ascription of Shakespeare's compliment of whiteness not just singly to the one or the other of his two most prominent patrons, Henry Wriothesley or William Herbert, as has been the modern critical proclivity to argue,[21] but to *both together asynchronously*, in the *Sonnets* and in *Venus and Adonis*, as well as unspokenly and by an implied temporal association with a play written around the same time, *The Merchant of Venice*.[22] The word 'faire' occurs 110 times in these three texts, which is eleven per cent of its total usage in the Shakespearean corpus; of the three texts the *Sonnets* has the highest occurrence rate at fifty-six, which is also one of the highest numbers of the word's incidence in any text in the corpus. As Stephen Greenblatt has affirmed, 'Shakespeare often conveys the sense of beauty's radiance with the word "fair" . . . [which] can denote lovely, clear, fine or clean, but it also has the distinct sense of shining lightness. And this lightness of hair and complexion in turn sets off the pink of blushing cheeks and the deep red of beautiful lips'.[23] Unsurprisingly (for the genre and the dedicatee) in the *Sonnets* the word 'beauty' features seventy-one times or once in nearly every two sonnets, which is twenty-four per cent of its total occurrence in Shakespeare (286 times). 'Fair' occurs with 'beauty' in the same sonnet, i.e. in association with it, nineteen times, or once in every eight sonnets, and in almost fifteen per cent of the combined occurrences of those two words (127 times).[24]

The historical grounds for conflating Wriothesley and Southampton as an expediently single, composite dedicatee of the three works are the similarities of the family histories of both figures and their frequent association in the records of their public appearances. The Wriothesley family's anxiety to consolidate their newfound rise to nobility in Henry Wriothesley corresponds to the Pembrokes's concern with the thinness of their dynastic issue in their sole heir William Herbert.[25] Both were pressed with marriage suits with the Earl of Oxford's family, both were insulted together by James I's son, the Prince, and both were burgesses of the city of Southampton, Wriothesley in 1591 and Herbert in 1603.[26] Both received the blessings of the newly crowned King James in 1603, Southampton on being released from imprisonment, and together with Pembroke on being installed as Knight of the Garter. They were both present at the investiture of Prince Henry as the Prince of Wales on 4th June 1610, and at the ceremony's feast Pembroke was the server and Southampton the carver. In addition to much else, both were concurrently active in the Virginia Company, with Southampton going on to serve as its Governor.[27] They were part of the two most powerful and outspoken aristocratic factions in Elizabeth's court – that of the Essex and the Sidney families.[28] Their analogous familial situations and the repeated closeness of their public appearances and careers underline their combined stature as a composite figure of eminence in the late Tudor and early Stuart public imagination.[29]

Whether the connection of both to Shakespeare occurred in a trip of the young Wriothesley to the family estate in Tichfield with Shakespeare in company, and joined by a still younger Herbert at *his* family's seat in en-route, as some have suspected,[30] or (in the case of Southampton) backstage in one of the London playhouses in the early 1590s when the Earl was reported to be 'frequent[ing] the theatres'[31] or whether the poet became a devotee of Pembroke when the Warwickshire-based George Carey introduced the latter to him, also backstage at one of the London playhouses but in the *late* 1590s, as G. V. Akrigg earlier and Duncan Jones later speculated,[32] may be indeterminable, but the identification of the exact circumstances of the commoner poet's linkage to the associative image of the two popular aristocratic icons in personal and poetic terms in a self-serving patronly culture that is always active and unpredictably connected is unnecessary. The uncertainties of the precise details of Shakespeare's linkage to Wriothesley and Pembroke, and of his adoption of their combined iconic image of ideality, are appropriate for the virtuality of a homosocial whiteness that the image represents.[33] That Southampton and Pembroke were *both,* and indistinguishably, an amalgamated dedicatee figure for Shakespeare's three late Elizabethan works named above is as much of a certainty as such an endorsement-driven society of delicate and direct allusiveness would expect.

II

If the nature of a white subjectivity is an exclusion of colours that can only produce a chromatic identification that is colourless since white is not a colour and can only be seen in the presence of other colours, the missing centre of whiteness's self-projection is like Jean Baudrillard's notion of a simulacrum, a copy 'without an original'.[34] The virtuality of that whiteness remains perpetually fading and lighting up, dying *and* living, continually nothing and something, forever an unilluminated imaged body achromically lit up and hence unseeable again. This is the 'insubstantiality' of the (white) self that Joyce Sutphen in her analysis of the trope of memory in the *Sonnets* postulates, something that is 'impossible to discern'.[35] The double-blindness of the seeing and the seen is the penumbra of the I/eye of whiteness that cannot see itself and that marks the limits of an ocular white subjectivity asserting itself as the focus of all sight.

Locked within the closed circle of an optical and psychic impairment, and struggling against it to write the phenomenal world in its own colourless colour, the narrative agent of whiteness's discourse, the self-directing seeing eye and the speaking I of the *Sonnets*, run conjoined disuniform loops of decay and revival that articulate not the extinction of whiteness but in fact its endless life as a continuous act of spectacular public self-voyeurism. Advertising the failing seeing of itself in public, the totality of the poems employs the verb 'see' and its synonyms no less than 174 times in 154 sonnets or on an average a little more than once in every sonnet of the cycle; that is, each and every sonnet in the cycle refers to the visual act in some form or the other.[36] They are deployed in the service of contrapuntal patterns of ruination and triumph of an explicitly invoked or implicitly understood white or 'faire' being-ness across a variety of personal situations that lace the expanse of the work, across both of its traditionally understood subsequences. In many of these asymmetrical cycles of decline and recovery, with their varied foregrounded personal situations, whiteness is an unspokenly default background identity because the unseeability of whiteness's pigmentary signature puts its self-projection naturally under erasure. The invisibility of whiteness's self-directing anteriority in large swathes of the topical conversations of the poems is fronted by a white poet enacting the rising and falling rhythms of a white male life in love with a male whiteness, or by extension a white maleness locked in a conflicted obsessive meditation of itself and projectively speaking to itself in the voice of the poet. The waves of whiteness's spiralling loops of hope and despair travel on a vertical and horizontal grid, the former within each sonnet across the *volta*, and the latter across clusters of sonnets articulating emerging and disappearing local ruminations, with the peak and the trough of each wave unevenly dispersed in length.

As the confident declaration of the desirable eugenic privilege of white breeding in the first line of the first sonnet degenerates into the stark prophecy of its closing couplet of the nihilism of selfish wasteful self-loving, 'or else this glutton be / To eat the world's due, by the grave and thee', so does the third sonnet in its descent from its initial hopefulness of a 'face . . . so fair [as] lovely April', to the hopeless prospect of its closing line: 'Die single, and thine image dies with thee'.[37] Paralleling the trough of 1 and 3, sonnets 7 and 8 deteriorate from the optimism of their opening statements of a resplendent sunrise (7) and joyful music (8), to the bitterness of fruitlessness 'So thou, thyself outgoing in thy noon / Unlooked on diest, unless thou get a son', and the mocking refrain of 'Sings this to thee: 'Thou single will prove none', ' even as sonnet 9 reinforces the tonal dip of both sonnets with the uniformity of its invective from its beginning diatribe against the self-consummation of 'a single life' to its sharp pronouncement of 'hate in that bosom sits / That on himself such murd'rous shame commits'. Conversely, 2, 4, 5, 6, extendedly populate the crests of whiteness's undulation in their swelling movement from despair and frustration to reassurance, hope and triumph, from the bankruptcy of aging to the 'new ma[king] of 'warm' 'blood' (2), from the prodigality of a reckless 'spend[ing]' of 'nature's bequest' to the hope of the extended life of beauty well 'used' (4), from the time wasting of uncaring youth to the survival of sweetness of 'flowers distilled' even in winter (5), and from the quiet defiance of a 'distilled' summer face's imperviousness against 'winter's ragged hand' to the resurgent conviction that whiteness's beauty is 'much too fair to be death's conquest' (6).

The upsurge expands in duration but the trough shortens, in the prolonged positivism of sonnets 10, 11, 12, and 13, and in the solitary sombreness of 14, for the former sonnets in the slow push from a whiteness 'unprovident[ly]' concerned with itself to one 'kind-hearted[ly]' 'mak[ing] . . . another self for love' of poetic fame ('me') (10), in the purposive drive from a 'best endowed' fairness's 'wan[ing]' to nature's select duplication of it in the fresh 'copy' of a progeny (11), in the gentle progression from the inexorable transience of fair 'beauty' to beauty 'breeding' to 'brave' time (12), and in the steady development of the patriarchal truism of 'sweet' 'beauty['s]' perpetual paternity (13). Against these hopeful sentiments 14 tracks a hopeless trajectory from the uncertainty of foretelling the future to the certain 'prognosticat[ion]' of 'the doom and date' of 'beauty' and with it of 'truth' (14). Whereas sonnets 15, 16, 17, 18, punctuate another sustained resurgence, of the triumph of fairness's poetic fame over time (15, 17, 18, 19) and of the superiority of fairness's own reproduced being over its poetic representation (16), 20's narrative of fairness's androgynous self-eroticism again falls away in the face of the fixity of its male anatomy: the 'one thing to my purpose nothing'.

As 20's brooding introspection of a homosocial whiteness's psycho-sexual quotidian exhausts the convention of compliment of the first seventeen breeding sonnets, whiteness's public self-exhibition extends over smaller cycles encapsulated within larger ones that carry forward earlier conversations asynchronously. From 21 to 126 nineteen uneven up and down loops of whiteness's despondency and exultation thread the poems, oscillating between the sorrow and pain of separation from fairness's beauty and its malignment and infection by sycophancy on the one hand, and the joy of fairness's praise as true, eternal, and poetically praiseworthy on the other, with a waxing and waning aesthetic and erotic personal investment in fairness's effigy sporadically undergirding that oscillation.[38] Also appearing in regular intervals are templates of fairness's beauty, first introduced in 18, that are often broadcast in direct declarative address without the dialogic relationship of a white poetic self in communion with its virtual image. These highlight the accumulated dividends as it were, the intellectual capital of whiteness, in each of its cyclic oscillations that are their foundational agenda to project. Echoing 18's summation of the undulations of whiteness's selective breeding theme ('Thou art more lovely and more temperate' than nature itself and 'Thy eternal summer shall never fade' 18.2, 9), and after 24 declares that summarizing agenda bluntly, 'Mine eyes have drawn thy shape' (24.10), 41 describes whiteness's privileged preferability, 'Gentle thou art, and therefore to be won / Beauteous thou art, therefore to be assailed' (41.5–6), 53 expositorily details whiteness's 'substance, whereof [it is] made' as the original of which 'Adonis' is the 'counterfeit', who 'Grecian tires' '[paint] new', of whom 'Spring's' 'beauty' is but a 'shadow' (53.1–10), 54 and 55 claims its eternal value, whose 'beauteous ... lovel[iness]' is 'distil[led] by verse' (54.13–14) and whose 'praise shall still find room / Even in the eyes of all posterity' (55.10–11).

Occurring in the approximate mid-point of the entire cycle of 154 sonnets, and therefore centrally speaking for the overall work's intentions, are six sonnets, 78, 79, 81, 82, 83, 84, that accelerate these panegyrics to their highest level to especially proclaim whiteness's cultural capital. While 79 inscribes its universal poetic godhead, 'what of thee thy poet doth invent ... in thee doth live' (79.7–12), 78 describes whiteness's cosmic munificence, whose 'eyes have taught the dumb... to sing, / And heavy ignorance to fly, / Have added feathers to the learned's wing, / And given grace a double majesty' (78.5–8). Likewise, as 82 and 83, echoing and extending 79's claim, pronounce whiteness's value beyond poetic description, 'Thou art as fair in knowledge as in hue, / Finding a limit past my praise' (82.5–6) and 'There lives more life in one of your fair eyes / Than both your poets can in praise devise' (83.13–14), 81 announces the eternality of its fame: 'Your name from hence immortal life shall have / ... When you entombed in men's eyes shall lie' (81.5, 8). Finally transcending the repetitiveness of earlier trailing conversations, 84 breaks out into a definitive statement about the unimpeachability of whiteness's integrity: 'you alone are you ... he that writes of you, if he can tell / That you are you, so dignifies his story' (84.2, 9). Subsequently, 93 and 112 add to these affirmations, as 93 does in a muted key with its calm belief that 'heaven in thy creation did decree / That in thy face sweet love should ever dwell' (93.9–10), and as 112 articulates more emphatically, 'you are my all the world.... / ... None else to me, nor I to none alive' (112.5, 8). The progressively finalistic note in these avowals – from the tentativeness of 18's 'Shall I compare thee ...', to 84's definitive 'you alone are you', and 112's 'None else to me, nor I to none alive', – thus sum up a straining project of whiteness' cultural self-writing, a public-private heralding of its own ontology and an enterprise in which it is both the looker and the looked at (that 'live[s] [it]self in the eyes of men' 16.12). This colour delimiting subjectivity is an ocular consciousness that sees itself and speaks itself through the ventriloquism of a client poet that is the seeing eye and the speaking I for it, a functionalism admitted insistently in 46 and 47's dichotomy between the 'eye[s]' jurisdiction of 'thy outward part' and that of the 'dear heart's part' that 'pleads' and 'sighs' i.e. speaks the emotions that sight engenders.

Yet, finality also postulates limits, not just because speech 'war[s]' with sight, epistemology fails sensory input, but also because the chromatic exclusionism of whiteness's self-performance is predicated on that which it excludes. Blackness's ontology predates whiteness, and is what the latter can only be led to in its projective examination of itself. As another closed solipsism that is also retrospective, meaning trying to cancel what already exists, the greater the effort of whiteness's abrogation of blackness the stronger is the emergence of blackness and its asservation of its ontological right of place. Thus, if 126, with its two clearly indicated missing last lines reflecting whiteness's eye's end of sight and its speaking I's termination of speech (that is, the seeing eye's failure to alight on any new objects and phenomena of empathy and the speaking I's corresponding inability to verbalize any fresh epistemologies of identification), marks the expiration of one macro cycle of whiteness extending over the first 126 poems,[39] sonnet 127 immediately inaugurates another circular struggle of whiteness's self-lighting – that of its wavering embrace of blackness. In this sense, however the *Sonnets* are read, 126 and 127 mark a pivotal point in its narrative of whiteness. If sight and speech are the principal agents for the prosecution of a white subjectivity, their failure in their blinding by the very whiteness they are trying to project (113's 'Incapable of more, replete with you') is in fact white consciousness's unspoken spur to compulsively shift from an exclusivist to an inclusivist ocular agenda, to transfer its attention to other regimes of vision, not to abandon itself in them but within which it can hope to find itself and against which it can strive to assert itself. White subjectivity's silent recognition of its limitations is thus not the end of its discursive life but the very means of its continuance, in a fresh course of repetitive striving whose equally demonstrative exhibitionism serves not to muzzle but to broadcast its ethnic ambition.

Blackness is both a polar textual construct and a historical reference, the former as a gendered figure of heterosexuality that irregularly interferes with whiteness's monosexual self-introspections, and the latter an allusive topical personification of a late Elizabethan material reality – a sizeable but growing black population that as I have elsewhere demonstrated can neither be acknowledged nor denied.[40] Proposed by Joel Fineman, and discussed by me elsewhere,[41] the self-expostulatory sonnets of fairness are accordingly the after-effects of the blackness sonnets that follow it in the text's chronology, composed after the writing of the black woman sonnets, and an attempt to thematically eclipse them. As a group of racially charged poems written possibly between the end of the 1580s and the early 1590s as was first proposed by a profusion of Victorian scholars,[42] these poems show off sensational innovation at the peak of the fiercely competitive sonnet writing rage of those decades, and were later positioned within a larger frame of white poems conceived initially as conventional epideictic compliment upon contact in London with the Southampton-Pembroke figures as they were frequenting the theatres and performances at that point in their careers.[43] Published only after the patronly relationship had endured beyond the point of failure and near the end of his writing career, these sonnets were first spurred by the promise of their powerful largesse as well as the new homosociality of Jacobean court culture.

A traumatic encounter of Shakespeare with an unnamed historical black woman upon his arrival in London (precisely when the incidence of archival mentions of black people in London reaches one of the highest levels in the documentary records)[44] urgently shadows the history of the black woman sonnets increasingly in the current scholarly moment. The semantic charge of the black woman sonnets' masked historical allusion to such an experience is expediently supplemented by the ugly-beauty or paradoxical praise convention about white women,[45] to make the figure of blackness a racialized misogynist fantasy of a woman the reality of whose race and gender is buried in the semiosis of literary artifact and male camp. As the spectrality of black woman-ness parallels the virtuality of a white maleness, a secondary semiosis thus coheres between whiteness fronting a maleness and blackness facing a femaleness. The efficacy of this complex double-semiotic design captures the culture of visible but subtle allusiveness that is the historical setting for the genre of the *Sonnets* and explains the fixity of modern critical orthodoxy that can entertain the euphemistic dark ladyship of a white Mary Fitton or an Iberian Jewish Emilia Lanyer but not that of the referentiality of a nameless historical black woman.[46] The later sonnets struggle to embrace blackness's cultural impropriety as they insist on performing the unnamed default position of a white aesthetic normalcy.

The only sonnet to formally name the triangular bind of fairness's 'pur[e]' maleness, blackness's 'evil' female-ness, and the poetic clientage that is intermediary to both, and for that reason long regarded as a 'key sonnet' for critics of all persuasions, a 'germ sonnet' for the entire work,[47] one of the more 'authentic' Shakespearean poems among the many that appeared in different collections before and after the publication of the *Sonnets* in 1609, including in the inaugural position in William Jaggard's pirated collection, the 'fuller poetic and narrative context' that 144 'seems to call for' in Duncan-Jones's estimation[48] is the dialecticism that fuels the chiasmic energies of whiteness's metaphysics. Appearing late in the cycle, it is whiteness's summation of the trajectory of its bipolar discourse:

> Two loves I have, of comfort and despair,
> Which, like two spirits, do suggest me still:
> The better angel is a man right fair,
> The worser spirit a woman coloured ill.
> To win me soon to hell my female evil
> Tempteth my better angel from my side,
> And would corrupt my saint to be a devil,
> Wooing his purity with her foul pride;
> And whether that my angel be turned fiend
> Suspect I may, but not directly tell;
> But being both from me both to each friend,
> I guess one angel in another's hell.
> Yet this shall I ne'er know, but live in doubt,
> Till my bad angel fire my good one out.
>
> —Sonnet 144

The politely lamenting posture (of 'comfort and despair') of the demands of competing loyalties ('Two loves') of the first two lines is a graceful spectacle of public soul cleansing that holds the promise of ethnic and sexual parity in the resolution of the conflict. Under that display is the quick syllogistic inversion of the coequality of the 'loves' of *both* entities that 'suggest me' (persuade me) as the cause of the comfort and despair (that I have *two* loves comforts me, that I have to choose between them makes me despair) by the apportioning of despair and lament as the *differing* effects of each: the 'better' one of 'the man right fair' and the 'worser' of 'a woman coloured ill'. Buried in that inversion is a second implied one, of the compulsive loving of the 'worser' entity despite her worseness, that solipsistically connects back to the first line's acknowledgement of 'Two loves have I', and recovers its scene of graceful impartiality. The obscurity of these compound ratiocinative reversals is strengthened by the professions of 'suspect . . . but not directly tell', 'guess', and 'ne'er know, but live in doubt' to articulate, despite the couplet's bitter venereal hope of the 'bad angel fir[ing] my good one out', the sense of an unresolvable paradox of choice whose only unstated outcome is an eternal Sisyphus-ian struggle of a 'better . . . fair[ness]' with a 'worse][r] . . . coloured ill'. This is the essential philosophical blueprint of whiteness's life, transcending the outcome of particular efforts such as 153 and 154's resignation to the decay and death of an incurable sexual infection.

In the uncertainty of endings is also the augury of beginnings. The incurability of the infection of 153, 154 is incomplete, left suspended, so that whiteness's 'death', forecasted by the schism that had broken out again between the sight of the eye and the speech of the I in 148, is not established but rhetorically proposed. The narrative aposiopesis of the cycle's ending is the prelude for the renewal of whiteness's self-projection.[49] If whiteness has been mauled, it must be repaired, rebuilt. If whiteness's casualty has been the fatal contamination of its 'purity' (144) by black female-ness's venereality, that sexual corruption and racial malignance are precisely what will be guarded against in other iterations of whiteness's self-performance, especially in *Venus and Adonis* and *The Merchant of Venice*, two works that share an immediate chronological adjacency with the *Sonnets*. As a cultural discourse, whiteness's gyrating self-projection in the *Sonnets* that Shakespeare starts writing at the very beginning of his career in the early 1590s, revises over the next two decades, and publishes at almost the end of it in 1609, is a master discourse framing his oeuvre and inevitably casting its pallor over its entirety, even if asynchronously and disjunctively.[50]

NOTES

Editor's note: Imtiaz Habib submitted his essay shortly before his passing, and I am honoured his estate has allowed us to publish his essay posthumously. I also wish to thank Jean Howard with whom I worked on the initial revisions to Habib's essay.

1. Carol Thomas Neely, 'Detachment and Engagement in Shakespeare's Sonnets: 94, 116, and 129', *Publications of the Modern Language Association of America* (1977): 83–95, available: http://www.jstor.org/stable/461416 (accessed 28 February 2014); Peter Erickson, 'Shakespeare Jungle Fever: National-Imperial Re-Visions of Race, Rape, and Sacrifice (review)', *Criticism* 43, no. 3 (2001): 358–60.

2. I am using 'homosocial' as being inclusive of the homoerotic, since as Paul Hammond has put it in his study of early modern homosexuality, 'homosocial relationships may set themselves up in opposition to homoeroticism; and they may be a repressed form of homoeroticism', *Figuring Sex Between Men from Shakespeare to Rochester* (Oxford: Oxford University Press, 2002), 9.

3. This dating is based partly on Katherine Duncan-Jones's view of the history of the *Sonnets*' composition: Katherine Duncan-Jones, ed., *Shakespeare's Sonnets* (London: The Arden Shakespeare, 2010), 1–28; and on those of several others such as, James Schiffer, ed., *Shakespeare's Sonnets: Critical Essays* (New York: Garland, 1999), p. 8; and Colin Burrow, *The Complete Sonnets and Poems*, ed. Colin Burrow (Oxford: Oxford University Press, 2008), 103–8.

4. Thomas Greene, '"Pitiful thrivers": Failed Husbandry in the Sonnets', in *Shakespeare and the Question of Theory*, ed. Patricia Parker and Geoffrey Hartman (New York: Columbia University Press, 1986), 232.

5. J. A. Burrow, *The Poetry of Praise* (Cambridge: Cambridge University Press, 2011), 2; Margreta De Grazia, 'The Scandal of Shakespeare's Sonnets', in *Shakespeare's Sonnets: Critical Essays*, ed. James Schiffer, 89–112 (New York: Garland, 1999), 102; Peter Herman, 'What's the Use? Or The Problematic of Economy in Shakespeare's Procreation Sonnets', in Schiffer, *Shakespeare's Sonnets*, 264.

6. William Birch, 'A Song between the Queen's Majesty and England' (1564), in *Elizabeth and Her Age*, ed. Donald Stump and Susan M. Felch (New York: W.W. Norton, 2009), 133; George Puttenham, 'Partheniads', in *Ballads from Manuscripts*, 2 vols, ed. F. J. Furnivall and W. R. Morfill (Hertford, UK: Stephen Austin and Sons, 1873), II: 57, 61, 73, 81–82, 126; John Davies, *The Complete Poems of John Davies*, ed. Alexander Grossart, 2 vols (London: Chatto and Windus, 1876), II: 131, 135, 160 (*Astroea* Hymns III and VIII, and *Orchestra* Hymn III) (John Davies was connected to the Pembroke family from the time of his grandfather (Grossart xiii–xiv); Ben Jonson, 'To the Immortal Memory and Friendship of . . . Sir H. Morison', in *the Norton Anthology of English Literature*, 2 vols, ed. M. H. Abrams et al (New York: W.W. Norton, 1993), I: 123–28; Alexander Dyce, *The Works of George Peele*, 2 vols, ed. A. H. Bullen, 'Eclogue Gratulatorie', II: 272.

7. John Clapham, *Narcissus* (London: Excudebat: Thomas Scarlett, 1591).

8. Walter Begley, *Is it Shakespeare?: The Great Question of Elizabethan Literature. Answered in the Light of New Revelations and Important Contemporary Evidence Hitherto Unnoticed* (London: J. Murray, 1903) 139; G. V. Akrigg, *Shakespeare and the Earl of Southampton* (London: Hamish Hamilton, 1968), 36.

9. Akrigg, *Shakespeare and the Earl of Southampton*, 36.

10. My translation of the original Spanish lines in Gustav Ungerer, ed., *A Spaniard in Elizabethan England: The Correspondence of Antonio Pérez's Exile*, 2 vols (London: Tamesis Books, 1976) 2: 267.

11. Thomas Nashe, *The Unfortunate Traveller and Other Works* (London: Penguin, 2006), n.p.

12. Barnabe Barnes, *The Poems of Barnabe Barnes: Parthenophil and Parthenophe, 1593. . . . A divine centvrie of spirituall sonnets, 1595. . . . Part II.*, 2 vols

ed. A. B. Grossart, (Manchester, UK: Private Subscribers, 1875) IS: 148. Akrigg cites all these complimentary pieces (*Shakespeare and the Earl of Southampton*, 33–40).

13. Henry Lok, *Poems of Henry Lok 1593-1597*, ed. A. B. Grossart (Blackburn, UK: Private Collections, 1871), 410.

14. Sidney Lee, 'Dictionary of National Biography, 1885-1900, Volume 26', n.d., Wikisource, available at: http://en.wikisource.org/wiki/Herbert,_William_(1580-1630)_(DNB00) (accessed 19 July 2014).

15. Quoted in Thomas Tyler, *The Herbert-Fitton Theory of Shakespeare's Sonnets: A Reply*, (London: D. Nutt, 1898), n.p.

16. John Aubrey, *Aubrey's Brief Lives* (Jeffrey, NH: David R. Godine Publisher, 1998), 145.

17. Duncan-Jones, *Sonnets*, 66.

18. Jonson's *Epigrams*, 'Dedication', lines 1–2; 19–20, available at http://hollowaypages.com/jonson1692epigrams.htm, (accessed 18 July 2014). For a close reading of the poem's attributes see, William Kolbrener, '"Man to Man": Self-Fashioning in Jonson's "To William Pembroke"', *Texas Studies in Literature and Language* 39.3 (1997): 290–3.

19. Park Honan, 'Henry Wriothesley', in *The Oxford Dictionary of National Biography*, ed. H. C. G. Matthew and B. Harrison (Oxford: Oxford University Press, 2004), available at: http://www.oxforddnb.com/templates/article.jsp?articleid=30073&back=#cosubject_3007,3 (accessed 23 July 2014).

20. Edith Snook, *Women, Beauty and Power in Early Modern England: A Feminist Literary History* (New York: Palgrave Macmillan, 2011), 40. Snook's discussion is focused with unnecessary narrowness on the Stuart regime and the effect of the seventeenth century advent of the English slave trade, but such ideological formations cannot credibly be assumed to have sprung up full blown suddenly in the seventeenth century, as my own work, *Black Lives*, has tried to make clear; Imtiaz Habib, *Black Lives in the English Archives 1500-1677: Imprints of the Invisible* (Lanham, MD: University Press of America, 2000).

21. For Wriothesley the most confident current advocate is Jonathan Bate, *The Genius of Shakespeare* (Oxford: Oxford University Press, 1998) 49, and for Herbert it is Katherine Duncan-Jones, *Sonnets*, 'Introduction', 52–68.

22. In the play, the fecklessness of Bassanio who is the precarious future of Christian Venice parallels the prodigality of both Southampton and Herbert who are the only hopes of their aristocratic lines' continuance.

23. Stephen Greenblatt, *Shakespeare's Freedom* (University of Chicago Press, 2010), 25. For Greenblatt, the count for the incidence of 'fair' across Shakespeare's *oeuvre* is 700.

24. All figures derived from simple word searches for 'fair', 'beauty', at the Open Source Shakespeare database at http://www.opensourceshakespeare.org/.

25. Cathy Shrank, 'Counsel, Succession and the Politics of Shakespeare's *Sonnets*' in *Shakespeare and Early Modern Political Thought*, ed. David Armitage, Conal Condren, and Andrew Fitzmaurice (Cambridge: Cambridge University Press, 2009), 111; Duncan-Jones, *Sonnets*, 55–69.

26. Charlotte Carmichael Stopes *The Life of Henry, Third Earl of Southampton: Shakespeare's Patron* (Cambridge: Cambridge University Press, 1922), 341, 344.

27. Robert Sean Brazil, '1609 Chronology: The Second Charter of the Virginia Company – May 23, 1609', in *1609 Chronology*, 23 May 2009, available at: http://1609chronology.blogspot.com/2009/05/second-charter-of-virginia-company-may.html (accessed 3 August 2014); Stopes, *The Life of Henry*, 443.

28. For Wriothesley and Herbert as the two most popular/powerful early modern English aristocrats see Alastair Bellany, *The Politics of Court Scandal in Early Modern England: News Culture and the Overbury Affair, 1603-1660* (Cambridge: Cambridge University Press 2007), 43–44; and Melissa Sanchez, *Erotic Subjects: The Sexuality of Politics in Early Modern English Literature* (Oxford: Oxford University Press, 2011), 91.

29. The amalgamation of Southampton and Pembroke into a composite figure of social and cultural ideality in the Elizabethan popular imagination as proposed here echoes Stephen Greenblatt's speculation to that effect (Stephen Greenblatt, *Will in the World: How Shakespeare Became Shakespeare* [New York: W.W. Norton, 2004], 227–28), Johanna Rickman's postulation of such an idea (Johanna Rickman, *Love, Lust, and License in Early Modern England: Illicit Sex and the Nobility* [Burlington, VT: Ashgate, 2008], 66–67), and parallels Kathrine Duncan-Jones's suggestion of a like composite for the 'Rival Poets'. For more historical grounds for a combined use of the two figures see Jonathan Bate, *The Genius of Shakespeare* (Oxford: Oxford University Press, 1998), who suggests that Shakespeare initially sought Southampton's patronage but when later Southampton's prospects of munificent patronage dimmed he switched to Pembroke (46–47, 58), and that the dedication (W.H.) was 'a sleight of hand assurance to Pembroke that he was the inspirer when he was in fact one of two male inspirers' (47).

30. Charles Hughes, ed., *Willobie His Avisa* (London: Sherrat and Hughes, 1904), xxi–xxiii.

31. Greenblatt, *Will in the World*, p. 32. Greenblatt's speculation is based on Rowland White's report in his letters to Philip Sidney's older brother, Henry Sidney [Sir Henry Sidney et al., *Letters and memorials of state: in the reigns of Queen Mary, Queen Elizabeth, King James, King Charles the First, part of the reign of King Charles the Second, and Oliver's usurpation*, ed. Arthur Collins, 2 vols (London: Printed for T. Osborne, 1746) II: 132].

32. Akrigg, *Shakespeare and the Earl of Southampton*, 193; Duncan-Jones, *Sonnets*, 66.

33. See note 2 above for the use of 'homosocial' and homosociality.

34. 'Jean Baudrillard - Simulacra and Simulations - XI. Holograms', trans Sheila Faria Glazer, n.d., available at: http://www.egs.edu/faculty/jean-baudrillard/articles/simulacra-and-simulations-xi-holograms/ (accessed 13 March 2014). Gwendolyn Audrey Foster, *Performing Whiteness* (Albany: State University of New York Press, 2003), ; Foster cites Baudrillard.

35. Joyce Sutphen, '"A Dateless Lively Heat": Storing Loss in the Sonnets', in Schiffer *Shakespeare's Sonnets*, 199–218; see 212. Even though Sutphen is not talking of a *white* self, per se, her point still holds in the context of a white self that I am working with here.

36. A simple search of the electronic text of the *Sonnets* on Open Source Shakespeare at http://www.opensourceshakespeare.org/ for incidences of the word 'see' and its synonyms produces the following: see 61 times; look 32 times; gaze 5 times; behold 7 times; witness 3 times; view 10 times; mark 4 times; and for words associated with seeing, eyes 35 times; sight 17 times; for a total 174 times in 154 sonnets.
37. All citations from the Shakespeare's *Sonnets* are from the Duncan-Jones ed., *Shakespeare's Sonnets*.
38. While particular peaks and troughs may vary in subjective readings, the steady undulation of the work's progress will still be apparent.
39. Duncan-Jones believes that this sonnet numerically marks 'the completion of two "grand climaterics"' *Sonnets*, 126. It is surely also interesting that her comment on sonnet 126 falls on page 126 of her edition!
40. See my *Black Lives*.
41. Joel Fineman, *Shakespeare's Perjured Eye: The Invention of Poetic Subjectivity in the Sonnets* (Berkeley: University of California Press, 1986), 35–43, and my book, *Shakespeare and Race: Postcolonial Praxis in the Early Modern Period* (Lanham, MD: University Press of America, 2000), 25–31.
42. Rollins, II: 242–72; esp. pp. 242–3, 249–52, 268–9, 271–2.
43. In addition to the Rowland Whyte's testimony cited earlier; see Michael R. Burch, 'Shakespeare Sonnets Analysis: Speculations, Intuition and Deduction', web essay available at http://www.thehypertexts.com/Shakespeare%20Sonnets%20Analysis.htm (accessed 13 March 2014); Lewis Frederick Bostelmann, *Rutland: A Chronologically Arranged Outline of the Life of Roger Manners, Fifth Earl of Rutland* (New York: Rutland Publishing, 1911), 9 (Shakespeare overheard complaining to the young earl of Rutland about getting good actors for female parts); Clara Longworth de Chambrun, 'The Inspirers of Shakespeare's Sonnets', *The North American Review*, 198 (1913): 132 (Herbert's father employed/organized companies of players); Honan (Southampton can be located at Gray's Inn in the early 1590s, among the many theatrical events that were common there).
44. See my *Black Lives*, 263.
45. For a study of this convention see Annette Drew-Bear, *Painted Faces on the Renaissance Stage: The Moral Significance of Face-painting Conventions* (Cranbury, NJ: Associated University Presses, 1994).
46. A good example of this automatic critical conviction is M. L. Stapleton's essay, '"My False Eyes": The Dark Lady and Self Knowledge', *Studies in Philology* 90.2 (1993): 213–30, wherein he sees the black figure as 'a literary character and a historical figure, a paradoxical – and now unfashionable – conjunction of selves' (214), without the slightest recognition of a historical black presence in her. Yet, the critical orthodoxy of a denial of a historical blackness in the poems is beginning to change, as is witnessed by Marvin Hunt's insistence ('Be Dark, but Not Too Dark: Shakespeare's Dark Lady as a Sign of Color', in Schiffer, *Shakespeare's Sonnets*, 369–90) and both De Grazia's tentative, and Dympna Callaghan's grudging, admissions (De Grazia, 'Scandal,' 106; and Callaghan, *Shakespeare's Sonnets* [London: Blackwell Publishing,

2007], 48–9), of the possibility of a historical black woman in the *Sonnets*. For an extended analysis of the early modern and modern critical politics of the non-representability of the historical black woman, see Chapter Two of my *Black Lives*, 'Colonialism's Homosocial Eugenics and Black Desire', 23–86.

47. Raymond Alden, ed., *The Sonnets of Shakespeare: from the Quarto of 1609 with variorum readings and commentary* (New York: Houghton Mifflin, 1916), 349, and Sidney Lee, quoted by Alden, 347.

48. Duncan-Jones, *Sonnets*, 6.

49. For the classical Greek rhetorician Quintilian, aposiopesis or 'the breaking of an expression before it is complete' (Hammond, *Figuring Sex Between Men*, 14) is a 'transitional' device used 'to introduce a digression or announce a change . . . in the conduct of . . . [the] argument', and for the Elizabethan grammarian, Puttenham it is a 'figure of interruption'; H. Baran, A. W. Halsall, and A. Watson, 'Aposiopesis', in *The Princeton Encyclopedia of Poetry and Poetics*, eds. Stephen Cushman, Clare Cavanagh, Jahan Ramazani, Paul Rouzer, 4th edn (Princeton, NJ: Princeton University Press, 2012), 60–1.

50. Anthony Holden suggests something similar when he says with the expectedly unbridled confidence of a Southampton-ist that 'Southampton's relationship with Shakespeare in the early 1590's . . . bequeathed . . . some of the finest poetry in the English language'. In *Shakespeare Found! A Life Portrait at Last: Portraits, Poets, Painters, Poems*, ed. Stanley Wells (Stratford-upon-Avon: Shakespeare Birthplace Trust, 2009), 59.

CHAPTER TWO

Staging the *Blazon*

Black and White and Red All Over

EVELYN GAJOWSKI

Few theoretical and critical approaches within contemporary Shakespeare studies and early modern English studies have generated more intellectual excitement, ethical considerations, and controversy than critical race theory. Indeed, as I revise my introductory paragraph to this contribution to Arthur L. Little, Jr.'s edited volume, *White People in Shakespeare*, in 2021 the Republican Party and radical right-wing media in the US have dislodged critical race theory from its relatively obscure home within academic and legal discourses, appropriating it and demonizing it as the most recent in a long line of wedge issues deployed to manipulate the US electorate to vote against its own best interests. At their outset, critical race studies were preoccupied with the theoretical question of whether race existed in the early modern period. However, a normative whiteness always already underlies the residue of this debate, as Little notes, regardless of one's theoretical position: 'whatever extent blacks or gays as we know them may or may not have existed in the Renaissance', as he puts it, 'such theoretical erasures leave in place an assumed and affective whiteness and straightness'.[1] Generally, critical race studies were preoccupied with non-white individuals, characters, and peoples. Whiteness has been, if not completely invisible, largely under-theorized, or un-theorized. Yet, as Valerie Wayne argues, 'it is this very whiteness that we need to learn to see'.[2] Attempting to redress this imbalance, this chapter, like this volume as a whole, attempts to analyse the significance of the 'assumed and affective whiteness' that Little notices – specifically, in both the Petrarchan discursive tradition, which yokes whiteness to redness, and in racist cultural discourse, which juxtaposes whiteness and blackness. I aim to analyse how the early modern drama of Shakespeare and his contemporaries embodies these poetic and cultural discourses, transforming them into semiotic codes on stage, especially in dramatic texts such as Shakespeare's *Titus Andronicus* or John Ford's *'Tis Pity She's a Whore*. I aim, further, to trouble both binaries – white/red and white/black – analysing their collision with each other, especially in dramatic texts such as Shakespeare's *Othello* or Elizabeth Cary's *The Tragedy of Mariam*.

THE WHITE/RED NEXUS

The moment in John Ford's *'Tis Pity She's a Whore* when Giovanni enters with Annabella's heart impaled on a dagger marks the most spectacular staging of the *blazon*, or the male anatomization of the female, on the early modern English stage. The drama is saturated with Petrarchan moments in which a male character idealizes a female character, constructing her as a love object, and Ovidian moments in which a male character denigrates a female character, constructing her as a sex object. Within Shakespeare's dramatic texts, Romeo's idealization of Juliet best exemplifies Petrarchan discourse, while Iago's and Othello's denigration of Desdemona best exemplifies Ovidian discourse.[3] At times, the drama is punctuated by theatrical moments that embody both discursive traditions, leading up to and culminating in Ford's spectacle: the rape, silencing and dismemberment of Lavinia in *Titus Andronicus*;[4] Romeo's Petrarchan rhetoric and worshipful stance below Juliet; Orlando's nailing love poems onto the trees in the Forest of Arden; Orsino's supine posture and Olivia's deconstruction of the *blazon*; Othello's reference to Desdemona's alabaster skin at the moment he murders her; Giacomo's masturbatory *blazon* over Innogen's sleeping body in *Cymbeline*;[5] Hermione stepping down from the pedestal in *The Winter's Tale*; the Duchess of Malfi's declaration to Antonio, 'This is flesh and blood, sir, / 'Tis not the figure cut in alabaster / Kneels at my husband's tomb' (1.1.445); John Webster's problematization of the character of Vittoria, and 'woman', generally, as *The White Devil*; and Elizabeth Cary's insistence on Mariam's whiteness in *The Tragedy of Mariam*. The colours white and red are integral to the *blazon*, or the anatomization of the female, in the literary inheritance of Shakespeare and his contemporaries. The *blazon* conventionally encodes female skin as lilies, snow, alabaster, or ivory, and female lips as roses, cherries, or rubies.[6] The female's white and red face was endlessly emblazoned, white and red evolving into shorthand for a standard of female beauty.[7]

During the twelfth century, troubadours in the south of France such as Guiraut de Borneil (*c*. 1138–1200) invented romantic love as a structure of thought in the Western tradition. While lords were called away to fight in the Crusades, ladies presided over castles and manors in their absence. Itinerant troubadours and minstrels literally sang for their suppers, having everything to gain – a meal and a bed – by praising the presiding female. Such were the material conditions underlying the origins of the Petrarchan discursive tradition. Eventually, this tradition came to construct females as love objects, rhetorically idealizing them, placing them, figuratively, in a position of power on a pedestal above the male speaker. It countered the Ovidian discursive tradition that constructs females as sex objects, rhetorically denigrating them, placing them, figuratively, in a position lower than the male speaker. A discursive tradition with a lengthier history, it originates in the classical world in texts such as *Ars Amatoria*.

The significance of 'the eyes' and 'the heart', the triad that makes possible intersubjectivity in an interpersonal psychodrama, is evident in the following poem by de Borneil. Rather than serving as the window of the soul, according to the conventional religious ideology of the time, the eyes serve as the window of the heart:

So through the eyes love attains the heart:
For the eyes are the scouts of the heart,
And the eyes go reconnoitering
For what it would please the heart to possess.
And when they are in full accord
And firm, all three, in the one resolve,
At that time, perfect love is born
From what the eyes have made welcome to the heart.
Not otherwise can love either be born or have commencement
Than by this birth and commencement moved by inclination.[8]

The emphasis on 'inclination' is significant. In opposition to the impersonal social practice of arranged marriage that early modern English dramatists transform into the dramatic device of enforced marriage in countless texts (e.g., Shakespeare's *The Taming of the Shrew*, *A Midsummer Night's Dream* and *Romeo and Juliet*, Mary Wroth's *Love's Victory*, and John Ford's *The Broken Heart*), de Borneil stresses the personal dimension – the radical notion of one individual choosing another.

Based upon the physical appearance of a real-life woman, Laura, Petrarch sets forth the rhetorical convention of female beauty in Italy in the 1300s that held sway for centuries: white skin, red lips, hair of golden filigree, and eyes like stars. He constructs Laura 'as a part or parts of a woman'.[9] His Sonnet 90 exemplifies his use of the *blazon*: 'She used to let her golden hair fly free. / For the wind to toy and tangle and molest; / Her eyes were brighter than the radiant west.'[10] Elsewhere, Petrarch constructs Laura's beauty in terms of white and red, describing her mouth, for example, as 'full of pearls and roses'.[11] Petrarchan anatomization and idealization of the female body simultaneously emphasizes her whiteness and occludes her sexuality – in effect, asexualizing her. Petrarchan discourse has the effect of wishing away 'the white woman's whole body' and therefore 'her sexual nature'. On the other hand, women who do not fulfil the stereotype of white fairness or beauty come to be constructed exclusively in terms of their bodies, or, more precisely, their sexuality. In early modern England, black women 'are praised for their materiality'.[12] Even as Petrarchan discourse associates female whiteness with fairness, beauty, and asexuality, Ovidian discourse associates female blackness with ugliness, even deformity, and sexuality.

In early modern England more than two centuries later, the emphasis is on self-dramatization: the discomfort of the sexual frustration of the male speaker in response to the refusal of the celebrated female to bestow her sexual favours on him. Sir Philip Sidney exemplifies this trend. The red-and-white colour scheme has become formulaic, as is evident in his description of Stella, or Penelope Deveraux Rich, in his sonnet sequence, *Astrophil and Stella*:

Queen Virtue's Court, which some call Stella's face,
Prepared by Nature's chiefest furniture,
Hath his front built of alabaster pure;
Gold is the covering of that stately place;
The door, by which sometimes comes forth her grace,

Red porphyr is, which lock of pearl makes sure,
Whose porches rich (which name of cheeks endure)
Marble mixed with red and white do interlace[13]

Stella's beauty is that of lilies and roses (Sonnet 100); her lips, 'blushing red' (Sonnet 43), are like roses and rubies. Indeed, the white/red aesthetic was influential enough to shape the social behaviour of early modern English women. Lead-based cosmetics created a chalk-white face with bright red cheeks.[14]

The conventional *blazon* structures Sonnet 15 from Spenser's *Amoretti*, using mercantile tropes from the realms of geographical exploration and commercial exploitation to catalogue the various parts of the female anatomy and equate them with valuable jewels and precious metals. The white/red colour scheme plays its conventional role: 'If Saphyres, loe her eies Saphyres plaine, / If Rubies, loe hir lips be Rubies sound: / If Pearles, hir teeth be pearles both pure and round; / If Yuorie, her forehead yuory weene; / If Gold, her locks are finest gold on ground; / If siluer, her faire hands are siluer sheene.'[15] The white racialization of the female is undeniable. However, in the context of European exploration and conquest of non-European cultures, something new is afoot: the male speaker represents the female body in terms of valuable commodities plundered from new worlds. The poetry of praise and the glorification of English females in the sonnet tradition eventually become a part of England's nationalist project – a way for England to define itself 'politically, culturally, and racially' and to establish itself as 'a dominant force on the world stage'.[16]

Shakespeare's Sonnet 130 performs an intervention into the Petrarchan discursive tradition. The speaker parodies conventions that have been, by the last decade of the sixteenth century, centuries in the making. The speaker deconstructs the conventional *blazon*, following the structure of cataloguing a woman's bodily parts but standing the *blazon* on its head by methodically inverting the stereotypical content – anatomical female part by anatomical female part:

My mistress' eyes are nothing like the sun;
Coral is far more red than her lips' red;
If snow be white why then her breasts are dun;
If hairs be wires, black wires grow on her head.
I have seen roses damask'd, red and white,
But no such roses see I in her cheeks. . .[17]

The humorous tone raises the question, 'Who or what is the butt of the joke?' Upon reading the three quatrains, we might think it is the 'mistress'; yet when we read the couplet, we realize that the speaker is equating the entire Petrarchan discursive tradition with 'false compare'. The sonnet stands on its own. But it takes on greater depth of meaning when we consider it not only in the context of Shakespeare's other sonnets but also in the context of centuries of the Petrarchan discursive tradition that, by Shakespeare's time, had become utterly calcified and clichéd. That is, dead. After traversing several centuries and several nations (Italy, France and England), the whiteness trope takes on a ghostly, death-like quality. By the mid-seventeenth

FIGURE 2: Literal graphic representation of the blazon in accordance with the Petrarchan discursive tradition, from Charles Sorel, *The extravagant shepherd: or, The history of the shepherd Lysis: an anti-romance* (London: Printed by T. Newcomb for Thomas Heath, 1654). Image from Monash University Library Special Collections.

century, a graphic in Charles Sorel's *The Extravagant Shepherd* visually parodies the *blazon*, literally representing teeth as pearls, lips as roses, eyes as stars, hair as golden wires, breasts as globes, and so on. The effect is grotesque (see Figure 2).

By the close of the sixteenth and the outset of the seventeenth centuries, the conventionalized rhetorical trope of the *blazon* gives way to its embodiment on the early modern English stage. The rhetorical representation of female dismemberment characterizes early modern English comedy; the physical enactment of female dismemberment characterizes early modern English tragedy. When male characters rhetorically anatomize the female, dramatists exploit the humorous potential of the situation. When male characters physically anatomize female characters, though, no one is laughing. This transition could be viewed as a battle between men – one that is first figuratively and then literally 'fought on the fields of woman's "celebrated" body'.[18] What happens in this transition from discourse to enactment, from metaphorical anatomizing of the female to literal dismemberment of the female, from poetic and comic genres to the tragic genre? More broadly construed, what are the implications of genre for gender? It is as though the potentially violent dismembering of the female body that is inherent in the rhetorical tradition of the *blazon*[19] finally becomes manifest, palpable. The *language* of woman hatred is not the same as *acts* of woman hatred: 'Misogyny is a way of speaking about, as distinct from doing something to, women. . . . Speech can be a form of action and even of social practice, or at least its ideological component.'[20] *Blazon* is the theory; dismemberment, the practice.

The homosocial relationships between pairs of male characters in Shakespeare's romantic comedies and love tragedies (e.g., Proteus/Valentine, Antipholus of Ephesus and Antipholus of Syracuse, Claudio/Benedick, Romeo/Mercutio, Antony/Enobarbus) dramatize romantic male desire for a female, on the one hand, and anti-romantic satirizing of the romantic male for having come under the influence of a female, on the other. In constructing the opposite sex, the romantics participate in idealizing, Petrarchan discourse while the anti-romantics participate in denigrating, Ovidian discourse. Yet in Shakespeare's comedies, we encounter a kind of character without precedent in the Western tradition: the articulate, assertive, and sympathetic female protagonist.

Two strands of comedy may be discerned on the early modern English stage – satiric comedy, represented by dramatists such as Jonson and Middleton, on the one hand, and romantic comedy, represented by dramatists such as Shakespeare, Greene, and Peele, on the other. As opposed to the satiric strand of comedy, wherein female characters are often objects of rival male characters' desire to be fought over, in the romantic strand of comedy female characters take centre stage. Indeed, they are often more interesting and memorable than their male counterparts. It is unusual for early modern English poets to view heterosexual relations from a female perspective.[21] Yet Shakespeare's female protagonists more often than not are the prominent figures in the dramatic worlds of his romantic comedies. Every time Shakespeare adapts a source to a comedy, he expands the roles of the female characters. His female protagonists, moreover, are typically more psychologically grounded, realistic, and mature than the male protagonists, as well as more generous and steadfast in their affections. In other words, they are subjects, not objects.

One of the most delicious moments in romantic comedy occurs during the initial encounter of Olivia and Viola/Cesario in *Twelfth Night*, when Olivia speaks, deconstructing the *blazon* in an ironic accounting of her own physical assets:

> O sir, I will not be so hard-hearted: I will give out divers schedules of my beauty. It shall be inventoried, and every particle and utensil labelled to my will. As, item, two lips indifferent red; item, two grey eyes, with lids to them; item, one neck, one chin, and so forth. Were you sent hither to praise me?
>
> —*TN* 1.5.238–43

In a manner similar to that of the speaker in Shakespeare's Sonnet 130, Olivia methodically describes each of the female anatomical parts that sonneteers celebrate – but in a matter-of-fact, prosaic way to parody, and repulse, Orsino's insipid Petrarchan overtures. The praise of female beauty is a legacy shaped 'by the male imagination for the male imagination'; it is the product of males talking about females to males.[22] Yet Olivia intervenes into that tradition, disrupting that legacy by inserting herself into it as a speaking subject and dislocating the male construction of her as a silent, idealized object. In doing so, she echoes Shakespeare's Juliet and other female protagonists and anticipates Pamphilia, the speaker in Mary Wroth's sonnet cycle, *Pamphilia to Amphilanthus*, with which her prose romance, *The Countess of Montgomery's Urania*, concludes.

Shakespeare's romances, or last plays, reanimate the clichéd formulas of Petrarchan discourse when villains and male protagonists alike express felt emotions: Iachimo's voyeurism of Imogen's sleeping body; Posthumus's tirade on eradicating 'the woman's part' from his masculine self (2.4.172); Leontes's wonder – 'O, she's warm!' – when Hermione steps down from the pedestal (5.3.109), a far cry from the accusatory outburst – 'Too hot, too hot!' – with which he initiates his pornographic fantasy of her infidelity (1.2.108). When Iachimo's voyeuristic gaze consumes Imogen's sleeping body in *Cymbeline*, he is overwhelmed by her beauty. According to the conventions of Petrarchan discourse, his eroticized *blazon* singles out her skin, lips, and eyes for praise, relying on the white/red code: 'fresh lily, / And whiter than the sheets! That I might touch! / But kiss, one kiss! Rubies unparagon'd, / How dearly they do't!' (2.2.15–18). As voyeur, Iachimo takes pleasure in the pornographic fantasy he weaves; as wager-maker, he reweaves that fantasy as a seduction fantasy for Posthumus's consumption. Savouring the beauty of the female whose honour he will sully, he takes visual and verbal pleasure in Imogen's body so intense that he nearly forgets his purpose. The bedchamber scene stages the deconstruction of idealizing Petrarchan discourse and exposes its underlying concern with seduction,[23] as romantic *blazon* gives way to seduction fantasy. The scene thereby provides a prime example in Shakespeare's dramatic texts of the theoretical phenomenon: *to-be-looked-at-ness*.[24] When a female is not only silent and passive but literally unconscious, the voyeur is able to enjoy the free play of his imagination over her body in what amounts to a masturbatory fantasy of omnipotence. The bedchamber scene dramatizes, in microcosm, the gendered power dynamics of the Petrarchan discursive tradition regarding the status of woman under patriarchy: man constructs meaning, while woman has meaning inscribed upon her.

It is shocking that Posthumus falls for the lie of Imogen's infidelity. When Iachimo's report detailing the artifacts of Imogen's bedchamber does not succeed in duping Posthumus, Iachimo (like Iago before him) readily provides 'ocular proof' (*Oth* 3.3.360) that focuses instead on two details of Imogen's person. His presentation of her manacle, or bracelet, causes Posthumus to doubt her, albeit temporarily. It is an unconventional use of the *blazon* as 'ocular proof' of female unfaithfulness, however, that succeeds in persuading Posthumus of her infidelity. Iachimo describes a unique anatomical detail, a 'cinque-spotted' mole (2.2.38), a black spot beneath Imogen's intimate bodily part, her left breast. To torture him further, moreover, Iachimo couches the lie of the sexual encounter in the language of consumption. It was the particular anatomical detail of the mole that aroused his sexual insatiability: 'By my life, / I kiss'd it, and it gave me present hunger / To feed again, though full' (2.4.136–38). The mole is one of many instances of the use of blackness to accentuate whiteness in early modern English literature and culture. In Iachimo's pornographic fantasy, the eroticized black mole set off against the whiteness of Imogen's skin exacerbates his appetite for her body.

It is worth noting the wager between Posthumus and Iachimo that sets the latter off on his unsuccessful attempt to violate Imogen's chastity. Nationalistic rivalry among male characters manifests itself as a contest over, through, and in female bodies:

> FRENCHMAN
> ... each of us fell in praise of our country mistresses, this gentleman at that time vouching – and upon warrant of bloody affirmation – his to be more fair, virtuous, wise, chaste, constant, qualified, and less attemptable than any the rarest of our ladies in France.
>
> IACHIMO
> That lady is not now living, or this gentlemen's opinion by this worn out.
>
> POSTHUMUS
> She holds her virtue still, and I my mind.
>
> IACHIMO
> You must not so far prefer her fore ours of Italy.
>
> POSTHUMUS
> Being so far provoked as I was in France I would abate her nothing, though I profess myself her adorer, not her friend.
>
> IACHIMO
> As fair and as good – a kind of hand-in-hand comparison – had been something too fair and too good for any lady in Britain.
>
> —*Cym* 1.5.57–72

Shakespeare dramatizes the contest among French, English, and Italian nationalities as a rivalry among female 'fairness', whiteness, beauty – all of which are equated with female virtue, chastity. The white racialization of the female that Petrarch initiates in his celebration of Laura and that Sidney, Spenser, and other English sonneteers continue takes centre stage.

Echoing the wager between Posthumus and Iachimo that structures the plot of *Cymbeline*, the rivalry among early modern English playwrights manifests itself as an Oedipal struggle for power. Increasingly, the female becomes the site of a disturbingly new kind of male competition that resolves itself over, through, and in the annihilation of the female body through which the drama sexualizes itself.[25] *Cymbeline* points the way to the sexualized theatrical spectacles that are contemporaneous with it and that follow it – *The Tragedy of Mariam*, *The White Devil*, *The Duchess of Malfi*, *The Changeling*, *The Broken Heart*, *'Tis Pity She's a Whore*. Jacobean theatre is about power – and the sexualized female body becomes the vehicle for its expression.

THE WHITE/BLACK NEXUS

Scholarship on the origins of race, racial representation and racial discourse has been characterized by disagreement. Historians argue for a medieval period that was 'pre-racial', asserting that 'race' was akin to twenty-first-century conceptions of 'ethnicity'.[26] Literary scholars disagree, asserting that racial difference played a significant role in the construction of premodern European identity.[27] Others challenge the view that medieval Europe was 'pre-racial'. The discourse that established 'the normativity of whiteness' (and, by implication, the deviance of blackness) is evident as early as the Middle English romance, *The King of Tars* (*c*. 1330), which, coincidentally, celebrates Christianity.[28] Constructions of whiteness and blackness can be traced to the early thirteenth-century German romance, *Parzival*, by Wolfram von Eschenbach. Both romances illuminate the tangled relationships between theological and biological notions of race in the premodern and early modern eras.[29] The racist associations with which we are familiar in the twenty-first century – of whiteness with goodness, purity, and innocence, and blackness with evil, sin, and guilt – were present in premodern Europe. The word 'race' had different denotations and connotations in the premodern era than it does in the twenty-first century, and this disparity is worthy of analysis.[30]

While Greek and Roman writers describe racial and character difference, they do not equate blackness with inferiority. Rather, it was the early Christian writers (e.g., Albertus Magnus, Bartholomaeus Anglicus, Gregory the Great, Paulinus of Nola) who initiated the associations of whiteness with goodness and blackness with evil.[31] The early Christian writers effectively initiate ideologies of racial difference as we know them today. This development occurs, in particular, in Christian constructions of the blackness of the Saracen, whose 'dark skin and diabolical racial physiognomy' were the most familiar, 'the most exorbitant embodiment of racial alterity'.[32] Strictly speaking, the Christian body did not have a race because 'the body of the other always carried that burden on its behalf'.[33] Thus, whiteness is invisible, while blackness is not. Evidence of colour prejudice and anti-Black sentiments have been traced to the founders of the Christian church such as Paul and Origen. According to the Roman Catholic formulation, blackness became equated with sin, demons and devils.[34]

In early modern literary scholarship, Ania Loomba challenges scholars' assertions that race issues cannot be analysed in early modern culture and literature because the concept, 'race', did not exist. The association of whiteness with goodness and blackness with evil derived, in part, from a Bible-centred conception of the world according to which humanity was measured by its 'geographical distance from the Holy Land; hence black people were devilish because they existed outside both the physical and the conceptual realm of Christianity'.[35] In early modern England, whiteness was viewed as primary – the default, the norm – whereas blackness was viewed as secondary, deviant. George Best's 1578 account of Genesis constructs blackness as a hereditary infection of blood (7: 264) and black skin as the result of polluted and polluting 'sexual transgression'.[36] Whiteness thereby functions as the 'originary truth', while blackness signifies a 'later horror', an 'accident or aberration', a 'jungle infestation'.[37] Throughout the development of these fluctuating ideologies of national identity, whiteness came to be equated with the European male 'self', while blackness came to be equated with the non-European female 'other'. Long before the English met people whose skins were black, the very words 'black' and 'white' were heavily charged with meaning: blackness signified death, mourning, baseness, evil, sin and danger; whiteness signified purity, virginity, innocence, good magic, flags of truce, harmless lies and perfect human beauty.[38]

WHITE DEATH[39]

The masculine emphasis of Elizabethan tragedy is apparent when we compare it to Jacobean tragedy. Generally speaking, the female characters in the dramatic texts of Kyd, Marlowe, Chapman, Jonson, and Tourneur are minor, conventional figures. Beaumont, Fletcher, Cary, Webster, Middleton, Dekker and Ford, however, shift the emphasis from male protagonist to female protagonist, from betrayer to betrayed. Woman seems to be 'the natural subject' of early modern English tragedy.[40] The phenomenon of the rise of the female protagonist in Jacobean tragedy has several roots. First, more translations of Euripides' dramatic texts were published in early modern England than those of any other classical playwright.[41] Euripides' texts are notable for their emphasis on female protagonists and the psychological dimension of human experience: *Medea, Andromache, Electra, The Trojan Women*. Too, females are inextricably bound up in sacrifice, particularly in those tragedies translated before 1560: *Hecuba* (1506), *Iphigenia at Aulis* (1506), *Alecestis* (1554), *Phoenissae* (1560), in addition to Sophocles' *Antigone* (1533). Woman doesn't just have a prominent place in sacrificial narratives – she is herself constructed as 'naturally sacrificeable'.[42]

A second reason for the rise of the female protagonist is the influence of Beaumont and Fletcher, who helped to turn the drama away from the masculine arenas of politics and history toward the study of intimate, emotional relationships. Third, the dramatists invented the tragic female protagonist at the very moment that interest in the position of women in early modern English society was being debated. The pamphlet controversy about the nature of 'woman' opened up a fruitful subject for interrogation on the part of the dramatists. When Beaumont, Fletcher, Cary, Webster, Middleton, Dekker and Ford dramatize the misery of enforced or forbidden desire, they emphasize the vulnerability of female characters in dramatic worlds governed by male characters and masculine ideals. Yet female protagonists are not merely sacrificed at the altar of masculine honour and ambition; they yearn for freedom from tyranny of patriarchal families and social conventions. A fourth reason for the rise of the female protagonist, then, is the dialectical relationship between subjectivity and power that structures the drama. Female subjectivity is defined *through* resistance on the part of individual protagonists to patriarchal institutions, practices and discourses. Even as the texts dramatize worlds in the thrall of patriarchy, they also valorise instances of female subjectivity in crisis under pressure. Indeed, female subjectivity is defined by that pressure.

White/red and white/black semiotic codes collide with each other in Elizabeth Cary's closet drama, *The Tragedy of Mariam*. Her interpolation of the two into her dramatic text is one of its striking features. They not only constitute the identity formation of the female protagonist and the female antagonist – they structure the dramatic action. Beginning with her subtitle, *The Faire Queene of Jewry*, on the title page of the 1613 edition and continuing throughout the dramatic action, Cary deploys Petrarchan conventions to describe Mariam. She repeatedly configures her female protagonist's skin in terms of its whiteness, its fairness – both of which constitute her beauty. Herod, Cary's male protagonist, does not appear until Act 4, enabling a range of female characters to dominate the dramatic action: Mariam; Alexandra; Doris, Herod's ex-spouse; Salome, Herod's sister; and Graphina, Herod's brother's lover. During Herod's absence in Rome, they vie for power and jockey for position by reading religious, ethnic and national differences within the white/black binary.[43]

More so than any other early modern English dramatic text, *Mariam* introduces female characters through references to their physical appearance.[44] Cary links competition to power and exploits female beauty as an instance of power. As the dramatic action of Shakespeare's *Antony and Cleopatra* suggests, female beauty influences politics. A descendant of David, Mariam's beauty embodies her racial and social superiority. It is 'matchless' (5.1.172), a standard against which other female characters are measured and found wanting. It exceeds that of not only Roman females, but also Biblical and Greek females. Mariam is constructed as a divine creature who is more beautiful than Caesar's Livia. Like her, Cleopatra is referred to in the text but is not represented on stage. As Alexandra – Mariam's mother – claims, had Antony met Mariam, he would have abandoned Cleopatra: 'He would have loved thee, and thee alone, / And left the brown Egyptian clean forsaken' (1.2.189–90). According to Alexandra, Antony would have preferred Mariam's white skin to Cleopatra's dark skin.

It is later in the dramatic action that Cary emphatically deploys whiteness tropes. Attempting to absolve himself of the moral culpability of having ordered Mariam's execution, Herod blames Salome for having manipulated him to do so. To accomplish this psychological and political two-step of plausible deniability, he rhetorically distances himself from Salome and contrasts Mariam's white skin and Salome's black skin. As Herod and Salome debate the complexion of Mariam's beauty, he uses the *blazon* rhetorically to anatomize Mariam's body according to the conventions of Petrarchan discourse: 'Her eyes like stars, her forehead like the sky' (4.7.451). Salome accuses Herod of having succumbed to a fit of raving, 'doting' (4.7.453) Petrarchism. Were he in possession of his faculties, he would see Mariam's eyes for what they are: 'ebon-hued' (4.7.454). She drily remarks, 'A sable star hath been but seldom seen' (4.7.455) – at once challenging Herod's construction of Mariam's beauty and deconstructing Petrarchan conventions.[45] Iago's strategy for undoing

Desdemona comes to mind: 'So will I turn her virtue into pitch' (2.3.349). Salome is as capable of blackening the reputation of her enemy as any early modern villain.

Only when Mariam is dead does she elicit Herod's most idealized references to her whiteness. Like historical and fictional monarchs who order others to carry out executions on their behalf, he expresses immediate regret. He configures Mariam's innocence of crime by fastening on the whiteness of her body: 'she was fair, / Oh, what a white hand she had, it was so white, / It did the whiteness of the snow impair' (5.1.149–51). His repetition of 'white', 'white', and 'whiteness' evacuates it of meaning. When Herod recounts his order of execution – 'My word, though not my sword, made Mariam bleed' (5.1.189) – he accentuates her innocence in a grotesque inversion of the white/red colour scheme of Petrarchan convention. Although violence occurs off stage, in accordance with Senecan convention, the female martyr's blood is rhetorically present on stage.

Mariam is structured around the racialization of demonized femininity, as well as the deracialization of sanctified femininity.[46] The epithets that Mariam and Herod hurl at Salome suggest the transvaluation of whiteness from its well-worn deployment in Petrarchan discourse to animate something fresh, something new: racist discourse. Cary's use of bodily complexion to accentuate status, cultural and religious difference is striking.[47]

In their confrontation in Act 1, Salome insults Mariam by denigrating her social status: 'Your daughter's betters far, I dare maintain, / Might have rejoic'd to be my brother's wife' (1.4.221–2). Mariam responds in kind: 'My betters far! Base woman, 'tis untrue, / You scarce have ever my superiors seen: / For Mariam's servants were as good as you, / Before she became to be Judea's queen' (1.4.223–6). Mariam asserts her racial purity and superiority over Salome's mixed-blooded status:

Though I thy brother's face had never seen,
My birth thy baser birth so far excell'd,
I had to both of you the princess been.
Thou parti-Jew, and parti-Edomite,
Thou mongrel: issu'd from rejected race

—*Mariam* 1.4.232–6

Mariam's insistence on Salome's 'baseness' and her own royalty are rooted in the Biblical story of Esau and Jacob. Salome is an Edomite, a descendent of Esau, who sold his birthright to his brother, Jacob. Mariam is an Israelite, a descendent of Jacob. Cary represents Mariam's and Salome's confrontation as a racialized difference between Edomites, those of Esau's lineage, and Israelites, those of Jacob's lineage.[48] The impurity and inferiority of Esau's lineage originate in his having married non-Hebrew women. Even though Salome and Herod are practitioners of Judaism, they embody a continuation of this tainted lineage. By the end of the confrontation between Mariam and Salome, Mariam rhetorically configures Salome's 'base' status in terms of her moral culpability: 'With thy black acts I'll not pollute my breath' (1.4.244). In accordance with the conventions of Senecan tragedy, Mariam's insults incite Salome to take revenge.

If Cary organizes a beauty critique around Mariam, she organizes an 'anti-beauty critique' around Salome.[49] Even as racist discourse associates vice with blackness, so too does misogynistic discourse associate vice with femininity. *Mariam* deploys both blackness and femininity in its construction of Salome. In Herod's confrontation with Salome in Act 4, he contrasts Salome to Mariam, constructing her as a 'black' 'other': 'You are to her a sun-burnt blackamoor: / Your paintings cannot equal Mariam's praise. . . . / Hence from my sight, my black tormentor, hence' (4.7.462–3, 513). Indeed, in the broader context of European history and literature, the 'extreme of otherness' is the black female.[50] His comparison pushes her off the human register altogether: 'when to her you have approached near, / Myself hath often ta'en you for an ape' (4.7.459–60). Salome's blackness, impurity and guilt underscore Mariam's whiteness, purity and innocence. For him, Mariam's whiteness signifies not only her racial superiority to Salome, but also her moral innocence of crime. In *Mariam*, as in *Othello* and in early modern English literature and culture generally, 'blackness is used to create a value for whiteness'.[51] Blackness exists to accentuate whiteness, the preferred colour for the patriarchal, imperialistic language of power over bodies – female, black, poetic, dramatic, geographic.

Mariam resonates with *Othello* in significant ways. Both tragedies culminate in a wife's execution by a husband who comes under the influence of a villain. Salome's role is complex, combining aspects of the roles of Othello, Emilia, and Iago. Like Desdemona, Mariam is constructed in terms of her whiteness/fairness/innocence. Like Othello, Salome is repeatedly configured in terms of her blackness. Whereas Shakespeare's intervention in tradition is his construction of a protagonist who is black, Cary's intervention is her construction of an antagonist who is black and female. Like Emilia, Salome speaks the most feminist lines in the dramatic text. She challenges the Jewish law that constructs divorce as an exclusively masculine privilege: 'I'll be the custom-breaker: and begin / To show my sex the way to freedom's door' (1.4.309–10). Like Emilia's attack on the double standard in *Othello*'s willow-song scene – 'Let husbands know / That wives have sense like them' (4.3.92) – Salome participates in emergent discourse, anticipating social practices that will become dominant only centuries later. However, far from being ignorant of Iago's plot to undo Desdemona and thereby to undo Othello, as is Emilia, Salome assumes the role of antagonist, manipulating Herod to order Mariam's execution. Emilia challenges us with her conflicting roles of servant to Desdemona and wife of Iago. Likewise, Salome challenges us with her conflicting roles of feminist divorcee and antagonist. As early modern England moves toward exploitation of African cultures and peoples, blackness begins to represent 'the destructive potential of strangeness, disorder, and variety', particularly when entangled with 'the familiar, and familiarly threatening, unruliness of gender'.[52] *Mariam*'s denouement, like that of *Othello*, insists that its female protagonist is a martyr and the antagonist is a survivor. Despite her whiteness and her innocence, Mariam ends up dead; despite her blackness and her guilt, Salome ends up alive. Cary destabilizes paradigms of whiteness and blackness that early modern English drama inherits from classical and medieval discursive traditions of gender and race. In the end, death takes on the valence of whiteness, as Mariam herself realizes: 'Now death will teach me: he can pale as well / A cheek of roses as a cheek less bright' (4.1.529–30).

CODA

John Ford's dramatization of incest in *'Tis Pity She's a Whore* is the most daring in early modern English drama. As the first English play to represent sibling incest as 'a passionate, all-consuming love story', it is startlingly original.[53] Giovanni expresses an aristocratic, romantic idealism toward and poetic adoration of Annabella. The conventions of the Petrarchan *blazon* structure his description of his sister:

> View well her face, and in that little round
> You may observe a world of variety:
> For colour, lips; for sweet perfumes, her breath;
> For jewels, eyes; for threads of purest gold,
> Hair; for delicious choice of flowers, cheeks;
> Wonder in every portion of that throne.
> Hear her but speak, and you will swear the spheres
> Make music to the citizens of Heaven.
>
> —*'Tis Pity* 2.5.49–56

Like *Romeo and Juliet*, *'Tis Pity* dramatizes a forbidden relationship; unlike Shakespeare's love tragedy, it challenges the universal incest social taboo.

Because this is tragedy, Annabella is, in the end, not only anatomized rhetorically, but undone, literally – caught in the crossfire between the two males in her life – husband and brother – both of whom are consumed with jealousy and obsessed with revenge.[54] Soranzo cannot tolerate the insult of cuckoldry although he is himself a cuckolder; Giovanni cannot abide the idea of Annabella with another man. Over the course of the dramatic action, his adoring Petrarchan rhetoric and stance degenerate into mad possessiveness. He comes to believe that Annabella and her life literally belong to him. When their secret relationship is revealed, he murders her to take revenge on Soranzo: 'Revenge is mine' (5.5.86), he says as he simultaneously kisses her and stabs her to death. Giovanni states that he murders Annabella to preserve her honour: 'To save thy fame and kill thee with a kiss' (5.5.84). However, no sooner does he stab her to death than he reveals the secret of their incestuous relationship to every character on stage: "Tis Annabella's heart; 'tis! . . . / I vow 'tis hers. This dagger's point ploughed up / Her fruitful womb and left to me the fame / Of a most glorious executioner' (5.6.29–32).

Dramatic conflict in Ford often resolves itself in a freeze-frame of ceremonial gesture. Giovanni's entry onstage with Annabella's heart skewered on his dagger (5.6.8) is one such tableau. The visual rhetoric of her bloodied anatomical part puts a grotesque twist on the coded white/red colour scheme that animates the conventional *blazon*. Yet Giovanni's dismemberment of Annabella inverts an earlier implied gesture on his part. He attempts, in their first exchange, to validate his declaration of his desire for her by offering her his dagger and inviting her to cut his body to his heart: 'And here's my breast, strike home! / Rip up my bosom; there thou shalt behold / A heart in which is writ the truth I speak' (1.2.217–19). His offer conventionally configures the anatomical part of his heart as the locus of his desire; his hope is that opening his body will enable her to understand, and respond sympathetically to, the forbidden nature of that desire. Eventually, Annabella reciprocates Giovanni's declaration of love, but she does not reciprocate his physical gesture. Rather, in 5.6, her impaled heart signifies Giovanni's futile attempt at utter possession of her. His objectification of her throughout the dramatic action culminates in his dismemberment of her. However, as is often the case in the drama of Shakespeare and his contemporaries, the most admirable expression in *'Tis Pity* is Annabella's generous devotion.

The territory spanned by the arc connecting Guiraut de Borneil's metaphorical troping of 'the eyes' as a window to 'the heart' in twelfth-century France, on the one hand, and the palpable spectacle of Annabella's heart impaled on Giovanni's dagger, on the other, is immense. Yet the shocking visual emblem of Annabella's off-stage dismemberment is an inevitable culmination of the discursive tradition that rhetorically anatomizes the female. Three decades before John Ford's *'Tis Pity*, the white/red and the white/black semiotic codes collide in the dramatic action of Elizabeth Cary's *The Tragedy of Mariam*. Despite its status as a closet drama, Cary's text serves as a catalyst in the transition that occurs in early modern English literature around 1600 – from the centuries-long tradition of the rhetorical *blazon*, on the one hand, to the embodiment of the *blazon* on the early modern English stage, on the other. In its dramatization of the ethical conflict between two constructions of femininity, *Mariam* associates whiteness with its protagonist, Mariam, and blackness with its antagonist, Salome. In the intricacy of its dramatization of both discourses of whiteness – gendered and racial – *Mariam* insists upon making the invisible visible. The *emblazoning* of historical, poetic, comic and tragic females – Laura, Stella, Lavinia, Juliet, Olivia, Desdemona, Innogen, Mariam, Annabella – creates a concomitant tradition of their white racialization. These females are deployed to do racial work, as well as gendered work. They are the embodiment of a whiteness that takes hold in early seventeenth-century England. The glorification of females in the sonnet tradition and the martyrdom of females in early modern English tragedy contribute equally to England's nationalist project. Both enable England and other white majority nations to define themselves and to establish their dominance on the world stage – imperialist forces, carrying out the 'white man's burden' in colonizing the black cultures of Africa, Asia, Australia and the Americas. The legacy of that problematic history consumes us still today.

NOTES

In revising this essay for publication, I am grateful for the generous, insightful suggestions of Arthur Little and the research assistance of Ariel Santos and Dorothy Vanderford. Earlier versions of portions of this material have appeared in other contexts, including conferences and journals such as the Shakespeare Association of America and *EMLS* (*Early Modern Literary Studies*).

1. Arthur L. Little, Jr., *Shakespeare Jungle Fever: National-Imperial Re-Visions of Race, Rape, and Sacrifice* (Stanford, CA: Stanford University Press, 2000), 6.
2. Valerie Wayne, ed., *The Matter of Difference: Materialist Feminist Criticism of Shakespeare* (Ithaca, NY: Cornell University Press, 1991), 11.

3. The theoretical concept, *theatrical subjectivity*, i.e. the disparity between female subjectivity and male objectification of the female – whether through romantic, idealizing, Petrarchan discourse; anti-romantic, denigrating Ovidian discourse; or idealizing and denigrating Orientalist discourse – characterizes Shakespeare's dramatic texts. See Evelyn Gajowski, *The Art of Loving: Female Subjectivity and Male Discursive Traditions in Shakespeare's Tragedies* (Newark: University of Delaware Press, 1992), 26–50 and 51–85.

4. When Demetrius and Chiron not only rape Lavinia but also cut out her tongue and cut off her hands, they 'deconstruct the Petrarchan conventions of the *blazon*, or the male anatomization of the female. They literally take her apart, accomplishing physically that which Petrarchan discourse performs rhetorically'. See Evelyn Gajowski, 'Lavinia as "Blank Page" and the Presence of Feminist Critical Practices', in *Presentist Shakespeares*, ed. Terence Hawkes and Hugh Grady, 121–40 (London: Routledge, 2007), 131.

5. I develop this point in greater detail in Evelyn Gajowski, 'Sleeping Beauty, or "What's the Matter?": Female Sexual Autonomy, Voyeurism, & Misogyny in Cymbeline', in *Re-Visions of Shakespeare: Essays in Honor of Robert Ornstein*, ed. Evelyn Gajowski (Newark: University of Delaware Press, 2004), 89–107.

6. Scholars who analyse the Petrarchan discursive tradition more thoroughly than I am able to do within the scope of this essay include: Leonard Forster, *The Icy Fire: Five Studies in European Petrarchism* (New York: Cambridge University Press, 1969); Stephen Minta, *Petrarch and Petrarchism: The English and French Traditions* (New York: Barnes and Noble, 1980); Roland Greene, *Post-Petrarchism: Origins and Innovations of the Western Lyric Sequence* (Princeton, NJ: Princeton University Press, 1991); Heather Dubrow, *Echoes of Desire: English Petrarchism and Its Counter Discourses* (Ithaca, NY: Cornell University Press, 1995); Kim F. Hall, *Things of Darkness: Economies of Race and Gender in Early Modern England* (Ithaca, NY: Cornell University Press, 1995); Natasha Distiller, *Desire and Gender in the Sonnet Tradition* (Houndmills, UK: Palgrave Macmillan, 2008). Hall identifies how early modern English poetry associates whiteness with beauty, innocence, and Christianity and blackness with ugliness, guilt, and non-Christianity.

7. Linda Woodbridge, 'Black and White and Red All Over: The Sonnet Mistress among the Ndembu', *Renaissance Quarterly* 40 (1987): 247–97. Woodbridge provides a comprehensive survey and detailed analysis of the white/red semiotic code that is visible in cultural rituals around the globe across time.

8. Guiraut de Borneil, *The Cansos and Sirvantes of the Troubador Guiraut de Borneil: A Critical Edition*, ed. R. V. Sharman (Cambridge: Cambridge University Press, 1989).

9. Nancy J. Vickers, '"The blazon of sweet beauty's best": Shakespeare's *Lucrece*', in *Shakespeare and the Question of Theory*, ed. Patricia Parker and Geoffrey Hartman, 95–115 (New York: Methuen, 1985), 267.

10. Francesco Petrarch, *The Canzoniere or Rerum Vulgarium Fragmenta*, trans. Mark Musa (Bloomington: Indiana University Press, 1996).

11. Dubrow, *Echoes of Desire*, 43.

12. Hall, *Things of Darkness*, 118.
13. Sir Philip Sidney, 'Sonnet 9', *Astrophil and Stella. Wherein the Excellence of Sweet Poesie Is Concluded* (London, 1591).
14. Woodbridge, 'Black and White and Red All Over', 253. For studies of face-painting and cosmetics in early modern English society and drama, see Frances Dolan, 'Taking the Pencil out of God's Hand: Art, Nature, and the Face-Painting Debate in Early Modern England', *PMLA/Publications of the Modern Language Association of America* 108.2 (1993): 224–39; Annette Drew-Bear, *Painted Faces on the Renaissance Stage: Moral Significance of Face-Painting Conventions* (Lewisburg, PA: Bucknell University Press, 1994; Farah Karim-Cooper, *Cosmetics in Shakespearean and Renaissance Drama* (Edinburgh: Edinburgh University Press, 2007).
15. Edmund Spenser, *Edmund Spenser's Poetry: A Norton Critical Edition*, ed. Hugh Maclean and Anne Lake Prescott (New York: Norton, 1992).
16. Hall, *Things of Darkness*, 66.
17. William Shakespeare, 'Sonnet 130', *Shakespeare's Sonnets*, ed. Katherine Duncan-Jones (London: Arden Shakespeare, 2010).
18. Vickers, 'The blazon of sweet beauty's best', 96.
19. Nancy J. Vickers, 'Diana Described: Scattered Woman and Scattered Rhyme', in *Writing and Sexual Difference*, ed. Elizabeth Abel (Chicago: University of Chicago Press, 1982), 96.
20. R. Howard Bloch, *Medieval Misogyny and the Invention of Western Romantic Love* (Chicago: University of Chicago Press, 1991), 4.
21. Female poets such as Isabella Whitney and Mary Wroth performed interventions in the Petrarchan discursive tradition, entering into it from subject positions. A rich body of scholarship has developed in recent years that analyses the ways in which early modern English women writers were influenced by their male-authored literary inheritance, yet performed interventions into it.
22. Vickers, 'The blazon of sweet beauty's best', 96.
23. Enorbarbus concludes his homage to Cleopatra on her barge at Cydnus by laying bare Ovidian discourse lurking just beneath the surface of Petrarchan discourse. As it turns out, her infamous 'infinite variety' about which he waxes poetic consists merely in her ability to defy masculine Roman sexual appetite: 'Other women cloy / The appetites they feed, but she makes hungry / Where most she satisfies' (2.2.246–8). Male Roman characters deploy Orientalist discourse to construct Cleopatra, and Egypt, as exotic, erotic 'others'. See Gajowski, *The Art of Loving*, 86–119.
24. Laura Mulvey, *Visual and Other Pleasures* (Bloomington: Indiana University Press, 1989), 19.
25. Lynda E. Boose, 'The 1599 Bishops' Ban, Elizabethan Pornography, and the Sexualization of the Jacobean Stage', in *Enclosure Acts: Sexuality, Property, and Culture in Early Modern England*, ed. Richard Burt and John Archer (Ithaca, NY: Cornell University Press, 1994), 197.

26. Robert Bartlett, *The Making of Europe: Conquest, Colonization, and Cultural Change, 950-1350* (Princeton, NJ: Princeton University Press, 1993).

27. Jeffrey Jerome Cohen, 'On Saracen Enjoyment: Some Fantasies of Race in Late Medieval France and England', *Journal of Medieval and Early Modern Studies* 31 (2001): 113–46.

28. Geraldine Heng, *Empire of Magic: Medieval Romance and the Politics of Cultural Fantasy* (New York: Columbia University Press, 2003).

29. Lisa Lampert, 'Race, Periodicity, and the (Neo-) Middle Ages', *Modern Language Quarterly* 65 (2004): 393.

30. Lynn T. Ramey, *Black Legacies: Race and the European Middle Ages* (Gainesville: University Press of Florida, 2014).

31. Cohen, 'On Saracen Enjoyment', 113–46.

32. Ibid., 114.

33. Ibid., 116.

34. Ramey, *Black Legacies*, 25–38.

35. Ania Loomba, *Gender, Race, Renaissance Drama* (New York: Manchester University Press, 1989), 42.

36. Sujata Iyengar, *Shades of Difference: Mythologies of Skin Color in Early Modern England* (Philadelphia: University of Pennsylvania Press, 2005), 9.

37. Little, *Shakespeare Jungle Fever*, 77, 308.

38. Peter Fryer, *Staying Power: The History of Black People in Britain* (London: Pluto Press, 1984), 35.

39. The phrase is Dyer's, in his last chapter, wherein he analyses cyborgs, zombies, and vampires in contemporary film; Richard Dyer, *White* (London: Routledge, 2017).

40. Little, *Shakespeare Jungle Fever*, 2.

41. Tanya Pollard, Conversation with the author, Launch party for publication of *As You Like It: Texts and Contexts*, ed. Pamela Brown and Jean E. Howard (Boston: Bedford/St. Martin's), New York, 22 March 2014.

42. Little, *Shakespeare Jungle Fever*, 2.

43. Hall, *Things of Darkness*, 184.

44. Ramona Wray, 'The Beauty Contest: Racial Aesthetics, Female Rivalry, and Elizabeth Cary's *The Tragedy of Mariam*', in Women's Writing about Beauty in Early Modern England, Renaissance Society of America Annual Meeting. New York, 29 March 2014.

45. But see Woodbridge, 'Black and White and Red All Over', who points out that the colour black (in reference to the eyes, in particular) plays a role that is nearly as significant in the Petrarchan *blazon* as does the white/red colour scheme.

46. Dympna Callaghan, 'Re-reading Elizabeth Cary's *The Tragedie of Mariam, Faire Queene of Jewry*', in *Women, 'Race', and Writing in Early Modern England*, ed. Margo Hendricks and Patricia Parker (London: Routledge, 1994), 176.

47. Hall, '*Things of Darkness*,' 185.

48. Callaghan, 'Re-reading Elizabeth Cary', 173.
49. Wray, 'The Beauty Contest'.
50. Hall, *'Things of Darkness'*, 67.
51. Ibid., 10.
52. Ibid., 28.
53. Sonia Massai, 'Introduction', in *'Tis Pity She's a Whore* by John Ford, ed. Sonia Massai, Arden Early Modern Drama (London: Bloomsbury, 2011), 1.
54. Eve Kosofsky Sedgwick theorizes the traditional love triangle in Western literature as a triangulation between two male characters and a female character: the rivalry between the two males is more intense than any love interest or desire on the part of either male for the female. The Annabella/Giovanni/Soranzo triangulation exemplifies her theoretical paradigm; Eve Kosofsky Sedgwick, *Between Men: English Literature and Male Homosocial Desire* (New York: Columbia University Press, 1985).

CHAPTER THREE

Red Blood on White Saints

Affective Piety, Racial Violence, and Measure for Measure

DENNIS AUSTIN BRITTON

> Oh how was the beauty of thy excellent composed body obscured with spots of bloud? How was the pure-white colour of thy skin made blacke and blew with bitter blowes, my most beautifull Iesus.
>
> —Saint Bernard, his Meditations: or Sighes, sobbes, and teares, vpon our Sauiours passion In memoriall of his death, 1611, p. 305[1]

The above epigraph from a 1611 English translation of Bernard de Clairvaux's *Meditations* magnifies the significance of the assumed colour of Christ's skin within the European medieval tradition of affective piety and, as I will argue, exemplifies a racializing aesthetics within Western Christian devotion from which Shakespeare's *Measure for Measure* draws. This English translation of *Meditations* suggests that the pious Christian is to be moved by an interplay of colour. Christ's 'excellent composed body' is 'obscured' by red blood, and his 'pure-white' beautiful body becomes less so when it is 'made black and blew'. Alongside establishing an alliterative antithesis between 'black and blew' and 'beautiful', the text suggests that colouring Christ's body and making it unbeautiful facilitates the production of the reader's '*Sighes, sobbes, and teares*'. This translation of *Meditations* isolates an important source of Western Christian affect within the crucifixion scene: the desecration of Christ's divine whiteness.

Isabella in Shakespeare's *Measure for Measure* similarly embodies a divine whiteness, one that draws emotional import from a racial aesthetics within the tradition of affective piety and its translation into the descriptions of female virgin martyrs. The colours white and red appear frequently in tales of female virgin martyrs, in which the virgin's beauty and white skin are stained with red blood. Shakespeare employs this imagery in *Measure for Measure*. Rather than give herself sexually to Angelo to save her brother's life, Isabella says that she would 'Th' impression of keen whips ... wear as rubies' (2.4.101).[2] Critics have noted that Isabella's simile invokes an image of the female virgin martyr, but the racial aesthetics deployed in legends of virgin martyrs and the emotions they elicit have gone unnoticed.[3] I argue that tales of female virgin martyrs were important to medieval race making. Moreover, they carry with them into the early modern period and beyond a visual aesthetics of racial violence, a racialization of Christian blood, and understandings of complexion that all establish Isabella as White.[4] The racial aesthetics of female virgin martyrdom in *Measure for Measure* also becomes evident when the image of Isabella's bleeding body is read alongside the play's trafficking in images of an eroticized darkness that provides a foil against which Isabella's whiteness is manifested. The racial aesthetics of virgin martyrdom, the affective piety enabled by it, and *Measure for Measure* all participate in a history that declares the sanctity of White people and blackens those who threaten them.

The 'passions' (*passio*) of the martyrs were intimately tied to *imitatio Christi*, and Candida R. Moss suggests that the 'Language of imitation is interwoven with ideals of discipleship and Pauline notions of "putting on Christ". Christ suffers *in* the martyrs and shares particular intimacy with them.'[5] Moreover, Moss argues,

> The identification of personal suffering with the sufferings of Christ . . . is part of a larger complex of practices in which members of the Jesus movement and early Christians sought to imitate Christ in aspects of their daily life. The association of personal with Christological suffering, therefore, was not solely the byproduct of theodicy; it was part of the mimetic practices that writers and church leaders sought to inculcate in their audiences.[6]

To be sure, the suffering of Christ and his wounded body are central to Christianity, but what I wish to consider here are the particularities of the bodies that medieval and early modern English Christians believed Christ suffered *in*.

I see the 'particular intimacy' that Moss mentions as being facilitated by the ways writers and artists from the Middle Ages forward recreate Christ in their own image. As Rosemary Radford Ruether argues,

> the whiteness of Christ in Western Christian culture is more than an artistic convention, depicting Jesus as 'like us', as Christian art in Africa or Asia might depict Jesus as looking like an African or Asian. It reflects certain assumptions in Western culture about the superiority of whiteness and the inferiority of 'non-whites', or people of 'colour'. This was a viewpoint particularly shaped in the sixteenth to twentieth centuries in Europe and the United States in the context of the enslavement of Africans and the conquest of indigenous peoples of the Americas. In order to claim that such forms of conquest and enslavement were appropriate, Spanish, English, Americans and other people colonizing and enslaving Africans and 'Indians' began to differentiate themselves as 'white', while styling the others as 'red' or 'black', although these colours were hardly literally the skin tone of any of these humans.[7]

For Ruether, the whiteness of Jesus in Western art cannot be separated from doctrines of white supremacy that justified conquest and slavery. She cites the sixteenth century as the origin of white supremacy as represented through art, but, as we will see, the supremacy of whiteness emerges earlier through an aesthetics of Christian martyrdom, especially that of female virgin martyrs.[8] When the medieval virgin 'puts on Christ', she puts on a White Christ like the one described by Clairvaux.

I would thus add to Moss's suggestion that the links that martyrologies made between the bruised and lacerated body of Christ and the body of the martyr were strengthened through establishing a similar visual aesthetics that in turn produced a similar affective response. If, as Sarah McNamer has suggested, medieval representations of Christ's passion 'had serious and particular work to do: to teach their readers, through iterative affective performance, how to feel',[9] then the patterning of the martyr's *passio* after The Passion would similarly teach readers how to feel about both martyrs and their oppressors. Readers were to be affected by the martyr's suffering body in ways similar to how they should be affected by meditating upon Christ's broken body, and a primary strategy that writers of martyrologies employed was to make white skin become red, black, or blue by people who were already 'coloured'. Losing bodily whiteness and becoming 'coloured' became something to be pitied.

The potent mix of affect, piety, and whiteness manifests itself clearly in tales of St. Katherine (or Catherine) of Alexandria, one of the most popular female saints in medieval England.[10] In addition, according to Karen A. Winstead, 'She was often designated God's favourite saint, second only to the Virgin Mary, and more lives were written about her than of any other virgin martyr.'[11] Modern scholars doubt she ever existed, but according to her legend the beautiful virgin was killed by the emperor Maxentius in the fourth century. Stories of her vary, but in various stories she is imprisoned and tortured after out-arguing fifty great philosophers sent by the emperor (some of whom convert to Christianity), is tortured, has her breasts cut off, and is beheaded.

St. Katherine's whiteness is an important feature in Middle English versions of the tale; it is the physical manifestation of her very character – her name comes from the Greek word, *katharos*, meaning pure.[12] In an anonymous thirteenth-century stanzaic account, the narrative asserts that whiteness equals saintliness. Katherine is first identified as white when she is tortured: 'They maden here body al red blood ren / That first was whyt as whales bon' (281–2).[13] Torture not only changes Katherine's body from white to red, but it also strips her of her beauty. Sherry Reames glosses 'whyt as whales bon' as 'A conventional image of beauty in Middle English poetry, meaning "as white as ivory"'.[14] The barbarity of the torturers, then, is accentuated by the fact that cruelty is enacted upon a young, beautiful, white, female body. Nevertheless, violence enacted upon the young, beautiful, white, female body proves necessary for establishing the surface of the body as a readable site of interiority and religious identity.

But scenes of tortured saints did more than link body and spirit. Ayanna Thompson argues that torture reveals not only religious but also racial truth. She notes in her analysis of medieval pictorial representations of torture, which often represent the torturers as Black pagans and Moors, that

> Whether the Moors are depicted as the torturers themselves or merely the servants of the torturers, their blackened presence easily encapsulates all of the differences between the Christians and their tormenters. The differences are written on their black skin, just as the Christian saints' and martyrs' holiness is written on their haloed white bodies . . . the black Moors are included in these

paintings because their skin announces their symbolic as well as religious, cultural, *and* physical difference.[15]

Torture thus helps reify the intimate connection between skin, body, and religious identity. *Life of St. Katherine* further reifies this connection by insisting that, ultimately, no act of violence upon the saint's white body can make her body anything other than White. The poem shores up the integrity of Katherine's spiritual and bodily whiteness by asserting that neither can be altered.

The *Life of St. Katherine* continues to sanctify the white body by demonizing non-white, black bodies.[16] After denying Katherine food for many days, the emperor tells Katherine that he will spare her life if she renounces Christ. She responds to his offer:

Thenne spak the mayden there sche stood
Among the Sarezynys so blak,
As Jhesu here taughte, that is so good,
With mylde wurdys withouten lak:
'Though I schole deye, thou may me trest:
Jhesu ne schal I nevere forsake;
For Jhesu love I am ful prest
Gladly here my deth to take.

'For though that thou bethynke thee
Aftyr peynys grete and sare
And doo hem alle to pyne me,
To suffre hem I wil be yare.
Nevere in my lyf, be God above,
My flesch, my blood ne wole I spare
To spende hem for that Lordys love;

—425–39

Katherine's whiteness is subtly alluded to when she speaks of not sparing her 'flesch' or 'blood', recalling the image of her white-as-whalebone body running with blood earlier in the poem. But more significant for unpacking the production of racial difference is the poem's transformation of the Roman oppressors into Black Saracens who are not only black but 'so blak'. Making the enemy black effectively whitens the Alexandrian virgin; in a poem where white skin testifies to the heroine's Christian identity, non-Christians are necessarily presented as black.[17]

This blackening and Islamizing of the Romans – we also learn at the very beginning of the poem that Maxenceus 'Mahoun heeld he for hys god', and that 'He was a Sarezyn ful tryst' (17 and 21) – might be read in light of a similar phenomenon that Jamie Friedman identifies in the fourteenth-century Middle English romance, *The King of Tars*, a tale in which a Black sultan becomes White after converting to Christianity: 'racial limits are foregrounded in this text precisely where they were indeterminate historically, in order to recuperate distinct communal boundaries and construct racial hierarchies that might maintain those boundaries. That foregrounding functions to guarantee a stable and central white Christian identity that was, in fact, the recent site of profound anxieties and longings.'[18] In this poem, Romans become Black Muslims to assert even further that white skin signifies Christian perfection.

Katherine's shed blood can also be read as working to establish her racial identity. Blood, after all, is an important carrier of religious and racial identity. According to Geraldine Heng, in the context of the crusades 'Christ's shedding of his blood for the salvation of Christians – a doctrine at the heart of corporate Christian identity, and one that is perpetually renewed at mass and in communion wine – meant that "shedding of *Christian* blood" by Muslims could become an occasion for consolidating Christian identity'.[19] Heng soon after poses the rhetorical question, 'In the contest of blood-letting, can there be a more succinct grasp of racial distinction than the articulation of fundamental differences in the identification of self from enemy?'[20] The stanziac *Life of St. Katherine* not only shows its affinities with crusade romances by turning Katherine's torturers into Muslims who believe in 'Mahoun', but also by asking the reader repeatedly to make connections between Christ and the martyr – the only other blood mentioned in the poem is Christ's.

But blood as a carrier of racialized religious identity is more fully established when Katherine actually becomes a martyr – the tale ends with a miracle of blood. Katherine's head is cut off, 'But for the blood the mylk out ran. / Above here stood that manquellere / He was ful blak, he was ful wan' (754–6). The miracle of Katherine bleeding milk is one part of the legend that is consistent across numerous versions of the tale, and this miracle testifies to her saintliness. Reames notes that the miracle of blood turned to milk 'is reported also at the executions of several other virgin martyrs and at least one male saint, the apostle Paul. In the cases of Katherine and the other virgins, the miraculous substitution operates most obviously as a sign of the saint's physical and spiritual purity, suggesting that she has transcended the natural, sexual functions of her earthly female body.'[21] The poem cannot allow even the possibility of having Katherine's whiteness compromised by sexuality, especially at the hands of a 'ful blak' man; since a woman's blood (from menstruation, a broken hymen, or even a blush) can variably point to her sexuality, having Katherine bleed red here may invoke an image of rape.[22] In this colour-obsessed poem, however, in which colours are repeatedly associated with bodies in order to establish racial and religious difference, Katherine's milk-blood should be understood as a final attempt to establish a bodily connection between whiteness and saintliness. Katherine's milk-blood is set against the black and wan complexion of the executioner (the 'manquellere', the man-killer) – lest readers forget, the poem insists, again, that the enemy of Christianity is Black. Additionally, inasmuch as martyrdom has long been understood as baptism by blood, a baptism that was understood as superior to water baptism, Katherine is baptized by and into whiteness at the poem's end, a baptism that seems to testify to her virgin purity in ways that the mere baptism by red blood would not.[23]

Katherine bleeds white, a final example that 'whiteness needs regular rearticulation in order to be remade continually as distinct'.[24] This 'regular rearticulation' occurs within and among the varied tales of female virgin martyrs. Similar to the thirteenth-century stanzaic *Life of Saint Katherine*, the accounts of virgin martyrs in the

Katherine Group – a group of thirteenth-century Middle English lives of the virgin martyrs St. Juliana, St. Margaret and St. Katherine – make a point of noting the white skin of the women being bloodied. In the account of St. Katherine's martyrdom, Maxentius 'commanded madly that she be stripped stark naked and her bare flesh and lovely body beaten with knotted scourges, and so it was done, so that her beautiful body seethed with blood'.[25] In the tale of St. Margaret of Antioch, after the virgin refuses to obey the Roman governor Olibrius and worship Roman gods, 'The accursed villains laid on so violently that her fair skin was broken all over and streamed with blood . . . . The executioners laid on so cruelly that the blood burst out and down her body like a stream from a spring'.[26] Later in this tale, after St. Margaret again refuses to denounce Christ, Olibrius 'furiously cried, "Strip her stark naked and raise her up high, so she may hang as payment for her insults and burn her body with lighted tapers"'.[27] Obedient to the command, 'the wretched menials did so at once, so that the snow-white skin blackened as it was scorched, and broke into blisters as it swelled all over, and her beautiful body crackled in the flame, so that there was an outcry from all those who saw the pitiful injury to her soft sides'.[28] Once again, we see an emphasis on the whiteness and beauty of the virgin martyr, but unlike the tales of Katherine discussed above and more so like the description of Christ's passion in Clairvaux's *Meditations*, we are given the affective response of witnesses to the torture. The tale betrays its emotional investment in white skin; white skin being made black is a pitiful sight. White skin gains its affective value – its ability to move the emotions of witnesses of the torture – at the very point that it is threatened by blackness, blueness, or redness.

The affective value of white skin in the English Christian imagination did not disappear after the Reformation. Early modern readers of Chaucer's *Second Nun's Tale* would have learned about St. Cecilia, that 'It is to seye in Englisshe hevenes lilie / For pure chaastnesse of virginitee; / Or, for she whitenesse hade of honestee' and after death 'Right so was faire Cecille the white'.[29] Additionally, in the first volume of *Acts and Monuments*, John Foxe recounts the martyrdom of the virgin Eulalia: 'but being glad and merry, abandoning from her mind all heaviness and grief, when, as out of a warm fountain, her mangled members with fresh blood bathed her white and fair skin'.[30] As in medieval accounts of female virgin martyrs before her, Foxe's Eulalia reflects an inner truth that is unaltered by torture. In Foxe we see that Protestant renderings of female virgin martyrs inherited medieval formulations that linked white skin and religious constancy. Rather than abandon the appeal to feeling that was so central to medieval European Christian devotion, English Protestants used images of beautiful bleeding White women to advance anti-Catholic sentiment.

Christian emotional investments in white skin thus crossed historical, generic, and confessional divides, and Shakespeare draws from the racializing aesthetics of martyrdom that were passed to the early modern period through tales of female virgin martyrs. Shakespeare's play, however, grapples with the following conundrum: can white skin signify spiritual and bodily purity in a world where White people give full license to their sexual desires? The play does not fully resolve this conundrum, but it does much to insist that pairing complexion with the aesthetics of martyrdom can shore up the belief that skin has the potential to indicate bodily purity and spiritual perfection.

Although a novice, the play introduces Isabella as a character whose saintliness is visible on her body. Upon first seeing her, Lucio says, 'Hail, virgin, if you be – as those cheek-roses / Proclaim you are no less' (1.4.16–17). Robert N. Watson suggests that 'Lucio translates the beginning of the primary prayer to the Virgin Mary, and then questions whether Isabella is actually suited for the role'.[31] The questioning itself, however, indicates that Lucio has some degree of physiognomic knowledge, especially regarding blushing. Although, as Sujata Iyengar has shown, blushing was not a stable signifier in the early modern period, it could be read as a sign of 'shamefastness', and 'a bashful reluctance about sexual matters'.[32] Additionally, the ability to blush itself was understood as indicating racial identity: 'Black Ethiopians and tawny Indians were thought to be unable to blush and therefore to experience shame.'[33] Shakespeare famously betrays the cultural belief that people with black and tawny skin could not blush and thus could not feel shame in *Titus Andronicus*; seeing the Black child of Tamora and Aaron, Chiron states, 'I blush to think upon this ignomy', to which Aaron, who is certainly shameless in the play, responds, 'Why, there's the privilege your beauty bears. / Fie, treacherous hue, that will betray with blushing / The close enacts and counsels of thy heart!' (4.2.114–17). Chiron's blush (and shame) are certainly different from Isabella's, but their blushes nevertheless render white bodies as uniquely equipped to show interiority.[34]

Lucio may be unsure if Isabella's blush is an accurate sign of virginity, but the play provides surety that Isabella's blush signifies a virginity that, through Lucio's allusion to the Hail Mary, is spiritually significant. The play then links virginity to saintliness. Lucio says to Isabella,

I hold you as a thing enskied and sainted,
By your renoucement, an immortal spirit,
And to be talk'd with in sincerity,
As with a saint.

—*MM* 1.3.34–7

Because of her 'renoucement', Isabella seems to have already passed into immortality. Becoming a nun would entail a general renouncing of the world, but given *Measure for Measure*'s strong focus on sexual desire, we should read her saintliness as a byproduct of her vow to remain a virgin. Although all nuns take a vow of celibacy, Lucio's comment elevates that vow by associating it with sainthood – no character in the play except Isabella appears uncontaminated by sexual desire.

The play goes on to suggest that sexual purity is white through repeatedly associating sexual deviance with darkness. When Lucio accuses the duke of sexual impropriety, the duke responds, 'you speak unskilfully: or if your knowledge be more, it is much darkened in your malice' (3.2.143–4). But Lucio swears he loves the duke, even as he continues to darken his reputation: 'The duke yet would have dark deeds darkly answered: he would never bring them to light' (3.2.170–2), and later in the play, 'if the old fantastical duke of dark corners had been at home, he had lived' (4.3.156). These alongside the fact that Isabella tells the duke that the success of the bed-trick relies on darkness – she is to arrive 'Upon the heavy middle of the night' (4.1.35) and 'repair i'th'dark' (4.1.43) – provide the background against which Isabella's whiteness shines all the more brightly.

Isabella's whiteness, however, needs to be differentiated from a fairness that seems to be a bit too promiscuous to describe a saint accurately. Upon first meeting her, Lucio also addresses Isabella as Claudio's 'fair sister' (1.3.19) and just a few lines later as 'Gentle and fair' (1.3.24) – these are the first two instances of the adjective in the play. Angelo, too, address Isabella as 'fair maid' (2.2.79) shortly after they meet. But Juliet is also fair: the duke says to her, 'Repent you, fair one, of the sin you carry?' (2.3.21). If Juliet can be fair even when in a state of sin, fair does not sufficiently represent the presumed connection between the external body and internal character embodied in the virgin martyr, nor can it – at least in *Measure for Measure* – produce the necessary affects for the canonization of whiteness.

Measure for Measure thus works through a particular racial problematic: how to make white skin signify superiority and purity when so many White people, even those like Angelo, are unable to restrain their sexual desires. To work through this problematic, the play engages multiple meanings of 'complexion', a word that appears three times in the play and variously denoted in the early modern period the body's humoral composition, affect, the physical appearance of the body, and skin colour.[35] In the first two occurrences of the word in *Measure for Measure*, complexion is rendered as particularly vulnerable to external forces. After Angelo's hypothetical sexual proposition, Isabella laments,

> Women? – Help, heaven! men their creation mar
> In profiting by them. Nay, call us ten times frail;
> For we are soft as our complexions are,
> And credulous to false prints.
>
> —MM 2.4.126–9

Isabella's comment suggests that women's complexions can be reshaped by gendered power relations; women and their complexions are soft and thus easily marred by male sexual aggression. The context in which this outcry occurs establishes a specific link between female complexion and sexual relations with men. Men's complexions, however, are also alterable. The disguised duke attempts to prepare Claudio for death by making life a thing to be hated because it is 'Servile to all the skyey influences' (3.1.9). The duke then proceeds to offer Claudio various reason why he should embrace death, including, 'Thou art not certain; / For thy complexion shifts to strange effects / After the moon' (3.1.23–5). The duke's understanding of the humoral body also renders men as subject to complexional change.

Isabella's complexion is different from that of ordinary men and women, however. The duke tells her not long after his discussion with Claudio, 'The hand that hath made you fair hath made you good. The goodness that is cheap in beauty makes beauty brief in goodness; but grace, being the soul of your complexion, shall keep the body of it ever fair' (3.1.179–83). Isabella is divinely constructed by a 'hand' that assured a correspondence between bodily fairness and goodness. In addition, the claim that Isabella's complexion has been ensouled by grace rather than affected by humoral forces suggests that her complexion is not subject to the penalty of human sin, death. The play does not allow us to understand this grace as delimited by a particular theological position: Lucio playfully insists early in the play, 'Grace is grace, despite of all controversy' (1.2.24–5). That said, recalling Lucio's 'Hail, Virgin' address at the beginning of the play and reading grace here through a Roman Catholic understanding of the Hail Mary, in which Mary is 'full of grace' and thus born without original sin, Isabella's complexion is produced by the very power so central to the theology surrounding Christianity's most important virgin, the Virgin Mary. Consequently, although both Juliet and Isabella may be fair, only Isabella's fairness can be read as indicating spiritual purity. The duke suggests that the body and complexion can be read as a true signifier of sexual and spiritual purity. Unlike the complexions that can be altered by the darkness of sexual sin, Isabella's complexion is saintly and full of grace.

Attending to the significance of Isabella's complexion – the correspondences between her whiteness, her soul, and her body – is essential for understanding her desire to be whipped rather than lose her virginity. She pronounces,

> were I under the terms of death,
> Th'impression of keen whips I'd wear as rubies,
> And strip myself to death as to a bed
> That longing have been sick for, ere I'd yield
> My body up to shame.
>
> —MM 2.3.100–4

In her willingness to have her blood shed, Isabella establishes herself among the virgin martyrs. She does not denote her own beauty or her whiteness explicitly, but she does not need to, given how integral white skin had already become in tales of female virgin martyrs. Isabella's blushing body is now imagined as a bleeding body, one that equally, though with greater potency, signifies her virginity and calls attention to her whiteness through being coloured red.

The problem is that Angelo does not respond as a pious Christian should. The image of a naked white virgin body becoming bloodied is supposed to inspire pity and piety, but instead it only seems to whet Angelo's sexual appetite, causing a tyrannical abuse of power. Angelo becomes like the pagan torturers in saint's lives and medieval painting that are often rendered black. He too is a character who hangs out in the play's 'dark corners', a racialized sexual discourse that paints those who give licence to sexual desire 'so blak' as to render Christianity and virginity white.[36]

We may assume that Angelo, Claudio, Juliet, the duke, and even Lucio are all White – White European is always the assumed identity of Shakespeare's characters unless they are specifically identified as being something different. But *Measure for Measure* insists on differentiating Isabella's whiteness from that of other characters in the play. Doing so, I suggest, privileges white skin as a site that has the *possibility* of – even if it does not always – truthfully denoting bodily and religious purity. Through sacrifice, white skin bears the possibility of redemption. Arthur L. Little Jr. has taught us that racial difference often becomes legible through sexual violence against women, and as he pointedly puts it, 'Real white men don't rape.'[37] That Angelo falls short of bloodying and raping Isabella makes his redemption and reincorporation into whiteness possible. *Measure for Measure* may not be able to assure its audience that all White people are saints, but it works hard to maintain that the saints are indeed White. The play reassures its audience that White people – through their whiteness – hold in their very racial makeup potentialities denied to Black and Brown people. People with white skin are uniquely capable of having their skin become a mark of sainthood, of having violence against their bodies read as imitating Christ's sacrifice that allows them to participate in the Christian plan of redemption, and of having violence against their bodies inspire pity.

NOTES

1. *Saint Bernard, his Meditations: or Sighes, sobbes, and teares, vpon our Sauiours passion In memoriall of his death. Also his Motiues to mortification, with other meditations. All done (as they are now) by W.P. Maister of Arts, in Cambridge* (London, 1611), 305.

2. All citations of Shakespeare's plays are from *The Arden Shakespeare Complete Works*, ed. Richard Proudfoot, Ann Thompson and David Scott Kastan (London: The Arden Shakespeare, 2001). Citations will appear parenthetically in the essay.

3. For example, see Julia Reinhard Lupton's *Afterlives of Saints: Hagiography, Typology, and Renaissance Literature* (Stanford, CA: Stanford University Press, 1994), esp. 110–19; Andrew Hadfield's 'Isabella, Marina, and St. Ursula', *Notes & Queries* 54.3 (2007): 292–93; and Katherine Gillen's *Chaste Value: Economic Crisis, Female Chastity and the Production of Social Difference on Shakespeare's Stage* (Edinburgh: Edinburgh University Press, 2017), 39–40.

4. Some scholars now suggest that 'White' should capitalized to draw attention to the fact that White is a racial designation. See Nell Irvin Painter, 'Why "White" should be capitalized, too', *The Washington Post*, 22 July 2020, https://www.washingtonpost.com/opinions/2020/07/22/why-white-should-be-capitalized/ (accessed 24 January 2021).

5. Candida R. Moss, *Other Christs: Imitating Christ in Ancient Christian Ideologies of Martyrdom* (Oxford: Oxford University Press, 2010), 3–4 (original emphasis).

6. Ibid., 19.

7. Rosemary Radford Ruether, 'Is Christ White?: Racism and Christology', in *Christology and Whiteness: What Would Jesus Do?*, ed. George Yancy (New York: Routledge, 2012), 101–13, esp. 102.

8. Medieval European Christian art was central to Europeans seeing themselves as 'white'. Madeline Caviness has noticed a shift that occurred in the second half of the thirteenth century. Whereas previously the colour white was reserved for clothing and the whites of eyes, in the second half of the thirteenth century, saints are painted with white skin, and in stained glass 'it had become the norm for glass-painters to use colourless glass instead of flesh tints'; Caviness, 'From the Self-Invention of the Whiteman in the Thirteenth Century to *The Good, The Bad, and The Ugly*', *Different Visions: A Journal of New Perspectives on Medieval Art* 1 (2008): 1–33, esp. 18. Responding to Caviness, Geraldine Heng writes, 'in their visual art, Latin Christian

Europeans not only came to depict their skin colour as white, but made whiteness literally transparent, invisible'; Heng, *The Invention of Race in the European Middle Ages* (Cambridge: Cambridge University Press, 2018), 183.

9. Sarah McNamer, *Affective Mediation and the Invention of Medieval Compassion* (Philadelphia: University of Pennsylvania Press, 2010), 2.

10. Sherry Reames, 'Katherine of Alexandria: Introduction', in *Middle English Legends of Women Saints*, ed. Sherry Reames (TEAMS Middle English Texts Series, 2003), para 2.

11. Karen A. Winstead, 'Saint Katherine', in *Chaste Passions: Medieval Virgin Martyr Legends*, ed. and trans. Karen A Winstead (Ithaca, NY: Cornell University Press, 2000), 115–17, esp. 115.

12. Reames, 'Katherine of Alexander: Introduction', para. 1.

13. *Stanzaic Life of Katherine*, in *Middle English Legends of Women Saints*, ed. Sherry Reames (TEAMS Middle English Texts Series, 2003). Citations will be included parenthetically in the essay.

14. Ibid., n282. On whiteness and the racialization of beauty, of course see Kim Hall's 'Beauty and the Beast of Whiteness: Teaching Race and Gender', *Shakespeare Quarterly* 41.4 (1996): 461–75.

15. Ayanna Thompson, *Performing Race and Torture on the Early Modern Stage* (New York: Routledge, 2013), 13.

16. Later in her analysis of seventeenth-century English plays about Christian-Muslim conflict, Thompson also suggests that the whiteness of the tortured is manifested via the blackness of the torturer; ibid., 49.

17. Maxenceus (Maxentius), although historically emperor of Rome, is identified as a 'Saracen' who serves Mahoun at the very beginning of the poem (15–21). Reames notes that this poem was likely written as an alternative to secular romance (para. 5). Reames also glosses 'Sarezynys so blak': 'The adjective here must be figurative rather than literally descriptive, referring either to their lack of enlightenment or more generally to their wickedness' (n426). Reames provides no explanation for why 'blak' *must* be read figuratively rather than literally. Divorcing the literal from the figurative is especially problematic in a poem where Christian saintliness is produced through literal torture to the virginal white body.

18. Jamie Friedman, 'Making Whiteness Matter: *The King of Tars*', *Postmedieval* 6.1 (2015): 52–63, esp. 55.

19. Heng, *The Invention of Race*, 122. Here Heng's analysis draws heavily from Tomaz Mastnack's 'The Muslims as Enemy of Faith: The Crusades as Political Theology', *Quaderni Fiorentini* 38 (2009): 143–200. On blood as a conveyer of racialized religious identity, also see my 'Flesh and Blood: Race and Religion in *The Merchant of Venice*', in *The Cambridge Companion to Shakespeare and Race*, ed. Ayanna Thompson (Cambridge: Cambridge University Press, 2021), 108–22.

20. Heng, *The Invention of Race*, 122.

21. Reames, *Stanzaic Life of Katherine*, n754.

22. The most complete study of blood as gendering the category of women in the Middle Ages is Peggy McCracken's *The Curse of Eve, the Wound of the Hero: Blood, Gender, and Medieval Literature* (Philadelphia: University of Pennsylvania Press, 2003). On how this image may invoke rape, see Arthur L. Little, Jr.'s reading of depictions of the rape of Lucrece in *Shakespeare Jungle Fever: National-Imperial Re-Visions of Race, Rape, and Sacrifice* (Stanford, CA: Stanford University Press, 2000), 39–48.
23. See my discussion of baptism and martyrdom in *Becoming Christian: Race, Reformation, and Early Modern English Romance* (New York: Fordham University Press, 2014), 169–71.
24. Friedman, 'Making Whiteness Matter', 58.
25. In Winstead, *Virgin Martyrs*, 40.
26. *Seinte Margarete*, in *Medieval English Prose for Women Sections from the Katherine Group and Ancrene Wise*, ed. Bella Millett and Jocelyn Wogan-Browne (Oxford: Clarendon Press, 1990), 44–85, esp. 53.
27. Ibid., 78.
28. Ibid., 75.
29. Geoffrey Chaucer, *Second Nun's Tale*, in *The Riverside Chaucer*, 3rd edn., ed. L. D. Benson (Boston: Houghton Mifflin Co., 1987), 226–69, esp. ll. 187–9 and 115.
30. John Foxe, *Actes and Monuments* (London: 1570), 144.
31. Robert N. Watson, 'False Immortality in "Measure for Measure": Comic Means, Tragic Ends', *Shakespeare Quarterly* 41.4 (1990): 411–32, esp. 425.
32. Sujata Iyengar, *Shades of Difference: Mythologies of Skin Color in Early Modern England* (Philadelphia: University of Pennsylvania Press, 2005), 106.
33. Ibid., 107.
34. See Mary Floyd Wilson's *English Ethnicity and Race in Early Modern Drama* (Cambridge: Cambridge University Press, 2003). She notes that although white complexions were not always viewed favourably in geo-humoral theories, such theories suggested that the ability of people with white skin to blush showed an inherent aversion to vice (158).
35. On humoral complexion as an aspect of early modern understandings of racial difference, see Floyd-Wilson, *English Ethnicity and Race on the Early Modern Stage*, and Gail Kern Paster, *Humoring the Body: Emotions and the Shakespearean Stage* (Chicago: University of Chicago Press, 2004).
36. We thus should read *Measure for Measure* as playing off the racialized tropes of rape and sacrifice that Arthur L. Little has discussed in *Shakespeare Jungle Fever*. Little's discussion of how Tarquin becomes black in his desire to rape a white Lucrece is especially resonant here (45–6).
37. Ibid., 58.

CHAPTER FOUR

Antonio's White Penis

Category Trading in The Merchant of Venice

IAN SMITH

I

Beginning in the 1950s, the idea of Antonio's 'strong homosexual inclination' entered into the modern critical tradition of *The Merchant of Venice*.[1] By the late 1990s, this interpretation had become so thoroughly influential that Mario DiGangi could write: 'At this stage in the development of theoretical and historical knowledges about early modern homoeroticism I prefer to bring a new text into the dialogue than take a position on a perennially debated play like *The Merchant of Venice*.'[2] Scholarly inquiry might not have exhausted the pertinent 'theoretical and historical knowledges about early modern homoeroticism', after all, especially if investigations were conducted in relative isolation from the consequential category of race. The silo-effects within early modern studies have been especially notable for the categories of queer sexuality and race that appear to inhabit different critical universes. I return to *Merchant*, therefore, hoping to re-engage the question of Antonio's sexuality in relation to race, specifically his whiteness, from the perspective of an intersectional critique. Before turning directly to the play, I would like to situate the questions my reading raises about whiteness and sexuality within a set of current concerns about the ideology of methods.

In her introduction to an edited collection of essays, that grew out of a 1993 Shakespeare Association of America seminar titled 'Race, Ethnicity, and Power in Shakespeare and his Contemporaries', Joyce Green MacDonald identifies what has become an orthodox view in early modern studies: that race is multiform and 'acquires its early modern force in tandem with some second or even third term'.[3] It would appear that the 2019 Folger Shakespeare Library symposium 'Intersecting the Sexual: Modes of Early Modern Embodiment' accepts a premise similar to MacDonald's about the category of early modern sexuality. Organized by DiGangi, this excellently executed symposium reached across the disciplinary aisle to propose a model that might serve as a generative blueprint for redirecting scholarship, especially around queer sexuality, in early modern studies. The programme description encourages methodological commitments to 'draw on theoretical models and methods from adjacent fields such as early modern race studies', to discover how 'the objects and questions foregrounded by such approaches advance the study of early modern sexuality beyond familiar paradigms'.[4] The programme's intersectional proposition suggests that much can be learned from exchange, meeting, collaboration, and even more from the crossing, co-mingling and intercourse of fields of knowledge, but such intersectional dialogue has been hobbled historically by the unacknowledged racial premise at the centre of early modern sexuality studies.

The symposium's critical, unstated term is, in fact, whiteness: for when was sexuality ever un-raced? Perhaps more to the point: when were the forms of sexual embodiment not ever deeply implicated in discourses of racial formation? Do we not continue to risk construing the sexual, even in the programme's careful formulation, as always *silently* white and, thereby, mask the specific racial dynamics that deserve our attention? Our discussion about the sexual must be properly conducted, therefore, on the terrain of whiteness which functions as the political proxy for the sexual. Not simply the idiosyncratic or unique identity of a single individual, but the product of fundamental social structures, whiteness constitutes a group mandate, bears the imprimatur of institutional authority, and is gifted the social levers of power and privilege. If systemic whiteness can be read as an extension of the *'racial dictatorship'* that Michael Omi and Howard Winant describe as endemic to the history of the United States,[5] then intersecting the sexual requires the kind of careful scrutiny that remains alert to the constant danger of radical appropriation. And if intersecting the sexual is meant to invoke the concept of intersectionality specifically,[6] then the theory's methodological investment in compound or overlapping forms of discrimination and oppression is rendered absurd by the unexamined, discordant, co-opting political agency of systemic whiteness that has historically informed the fields of early modern and sexuality studies.

II

Merchant's paradigmatic reference to 'a pound of flesh' (3.3.33)[7] has figured largely in the critical anatomies of Antonio's sexual desires, beginning with the quest for the identity and specific location of that bodily pledge. The 'part' (1.3.144) for the whole, in this instance, has been the synecdochic subject of much critical speculation, leading to interpretations of Antonio's sexuality as manifest in the homoerotic and performative gift of his flesh to Bassanio where the rhetoric of complete bodily surrender encodes the willed intensity of physical and sexual ardour. Antonio's gift of his incised body, Arthur L. Little, Jr. suggests, stands in deliberate counterpoint to the trappings and conventions of dowries and hymeneal bloodletting in traditional marriage practices.[8] Little sees in Antonio's conscious and direct assertions of homoerotic love a challenge to an increasingly stifling heteronormativity institutionalized and reinvigorated in the social idea of marriage. But Antonio's confession in the courtroom that he is 'a tainted wether of the flock' (4.1.114) acknowledges his outsider status as the gelded ram whose castration brings to the fore, once more, a body 'part' whose cutting neutralizes Antonio's homoerotic expenditure of flesh. In what context does this admission of failure make sense, constituted as it is in specifically racial terms of 'tainted' or black genital flesh? The 'tainted' flesh might, at first, appear discontinuous, something of a surprise, but I propose that Antonio's citing of blackness is consistent with the ideology of binary racialism in Venice that has insisted on his own careful racial construction as a white man throughout the drama.

Whiteness is a major concern of Shakespeare's *Merchant*.[9] In making this claim, I depart from a longstanding practice of posing the play's dramatic conflict between the main protagonists, Antonio and Shylock, in terms of their respective religious affiliations. The orthodox critical approach, supplemented by a theatrical tradition initiated by Henry Irving's 1879 landmark interpretation of Shylock, 'has focused the attention of western audiences on the question of whether the play is anti-Semitic'.[10] Not surprisingly, therefore, James Bulman has argued that in performance, at least, 'perhaps no play by Shakespeare has been subject to the pressures of history – or in the words of Jonathan Miller, "held hostage to contemporary issues" – more forcibly than *The Merchant of Venice*'.[11] In this essay, I take Shakespeare's own perspective seriously, returning to focus on the author's titular character, Antonio the merchant. Examining Antonio's whiteness allows for a renewed consideration of what 'the pressures of history' might mean in an Anglo-American context given whiteness's formative influence in our political evolution. Importantly, the emphasis Shakespeare places on Antonio's whiteness sheds new light on the dramatic action, especially pertinent when, as in Antonio's case, his whiteness and sexuality are posited as conflicting forms of identity. In Judith Butler's well-known analysis of gender formation, she argues that gender, as commonly understood and experienced, is contingent on 'the idealization of the heterosexual bond'. Gender, she maintains, 'is the forcible citation of a norm', but that norm is co-extensive with the enforced canons of heterosexuality and, as a result, sexuality is the ideological predicate for gender and its performance.[12] A similar argument can be made about whiteness and the degree to which racial performativity is constrained by the emerging demands and growing idealization of heterosexuality. Antonio's commitment to whiteness as a performed Venetian identity, in this city-state where commerce matters, forces him to engage in category trading – race for sexuality – in a transactional exercise that is not unfamiliar to the trafficking merchant. In short, whiteness is an expression of a sexuality – whiteness *is* a sexuality – in *Merchant*, and any departure from *its* idealization marks a venture into its literal opposite: blackness and corresponding notions of deviance that are assiduously avoided and denigrated as un-Venetian.

III

The beauty of Venice and the republic's political institutions, as attested by international visitors, are recorded in Cardinal Gasparo Contarini's *The Commonwealth and Government of Venice* (1543).[13] Elisabeth G. Gleason acknowledges the treatise's reputation in establishing the perfection of the Venetian government but argues that the work's idealism must be read within the context of Contarini's negotiations of the peace of Bologna that demoted Venice's military standing.[14] Gleason proposes that 'by reading between the lines an image of the

Venetian state and constitution in Contarini's day begins to emerge, an image that is more problematic than appears on the surface'.[15] In Shakespeare's treatment of foreigners in Venice, for instance, he debunks the myth of a commercial centre celebrated for the harmonious and 'wonderful concourse of strange and forraine people' by revealing the divisive religious conflict inherent in the practices of moneylending that was the lifeblood of city business.[16] In this essay, I wish to forego the familiar coverage of religious hate or the purported ideals of the government and justice system to address Shakespeare's exploration of whiteness, not between the lines as Gleason advertises, but in the words, beginning with the playwright's repeated use of 'fair'. Appearing thirty-five times in the text (with an additional five variant uses of 'fairer', 'fairest', and 'fairness), 'fair' might be construed, at first glance, as Shakespeare's gesture toward the myth of Venice that Contarini's text initiated, signalling 'the beautie and magnificence' of a city incomparable 'either in glory or goodlinesse'.[17] A closer examination of *Merchant* reveals that the culture's idealization of racial whiteness, not the beauty of physical structures or governmental organization, becomes the focus of Shakespeare's demystification of beauty in Venice.

Lancelot, immediately after switching service from Shylock to Bassanio, with the promise of 'a livery / More guarded than his fellows' (2.2.147–8), calls attention to his white skin in a statement denoting the swearing of an oath by laying the palm of his hand on a Bible: 'well, if any man in Italy have a fairer table which doth offer to swear upon a book' (2.2.151–2). The acknowledgment that Italians have fair skin ('fairer table') is exceeded only by the comparatist and competitive argument that good fortune across the Italian peninsula is measured by degrees of racial whiteness. As a Venetian from the lowest social ranks, Lancelot reproduces the competitive ideology – who's the fairest, whitest, of them all – that is consistent with a market economy. Similarly, the play makes explicit the relation between 'fair' and somatic whiteness in Lorenzo's adoring veneration of Jessica's white hand upon receiving a letter written by her: 'I know the hand, in faith, 'tis a fair hand, / And whiter than the paper it writ on / Is the fair hand that writ' (2.4.11–13). In addition to the explicit equation of 'fair' beauty and whiteness, the pun on 'writ' as legal warrant suggests the kind of written document emanating from the state that ensures the stable intercourse of commerce and official sanction of whiteness.[18] Jessica's escape with her father's wealth highlights further the compensatory measures taken to supplement even her hyperbolic fairness, that is whiter than paper (again the comparatist trope), as she mints herself into living currency – 'I will make fast the doors, and gild myself / With some moe ducats' (2.6.49–50) – fit for the economy of racial capitalism.

Farah Karim-Cooper explains that in his works Shakespeare draws on the significance of hands as maps to identity and moral character in early modern culture.[19] However, Shakespeare goes further and grounds this reading of manual body parts in a discourse of racial whiteness that sets forth the unique terms of Venetian human and social value. 'Insofar as parts were imagined as dominant vehicles for the articulation of culture', write David Hillman and Carla Mazzio, 'the early modern period could be conceptualized as an age of synecdoche'.[20] As parts for the whole, therefore, Lancelot's and Jessica's hands bring into focus the cultural investment in corporal synecdoche that reveals not only the obsession with white bodies 'writ' large, but also the corporate value attached to whiteness in the Venetian social body. Jessica's case, for instance, makes clear that not all forms of whiteness are counted equal, and the city's investment in international commerce forces into view the multiple forms of human whiteness of its business community that, in turn, intensify an already extreme cultural programme of racial exclusivity. Moreover, the rhetorical signature of comparison, marking degrees of fairness, highlights the pervasive mindset of commercial competition that binds itself to race while insisting on whiteness as the standard from which no racial deviation will be tolerated.

Not surprisingly, therefore, Morocco's entry in the play makes plain what everyone already knows: a culture of competitive forms of whiteness is a particularly inhospitable environment for a black African. Moreover, racial synecdoche is even more striking here when not just a body part but one's skin colour is taken to represent the totality of one's identity. His opening declaration, 'Mislike me not for my complexion' (2.1.1), acknowledges Venice's hostile white climate that would subvert his bid for Portia among the several suitors, his colour being reviled even before his arrival as the 'complexion of a devil' (1.2.129). Thus, when Bassanio praises Portia's fairness, the language is fraught, suggesting that beauty is but one component of the woman who represents the archetype of Venetian whiteness inscribed in the commercial ethos of capitalist venture, all of which is symbolized in the casket lottery. Shakespeare's verbal insistence on 'fair' in Bassanio's description of her animates the rhetorical figure antanaclasis (different meanings of a repeated single word) that calls attention to her whiteness: 'In Belmont is a lady richly left / And she is fair, and – fairer than the word – / Of wondrous virtues, – sometimes from her eyes / I did receive fair speechless messages' (1.1.161–4). The Venetian comparative racial tic, 'fairer than the word', returns to defamiliarize 'the word' *fair* itself in a metalinguistic calling out of its multiple meanings. Belmont, Portia's home, meaning 'beautiful mountain', which she also refers to as her 'fair mansion' (3.2.168), represents the metaphorical pinnacle of whiteness for which she stands. The multiple occurrences of 'fair Portia' (1.1.181), 'Fair lady' (3.2.139), or 'thrice-fair lady' (3.2.146), especially potent when articulated by the black Moroccan (2.7.43, 47), can no longer be regarded as merely complimentary of her beauty or innocuous civil overtures of respect. Each instance reminds the audience of her totemic status, the epitome of interlocking Venetian values of whiteness, the economy of nascent capitalism and the comparatist, competitive commercial logic that militates against unwelcome forms of blackness in the social sphere. As such, whiteness as beauty is rigorously reconceptualized by Shakespeare to address a culture of white supremacy in Venice and its corollary, institutional bias expressed as anti-blackness. The culture of whiteness in Venice, as presented by Shakespeare, provides the backdrop against which Antonio's whiteness is made legible and better understood.

IV

The early modern social construct of male friendship has been useful for commentators who advance a homoerotic reading of the relationship between Antonio and Bassanio whereby friendship's homosocial bonds are sufficiently expansive to include same-sex intimacies.[21] 'Amity', writes Steve Patterson, 'represented friendship as an identity premised upon the value of same-sex love which codified passionate behaviours between men'.[22] Notably, exemplary friendships are structured in sameness in the literary and humanist tradition. Titus and Gisippus, the celebrated friends of Sir Thomas Elyot's *The Governour* (1531), 'semed to be one in fourme and personage, so, shortly after acquaintaunce, the same nature wrought in their hartes such a mutuall affection, that their willes and appetites daily more and more so confederated them selfes'.[23] The sexually charged language of shared 'willes' and 'appetites' registers, to borrow Jeffrey Masten's apt descriptors, 'an *equitable* jouissance' based in the 'erotics of similitude'.[24] This founding principle of friendship's mutuality is neatly emblematized in John Florio's 1599 translation of Montaigne's 'Of Friendship': 'If a man vrge me to tell wherefore I loved him, I feele it cannot be expressed, but by answering; Because it was he, because it was my selfe.'[25] Far from being a sentimental indulgence, passionate friendships served a critical social purpose in securing the personal ties that generated economic stability among a male elite. Similitude became the ideal sign of an exclusive male network where the reciprocity in values, interests, behaviours and wealth enhanced the health of the fraternity. Undifferentiated on the surface, male friendship's mutual economic benefits enjoyed social distinction in contrast to sodomy that, in theory, at least, signalled disorder.[26]

I have briefly retraced the critical terrain of male friendship because I wish to call attention to the glaring omission that has long stood at the centre of these scholarly observations. If, as Elyot writes, the famous friends are 'one in fourme and personage', Shakespeare has dramatically extended similitude to include racial whiteness among friends to insist on the physical resemblance that characterizes that union and highlight the emerging social awareness of skin colour as having a culturally binding authority. Lorenzo, extolling Antonio to Portia as 'How dear a lover of my lord your husband' (3.4.7), elicits her response that is steeped in the classic rhetoric of similitude of early modern male friendship, identifying Antonio and Bassanio's 'like proportion / Of lineaments, of manners, and of spirit; / Which makes me think that this Antonio, / Being the bosom lover of my lord, / Must needs be like my lord' (3.4.14–18). The emphatic attention to their similarity in physical build and appearance ('proportion' and 'lineaments')[27] is set in relief by the silently attending servant Balthazar, who bears the same name of the black African among the Three Magi according to tradition. If 'amity excludes even as it invites',[28] the gender and racial exception to friendship's networks is made patently clear for Portia and the black Balthazar even as it reifies the physical bonds of whiteness that are manifest in the beauty of the men's sinuous muscularity, 'proportion' and 'lineaments'.

Thus, when Shylock demands from Antonio 'an equal pound / Of your *fair* flesh' (1.3.142–3, italics mine), he attacks the powerful intersection of whiteness and beauty that is Venice. Overlooked in the critical literature, this careful description of 'fair flesh' inserts Antonio within the city's white racial continuum, and 'equal' revives the racial dimension of reciprocity. The Jewish outsider's disgust at the treatment he suffers is given its ideological formulation in the legal codification of the bond. Through the bond's calling out of Antonio's whiteness as forfeit, Shylock expresses his resentment of the aggressive institution of whiteness as 'fair' – meaning beautiful, just and moral – when it has been the basis of an oppressive racial supremacy that continues to disempower and shame the Jew. Importantly, inasmuch as Shylock interpellates Antonio's whiteness in the specifications of the forfeit, he accomplishes an equally complex task in setting whiteness and homoeroticism at odds in his repeated conjunction of 'friend' and 'kind' or 'kindness'.[29] Shylock's taunting bid for social acceptance, 'I would be friends with you, and have your love' (1.3.131) has an interpellative, calling-out effect for Antonio's homoerotic propensities. That overture is met with Antonio's firm rejection even as Shylock's deliberate use of 'kind' – 'This is kind I offer' (1.3.135) – foregrounds the same-sex affinity, material generosity and racial similitude that underwrite Shakespeare's reconceptualization of male friendship in his era of race consciousness. The biblical prohibition against charging a brother interest was still influential in early modern European cultures,[30] so the rejection of Shylock's friendly offer of an interest-free loan promotes, instead, 'kindness' (of the same kind, similar) as sexual, gender and racial sameness as the proposition left on the negotiating table to which Antonio unwittingly assents.

Whiteness and sexuality are thus held in heightened tension, and Shylock makes both visible as pertinent categories to Antonio's life in the commercial city. Nowhere is this tense pairing more palpably evident than in Shylock's demand for the pound of 'fair flesh'. According to James Shapiro, questions concerning the exact site of cutting and extraction of the pound of flesh are animated by the early modern use of 'flesh' to mean 'penis'.[31] But it is the 'fair flesh' or white penis that Antonio is prepared to sacrifice in this spectacular performance of homoerotic giving. And while Antonio's pledge to support Bassanio has drawn critical attention – 'My purse, my person, my extremest means / Lie all unlock'd to your occasions' (1.1.138–9)[32] – the pun on 'purse' meaning 'genitals' acquires fuller dramatic significance insofar as it iterates the coupling of male sexual organs and racial whiteness in Antonio's attempt to enforce a stable ideological and acceptable social bond between the two.[33] The extravagance of the gesture and its accompanying rhetorical hyperbole mark the stretching point of an idea under extreme social pressure. The white penis as synecdoche stands in for the whole physical body as an openly sexual gift; but the merchant's phallus emblematizes Venice's culture of whiteness into which Antonio wishes to insert his penile homoerotics that borders on sodomy.

When does the orderly homosociality of male friendship become disruptive by venturing into the realm of sodomy? Critics have pointed out that the economic shifts of nascent capitalism dramatized in *Merchant* rendered the traditional economic and homoerotic benefits of the male friendship system less efficient and effective. In the Venetian culture of commerce, Shakespeare demonstrates how 'economics is inextricably bound to sex and, more specifically, how sexual reproduction is bound to economic reproduction'.[34] That is, the imperative of heterosexual sex becomes one with the nascent culture of capitalism to assign value to reproduction of wealth and children whose monetary pre-history is inscribed in *tokos*, in Greek signifying 'child' and 'interest on an investment'.[35] Central to my reading, therefore, is the recognition that Venice's culture of whiteness is environmentally congruent with the evolving reproductive episteme of capitalism and heterosexual marriage. In this commercial world newly affined to burgeoning heterosexual reproduction, whiteness becomes an expression of legitimate, economically compatible sexuality. In short, whiteness has become a sexuality.

In Antonio's attempts to couple whiteness and homoerotic desire, he is pushing against the limits set by the capitalist principles that cannot recognize nonreproductive sentiments and practices. His whiteness that situated him within friendship's repetitive (not reproductive) logics of similitude collapses in the courtroom scene when he fears the punishment of legal retribution: 'I am the tainted wether of the flock' (4.1.114). The evocation of the castrated ram brings to the fore, once more, the white penis whose phallic power is endangered. On one level, 'the mercantile world of Venice, devalues the erotic possibilities of male friendship nearly to their vanishing point', argues Patterson, and 'would not only nullify Antonio's love but turn the merchant himself into a kind of hapless, friendless 'other' – possibly a sodomite'.[36] Antonio admits failure in his attempts to join homoerotic love to new capitalist principles; the castrated ram has no place in the commerce of reproduction. On another level, the striking use of the word 'tainted' is key to understanding the arc of Antonio's journey into identity. Within the current mercantile and sexual economy, homoerotic love becomes a transgression whose reconfiguration as sodomy is identified by its stain or indelible mark of shame. 'Taint', understood as a legal infraction, might suggest the criminal offence of sodomy in language befitting the courtroom scene.[37] In the racially white-dominant exclusive world of Venice, 'tainted', meaning 'stained, tinged; contaminated, infected, corrupted', takes on the specific contrastive sense of blackness.[38]

The association of 'tainted' with blackness, however, calls to mind the early modern tendency to project sodomy onto foreign others, thereby aligning Antonio with Morocco.[39] Importantly, upon his entry, Morocco not only has to beg for racial inclusion, but his additional offer to incise his flesh to prove his love also reveals an appeal for heterosexual legitimacy. His desperate need to prove his heterosexuality suggests a biased, pre-existing intellectual framework that conjoins blackness and sodomitical acts. The play's two dramatic moments of bodily incision highlight the contrast between Morocco's black flesh and Antonio's 'fair', white body. The two men never meet, so this perception of their structural reciprocity operates entirely at the level of audience members whose intellectual engagement Shakespeare elicits. In Venice's white world, blackness is troubling, expendable (as in Lancelot's cavalier impregnation of a young black woman), or to be avoided, and Antonio's white penis graphically demonstrates his will for whiteness even while its desultory queerness struggles for legitimacy in the new economy. In the end, Antonio's initial racial contrast to Morocco disintegrates, resulting in a new and culturally undesirable similarity: the once-white now black phallus is excised, leaving Antonio the 'tainted wether of the flock', the black homosexual or sodomite, set apart racially and sexually from the rest, and made a superfluous nonentity by his journey into blackness. Shylock, having divined the combustible crux of Antonio's sexuality and race, now sees his rival similarly 'stained' with social 'shames' (1.3.132) reminiscent of the daily denigrations of the moneylender. Antonio's struggle throughout, results from his acquiescence to the culture's racial and sexual discipline that, with acute irony, makes demands of its queer citizens in terms the merchant understands too well: trading his sexuality for race, wanting the privileges of whiteness even while he desperately sought a love the mercantile economy rendered useless.

V

In this section, I tease out the historical prolongations of the play's insights for sexuality and race where whiteness continues to serve as political currency in the social barter of identities. Scholars have alerted us to the idea of race trading in United States history that is evident, for example, in Bacon's Rebellion of 1676 when a Virginia gentleman, bent on the eradication of Indians, opposed the governor William Berkeley who saw the political benefits of stability in maintaining friendly relationships with certain Indian groups.[40] When local insurrection turned into civil war, Bacon built a rebel group that included indentured servants and some slaves; within months, however, Bacon died of dysentery, and Berkeley re-claimed his authority. Ibram X. Kendi argues that the outcome of Bacon's rebellion, a coalition of white labourers, blacks and servants, became a political object lesson: 'Rich planters learned from Bacon's Rebellion that poor Whites had to be forever separated from enslaved Blacks. They divided and conquered by creating more White privileges. In 1680, legislators pardoned only the White rebels; they prescribed thirty lashes for any slave who lifted a hand "against any Christian" (Christian now meant White)'.[41] Two hundred years later, writes Michelle Alexander, '[h]istory seemed to repeat itself' in a manner that destroyed the gains of Reconstruction through promises of white affiliation at the expense of black disenfranchisement using segregation laws 'designed to encourage lower-class whites to retain a sense of superiority over blacks'.[42] And it was of these Reconstruction-era political manoeuvres that the notion of a 'racial bribe', following W. E. B. DuBois's analysis, became the incisive formulation for a recurring pattern of trading the possibilities of real political liberation or economic betterment for the social legitimacy of whiteness that has extended into the twentieth-first century.[43]

The well-documented practice of category trading is not, however, limited to transactions of class and race. It does, however, function as the historical primer that makes legible other coalitions of whiteness that are defensively deployed to contain expressions of subversive, non-conforming sexualities. In his provocatively titled 'Why I Hate Abercrombie & Fitch', Dwight A. McBride examines the 1990s fashion craze as an anthropological phenomenon in gay cultural spaces that held considerable value for conservative, gay white men.[44] Documenting Abercrombie's beginnings in 1892, McBride traces its particular marketing strategy as a high-end establishment whose professional outdoorsman appeal signalled the fixation on masculinity that its clientele, including men like Hemingway, espoused. The intoxicating combination of whiteness, masculinity and leisure became Abercrombie's unique brand so that the company's successful revitalization, after a twenty-year slide in the 1990s, under the leadership of Michael Jeffries marked a continuity in the signature appeal, not a new departure. McBride is forthright in his critique of Abercrombie's racist management practices that are reflected in its 'legacy of an unabashed consumer celebration of whiteness, and of an elite class of whiteness at that'.[45]

The high visibility of Abercrombie clothing in gay spaces at that time speaks to the predominantly gay white male predilection for what are fairly ordinary-looking products and the cultural meaning wearing them affords. Where conservative ideology held gay identity as antithetical in the 1990s era of so-called family values, certain gay white men could trade their sexuality for whiteness, masculinity and financial cachet, which would earn the conservative seal of social approval. In this instance, McBride writes, 'we are dealing with a group of people who understand themselves – but for this critical difference that their sexuality makes – as in line to be the beneficiaries of their white birthright in the United States: to be and to receive the mantle of whiteness and all the privileges it entails'.[46] McBride is insistent on the outcome of what I conceive as category trading: the collusion of whiteness that is a continued reinvestment in a racist and homophobic status quo. The terminology of the 'racial bribe' attributed to historical enticements to white identification draws on the metaphor of a social drama of racial persuasion directed by one group toward another. Category trading, as I have used it in my analysis of *Merchant* and to describe the behaviours of McBride's white subjects, emphasizes the hegemonic self-fashioning of men with an agential investment in whiteness that, simultaneously, minimizes their gay sexual identities.

VI

In closing, I return to the 'Intersecting the Sexual' symposium, with which I began to pose the obvious and still pressing question: in the field of early modern studies, have scholars been guilty of category trading, preferring to distance race in order to avoid having to question the politics and pleasures of whiteness? The general query of the symposium can be read as a public invitation to expanded scholarship and as a confession that the discipline of early modern sexuality studies has indeed been constitutionally white. Moreover, when we speak of disciplines, we engage often in yet another form of masking: of the actual persons who produce scholarship in a white-dominant field. The analytical focus on Antonio's white penis is not meant to constrain the scope of gender reference, but, rather, to indicate the exclusivity of whiteness enshrined as an identity of power. Race and racial identification *do matter* in life as in scholarship though the latter consequence pretends to be an open secret. Eric Knowles and Kaiping Peng in their study 'White Selves' state that 'racial identification . . . shapes personal beliefs [and] intergroup behaviour'; they argue further that whiteness is other-dependent and that the greater the exposure of whites to non-whites, the greater the awareness of one's white centrality and belonging to an ingroup.[47] Category trading as I have described it constitutes a failure to understand the importance of coalition building for a better and authentically inclusive society on all levels – personally, professionally and politically. It also constitutes a troubling re-commitment to white supremacy. Because of the divisiveness of category trading, we find ourselves in the academy still having to address the bifurcations in research and make urgent appeals to repair the damage of intellectual isolation. Since disciplines are populated by scholar-persons, we must consider, finally, the extent to which intersecting the sexual, a seemingly reasonable and welcome enterprise, might, nevertheless, run the risk of co-opting and appropriating blackness for its own peculiar ends, recapitulating one of the most familiar and destructive paradigms of American history.

I have emphasized, as have many with investments in intellectual activism and social change, the importance of collaboration that requires not just respecting (which can exist as a conditioned intellectual reflex of a self-confessed progressive age) but recognizing the humanity of others *because of* our differences. Audre Lorde, who taught us a good deal about the productive dialectic of difference, notes: 'Without community, there is no liberation, only the most vulnerable and temporary armistice between an individual and herself.'[48] Importantly, 'theory alone cannot wipe out racism', announce Cherríe Moraga and Gloria Anzaldúa,[49] meaning that academic work, by itself, can become an illusion. The positions taken and intellectual lineages announced with passion can be, in reality, simply a mask for action, a performative passing, if you will, that is supposed to display socially conscious selves but means little if not grounded in the deep recognition of others, and others in ourselves, *as* a form of action. The would-be reformed, modern Antonios cannot simply be caught repeating the shame, disgust, or distrust of blackness; that is unacceptable. At the same time, the call for intersecting the sexual, as a disciplinary re-direction that should occupy early modern studies, must also imagine and act on stepping out from the shadows of the merely academic and engage scholar-persons in a serious, meaningful action without surrendering to the lure of category trading or its alternative, the insufficiently reflective turn to early modern race studies, that is intellectual passing.

NOTES

1. E. E. Krapf, 'Shylock and Antonio: A Psychoanalytical Study on Shakespeare and Antisemitism', *The Psychoanalytic Review* 42 (1955), 118. For the historical perspective on homoerotic readings, see Seymour Kleinberg, '*The Merchant of Venice*: The Homosexual as Anti-Semite in Nascent Capitalism', *The Journal of Homosexuality* 8 (1983): 113–26.

2. Mario DiGangi, *The Homoerotics of Early Modern Drama* (Cambridge: Cambridge University Press, 1997), 28.

3. Joyce Green MacDonald, *Race, Ethnicity, and Power in the Renaissance* (Madison, NJ: Fairleigh Dickinson University Press, 1997), 13.

4. The quoted words are taken from the description of the symposium titled 'Intersecting the Sexual: Modes of Early Modern Embodiment', sponsored by the Folger Shakespeare Library and organized by Mario DiGangi, from November 14–16, 2019.

5. Michael Omi and Howard Winant, *Racial Formation in the United States* (New York: Routledge, 1994), 65. For their examination of racial dictatorship and European conquest, see 61–9.

6. See the landmark essays by Kimberlé Crenshaw, 'Demarginalizing the Intersection of Race and Sex: A Black Feminist Critique of Antidiscrimination Doctrine', *University of Chicago Legal Forum* (1989): 139–68; and 'Mapping the Margins: Intersectionality, Identity, and Violence Against Women of Color', *Stanford Law Review* 43.6 (1991): 1241–1300.

7. *The Arden Shakespeare Complete Works*, ed. Richard Proudfoot, Ann Thompson and David Scott Kastan (London: The Arden Shakespeare, 2001). All quotations follow this edition.

8. Arthur L. Little, Jr., 'The Rights of Queer Marriage in *The Merchant of Venice*', in *Shakesqueer: A Queer Companion to the Complete Works of Shakespeare*, ed. Madhavi Menon (Durham, NC: Duke University Press, 2011), 216–24, esp. 221.
9. I began this inquiry into whiteness in *Merchant*, on which this essay builds, but in completely different investigatory directions, in 'Shakespeare and the Philologies of Race', Panel Session, Shakespeare Association of America, Forty-Sixth Annual Meeting, March 2018.
10. James C. Bulman, *The Merchant of Venice* (New York: Manchester University Press, 1991), 143.
11. Ibid.
12. Judith Butler, *Bodies that Matter: On the Discursive Limits of 'Sex'* (New York: Routledge, 1993), 232.
13. Cardinal Gasparo Contarini, *The Commonwealth and Government of Venice*, trans. Lewes Lewkenor (London: John Windet, 1599), sig. Av.
14. Elisabeth G. Gleason, 'Reading Between the Lines of Gasparo Contarini's Treatise on the Venetian State', *Historical Reflections/ Réflexions Historique* 15.1 (1988), 251–270, esp. 252.
15. Ibid.
16. Contarini, *The Commonwealth and Government of Venice*, 1.
17. Ibid.
18. *OED*, n. 3d. In law: 'A written command, precept, or formal order issued by a court in the name of the sovereign, state, or other competent legal authority, directing or enjoining the person or persons to whom it is addressed to do or refrain from doing some act specified therein.'
19. Farah Karim-Cooper, *The Hand on the Shakespearean Stage: Gesture, Touch and the Spectacle of Dismemberment* (London: Bloomsbury, 2016), 6.
20. David Hillman and Carla Mazzio, eds., *The Body in Parts: Fantasies of Corporeality in Early Modern Europe* (New York: Routledge, 1997), xiii–xiv.
21. Bruce R. Smith, *Homosexual Desire in Shakespeare's England: A Cultural Poetics* (Chicago: University of Chicago Press, 1994), esp. 66–9. On friendship, see Alan Bray, *The Friend* (Chicago: University of Chicago Press, 2003).
22. Steve Patterson, 'The Bankruptcy of Homoerotic Amity in Shakespeare's *The Merchant of Venice*', *Shakespeare Quarterly* 50.1 (1999): 9–32, esp. 10.
23. Sir Thomas Elyot, *The Boke Named the Governour*, ed. Henry Herbert Stephen Croft, Vol. 2 (London: Kegan, Paul, Trench, & Co., 1883), 134.
24. Jeffrey Masten, *Textual Intercourse: Collaboration, Authorship, and Sexualities in Renaissance Drama* (Cambridge: Cambridge University Press, 1997), 35. See *OED*, 'will' n.2: 'Carnal desire or appetite'.
25. Michel de Montaigne, *Essais*, trans. John Florio (London: Melch. Bradwood, 1613), 92.
26. Patterson, 'The Bankruptcy of Homoerotic Amity', esp. 3–4; Little, 'The Rights of Queer Marriage', 216.

27. *OED*: 'proportion', n.5: 'Form, shape; configuration (of limbs of the body, etc.); 'proportion', n.1.a, also implies the balanced symmetry of the bodily form, 'due relation of one part to another; balance, symmetry, harmony.' Similarly, 'lineament', n.2.a: 'A portion of the body, considered with respect to its contour or outline.' Mahood, the Cambridge editor of the play, glosses 'lineaments' as 'appearance, build' (141).

28. Patterson, 'The Bankruptcy of Homoerotic Amity', 23.

29. The number of verbal instances of 'friend', 'friendship', 'kind', and 'kindness' in 1.3 only is striking – a total of 12 clustered closely together. On the use of 'kind' in the play, but without my current argument about racial whiteness, see Amy Greenstadt, 'The Kindest Cut: Circumcision and Queer Kinship in *The Merchant of Venice*', *ELH* 80.4 (2013): 945–80.

30. Greenstadt, 'The Kindest Cut', 946. Deuteronomy 23:20. 'Unto a stranger thou mayest lend upon usury, but thou shalt not lend upon usury unto thy brother, that the Lord thy God may bless thee in all that thou settest thine hand to, in the land whither thou goest to possess it.' (GNV)

31. James Shapiro, *Shakespeare and the Jews* (New York: Columbia University Press, 1996), 121–2; Alan Sinfield, *Shakespeare, Authority, Sexuality: Unfinished Business in Cultural Materialism* (New York: Routledge, 2006), 56. One of the possible sources of *Merchant*, Alexander Silvayn's *The Orator*, makes explicit mention of male genitals: 'what a matter were it then, if I should cut off his privie members', in *Narrative and Dramatic Sources of Shakespeare*, ed. Geoffrey Bullough, Vol. 1 (New York: Columbia University Press, 1977), 484.

32. Kleinberg, '*The Merchant of Venice*: The Homosexual as Anti-Semite', esp. 20.

33. *OED*: 'purse', n.7.a.

34. Little, 'The Rights of Queer Marriage', 219.

35. On the meaning of *tokos*, see Rex Gibson, ed., *The Sonnets*, by William Shakespeare (Cambridge: Cambridge University Press, 1997), 25.

36. Patterson, 'The Bankruptcy of Homoerotic Amity', 23.

37. Jonathan Gil Harris, *Sick Economies: Drama, Mercantilism, and Disease in Shakespeare's England* (Philadelphia: University of Pennsylvania Press, 2004), 52.

38. *OED*, 'tainted', adj. 1.a.

39. Ian Smith, 'The Queer Moor: Bodies, Borders and Barbary Inns', in Jyotsna Singh, ed., *A Companion to the Global Renaissance 1550–1660: English Culture and Literature in the Era of Expansion* (Oxford: Blackwell, 2009), 190–204.

40. Edmund S. Morgan, *American Slavery, American Freedom: The Ordeal of Colonial Virginia* (New York: Norton, 1975), 250–70.

41. Ibram X. Kendi, *Stamped from the Beginning: The Definitive History of a Racist Idea in America* (New York: Nation Books, 2016), 53–54.

42. Michelle Alexander, *The New Jim Crow: Mass Incarceration in the Age of Colorblindness* (New York: New Press, 2012), 34.

43. Alexander, 34; W. E. B. DuBois, *Black Reconstruction in America* (Oxford: Oxford University Press, 2007), 573; for its twenty-first century iterations, see Ta-Nehisi

Coates, *We Were Eight Years in Power: An American Tragedy* (New York: One World, 2017), 341–67.

44. Dwight A. McBride, *Why I Hate Abercrombie & Fitch: Essays on Race and Sexuality* (New York: New York University Press, 2005), 59–87.
45. Ibid., 64.
46. Ibid., 84.
47. Eric Knowles and Kaiping Peng, 'White Selves: Conceptualizing and Measuring a Dominant-Group Identity', *Journal of Personality and Social Psychology* 89.2 (2005): 223–41, esp. 223.
48. Audre Lorde, 'The Master's Tools Will Never Dismantle the Master's House', in *This Bridge Called My Back: Writings of Radical Women of Color*, ed. Cherríe Moraga and Gloria Anzaldúa, 2nd edn (Berkeley, CA: Third Woman Press, 2002), 107.
49. Moraga and Anzaldúa, eds., *This Bridge Called My Back*, 63.

CHAPTER FIVE

'Envy Pale of Hew'

Whiteness and Division in 'Fair Verona'

KYLE GRADY

Whiteness is a central concern in Shakespeare's *Romeo and Juliet*. Most immediately, the tragedy privileges fairness: a ubiquitous descriptor of beauty in the period inextricable from ideologies of racial difference. As is often conventional in early modern English literature, the term is so liberally applied that it registers as a norm. Romeo describes Juliet as 'the fair daughter of rich Capulet' (2.2.58), while Juliet regards Romeo as 'fair Montague' (2.1.140). Even when Benvolio hopes to convince Romeo that Rosaline is not especially attractive – suggesting that Romeo compare Rosaline with 'all the admirèd beauties of Verona' (1.2.84) – Benvolio first calls her 'fair Rosaline' (1.2.83). Romeo's recalcitrant response to the idea that he 'examine other beauties' (1.1.221) plays with fairness's broad applicability in Verona:

> 'Tis the way
> To call hers, exquisite, in question more.
> These happy masks that kiss fair ladies' brows,
> Being black, puts us in mind they hide the fair.
> He that is stricken blind cannot forget
> The precious treasure of his eyesight lost.
> Show me a mistress that is passing fair;
> What doth her beauty serve but as a note
> Where I may read who passed that passing fair?
>
> —*RJ* 1.1.221–9

Romeo's argument describes a preponderance of phenotypic whiteness. His observation that 'these happy masks that kiss fair ladies' brows, / Being black, puts us in mind they hide the fair' describes Verona's women as racially homogenous. In order for his conceit to work, white faces must consistently lie behind these masks. Moreover, in Romeo's formulation, even the exceedingly fair can be surpassed. In Verona, fairness seems to give way to more fairness.

Romeo's aphoristic notion that too much of one thing can 'put us in mind' of the other identifies some of the racial stakes entangled with the play's preponderance of fairness. To distinguish between the phenotypically white, Romeo renders those whom we might call the comparatively 'less fair' of Verona through the racializing language of blackness. When he first sees Juliet and regards her as 'a snowy dove', he differentiates her from her otherwise fair peers by imagining Juliet 'trooping with crows' (1.5.45). Romeo furthers his un-fairing of some portion of Verona's phenotypically white women when describing Juliet 'As a rich jewel in an Ethiope's ear' (1.5.43). The allusion draws a comparison between white and black, one that emphasizes Juliet's value through juxtaposition with African difference. As Kim F. Hall explains, 'the binaries of black and white might be called the originary language of racial difference in English culture'.[1] In that sense, such a formulation is unsurprising. That said, why is the language of racial difference employed here to draw hierarchies among Verona's abundantly fair and racially homogenous people?

Scholars have long acknowledged *Romeo and Juliet*'s lack of a coherent central problem, citing the arbitrary nature of the feud between the Capulets and Montagues. As Susan Snyder argues, the play 'becomes, rather than is, tragic'.[2] What Naomi Conn Liebler notes as the play's lack of a 'complex dilemma or soliloquy-debated decision to act that mark, for example, *Julius Caesar*, *Hamlet*, *Othello*, or *Macbeth*'[3] gives the impression that Verona is on the precipice of tranquillity. The Capulets and Montagues – marked as 'alike in dignity' in the play's first line (Prol.1.i) – have no appreciable differences in need of surmounting. But, as Romeo's sense of Verona as a site in which fair people surpass the already 'passing' fair makes clear, racially organizing logic circulates among the otherwise all white population. Such notions of supersedure engender the potential to envision, as Romeo does, 'Ethiope[s]' where there are none. These conceptual reorganizations are not only representative of the arbitrary nature of racial hierarchization. They also serve to demonstrate that otherwise white spaces like 'fair Verona' are pressured by an iteration of the exclusionary processes that produce the category 'white people'.[4] Indeed, as whiteness begins to figure in the early modern period as an aspirational concept – one at once attached to phenotype, but one more specifically formulated and reformulated as a category of privilege – even marked similitude can become subject to racialized routines of differentiation.

THE AHISTORICISM OF WHITE 'NORMATIVITY'

The term 'white people' was not universally available for the early modern English. That said, it is important to note that whiteness, both today and in the early modern period, need not refer to itself in order to operate as a mode of community formation. Alan Sinfield's description of ideology is helpful for understanding how such organization occurs. For Sinfield, 'ideology produces, makes plausible, concepts and systems to explain who we are, who the others are, how the world works' and its strength 'derives from the way it gets to be common sense; it "goes without saying"'.[5] If more modern-day analogues are any indication, whiteness actually holds a particular power by remaining unnamed. As Peggy McIntosh writes in her well-known 'Unpacking the Invisible Knapsack', 'whites are taught to think of their lives as morally neutral, normative, and average, and also ideal'.[6] Identifying oneself as a white person and concomitantly pointing out the whiteness of one's group runs counter to this socialization. Such a self-identification erodes the powerful fiction of the white perspective as objective and universal. It attaches an identity to those dominant politics that are often erroneously considered unbiased in contrast to the identity politics ascribed to marginalized groups.

Whiteness also maintains conceptual power by reflexively appearing a stable and given category. For example, the fact that, as Nell Irvin Painter points out, 'most Americans envision whiteness as racially indivisible'[7] delimits our view of whiteness as either a historical construct or a category in a perpetual state of reorganization.[8] And when the notion of race as a construct is taken up in the dominant view, it is often done so in a way that evacuates the historical and contemporary centrality of whiteness to regimes of racism and racial violence.[9] But as Ta-Nehisi Coates aptly observes when discussing the formation of modern-day whiteness, 'the process of washing the disparate tribes white, the elevation of the belief in being white' was achieved 'through the pillaging of life, liberty, labor, and land'.[10] Ignorance of and discomfort with the exploitative and often violent means through which whiteness has historically been – and continues to be – constituted readily skews dominant discourse away from sustained interrogation of whiteness and its history.

Certainly, early modern studies does not talk enough about whiteness, even though racial inclusivity depends on our ability to make visible the inherent biases of a white positionality as a necessary counterpoint to the dominant cultural assumption that only people of colour have an identity-based politics. The field of early modern studies remains a venue in dire need of such a corrective. Comprehensive studies of race and its relationship to power in early modern England – work often done by people of colour – has historically been linked to a particular politics.[11] Moreover, many scholars of colour self-consciously interrogate such politics as a means of bracketing their research.[12] Yet, it is still uncommon for white scholars in early modern studies to reflect on their own professional positionality, even though our field is predominantly white. The lack of discourse about whiteness's influence on the field of early modern studies – an example of 'the luxury of *not* thinking about race' that Hall importantly identifies as endemic to the field[13] – enables the notions of neutrality and normativity that help 'maintain white privilege'.[14] The absence of an ongoing interrogation of white positionality in studies of early modern England represents an even more problematic oversight when considering that the vast majority of our objects of study concern the lived and fictional lives of white people. As Ian Smith argues, 'The failure among critics to routinely remark whiteness as a fully realized racial category in all-white plays – that is, where all the characters are presumed to be white, unless otherwise noted – enables the normative invisibility of whiteness, which is a sign of its hegemony'.[15] Smith's injunction accurately identifies the often-ignored stakes of racial positionality in early modern studies. Interrogating one's own racial position is essential for better understanding one's relationship to power – cultural, institutional and professional – as well as one's relationship to history.

PHENOTYPIC WHITENESS AND COMMUNITY FORMATION IN 'FAIR VERONA'

In *Romeo and Juliet*'s Verona, phenotypic whiteness provides some means of group identity, even while the exclusionary concept of 'white people' is in the process of being formulated. If we consider the term 'white' as indicating a '"genre" of humanity', which is the criteria employed by Gary Taylor to consider when whiteness became a concept akin to what it is today, *Romeo and Juliet* does not pass the test.[16] For example, the word white only refers to women in Shakespeare's tragedy, while male characters like Romeo are described by the interrelated term 'fair'.[17] The Elizabethan English had the 'originary language of racial difference' expressed in the binaries of Hall's formulation – Juliet's physical beauty is set in contrast to the blackness of an 'Ethiope', just as Othello's 'sooty bosom' (1.2.71) is disparagingly rendered in comparison to Venice's 'curléd darlings' (1.2.69) – yet they did not fully comprehend or mark the side of the binary in which they placed themselves. Furthermore, references to phenotypic whiteness in early modern England were not necessarily straightforward. Nor were they inherently favourable, a point made clear in Mercutio's criticism of Rosaline. After hearing that his friend failed to return home the night after the Capulet banquet, and mistakenly believing Rosaline the cause, Mercutio characterizes her as a 'pale hard-hearted wench' (2.3.4). The line correlates Rosaline's romantic rejection of Romeo – her hard-heartedness – with green sickness, a condition historically believed to affect virgin women and for which a symptom was pallor.[18]

Regardless, we would be right to assume that Mercutio's insult is tailored to someone that we – in the modern day – would identify as a white person (and not just because Romeo earlier identified Rosaline as having 'passed that passing fair'). Mercutio's subsequent lines reaffirm the phenotype of his target of derision. Some ten lines later, he proclaims Romeo 'already dead, / stabbed with a white wench's black eye' (2.3.12–13), a phenotypic description that would not earnestly apply to a black person today or in the early modern period.[19] Such descriptors – pale, fair and even white – serve a metonymic function for a white person, albeit in the absence of that particular referent. And this phenomenon is part of what makes the historical concept of a 'white people' so difficult to parse. As Taylor succinctly puts (in terms that recall Sinfield's notion of ideology) 'in Elizabethan English, the opposite of *black* was *us*'.[20] Thus, to speak of whiteness in an Elizabethan text is to speak of an 'us' that included people who were fair, pale, white and sometimes brown (but only brown in the way that white people can be brown). And that 'us' did not include people of colour (people, for example, who were brown in the way that people of African descent are imagined to be brown).[21] Such an 'us' sets the tacit phenotypic dimensions of belonging in Verona.

DESIRE AND DIVISION

Through the lens of neutrality and normativity often erroneously ascribed to whiteness, *Romeo and Juliet* may simply appear a play about people who find love across a great fracture in their community. But such a reading excises the racial and cultural parameters of Verona's 'us'. Moreover, it presumes that phenotypic whiteness holds no influence for the play or for its lovers, even while it certainly does. Intraracial coupling is rarely noted as such in either its historical or contemporary iterations, but Romeo and Juliet's intraracial desire is not hidden either. Convinced that he may never see his lover again, Romeo turns, for example, to the corporeal, recalling 'the white wonder of dear Juliet's hand' (3.3.36). And Juliet, who can see past Romeo's name, openly articulates the centrality of his body to her desire:

> 'Tis but thy name that is my enemy.
> Thou art thyself, though not a Montague.
> What's Montague? It is nor hand, nor foot,
> Nor arm, nor face, nor any other part
> Belonging to a man.
> —*RJ* 2.1.80–4

Inasmuch as Juliet's concluding reference also encompasses anatomy associated with reproduction, it brings to mind the endogamous implications of Shakespeare's sonnet 1, in which the speaker asserts 'Of fairest creatures we desire increase'.[22]

That said, even once Verona's phenotypic dimensions are acknowledged, it would be inaccurate to consider such a quality the sole means of bounding the hierarchized idea of 'white people'. While the term 'fair' functions as an oft-repeated referent in the play for phenotypic whiteness (and indeed, an attribute central to the eponymous characters' connection), it also denotes a variety of other favourable qualities. Historically, the term indicated everything from beauty, to honour, to wealth. But its early modern denotation 'of an abstract quality personified' (*OED*) more clearly encapsulates the exclusionary, hierarchizing and frequently arbitrary grounds upon which whiteness has historically been constructed. Consider how the play's Chorus recharacterizes Romeo's estimation of Rosaline in comparison to Juliet, declaring 'That fair [Rosaline] for which love groan'd for and would die, / With tender Juliet match'd, is now not fair' (1.5.146–7). Rosaline, of course, has not ceased to be phenotypically white, nor have any of her other qualities or attributes changed. Regardless, her relegation refigures her as 'not fair', a status in direct conflict with the communal confines set by the Chorus's initial introduction of the community as 'fair Verona' (Prol.i.2).

There is a precarity to fairness ostensibly borne out of its preponderance. Verona's homogeneity engenders increasingly arbitrary grounds upon which to construct hierarchies, a condition entangled with the tragedy's core tension. The otherwise inexplicable feud concerns likeness – 'Two households, both alike in dignity' (1. prol.1).[23] But it is as though that likeness does not yet include a secure and shared sense of 'us', to return to Taylor's notion of Elizabethan racial self-identification. That something akin to racial strife emerges from this similitude is perhaps most immediately demonstrated by the tragedy's amenability to interracial explication. For example, in David Leveaux's 2013 rendition of the tragedy, Romeo and Juliet are cast as white and black respectively. As Ian Munro notes, Leveaux's casting choice 'is clearly intended to have some kind of explanatory effect regarding the civil strife of the play'.[24] For his part, Arthur Laurents, the author of *West Side Story*'s book, considered the overt racialization of the feud in his famous rendition an improvement, stating: 'the thing I'm proudest of in telling the story is why [Anita] can't get the message through: because of prejudice. I think it's better than the original story'.[25] In some sense, we might see Laurents's introduction of interracial conflict making legible the racialized tension inherent to the original play.

That said, the overtly interracial paradigm was available to Shakespeare, who likely wrote *Titus Andronicus* before adapting *Romeo and Juliet*. As Lynda Boose explains, 'the black male-white female union is, through this period and earlier, most frequently depicted as the ultimate romantic-transgressive model of erotic love'.[26] That Shakespeare would go on to write such plays as *Othello* and *Antony and Cleopatra* suggests that the racialized dimensions of *Romeo and Juliet* – the core aspects of the tragedy so amenable to interracial adaptation – were not rendered between phenotypically white factions in lieu of a more overtly racialized alternative. Rather, such dimensions more accurately concern strife specific to developing notions of whiteness. Certainly, as the early modern English seek to further differentiate white from black, fair from 'not fair', and as the bounds of belonging expand and contract accordingly, phenotypically white spaces experience interrelated racial pressures. Anti-blackness comprises a particular and persistent form of violent exclusion, one that renders black people unassimilable in white-dominated society. But the exclusionary category 'white people' has not historically been inclusive solely on the basis of phenotypic whiteness. Its parameters have repeatedly shifted, frequently in ways irrespective of any other coherent organizing principle outside of asserting and maintaining racial hierarchy. Through such processes, otherwise incomprehensible divisions can be engendered out of similitude.

Consider Shakespeare's source text, Arthur Brooke's *Tragical Historye of Romeus and Juliet*, which contextualizes the feud by further emphasizing its grounding in similitude. As Brooke writes,

> A wonted use it is, that men of likely sort,
> (I wot not by what fury forced) envy each other's port.
> So these, whose egall state bred envye pale of hew,
> And then of grudging envyes roote, blacke hate and rancor grewe.[27]

The lines begin by claiming that it is common, or a 'wonted use', for 'men of likely sort' to 'envy' one another. Yet the speaker's parenthetical subsequently attenuates the applicability of this general rule in favour of some unknown motivation – some 'fury' the speaker 'wot not'. In lieu of a clear reason, the poem turns to the discourse of white and black as a means to expound upon the nature of the conflict. Whiteness, figured as 'envye pale of hew', becomes the most apt means of expressing the condition 'bred' from discontentment with equivalence. Whiteness as a 'hew' or 'hue' factors, of course, as a colour, one that carried a phenotypic denotation in the early modern period that could reference 'External appearance of the face and skin, complexion' (*OED*). Yet the homonymic resonance of 'hew' as a term for cutting and dividing is apt, given that the feud engenders fracture among 'men of likely sort'. Here, whiteness appears to develop and divide in the pursuit of hierarchy. That this division engenders 'hate and rancor' deemed 'black' by the speaker is also of particular note, suggesting that Verona's division is capable of producing, out of whiteness, a characteristic that signalled racial alterity to the early modern English.

INTRARACIAL RIOTS, INTRARACIAL RECONCILING

The solution to the problem raised by Brooke's poem is ostensibly simple. As Friar Laurence explains in Shakespeare's rendition, Romeo and Juliet's 'alliance may so happy prove / To turn [their] households' rancour to pure love' (2.2.91–2). Part of what makes *Romeo and Juliet* tragic is that Verona forgoes this path toward unity. The tragedy is only amplified by just how idyllic a harmony Verona might be able to sustain. A return to Brooke demonstrates that the town Shakespeare inherits is introduced as near perfect, save for its feud. Brooke writes that Verona is

> Bylt in an happy time, bylt on a fertile soyle,
> Maynteined by the heavenly fates, and by the townish toyle.
> The fruitful hilles above, the pleasant vales belowe,
> The silver streame with chanell depe, that through the towne doth flow,
> The store of springes that serve to use, and eke for ease
> And other moe commodities, which profite may and please[28]

Brooke's Verona is a place built for prosperity. Likewise, in Shakespeare's rendition, there is no notable economic strife. Even the act of lamenting is spared no expense, with both Capulet and Montague pledging to erect 'statue[s] in pure gold' (5.3.298) to memorialize the dead Romeo and Juliet. Given the lack of other pressing social or economic problems, *Romeo and Juliet* offers a clearer sense of the arbitrary lines of division instated through disputes over attaining and retaining whiteness. Yet given the appreciable similitude over which the conflict is waged, the tragedy concomitantly emphasizes Verona's pronounced potential for intraracial unification.

Despite sixteenth-century London's comparative economic challenges, the city in many ways experienced analogous conflicts. As Liebler notes when drawing affinities between the fictional Verona and late-sixteenth century London, 'both were cities desperately struggling to control their unruly populations'.[29] London, of course, was markedly less insulated from the outside world. And as Ania Loomba points out in summarizing notable instances of unrest in the city that took place over the course of the sixteenth century, a great deal of civil conflict concerned the presence of strangers and aliens – terms that 'were employed for non-English Europeans as well as Africans and Jews':

> In 1517, there was [a] violent riot against foreign artisans resident in London; in the same year, a preacher had moved his audience to violence by proclaiming that the increase in English poverty was due to the influx of aliens, and that God had earmarked that land exclusively for Englishmen . . . In 1551, about 500 citizens had demonstrated before the mayor of London, threatening to kill foreigners. In 1595, tradesmen rioted against 'strangers' in Southwark. Such hostile demonstrations were frequent, the result of growing anxieties about being engulfed by outsiders.[30]

It is important to note that over the course of the century glossed by Loomba, the line between who might be considered a phenotypically white foreigner and who might be marked as a phenotypically white English person blurred. While *Romeo and Juliet*'s Verona and early modern London struggled under starkly different conditions, both city's tensions demonstrate the ways in which phenotypic whiteness provided precarious but, in many instances, feasible means of constituting community.

The first of the events noted by Loomba – the 'Evil May Day' riot of 1517, in which a mob of some thousands of London's labourers rioted against those they deemed 'foreigners' – serves as an instructive example. The conflict most immediately manifests as intraracial in drawing division between 'native' Londoners, a fact famously encapsulated by Sir Thomas More's unsuccessful attempts at quelling the anger of his fellow countrymen. Yet it is also important to consider that many of the phenotypically white European targets of the mob would in time help to comprise the population we would now understand as white Londoners. As Graham Noble points out in his overview of the riot,

> As time passed, those groups targeted by the mob in 1517 were gradually assimilated into London society, inter marrying and bringing up their own children as Londoners. Their place as 'aliens' or 'strangers', struggling to make a living and despised by a minority of the native population, was taken – and still continues to be taken in the twenty-first century – by new waves of immigrants from diverse regions of the world.[31]

Not all of those considered strangers would find assimilation quite as attainable as Noble outlines. Phenotypic difference remains a basis for exclusion in white dominated societies. And English identity was in part developed through longstanding exclusionary ideologies like anti-Semitism.[32] That said, Noble's observation is helpful for recognizing that, for many phenotypically white Europeans, barriers to belonging in sixteenth-century England proved far less concrete than they initially appeared.

Noble terms the unrest 'The Race Riot of 1517',[33] despite it almost exclusively targeting and taking place among the phenotypically white. Indeed, such contractions and expansions of English belonging – both short-lived and persistent – are entangled with issues of racial organization. As Arthur L. Little, Jr. argues concerning Elizabethan attempts to banish Black people, Jesuit priests, the Irish and gypsies, 'the rhetoric of deportation ... makes evident ... the contours, however inchoate, of the establishment and deployment of a racial whiteness'.[34] To return to Coates, who considers the more modern-day, American expansion of 'white people' to include some of those groups previously marked as 'others' in sixteenth-century England, 'The new people were something else before they were white – Catholic, Corsican, Welsh, Mennonite, Jewish – and if all our national hopes have any fulfilment, then they will have to become something else again.'[35] When considering the shifting confines of whiteness – its barring and later admittance of groups like Catholics or the Irish – it is essential to emphasize a key limitation. Whiteness has consistently worked to violently exclude those seen as phenotypically black. Elizabethan London's warrants to deport 'Negroes and blackamoors' precede England's eventual dominance of the transatlantic slave trade, further solidifying hierarchical racism that persists into the modern-day.[36]

Even while *Romeo and Juliet* begins to play out a contest of exclusivity intrinsic to the developing notion of 'white people', Verona still comprises a population for whom a shared identity will become attainable under those same bounds. Brooke's *Romeus and Juliet* offers a key means for understanding the possibilities for Verona's unification, even amid its intramural fracture. There, 'race' appears as a central term. The poem employs the word in the familiar early modern sense of family, describing Romeo as 'of race a Montague'.[37] However, Brooke's poem concomitantly uses the term in contradistinction to the concept of a familial line. For Brooke, Montague and Capulet are 'two aunceint stockes, which Fortune high dyd place / Above the rest, indewd with welth, and nobler of their race.'[38] In this formulation, 'stockes' stands in for 'family' or 'house', and 'race' denotes the larger group to which both families belong. The two usages concomitantly offer racial division as well as intraracial affinity.

Brooke also expands the racial bounds of Verona to exceed its two preeminent families. When describing the approval Juliet receives at the Capulet feast, the poet writes that 'she the cheefe prayse wan that night from all Verona race'.[39] When considering the indiscriminate standard for invitation to the gathering, the phrase appears to apply quite broadly:

No lady fayre or fowle, was in Verona town,
No knight or gentleman of high or lowe renowne,
But Capilet himselfe hath byd unto his feast,
Or by his name in paper sent, appoynted as a geast.[40]

In contrast to Ivan Hannaford's sense that 'at this stage in English history, to belong to a race was to belong to a noble family with a valorous ancestry and a profession of public service and virtue',[41] Capulet's guestlist includes quite ignoble nobility, featuring 'fowle' ladies and gentleman of 'lowe renowne'. In that sense, Brooke's usage of race ostensibly encroaches on the more modern-day connotations of the word, identifying something like Verona and its culture as a racial grouping. It appears to describe a 'genre' of people – to use Taylor's formulation – however parochially defined. In recognizing the identitarian potential of Brooke's usage of the term 'race', we might also realize that part of what enables Verona's concluding attempt at reconciliation – that is, the uniting of a community after the deaths of the play's eponymous characters – is the town's ability to envision itself as racially cohesive.[42]

That said, whiteness often finds its most cooperative expression by asserting lines of exclusion relative to that which is factored as more overt difference. Verona's failure to fully recognize its whiteness is perhaps due to the lack – at least locally – of such difference. But in an early modern London marked by various forms of hardship, often blamed on the presence of foreign populations, the real tragedy of *Romeo and Juliet* might readily have figured as the fictional town's inability to indulge in its racial homogeneity. Romeo's paradoxical claim that 'There is no world without Verona walls' (3.3.17) suggests that the insulated bounds of Verona supersede all that which lies outside. Yet in asserting the preeminence of the insular, Romeo in many ways rejects that which enables the very notion of 'fair Verona'. Indeed, one lesson the tragedy appears to offer is that the hierarchizing routines of whiteness will turn inward in the absence of other difference through which to fabricate exceptionalism.

NOTES

1. Kim F. Hall, *Things of Darkness: Economies of Race and Gender in Early Modern England* (Ithaca, NY: Cornell University Press, 1995), 2.

2. Susan Snyder, *The Comic Matrix of Shakespeare's Tragedies: Romeo and Juliet, Hamlet, Othello, and King Lear*, 1st edn (Princeton, NJ: Princeton University Press, 1979), 57.

3. Naomi Conn Liebler, '"There Is No World without Verona Walls": The City in *Romeo and Juliet*', in *A Companion to Shakespeare's Works, Volume 1: The Tragedies*, ed. Richard Dutton and Jean E. Howard, 303–18 (Malden, MA: Blackwell, 2005), 304.

4. We might consider the making and remaking of early modern whiteness, particularly as a means through which to assert racial hierarchy, in relation to American whiteness. As Ta-Nehisi Coates explains regarding more modern-day constructions of whiteness, '. . . the process of naming "the people" has never been a matter of genealogy and physiognomy so much as one of hierarchy. Difference in hue and hair is old. But the belief in the preeminence of hue and hair, the notion that these factors can correctly organize a society and that they signify deeper attributes, which are indelible – that is the new idea at the heart of these new people who have been brought up hopelessly, tragically, deceitfully, to believe that they are white'; Ta-Nehisi Coates, *Between the World and Me* (New York: Spiegel & Grau, 2015), 7.

5. Alan Sinfield, *Faultlines: Cultural Materialism and the Politics of Dissident Reading* (Oakland: University of California Press, 1992), 32.

6. Peggy McIntosh, 'White Privilege: Unpacking the Invisible Knapsack', in *Race, Class, and Gender in the United States: An Integrated Study*, ed. Paula S. Rothenberg (New York: Macmillan, 2004), 189. McIntosh identifies this observation as belonging to a colleague, Elizabeth Minnich, who grew up with an experience similar to McIntosh's.

7. Nell Irvin Painter, *The History of White People*. Illustrated edn (New York: W.W. Norton, 2011), xi.

8. Painter's project reaches as far back as antiquity to better understand whiteness.

9. As an important counter to this trend in early modern studies, Peter Erickson and Kim F. Hall importantly assert that 'The narrow focus on fluidity can reinforce a tendency to approach race purely as an abstraction, thus ignoring the implications of living as a raced subject then and now as well as the political urgency many of us feel in doing this work', Peter Erickson and Kim F. Hall, '"A New Scholarly Song": Rereading Early Modern Race', *Shakespeare Quarterly* 67.1 (2016): 1–13, esp. 11.

10. Ta-Nehisi Coates, *Between the World and Me* (New York: Spiegel & Grau, 2015), 8.

11. For example, Bartels notes that 'the Moor came into scholarly discussion as an "African", not coincidentally in the era of the civil rights movement, when "Africa" was providing an empowering collective base for black power and pride', Emily C. Bartels, 'Introduction: On Sitting Down To Read Othello Once Again', in *Speaking of the Moor: From 'Alcazar' to 'Othello'* (Philadelphia: University of Pennsylvania Press, 2010), 10. While such a confluence of political and scholarly interest is worthy of investigation, such an examination is incomplete without a corollary investigation of

the politics of whiteness and its influence on scholarship. For an important analysis in that vein, see Little, who productively asks 'Is Shakespeare or the Renaissance/early modern period white property?'; Arthur L. Little, Jr., 'Re-Historicizing Race, White Melancholia, and the Shakespearean Property', *Shakespeare Quarterly* 67:1 (2016): 84–103, esp. 88.

12. See Little, 'Re-Historicizing Race', esp. 84–6, who begins his investigation of the centrality of whiteness in Shakespeare studies with a discussion of his own racial positionality as a black scholar.

13. Hall, *Things of Darkness*, 255.

14. Ibid.

15. Ian Smith, 'We Are Othello: Speaking of Race in Early Modern Studies', *Shakespeare Quarterly* 67.1 (2016): 107.

16. Gary Taylor, *Buying Whiteness: Race, Culture, and Identity from Columbus to Hip-Hop* (New York: Palgrave Macmillan, 2005), 3.

17. As Taylor explains, 'in the plays of Shakespeare and his contemporaries, a brown complexion was "manly", and brown-faced men were described as "handsome" and "honest"', *Buying Whiteness*, 36.

18. See Lesel Dawson, *Lovesickness and Gender in Early Modern English Literature* (Oxford: Oxford University Press, 2008), esp. 49–59.

19. Critics have productively read this line from Mercutio in a variety of ways, although it has not yet been realized for its racial connotations. For example, Utterback argues that the lines confirm Mercutio's bellicose inclination, Raymond V. Utterback, 'The Death of Mercutio', *Shakespeare Quarterly*, 24.2 (1973): 105–16, esp. 108. Lewis analyses their allusion to Cupid, Alan Lewis, 'Reading Shakespeare's Cupid', *Criticism*, 47.2 (2005): 177–213, esp. 183–4. And Wells connects the line to the play's satirical use of Petrarchan imagery, given its confirmation of Romeo as a Petrarchan lover with premonitions of an early death, Robin Headlam Wells, 'Neo-Petrachan Kitsch in *Romeo and Juliet*', *Modern Language Review*, 93.4 (1998): 913–33, esp. 916.

20. Taylor, *Buying Whiteness*, 35.

21. Indeed, there is clear difference between the '"handsome" and "honest"' brown faced white men that Taylor discusses (ibid, 36), and a representation like Othello, whose darker skin unequivocally marks him as a racial other.

22. For an examination of whiteness in Shakespeare's Sonnets, see Kim F. Hall '"These Bastard Signs of Fair": Literary Whiteness in Shakespeare's Sonnets', in *Post-Colonial Shakespeares*, ed. Ania Loomba and Martin Orkin (London: Routledge, 1998).

23. The repeated violence is described by the Prince as being 'bred of an airy word' (1.1.82). As Liebler notes, 'no one in Verona seems to remember or care what that "airy word" was that started the feud', Liebler, 'There Is No World', 315.

24. Ian Munro, 'Performance History', in *Romeo and Juliet: A Critical Reader*, ed. Julia Reinhard Lupton, 53–78 (London: Bloomsbury Publishing, 2016), 67.

25. Ibid., 609.

26. Lynda Boose, '"The Getting of a Lawful Race": Racial Discourse in Early Modern England and the Unrepresentable Black Woman', in *Women, 'Race', and Writing in the Early Modern Period*, ed. Margo Hendricks and Patricia Parker (New York: Routledge, 1994), 41. Celia R. Daileader puts the narrative function of the interracial paradigm into starker terms (and ones especially relevant to the quandary offered by *Romeo and Juliet*), calling it 'the ultimate in "star crossed love"'; *Racism, Misogyny, and the* Othello *Myth: Inter-racial Couples from Shakespeare to Spike Lee* (New York: Cambridge University Press, 2005), 16. Daileader also notes that 'inter-racial productions [of *Romeo and Juliet*] almost inevitably cast Romeo, not Juliet, as black'; ibid., 7.

27. Arthur Brooke, 'The Tragicall Historye of Romeus and Juliet', in *Narrative and Dramatic Sources of Shakespeare*, ed. Geoffrey Bullough (New York: Columbia University Press, 1957), 31–34.

28. Ibid., 3–8.

29. Liebler, 'There Is No World', 307.

30. As Loomba notes, the 1517 riot is part of the plot of *Sir Thomas More*, a play to which Shakespeare is believed to have contributed. For a discussion of the events of 1517 and their culmination into what is known as 'Evil May Day'; Ania Loomba, *Shakespeare, Race, and Colonialism* (New York: Oxford University Press, 2002), 15–16). See also Graham Noble, '"Evil May Day": Re-Examining the Race Riot of 1517', *History Review* 61 (September 2008): 37–40.

31. Ibid., 40.

32. See Heng, who demonstrates the operation of racial thinking in the European Middle Ages, in part, through an analysis of medieval England's violent and exclusionary treatment of Jewish people; Geraldine Heng, *The Invention of Race in the European Middle Ages* (Cambridge: Cambridge University Press, 2018).

33. Noble, 'Evil May Day', 37.

34. Little, 'Re-Historicizing Race', 100.

35. Coates, *Between the World and Me*, 7. Religion, of course, continues to factor in racially hierarchizing discourse. For example, see Heng, *The Invention of Race*.

36. For an analysis of the warrants' dehumanizing rhetoric specific to 'blackamoors' in comparison to rhetoric employed to expel groups like the Irish, see Emily Weissbourd, '"Those in their Possession": Race, Slavery, and Queen Elizabeth's "Edicts of Expulsion"', *Huntington Library Quarterly* 78.1 (2015): 1–19. Contextualizing the warrants alongside the Iberian slave trade, Weissbourd argues that they 'assume the status of "blackamoores" as objects or commodities. A comparison of the open warrants with the expulsions of vagabonds, Jesuits, and Irishmen . . . makes this point still clearer. These latter groups are all described as threatening undesirables in proclamations of expulsion; nonetheless, the proclamations treat them as subjects with agency. . ... The "blackamoores", by contrast, are consistently described in both the open warrants and the correspondence in the Cecil papers as property', ibid., 17.

37. Brooke, 'The Tragicall Historye of Romeus and Juliet', 53.

38. Ibid., 25–26.
39. Ibid., 248.
40. Ibid., 159–62.
41. Ivan Hannaford, *Race: The History of an Idea in the West* (Woodrow Wilson Center Press, 1996), 175.
42. It is worth pointing out that Capulet initially overlooks the feud in his approach to Romeo. When Romeo's presence at the ball is brought to Capulet's attention, he decides that Romeo 'shall be endured' (1.5.86), and even takes the opportunity to praise the young Montague, stating: 'He bears him like a portly gentleman, / And, to say truth, Verona brags of him / To be a virtuous and well-governed youth.' (1.5.74–80). See Kottman, who argues that 'Because Romeo does not appear at the feast as an external enemy, but as a "virtuous and well-govern'd youth" about whom "Verona brags", his presence bears witness to openness *within* the ancient family that, like the chink in the wall between the houses of Pyramus and Thisbe, had been there all along', Paul A. Kottman, 'Defying the Stars: Tragic Love as the Struggle for Freedom in *Romeo and Juliet*', *Shakespeare Quarterly* 63.1 (2012): 1–38, esp. 16.

CHAPTER SIX

'Shake Thou to Look on't'

Shakespearean White Hands

DAVID STERLING BROWN

White hands are all over Shakespeare. And those white hands touch on so much that is critical to interrogations of race and racism. With the notable exception of *Antony and Cleopatra*, a play in which the 'white hand' is an anomaly, Shakespeare's white hands manufacture unambiguous meaning that allows the dramatist to compose a socially, politically and culturally significant narrative about whiteness, masculinity and femininity that Antony's, and Cleopatra's, presence subverts. Specifically, the phrase 'white hand', which belongs to women physically and men rhetorically, is a highly scrutinized object and recurring motif in the canon, which does not highlight the phrase 'black hand', perhaps predictably so. Beginning with *Love's Labour's Lost* and ending with *The Winter's Tale*, the phrase 'white hand' appears several times in at least seven plays and across all genres[1] – comedy, tragedy, history and romance.[2] In these other plays that enable the interrogation of race,[3] this corporeal extremity is always unmistakably attached to a white body – a woman's body. The white hand functions as a fundamental agent of 'white self-fashioning'[4] that is inherently feminized, always through masculine articulation, in discourse centred on commitment, love, beauty, virtue, honour, validation, modesty, sexual purity and domestic concerns.[5] Yet, as Arthur L. Little, Jr. observes in *Shakespeare Jungle Fever*, 'However much whiteness seems to communicate an authentic cultural sense of purity, divinity and power, it remains a theatrical device', and thus inauthentic.[6] I contend that this dramatic device, the image of the white hand that, according to Little '*works* as the primary penning and pinning agent – authorizing and flaunting, securing and insisting on the white woman's claim to sexual and racial purity', is deployed for maximum racial and rhetorical impact in *Antony and Cleopatra*.[7]

As Katherine Rowe[8] and Farah Karim-Cooper reveal in their respective studies, hands were an important symbol in the early modern period, particularly white women's hands. In *The Hand on the Shakespearean Stage: Gesture, Touch and the Spectacle of Dismemberment*, Karim-Cooper offers an astute analysis of this bodily extremity. She argues, 'Shakespeare's texts demonstrate how the hand was perceived as a powerful instrument of human exchange, emotional expression, self-scrutiny, character and identity.'⁹ As an appendage of white self-fashioning, the white hand carves out a lady's social place and directs her way of being in the world. In thinking specifically about *Antony and Cleopatra* and early modern culture, it is crucial to note that 'while the code of manners established for the hand in polite society was in continuous flux, there was a distinctive set of rules advising men, women, children and servants about their hand behaviour, such as when it is appropriate to kiss the hand of a social superior'.¹⁰ Additionally, 'kissing the monarch's hand was not only a ritualistic gesture, but it was also a sign of the privilege and honour of the kisser'.¹¹ By knowing what certain hand gestures, or even the placement of hands, mean, we can begin to see why Antony gets so incensed by Thidias' behaviour, as it is not just Antony's language, which I will soon examine, but also the play's action that sanctions the Roman's self-conscious whitening of the Egyptian Queen and that causes great friction, racial anxiety and domestic discord.¹²

SHAKESPEARE'S WHITE HANDS

Besides Antony, a number of Shakespearean men speak of the white hand of a lady, which often provides, or provided, some sense of security and comfort for the male figures: In *Love's Labour's Lost*, Shakespeare draws out the connection between whiteness and female beauty when Holofernes reads, 'To the / snow-white hand of the most beauteous Lady / Rosaline' (4.2.130–2). This point regarding beauty, naturalized by the modifier 'snow', is bolstered when Berowne says, 'And Rosaline they call her. Ask for her, / And to her white hand see thou do commend / This seal'd-up counsel' (3.1.165–7). It is as though the whiteness of the lady's unstained hand is what makes it and her, by extension, worthy of male attention, a point that *Antony and Cleopatra* also illustrates. Pandarus, in *Troilus and Cressida*, moves beyond a superficial reference to the white hand: In fact, his speech showcases a keen fixation on the woman's white hand when he references Helen's hand twice, saying, 'But to prove to you that Helen loves him: she / came and puts me her white hand to his cloven chin' (1.2.119–20), and a few lines later, 'Indeed, she has a marvellous white / hand, I must needs confess (1.2.137–8). In addition to complimenting the hand, his concentration on the placement of it suggests it mattered greatly when and how a lady's white hand came into contact with something.

Troilus and Cressida is not alone in its utilization of the white hand motif as an object of proof and validation, for *Henry V*'s Orleans claims, 'By the white hand of my lady, he's a gallant / prince', regarding the Dauphin (3.7.93–4). The white woman's hand is a pedestalized patriarchal fixture that white men can possess in the domestic context; the power of ownership permits men to channel at will the woman's constancy to prove their own. Similarly, in *As You Like It*, Orlando proclaims to the cross-dressed Rosalind, 'I swear to thee, youth, by the white hand of / Rosalind, I am that he, that unfortunate he' (3.2.384–5). In this instance, the hand functions as assurance of, as well as a kind of insurance for, Orlando's self-identification. In pledges that involve distinguishing something about oneself, the white hand assumes an instrumental role as we also see in *The Winter's Tale*. Reflecting on the past, Leontes reminisces about Hermione's white hand, noting,

'Why, that was [. . .] / Ere I could make thee open thy white hand, / And clap thyself my love; then didst thou utter, / "I am yours forever"' (1.2.101–5). Again, white masculine power prevails as Leontes reflects on what he could 'make' Hermione do with her body. And even *Twelfth Night*'s Fool asserts, in an otherwise nonsensical reply to Sir Andrew, 'My lady has a white hand' (2.3.27). Despite its randomness, his statement denotes how the lady's white hand is a recognizable racialized symbol whose meaning, which is linked to domestic relations and relationships, transcends class boundaries. The white hand is important to him just as it is important to Antony. In the canon, then, Shakespeare depicts the white hand as indisputable white prop(erty),[13] and even male property, that overtly and covertly validates white patriarchal power and verifies honour associated with the white identity. When transplanted onto Cleopatra's Black body, the white hand effectively elucidates crucial messages about whiteness, about its perceived beauty, its domestic importance, its need for protection and preservation and more;[14] Blackness, which is a diversion in Shakespeare's play, can only be of tangential importance when it is so purposely displaced by whiteness.[15]

BE(ING) WHITE

Marginalized by members of the dominant culture, Cleopatra figuratively evolves into a racially hybrid scapegoat that highlights the instability of white racial superiority, as there is an attempt to erase her racial identity by imposing whiteness on her.[16] Matthieu Chapman, Imtiaz Habib and Francesca T. Royster, to name a few critics, acknowledge the problematic nature of racial categories and racialized terms with respect to Cleopatra; the indiscriminate term application in the early modern period is reinforced by Cleopatra's being 'black' (1.5.29) and 'tawny', adding to the confusion about how to identify her racially in Shakespeare's play (1.1.6).[17] And this racial volatility is, perchance, what leads Antony, and scholars, to transform Cleopatra into a figure whose seeming 'racial ambiguity' authorizes (mis)readings of her as other than what Shakespeare so deliberately created her to be – a Black African figure – despite the fact that his 'treatment of her is not historical', as some critics and historians note.[18] In the playtext, Cleopatra's borrowed whiteness conveniently permits Antony to describe her bodily hue in opposition to Blackness in the climax when he encounters Thidias, a Roman messenger of Caesar's, kissing Cleopatra's hand.[19] In this pivotal moment, which scholars have not thoroughly explored, she ceases to be Black as her racial identity aligns with that of Antony's deceased and living fair-skinned wives, Fulvia and Octavia, respectively:[20] Egypt's queen curiously becomes a 'lady' with a 'white hand' (3.13.141).[21] A deliberate dramatic choice, the metaphorical white hand generates a colour conversion that enables Antony to claim Cleopatra as his white prop(erty);[22] for the primary purpose of articulating the centrality of whiteness, Cleopatra becomes a prop as she endures the Roman's exploitative and manipulative appropriation of her dark body.[23] Putting a critical finger on the white hand scene opens up possibilities for grasping the 'kinds of power relations [that] are reproduced within our own discipline' and allow whiteness and its impact to remain invisible.[24]

Tracing the specific white hand allusions within Shakespearean drama exposes how Antony's warning to Thidias stands out among all such specific 'white hand' references, especially because the rhetorical tone lacks the usual emblazoning. After having Thidias whipped, Antony chides him, 'Henceforth / The white hand of a lady fever thee, / Shake thou to look on't' (3.13.140–2).[25] That Antony says this to another white man while in Egypt is interesting because the general phrase 'white hand of a lady' is not specific to Cleopatra, though it peculiarly includes her.[26] And in the play, characters use 'lady' in reference to Cleopatra and Octavia, affirming the focus on whiteness here as a deliberate and strange racialized moment that *re*affirms, as Celia Daileader contends, 'the central lie of masculinist-racist power, wherein white women become scapegoats for a system of racial oppression that is almost entirely run for the benefit of white men'.[27] Antony's assertion of Cleopatra's borrowed whiteness, an assertion that some scholars have reiterated in their analyses of the play, is as much an attempt to fool others as it is an attempt to fool himself.

Given this, the white hand scene is unsurprisingly perverse in its disrespect toward the Queen. Cleopatra's white hand is an anomaly in Shakespeare's oeuvre, supporting the notion that 'the subject of race is peculiarly visual'.[28] This fact should give us pause and make us wonder about the efficacy of Antony's rhetoric as well as the symbology of the Queen's hand, which is being actively misread in multiple ways. For the hand to be acceptable, and by that I mean beautiful, by early modern standards, it has to become 'white'. In the context of Gretchen Gerzina's claim that 'the English only began to see themselves as "white" when they discovered "black" people', Cleopatra's whitening acts may be read as a necessary climactic metamorphosis, one that puts understanding the symbolic weight of binary racial opposition on her already taxed 'female body [that] itself becomes the ground on which race, culture, and cultural affiliation can be promoted'.[29]

As Joyce Green MacDonald rightly suggests, 'The more [whiteness] remains unannounced, unarticulated, the more it may be said to be in operation. Not merely about skin color, early modern whiteness works to naturalize and normalize the operations of existing hierarchies of race, nation, and sexuality. Whiteness articulates cultural authority.'[30] Antony's 3.11 'mutiny' speech (lines 12–15) solidifies the hierarchically racialized connection between 'brown' and 'white', dark and light, that Cleopatra initiates with her concerns about Roman Octavia's hair colour in 2.5 (lines 115–16) and 3.3 (lines 34–7). Thus, when Cleopatra's hand magically morphs into a white one, it (and the dark body to which it belongs) becomes symbolically beautiful and worthy of white male protection, reiterating how 'whiteness is a construct of convenience and improvisation'.[31] Cleopatra's hand signifies inferiority, which Antony's colour conversion reinforces since, according to Kim F. Hall, 'The language of dark and light is part of a white supremacist ideology and persists as a common way of making people [of African descent] inferior.'[32] Although Antony claims Cleopatra as '[his] love', his whitening of her makes that love questionable (1.1.26).[33] Karim-Cooper acknowledges that 'inferior hands include hands that are deformed, unmanicured, old and withered, mis-coloured or rough from manual labour'.[34] If one thinks of the 'white hand' articulation as a rhetorical gesture that emphasizes Cleopatra's swarthy hand as 'mis-coloured', as in not white and perhaps older because it is 'wrinkled deep in time', then the Thidias scene serves to illuminate Antony's underlying racial prejudice, which forces him to mutilate Cleopatra by attaching a white hand to her body, figuratively speaking (1.5.30). Moreover, the Thidias episode implies that Cleopatra's white hand encapsulates Shakespeare's authorial conformity to social norms regarding English beauty standards.[35] Once Antony thinks his relationship with Cleopatra is threatened, or that her honour and loyalty have been compromised, he begins to turn on her at the end of the play's climax, which marks an incredible shift in their relationship.[36]

In this 'transaction of power that employs distinct, identifiable personal features as the tools of negotiation', Antony's rather insulting message to the Queen is clear.[37] Whiteness is instilled with intangible authority that is universally recognizable; moreover, it seems that whiteness is instilled, paradoxically so, with powerful stereotypes that reify its presumed superiority. Nevertheless, racialized whiteness is a social construct. The white hand should 'fever' Thidias and, moving forward, he should tremble at its sight because violating whiteness, especially the white femininity that Antony presents as an extension of his masculine power, means violence for the violator. For an English audience, Antony's reproval of Thidias would have been apt: 'The Romans were *the* model of an imperial and civilizing masculinity, and their empire served as a nostalgic model for an early modern England that strongly desired to perform (and thereby prove) its own imperial and masculine identity.'[38] Antony's reaction is an early example of white intimidation, which is itself a by-product of white supremacy, as the Roman triumvir indicates that the very appearance of whiteness should make people shudder.[39] That is to say, Thidias has now learned he should intuitively fear the presence of a lady's white hand. It is Antony's hope that Thidias' being whipped will condition him to avoid instinctually looking at or being 'so saucy with the hand of' a lady (3.13.99); the aggression is an assertion of Antony's male dominance over both Thidias, who represents Caesar, and Cleopatra.

OWNING WHITENESS

The Roman triumvir's attempted ownership of Cleopatra is most evident in the connection I draw between 3.13 and 4.8. Antony succinctly affirms for Cleopatra that he is upset because she allowed a 'feeder' to 'be familiar with / My playfellow, your hand', which specifically becomes a white hand just a few lines later (3.13.126–7). As Cheryl I. Harris argues, 'Possession of property includes the rights of use and enjoyment.'[40] The possessive 'my' makes the hand Antony's white property. At this point, his prior submission to the Queen seems more like a ruse in retrospect; even though they are not married he views her (white hand) as belonging to him. This is another reason why Thidias must 'shake' with fear to look, because Antony did not authorize his touching the hand that plays with him (Antony) sexually and romantically. 'Fears about profane touches and the ugliness of spotted or deformed hands are embedded in the misogynistic writing about witchcraft, diabolism and in the xenophobic anxieties about foreigners in this period', as Karim-Cooper explains.[41] Antony's misogynistic language is infused with racial anxiety: his misogynoir reminds us that Cleopatra is neither Fulvia nor Octavia.[42] She is not white.

As I previously suggested, Cleopatra's tawny hand is 'mis-coloured' and therefore somewhat deformed, visually speaking. Given this, I propose that Antony defines

Thidias' actions as disrespectful because of his own deeply internalized beliefs about white racial superiority that sometimes cause him to see Cleopatra as the 'cunning' (1.2.152), 'enchanting' (1.2.135) non-white 'witch' (4.12.47) who has him bound in 'strong Egyptian fetters' (1.2.122). His words implicate him in the Roman anti-Black racism shown toward Egypt;[43] he deploys 'the powers of [descriptive] distortion that the dominant community seizes as its unlawful prerogative'.[44] The major takeaway is that no one can touch Antony's transformed white property, the Queen, unless he says so. He is the master of this feminine possession, so he thinks.[45] Antony views himself as superior to the Queen, certainly in terms of gender and possibly in terms of race, for when Antony feels threatened by other white men – namely, Thidias and Caesar – he reacts aggressively toward Cleopatra to control her with his histrionic emotions; when these other men encroach upon his Egyptian territory, he responds defensively. Yet, the power he thinks he holds over Egypt accentuates a fundamental double standard that solidifies how he operates with a sense of 'white male supremacy', which Ijeoma Oluo argues 'has been in place in white culture since before white people thought of themselves as white'.[46] I specifically apply white male supremacy here because in 4.8 Antony has no problem with Scarus touching, at Antony's request, the Queen's hand, his 'playfellow' (lines 22–4).

The Queen's white hand makes her a direct foil to virtuous white women such as Antony's wife Octavia. The existence of and references to Antony's official spouse remind us that: Cleopatra is not a wife; she lacks the ideal beauty and 'patien[ce]' embodied by virtuous white women (4.12.38); she is viewed as a 'gipsy' (1.1.10) and 'whore' by the play's Romans (4.12.13);[47] and she is, most obviously, not Roman.[48] Before Antony falls on his sword in 4.14, his last words to Cleopatra are harsh. Infuriated that 'this foul Egyptian hath betrayed [him]' once more (4.12.10), Antony verbally assaults her:

> Vanish, or I shall give thee thy deserving,
> And blemish Caesar's triumph. Let him take thee,
> And hoist thee up to the shouting plebeians:
> Follow his chariot, like the greatest spot
> Of all thy sex; most monster-like, be shown
> For poor'st diminutives, for doits; and let
> Patient Octavia plough thy visage up
> With her prepared nails.
>
> —4.12.32–9

The trafficking of Cleopatra's body, first handed to Scarus and then envisioned as being turned over to Caesar, adds to the air of white patriarchal supremacy perpetuated by the male characters. Moreover, Antony's use of 'foul' racializes this moment since, in addition to meaning physically loathsome, wicked, ugly and morally/spiritually polluted, the term means dirty, soiled and full of dirt.[49] To see the foul Egyptian is to see her as dark – physically, spiritually sullied.

The threat of disfigurement is interesting because, to an extent, Antony already maimed her body when he rhetorically bleached or detached replaced her hand with a white one.[50] While enraged, Antony derives pleasure from the thought of Caesar imprisoning Cleopatra and making money off her physique that is on display among the common people in the Roman streets.[51] The white man sees this woman's body as profitable and available for economic exploitation. Thus, Cleopatra is a dual spectacle, an early modern minstrel sideshow within the play, which feeds the offstage audience's interests just as much as she feeds the curiosities of the characters around her. We could call the latter group an onstage audience since Cleopatra, the character, was performed on the early modern stage by a white male actor and since Cleopatra, as a character, also performed for the dominant culture the perceived monstrousness and impropriety of her femininity.[52] Caesar's seizure of Cleopatra would be empowering for the white Roman figures because capturing the Queen typifies successful white dominance. Antony passing her off to his Roman brethren ensures the perpetuation of violent white supremacy,[53] guaranteeing her being mastered by white hands,[54] and then continue "and guaranteeing, too, that Cleopatra 'shall' die' (4.12.47).

Egypt's queen knows she cannot wholeheartedly trust the questionable intentions of the white Romans. Her apprehension works in her favour; it allows her to assume rightfully that Caesar wants to parade her through Rome as a sign of his masculine strength and white dominance. Cleopatra, however, plans to use the power of *her* white hand to master herself and 'by some mortal stroke, / [. . .] defeat [Caesar and Rome]' (5.1.64–5). At the play's conclusion, the Queen of Egypt overpowers whatever white masculine holds might exist on her in order to own her end. She calls attention to this when, in imagining her future in Rome, she winces at the thought of 'some squeaking Cleopatra boy [her] greatness / I'th' posture of a whore' (5.2.220–1). In not wanting to experience this, Cleopatra offers another reason why she must inflict violence on herself with her own hands.

The alteration of 'boy' into a verb sheds light on the boy actor who would have played her part on the early modern stage. Implied in her lines is that she is too much woman for a white boy; she is too magnificent for Caesar and the actor underneath who plays her.[55] By killing herself, Antony's lover asserts through action that she will not be played, as in mocked in Rome's streets, ever.[56] She employs the white hand, her white hand, to fight the encroaching white male power that wants to assume control of her body yet again. Until the end, the tension between Black and white is evident, but paradoxically reconciled through Cleopatra's self-destruction. When Caesar finally encounters the dead Cleopatra, he does not see the boy actor; rather, he 'see[s] performed that dreaded act which [he] / So sought'st to hinder' (5.2.331–2). He did not intend to prevent the Queen's death for her benefit; that was all for his advantage. Cleopatra herself does not 'shake' at the sight of the white hand. In the end, the Egyptian monarch has the royal authority to own and 'ruin' her 'mortal house', and consequently undermine white supremacy (5.2.50), deal a blow to Roman Caesar, and mock his 'ass / Unpolicied!' (5.2.307–8).

FAIR WEAPONS OF MASS DESTRUCTION

As a counterexample among the appearances of the white hand motif Shakespeare, *Antony and Cleopatra* figures the incessantly conquering white hand as a dangerous thing. For all that *Antony and Cleopatra* articulates about whiteness, by the play's conclusion we discover that violence, murder, and suicide seem invariably attributable to white hands regardless of any character's dominant bodily hue: 'if black Cleopatras seduce[, then] white ones kill themselves'.[57] Returning to 3.13 and Cleopatra's white hand, it is possible to see this moment as both a physical Black-to-white conversion and Antony's recognition of the literal white part of the Queen's hand, the palm side.[58] Through the latter reading, the Black body is always hybrid and 'the hand of death' is white (4.9.34). As a symbol, the white hand instils fear because of its inextricable connection to violence and death.

Moreover, the white hand's penchant for violence foreshadows Cleopatra's own death. The Queen's failed first attempt to slay herself in 5.2 occurs when she learns that Caesar's men have stormed her monument; here, the stage directions read, 'drawing a dagger', signalling Cleopatra's suicidal agenda as she says, 'Quick quick, good hands' (38). The address to the hands highlights what such hands are capable of. Rather than allow the Romans to take her, Cleopatra prefers to take her own life because, for the overpowered Egyptian, to borrow from Frantz Fanon's discourse on natives, 'violence is a cleansing force [that] [. . .] makes [her] fearless and restores [her] self-respect'.[59] Ironically, these 'hands [that lack[ed]] nobility' for striking the Messenger (2.5.83), and attempting to kill him earlier in the play, become 'good hands' after Antony whitens them; Cleopatra also becomes a 'good lady' after that scene as well (5.2.193).

Despite its less than flattering associations with violence here, whiteness gets equated with goodness, beauty and innocence.[60] And we are conditioned to see the virtuousness that fosters positive assessments of what undeniably amounts to white brutality.[61] That is to say, destructiveness transmutes into constructiveness. The Romans, the white people and therefore their white hands, are depicted negatively as untrustworthy; however, Cleopatra's hands still encourage a positive critique of whiteness because they are, according to the Queen, the only hands she will 'trust' (4.15.51).[62] At best, whiteness maintains bifurcated, and confusing, meaning in *Antony and Cleopatra* and in contemporary times as well: By killing the Queen, the bad-good white hands do something destructive that is presented and interpreted as constructive. In so doing, the hands expose the automatic ability for intention to be *always* positively skewed as one of the quintessential privileges of whiteness. With all the chaos caused by white hands – fair weapons of mass destruction – it is hard to fathom how white supremacy exists as a reliable or useful metric against which to measure Others' inferiority. Furthermore, it is hard to fathom how white supremacy can be taken so seriously and so fiercely drive white people's social, political and personal ideologies, for it appears we all have white hands but, alas, all white hands are not created equal – not even Shakespeareans' or Shakespeare's.

NOTES

1. Attention to white women's hands exists in other Shakespeare plays, though the phrase 'white hand' might not be the specific language used. For example, Romeo mentions 'the white wonder of dear Juliet's hand' (3.3.36). Elsewhere in *Troilus and Cressida*, we encounter the line: 'O, that her hand, / In whose comparison all whites

are ink' (1.1.55–6). In *Titus*, Marcus refers to Lavinia's 'lily hands' as he studies her body in the scene where we find her ravished and mutilated (2.4.44). Shakespeare's titular character observes Desdemona's hands in *Othello*: 'Give me your hand. [*She gives her hand*.] This hand is moist my lady' (3.4.36). And in *The Winter's Tale*, Florizel says to Perdita: 'I take thy hand, this hand, / As soft as dove's down and as white as it, / Or Ethiopian's tooth, or the fanned snow that's bolted / By th' northern blasts twice o'er' (4.4.362-4). Additionally, Arthur L. Little, Jr., observes in *Shakespeare Jungle Fever* that white hands also matter in other texts, such as those that centre on the figure of Lucrece. See Arthur Little, Jr., *Shakespeare Jungle Fever: National-Imperial Re-Visions of Race, Rape, and Sacrifice* (Stanford, CA: Stanford University Press, 2000), 29–48. All the Shakespearean quotations in this chapter are from *The Arden Shakespeare Complete Works*, ed. Richard Proudfoot, Ann Thompson and David Scott Kastan (London: The Arden Shakespeare, 2001).

2. As Matthieu Chapman acknowledges, 'Dramatists wrote black characters in no fewer than seventy plays.' See 'The Appearance of Blacks on the Early Modern Stage: *Love's Labour's Lost*'s African Connections to Court', *Early Theatre* 17.2 (2014): 86.

3. For additional, new scholarship on whiteness and Shakespearean drama, see David Sterling Brown, with Patricia Akhimie and Arthur L. Little, Jr., "Seeking the (In)Visible: Whiteness and Shakespeare Studies," *Shakespeare Studies* Forum (Vol. 50, 2022).

4. Peter Erickson "God for Harry, England, and Saint George': British National Identity and the Emergence of White Self-Fashioning', *Early Modern Visual Culture: Representation, Race, Empire in Renaissance England*, ed. Peter Erickson and Clark Hulse, 315–45 (Philadelphia: University of Pennsylvania Press, 2000), 322. For an explanation of 'self-fashioning' and its 'governing conditions' see Stephen Greenblatt, *Renaissance Self-Fashioning: From More to Shakespeare* (Chicago: University of Chicago Press, 1980), 8–9.

5. See Imtiaz Habib, *Shakespeare and Race: Postcolonial Praxis in the Early Modern Period* (New York: University Press of America, Inc., 2000), 4. And Arthur L. Little, Jr. 'Re-Historicizing Race, White Melancholia, and the Shakespearean Property', *Shakespeare Quarterly*, 67.1 (Spring 2016): 91–2.

6. Little, *Shakespeare Jungle Fever*, 161.

7. Ibid., 48.

8. Katherine Rowe, *Dead Hands: Fictions of Agency, Renaissance to Modern* (Stanford, CA: Stanford University Press, 1999).

9. Farah Karim-Cooper, *The Hand on the Shakespearean Stage: Gesture, Touch and the Spectacle of Dismemberment* (London: The Arden Shakespeare, 2016), 4.

10. Ibid., 6.

11. Ibid., 45.

12. Erickson, 'God for Harry', 331.

13. Building on Cheryl I. Harris's work, Little discusses 'whiteness as a form of property'. See 'Re-Historicizing Race', 89. These 'white hand' passages indicate that for both

white and Black people 'racial identity remains an important component of social appraisal'. See Robert M. Entman and Andrew Rojecki, *The Black Image in the White Mind: Media and Race in America* (Chicago: University of Chicago Press, 2001), 1.

14. Considering that 'Shakespeare's plays refer back and forth among themselves', the placement of the white hand in *Antony and Cleopatra* is even more fascinating and fitting, especially in terms of genre, since the most prominent Black Shakespearean figures – Aaron, Othello and Cleopatra – are bound to the tragedies. See Lawrence Danson, *Shakespeare's Dramatic Genres* (Oxford: Oxford University Press, 2000), 7.

15. As a very specific kind of distraction for Antony, Cleopatra's Blackness, and her affair with the Roman triumvir, calls 'attention to the sexual dimension of politics'. See Melissa E. Sanchez, *Erotic Subjects: The Sexuality of Politics in Early Modern English Literature* (Oxford: Oxford University Press, 2011), 11.

16. Additionally, since 'the countries bordering the Mediterranean[, including Egypt,] were another frequent source of supply [of black slaves]', I want to suggest that this reality may have influenced Shakespeare's choice to blacken the Egyptian Queen; Blackness aligns her with those who are thought of as needing to be dominated. See Gustav Ungerer, 'The Presence of Africans in Elizabethan England and the Performance of *Titus Andronicus* at Burley-on-the-Hill, 1595/96', *Medieval and Renaissance Drama in England* 21 (2008): 31. Virginia Mason Vaughn reminds us that 'as early as the 1570s black Africans were in England, working as household servants, prostitutes, and court entertainers'. See *Performing Blackness on English Stages, 1500–1800* (Cambridge: Cambridge University Press, 2005), 77. Anthony Gerard Barthelemy posits, 'Attitudes toward black people in the seventeenth century were formulated in an environment that had not distinguished between the traditional Christian view of black people as devils and the then not entirely unfamiliar African.' See *Black Face, Maligned Race: The Representation of Blacks in English Drama from Shakespeare to Southerne* (Baton Rouge: Louisiana State University Press, 1987), ix.

17. See Matthieu Chapman *Anti-Black Racism in Early Modern English Drama: The Other 'Other'* (London: Routledge, 2017), 8. Also see Habib, *Shakespeare and Race*, 3. Francesca T. Royster, 'White-Limed Walls: Whiteness and Gothic Extremism in Shakespeare's *Titus Andronicus*', *Shakespeare Quarterly* 51.4 (Winter 2000): 448. Dympna Callaghan reads Cleopatra as a 'symbol of woman, of female sovereignty, of racial difference'. See *Shakespeare Without Women: Representing Gender and Race on the Renaissance Stage* (New York: Routledge, 2000), 7.

18. *Northrop Frye on Shakespeare*, ed. Robert Sandler (New Haven, CT: Yale University Press, 1986), 124. See also Celia R. Daileader, 'The Cleopatra Complex: White Actresses on the Interracial 'Classical' Stage', *Colorblind Shakespeare: New Perspectives on Race and Performance*, ed. Ayanna Thompson, 205–220 (New York: Routledge, 2006), 205, 209, 213. Francesca T. Royster, *Becoming Cleopatra: The Shifting Image of an Icon* (New York: Palgrave Macmillan, 2003), 17–20. Little, Jr. calls attention to the debate about Cleopatra's race when he notes, 'Whether white or black Cleopatra finds herself the object of racial passing.' See Little, *Shakespeare Jungle*, 24. Also see Farah Karim-Cooper, who argues, 'While Shakespeare suggests the readability of hands, he simultaneously alludes to the elusiveness of the self upon the surface of the body when people misread hands and their gestures.' See Karim-

Cooper, *The Hand*, 24. Vanessa Corredera claims, 'Today's conceptions of race are no more stable or biologically based than those constructed in the early modern period.' See 'Not a Moor Exactly: Shakespeare, *Serial*, and Modern Constructions of Race', *Shakespeare Quarterly* 67.1 (2016): 43.

19. Blackness enables Shakespeare's Cleopatra to fulfil the 'common stereotype of black women as particularly promiscuous and sexually immoral'. See Melissa V. Harris-Perry, *Sister Citizen: Shame, Stereotypes and Black Women in America* (New Haven, CT: Yale University Press, 2011), 54.

20. Little, Jr., briefly acknowledges but does not offer an extensive critique of this moment. See Little, Jr., *Shakespeare Jungle*, 168.

21. Although 'female 'blackness' [could be] metaphorical' in the Renaissance, Cleopatra's physical Blackness makes her holistically, and therefore unquestionably, Black. See Lara Bovilsky, *Barbarous Play: Race on the Renaissance Stage* (Minneapolis: University of Minnesota Press, 2008), 39.

22. For more on 'white property' (my parentheses added), and white transformation, see Cheryl I. Harris, 'Whiteness as Property', *Harvard Law Review* 106.8 (Jun. 1993): 1707–1791; esp. 1709. Also see Little, 'Re-Historicizing Race', 88. For more on Cleopatra's colour conversion, see Little, Jr., *Shakespeare Jungle*, 163.

23. Daileader, 'Cleopatra Complex', 207.

24. Thomas K. Nakayama and Robert L. Krizek, 'Whiteness: A Strategic Rhetoric', *Quarterly Journal of Speech* 81.3 (1995): 291–309, esp. 303.

25. Antony's language shows how 'discourses of race and gender are not fully separable in the early modern period and indeed possess numerous identity features'. The Queen's hand represents a complicated intersection of Blackness, whiteness, masculinity and femininity. See Bovilsky, *Barbarous Play*, 39.

26. In *Antony and Cleopatra*, the Egyptian Queen makes references to her 'bluest veins' and being 'pale'. These references have served as support for some scholars, such as Royster, seeing Cleopatra as 'explicitly emphasiz[ing] her whiteness'. I want to acknowledge, however, that it is possible for Black people, depending on how dark they are, to become pale and it is also possible for some Black people to see the blue of their veins, myself included. Cleopatra's blue vein and pale skin references are insufficient evidence of her whiteness, just as references that might mention tanned skin would be unreliable markers of unquestionable whiteness, as it is possible for Black people to become darker when exposed to the sun. See *Becoming Cleopatra*, 18.

27. Daileader, 'Cleopatra Complex', 211.

28. See Entman and Rojecki, *The Black Image*, xv.

29. Gretchen Gerzina, *Black England: Life before Emancipation* (London: John Murray, 1995), 5. Also see Joyce Green MacDonald, *Women and Race in Early Modern Texts* (Cambridge: Cambridge University Press, 2004), 23.

30. See MacDonald, *Women and Race*, 36–37.

31. Susan Briante, 'Seeing White: The Painful Ways the World Teaches Race and Color', *Guernica/A Magazine of Global Arts & Politics*, 9 October, 2017, https://www.

guernicamag.com/seeing-white/. The ability for the colour of Cleopatra's hand to shift rhetorically also speaks to the fact that skin 'was a contested and unstable boundary' in the early modern period. See Kimberly Poitevin, 'Inventing Whiteness: Cosmetics, Race, and Women in Early Modern England', *Journal for Early Modern Cultural Studies* 11.1 (Spring/Summer 2001): 78.

32. See Kim F. Hall, *Things of Darkness: Economies of Race and Gender in Early Modern England* (Ithaca, NY: Cornell University Press, 1995), 266. For more on Cleopatra's 'racial and sexual conversion' see Little, Jr., *Shakespeare Jungle*, 163.

33. Ania Loomba asserts, 'Early modern plays about the East remind us that the discourses of 'modern' racism were shaped by vocabularies of love and war appropriated from worlds that are today regarding as being on the 'other' side of temporal, ideological, and geographic borders.' See 'Periodization, Race and Global Contact', *Journal of Medieval and Early Modern Studies* 37.3 (Fall 2007): 614.

34. Karim-Cooper, *The Hand*, 62.

35. Roman Octavia's beauty, alluded to twice in the play, is couched in positive terms (see 2.2.136 and 2.2.240).

36. Reinforcing my point, François Laroque argues, 'Like the 'o'erflowing Nilus' (1.2.46), Cleopatra, as Africa, threatens Antony and the whole Roman world with dissolution and with the erasing of identity in its 'colonial economies of desire'. See 'Italy vs. Africa: Shakespeare's Topographies of Desire in *Othello, Antony and Cleopatra* and *The Tempest*', *Shakespeare Studies* 47 (2009): 10. Also see Francesca T. Royster, 'Cleopatra as Diva: African-American Woman and Shakespearean Tactics', in *Transforming Shakespeare: Contemporary Women's Re-Visions in Literature and Performance*, ed. Marianne Novy (New York: St. Martin's Press, 1999), 106. And for a general take on the idea of the threatening Black woman see Lynda E. Boose, 'The Getting of a Lawful Race: Racial Discourse in Early Modern England and the Unpresentable Black Woman', in *Women, Race, and Writing*, ed. Margo Hendricks and Patricia Parker (New York: Routledge, 1994), 49.

37. Ian Smith, *Race and Rhetoric in the Renaissance: Barbarian Errors* (New York: Palgrave Macmillan, 2009), 8.

38. See Little, Jr., *Shakespeare Jungle*, 103.

39. This white hand scene, particularly the whipping, makes me think of Emmett Till, a Black boy who was lynched by two white men in Mississippi in 1955 for allegedly whistling at/flirting with a white woman. The horrific consequence for his supposed transgression was meant to instil fear in Black people, especially boys and men, and illustrate the white male exertion of authority over the white female body that is, according to history, always in need of protection. On 7 March 2022, the Emmett Till Antilynching Act became federal law in the United States, 67 years after Till's lynching-murder. See https://en.wikipedia.org/wiki/Emmett_Till_Antilynching_Act#Background

40. See Harris, 'Whiteness as Property', 1734.

41. *The Hand*, 63. Chapman points out that 'for hundreds of years, at least since the crusades, the English held a widespread belief that fairness or whiteness was

equivalent with beauty, modesty, and good and blackness was equivalent with ugliness, promiscuity, and evil'. See Chapman, 'The Appearance of Blacks', 78. For more on African sexuality, and the meaning of whiteness and Blackness, see Winthrop D. Jordan, *White Over Black: American Attitudes toward the Negro, 1550–1812* (Chapel Hill: University of North Carolina Press, 1968), 5–8, 33.

42. Antony's anxiety is multifaceted, and it makes sense given that 'sexual intercourse between members of different groups was the kind of crossover that generated the greatest anxiety'. See Ania Loomba, '"Delicious Traffick": Racial and Religious Difference on Early Modern Stages', in *Shakespeare and Race*, ed. Catherine M. S. Alexander and Stanley Wells (Cambridge: Cambridge University Press, 2000), 213.

43. John Michael Archer posits, 'Antony himself assumes the Roman discourse that renders Cleopatra whore and trickster, a darkened remnant whose false soul turns antiquity into a conjurer's cheat, like the rigged game of fast and loose.' See 'Antiquity and Degeneration in *Antony and Cleopatra*', in *Race, Ethnicity, and Power in the Renaissance*, ed. Joyce Green MacDonald (London: Associated University Presses, 1997), 151.

44. Hortense Spillers, 'Mama's Baby, Papa's Maybe: An American Grammar Book', *Diacritics* 17.2, Culture and Countermemory: The 'American' Connection (Summer 1987): 64–81; esp. 69.

45. His words and actions are a reminder that early modern images of Black women, in art and literature, have 'little to do with actual black women'. See Kim F. Hall, 'Object into Object: Some Thoughts on the Presence of Black Women in Early Modern Culture', in *Early Modern Visual Culture: Representation, Race, Empire in Renaissance England*, ed. Peter Erickson and Clark Hulse (Philadelphia: University of Pennsylvania Press, 2000), 346.

46. Ijeoma Oluo, *Mediocre: The Dangerous Legacy of White Male America* (New York: Seal Press, 2020), 3–4.

47. Barthelemy recalls that 'the popular notion that black women were whorish could be heard on the English stage as early as Shakespeare's *The Merchant of Venice*'. See *Black Face*, 124.

48. As Royster articulates, 'Moderation and restraint were to Elizabethans the quintessential Roman virtues.' As such, it would be odd for Shakespeare's Cleopatra to be white from the play's start; in the role of white whore, she would potentially alienate the early modern audience. See 'White-Limed Walls', 448.

49. See 'foul' in the *Oxford English Dictionary*.

50. Daileader calls attention to the historical whitening, lightening of Cleopatra: 'That time bleached her is an ideologically useful accident, but an accident all the same.' See 'The Cleopatra Complex', 209.

51. Antony's behaviour demonstrates how 'imperialism can[not] be understood without reference to ideologies of race'. See Ania Loomba, 'Early Modern or Early Colonial?', *Journal for Early Modern Cultural Studies* 14.1 (Winter 2014): 147.

52. For more on the performativity of Blackness and character profiling, see my essay, '"Is Black so Base a Hue?": Black Life Matters in Shakespeare's *Titus Andronicus*', in *Early*

Modern Black Diaspora Studies (New York: Palgrave Macmillan, 2018). On African monstrosity, see Mary Floyd-Wilson, *English Ethnicity and Race in Early Modern Drama* (Cambridge: Cambridge University Press, 2003), 19. Also see David Sterling Brown, 'I Feel Most White When I Am . . .: Foregrounding the "Sharp White Background" of Anchuli Felicia King's *Keene*', *Shakespeare Bulletin* 39.4 (Winter 2021): 584–7.

53. Frantz Fanon, *The Wretched of the Earth*, trans. Constance Farrington (New York: Grove Press, 1963), 43.

54. Saidiya Hartman suggests that 'history is an injury that has yet to cease happening'. Given the pervasiveness of global anti-Black violence, I agree with Hartman's assessment of the metaphorical open wound that is the Black existence, which remains subject to mastering today. See 'The Time of Slavery', *The South Atlantic Quarterly* 101.4 (Fall 2002): 772.

55. Antony refers to Caesar as a 'boy' a few times in the play (see 3.13.17; 4.1.1; and 4.12.48).

56. Joseph Roach claims, 'Performance [. . .] stands in for an elusive entity that it is not but that it must vainly aspire both to embody and replace'. The young actor boy-ing Cleopatra's greatness vainly plays the woman who cannot be played. See *Cities of the Dead* (New York: Columbia University Press, 1996), 3. See also Callaghan, *Shakespeare Without Women*, 12. Also see 'play me' in Urban Dictionary: https://www.urbandictionary.com/define.php?term=play%20me

57. Little, Jr., *Shakespeare Jungle*, 170.

58. As Peter Erickson and Kim F. Hall posit, 'Early modern race studies places more emphasis on race, not less, and increases the opportunities for discussing race by focusing on new directions for analysis.' For early modern race studies, then, Cleopatra's white hand is an incredibly valuable object. See "A New Scholarly Song': Rereading Early Modern Race', *Shakespeare Quarterly* 67.1 (2016): 5.

59. Fanon, *The Wretched of the Earth*, 94. With self-respect restored, 'there is finally no frivolous or politically irresponsible queen in Shakespeare's play. Throughout, she poses her theatrical body against Rome's inevitable conquest of Egypt'. See Little, Jr., *Shakespeare Jungle*, 155. Habib describes Cleopatra's suicide as 'the subaltern's act of posthumous self agency within the discourse that is writing it, its ultimate denial of its own scriptability'. See *Shakespeare and Race*, 16.

60. Speaking in relation to the mid-nineteenth century, Robin Bernstein notes that by that historical point 'innocence was raced white'. I propose that *Antony and Cleopatra* also presents a symbolic equivalent to racial whiteness as innocence and goodness. See *Racial Innocence: Performing American Childhood from Slavery to Civil Rights* (New York: New York University Press, 2011), 4.

61. Patricia J. Williams comments on how Black people are conditioned to see themselves in a white society; and I want to add to her language slightly by arguing that whites in a white society are conditioned from infancy to see in themselves all the positive qualities to which Black people are generally denied automatic access. Goodness and virtue, for instance, are alleged intrinsic aspects of the white identity that allow white

people's bad behaviour to be always questionable. See *The Alchemy of Race and Rights* (Cambridge, MA: Harvard University Press, 1991), 62.

62. The white hand scene is a literary 'exploited distorted representation of [the] black [woman]' that hands her a sliver of acceptability. See Patricia A. Turner, *Ceramic Uncles & Celluloid Mammies: Black Images and Their Influence on Culture* (New York: Anchor Books, 2000), 11.

CHAPTER SEVEN

'Pales in the Flood'

Blood, Soil, and Whiteness in Shakespeare's Henriad

ANDREW CLARK WAGNER

In late 1648, Leveller pamphleteer and New Model Army printer John Harris published a series of pro-Parliamentary newspapers under the title *Mercurius Militaris*. Harris had come to printing and publishing by accident. Previously a stage actor, he was forced into a new line of work following the closure of the theatres by the Long Parliament in 1642.[1] The Levellers sought to tear down social hierarchies and derived their name from a 1607 rural uprising in which a group of rioters razed the fences and hedges of a local landlord.[2] It is not hard to imagine Harris's theatrical background serving him in his new line of work as a Leveller journalist. Like their predecessors, the Levellers had clear antagonists and dramatic tactics. Indeed, in an earlier pamphlet, he rails against the French for only wanting to see an English play performed 'but once':

> The French (so further speakes intelligence) desiring to see an English Play acted but once – : Geographers indeed do speake of a Nation that is naturally fickle. Besides, if that Play were one of 2 or 3 that I could name in Shakespeare, it were incredible newes to me they would see it (quite out) once.[3]

For Harris, the theatre is a crucial marker of Englishness both because of England's ownership over a rich literary tradition – in this case, Shakespeare – and because the English possess a uniquely discerning literary taste. Reading Shakespeare discloses Englishness and offers an expansive conceptual reservoir for imagining what it means to be English. Harris frequently invokes Shakespeare's tragedies to define the tyranny of Charles I as a Roman perversion.[4] In the dynastic struggles for the English crown depicted across Shakespeare's two historical tetralogies, Harris discovers another basis for the seventeenth century's long-raging civil wars: the degradation of England's racial genealogy.

Those history plays were on Harris's mind in a 19 October 1648 dispatch of *Mercurius Militaris*. Questioning King Charles I's divine right to the throne – 'Did God drop down the oyl, or send a messenger with it?' – Harris associates the material symbols of divine monarchy, oil, with the messengers of divine authority, angels.[5] He then connects James I's claim to the monarchy with Richard III's usurpation of the throne, suggesting the monarchy has been perverted for generations: 'Who desided the question then, and divers times since, which was the bastard brood, and which was the Royal blood?'⁶ In a dispatch from the following week, Harris proposes another source for the monarchical impurities plaguing England in the middle of the seventeenth century:

> Where are now the old English spirits? [. . .] [T]hey would even sink into their ashes, and desire to dwell in the Caverns of the earth, rather then to see such degenerated sprouts from their roots, who having, liberty put into their hands, will so basely betray it into the most bloody Tyrants; nay, would they not defie us from relating to their stock, and suppose, that the Boars of *France* and *Negroes* in *Barbary* were transformed into English habits.⁷

Harris first conjures the ancient past to introduce a disjunction between ethereality and base materiality: the 'old English spirits' would, if they knew the depravation being visited upon their native land, 'sink into their ashes, and desire to dwell in the Caverns of the earth'. Harris's imagery calls to mind the terraforming force of the rural terrorists from whom the Levellers derived their name, and just as those rioting peasants resisted the enclosure of private land which occluded access to free, arable land, so too is Harris's language curiously generative: the collapse of those 'English spirits' serves as the root and soil for 'sprouts', howsoever 'degenerated' those descendants may be. The monarchy's collapse into a corrupted, material – and in this case, bodily – substance is made visible in his 'bloody Tyrants'. What ultimately explains the debasement of the English, however, is a genealogical disconnection from the stock of their forebears, the interloping 'Boars of France and Negroes in Barbary'. Harris here extends his rage into explicitly racial territory.

For Harris's white, English readers, genealogical connections to the past are always personal, represented through a seemingly unending chain of fathers and mothers. In his 19 October 1648 entry, Harris explores this mode of relating to the past: 'How came King Jamee to his power? From her Cozen, or my aw Uncle, or my Aunt, or my awe Grandam, or my Beldam?'⁸ The blurring of monarchical and personal genealogies set against a depersonalized group of others constitutes a fundamental mode through which ideas about whiteness become racial: through the 'conferral of otherness made visible only through collective characterization', which renders Harris's white readers, by contrast, a fully human set of individuals.⁹ Harris thus differentiates English whiteness from French whiteness and African blackness. The suggestion, moreover, that these intrusions upon English racial purity threaten 'English habits' solidifies, in its connection of habits-as-behaviour with habits-as-clothing, the centrality of the theatre in this story of racial, English whiteness. The materiality of blood, ashes and earth provides shape and form to an otherwise disparate constellation of ideas, transmuting notions of genealogy, monarchy and Englishness into bodies instrumentally capable of imagining a racial whiteness that is disembodied and pure. Degraded blackness constitutes a materiality that simultaneously supports and dissimulates the presence of a whiteness obscured by a mask of bloody earth or ashen mud.

The story Harris tells here is exemplary insofar as it highlights a racial epistemology I wish to explore in much greater detail in the following pages. But Harris's story could well have been told by any English reader of Shakespeare, then or now, and indeed points to ideas of Englishness and whiteness that thread themselves through much of Shakespeare's dramatic work. This chapter explores genealogies of English whiteness in Shakespeare's second tetralogy: *Richard II*, *Henry IV Parts 1* and *2*, and *Henry V*. These dramatic and monarchical deployments of genealogy attest to the persuasive force of natural and innate pedigrees; the past, in its immutability, justifies the present. Genealogies are narrative constructions assembled with chosen ends in sight, and monarchs are born inevitably into worlds that mandate their dominion. Two genealogies, for example, might be constructed out of the story of John Harris and the Levellers: in one, the Levellers stand 'at the headwaters of liberalism's most democratic and egalitarian branch', as 'harbingers of the democratic revolutions of later centuries'.[10] In another genealogy, their tactics are adopted by a group in Ireland known variously as the Levellers and the Whiteboys, so called because they wore their shirts outside their jackets to aid recognition, and whose tactics were in turn adopted by the 'Ku Klux Klan, whose origins have been traced directly to them'.[11] These genealogies are not distinct; Charles W. Mills has argued that liberalism 'has historically been a racial liberalism', and the social contract 'has really been a racial one'.[12] In what follows, I investigate the origins of these genealogies within Shakespeare's histories, locating eddies of whiteness at the 'headwaters of liberalism'. In their muddled origins, at the river's source, the futures imagined within Shakespeare's dramatic renderings of history begin to appear fathomless. We begin, appropriately enough, with rivers.

* * *

In the opening scene of Shakespeare's *Henriad*, Henry Bolingbroke, the future King Henry IV, challenges Thomas Mowbray, the Duke of Norfolk, to a duel, comparing Norfolk's murder of Gloucester to the murder of Abel. Mowbray 'Sluiced out his innocent soul through streams of blood; / Which blood, like sacrificing Abel's, cries, / Even from the tongueless caverns of the earth, / To me for justice and rough chastisement' (1.1.103–6). Bolingbroke's fusion of blood, soil and genealogy both locates John Harris's 'caverns of the earth' and supplies, in its sensitivity to the inherited impurity of Mowbray's misdeeds, an essentially racial interrelation of past and present. Abel's cries – and Gloucester's – are of a genealogy denied; Abel's obverse is the wandering Cain who founds cities. Cain, a farmer who bears a mark, soaks the soil with Abel's blood and renders it infertile. Bolingbroke's mythic wrangling places himself within a lineage alongside, but separate from, the city dwellers descendent of Cain.[13] We might then posit a connection between the Levellers and the itinerant, farming poor who resisted the enclosures of English land that facilitated the grazing of livestock. But the *Henriad* does not simply imagine the English participating in one genealogy or another, nor is the murder of Abel, strictly speaking, 'a foreclosure of otherness, which is represented by the original sacrifice of the brother'.[14] Rather, the *Henriad* repeatedly engages with genealogy as an opportunity to make meaning out of the historical record, to craft history from the bare elements of chronicle. Available to certain characters but unavailable to others, Shakespearean racial genealogies produce figures who are simultaneously the arbiters of historical meaning and the issues of its creative force, endlessly fecund in the face of infertility, marking and unmarking at will the boundaries of English identity and soil: defining and redefining 'streams of blood' as violent symbols of conquest and seminal fountains of identity.

Rivers mark the natural boundaries between England, Wales and Scotland. But as Henry 'Hotspur' Percy demonstrates in *Henry IV, Part 1*, what is natural is not always permanent. Before they take the field against Henry IV and his son Hal, the rebels Glendower, Mortimer and Hotspur meet with a map of the island of Great Britain to divide their future territories. The appearance of the map is explicit – Hotspur forgets the map, but Glendower has remembered it – and as is the case when maps appear on the Shakespearean stage, the audience is prepared for geographical manipulation. The map serves as a tool to divide the landscape of their united (and severable) kingdoms, both reflecting and informing the natural features of the island of Britain. Hotspur is dissatisfied with his share, which is the 'remnant northward lying off from Trent', the southwest being given to Mortimer and Wales to Glendower (3.1.78). Hotspur does not like the path of the river Trent, which 'comes me cranking in', cutting him off 'from the best of all [his] land' (3.1.97–98). The resulting loss is a 'monstrous cantle out', a 'huge half-moon' gutted from his territory, and so he warns of a solution he may pursue: to dam up the river, so that it runs 'fair and evenly', 'smug and silver' in a newly straightened course (3.1.99–102). The river Trent is notoriously fickle and changing, and Hotspur will have none of that uncertainty. The Trent would do well to run 'smug' – clean, pure, and neat – and 'fair' – clean, pure, and white – in a newly fashioned course (3.1.101–2). Glendower's protestation – 'Not wind? It shall, it must, you see it doth' – evaporates in the face of Hotspur's reality-bending manipulations (3.1.105). Your kingdom will be diminished, Hotspur declares, winnowed out one small charge by one small charge, as the Trent moves farther and farther west, cantling Wales silver half-moon by silver half-moon. Hotspur's gambit challenges the immutability of nature, rejecting the notion that what is natural is fixed and constant. He does not take exception with the authority of the archbishop to divide the land in this fashion, or with using the river as a boundary between his lands and those of Mortimer and Glendower. He simply moves the river, clarifies its path, straightens its course.

In its construction of and ownership over natural orders which are at once fixed and mutable, Hotspur's focalization of identity, nature and property typifies the way whiteness becomes racialized within the *Henriad*. In shifting the course of the Trent, Hotspur not only refashions the internal boundaries of the kingdom – just as Henry V will proleptically recreate the external boundaries of his own unified kingdom, claiming dominion over an empire that includes the kingdom of France – but also clarifies the functions of a newly racial whiteness in relation to English history and identity. Henry V will unify the British Isles during his French campaign, and in this earlier moment, the rebels seek an alliance between otherwise disparate factions, regions, and nations. Hotspur's rash behaviour – he later suggests to Mortimer his outburst had arisen from a visceral disgust with Glendower's stereotypically Welsh habits of behaviour – reminds Glendower that his participation in this alliance is tenuous and revocable. Throughout the entire tetralogy, key figures enforce the internal and external borders of whiteness, reminding audiences and readers about those who are not white: Richard II pursues 'Irish wars' to his ruin (*R2*, 1.4.62); *Henry IV, Part 1* is scarcely underway before Henry IV is desiring to 'chase these pagans in those holy fields' (*1H4*, 1.1.24); the Bishop of Carlisle celebrates the deceased Norfolk's battles against 'black pagans, Turks, and Saracens' (*R2*, 4.1.95). The *Henriad*'s persistent interest in breaking down and re-establishing borders of identity signals its investment in racial whiteness and its capacity 'to temporarily dissolve other social differences – sex, age, class, region and nation – into a delusion that the people labelled white have more in common with each other than they do with anyone else, purely because of what they are not'.[15] When Hotspur threatens to move the Trent, he tests the constitution of whiteness by manipulating its internal borders.

Rivers link a people to a place and inform notions of identity, and English rivers are no different. Lisa Hopkins notes that in 'English writing of the time, the primary markers of [Wales's] geographical and cultural difference from England are rivers'.[16] In his *Description of England*, William Harrison claims that English waters are plainer and less supernatural than rivers described by writers from other times and places: '[Y]et can I not find by some experience that almost anie one of our rivers hath such od and rare qualities as divers of the maine are said to be indued withall.'[17] Unlike rivers foreign and ancient, waters in England do not cause laughter, or cure gout, or cause the drinker to lose her teeth; nor do they make men effeminate, or dye wool scarlet.[18] The 'like whereof are not to be found in England, [. . .] but that which is good, wholesome, and most commodious for our nation. We have therefore no hurtfull waters amongst us, but all wholesome and profitable for the benefit of the people.'[19] In its depiction of placidity, Harrison's description of English rivers constitutes a project not unlike Hotspur's, which is to construct English identity as both natural and pure: English waters are nothing more, or less, than clean and wholesome.

The proposed path of Hotspur's Trent will be 'silver' and 'fair' not simply because the boundary it forms will be fairer to Hotspur. Rather, the river will become fair in its refashioning. Hotspur's riverine imaginings lay bare the nonracial aspirations of racial whiteness. To be 'fair' is not to be without blemishes, but to reckon oneself unblemished – to have been created pure. Hotspur attempts to rewrite the historical record, erasing blots at will: what is white was always already white. The assertion requires historical erasure and refashioning made 'fair and evenly', without cranks, cantles, angles, or nooks. Although Hotspur's articulation of racial whiteness appears to end with his demise, the project will be taken up by the begetter of his violent death. When Hotspur turns to 'dust', Hal transforms Hotspur's racial mappings into 'food' not just 'for worms' but also the grist of racial genealogy (*1H4*, 5.4.84–6). As *Henry V* looms, the *Henriad* heightens its resonances between past and present, and even the civil wars, a fascination for Shakespeare's audiences, come to represent a kind of inevitable and clarifying justification of royal power, despite Elizabeth I's concern that she herself is represented in the figure of Richard II.[20] The *Henriad* is simultaneously open and resistant to analogical readings: Elizabeth is Richard II as much as she is the bride of Henry V, Katherine of France, and so too, I will suggest, Katherine's descendant. Although James VI of Scotland was already a rumoured successor, his ascension was neither consoling nor even assured, and 'as a foreigner he faced a common law prohibition against alien land inheritance in England'.[21] If England's future monarch was to arrive from a foreign land, the *Henriad* grapples with a racial answer to the question of an English identity in desperate need of plasticity. If one function of myth is to mediate change, the *Henriad*'s experimentations with biblical myths and English history make sense of the end of Elizabeth's reign. The Shakespearean innovation is to craft a solution to the problem of genealogy without an heir. If blood and genealogy can be transcended, how does racial whiteness replicate itself, and through which vessels? Into the gap between Elizabeth and her successor, between an English queen and a Scottish king, the women of the *Henriad* come 'pouring like the tide into a breach' (*H5*, 1.2.149).

* * *

Whiteness creates itself in the *Henriad* through the enforcement of external and internal boundaries. At the outset of both *Henry IV, Part 1* and *Henry V*, invasions nearer to home foreclose the possibility of military excursions abroad, and in both cases, incursions across the internal borders of the island of Britain are encoded as feminine perversions. In the earlier play, Westmoreland brings news to Henry IV that Mortimer has been captured by Glendower, and refers obliquely to rumoured treatment of the English dead:

> A thousand of his people butchered,
> Upon whose dead corpse' there was such misuse,
> Such beastly shameless transformation,
> By those Welshwomen done as may not be
> Without much shame retold or spoken of.
>
> —*1H4*, 1.1.42–6

The 'tidings of this broil / Brake off our business for the Holy Land', laments Henry (*1H4*, 1.1.47–8). The supposed defiling of English bodies at the hands of Welsh women haunts Henry's imperial ambitions. Although English rivers may not, as those ancient writers report, turn men effeminate, crossing the River Wye into Wales threatens to destabilize both Englishness and masculinity.

River crossings threaten again in *Henry V*, but this king has read his history. Near the beginning of the *Henriad*'s final play, as Henry V is persuaded to make plans against the French, he recalls an imminent danger for a defenceless England, 'the Scot, who will make road upon us / With all advantages' (*H5*, 1.2.138–9). 'They of those marches', Canterbury promises, 'Shall be a wall sufficient to defend / Our inland from the pilfering borderers' (*H5*, 1.2.140–2). But Henry disagrees:

> For you shall read that my great-grandfather
> Never went with his forces into France
> But that the Scot on his unfurnish'd kingdom
> Came pouring like the tide into a breach,
> With ample and brim fullness of his force,
> Galling the gleaned land with hot assays,
> Girding with grievous siege castles and towns;

That England being empty of defence,
Hath shook and trembled at th'ill neighbourhood.

—*H5*, 1.2.146–54

Henry's sense of history is expansive, the connection with the past both personally genealogical and broadly available to his English subjects: 'For you shall read', he begins, about 'my great-grandfather'. The image Henry paints is of a country 'unfurnish'd' without its army, 'empty of defence', shaken, trembling, breached. So long as the Scottish remain a dangerous foe, no expedition into France can be sustained. The portrayal of England as a fragile vessel – one empty without men – persists throughout the *Henriad* as a way of feminizing the landscape, beginning as early as Gaunt's personification of England as '[t]his blessed plot, this earth, this realm, this England, / This nurse, this teeming womb of royal kings' (*R2*, 2.1.50–1). The land teems only with its 'royal kings', without which England is but an 'unfurnish'd kingdom'. England becomes the site and source of an English racial bloodline, albeit one threatened by its feminized, porous landscape.

Across these moments, the *Henriad* creates a shared racial identity defined by the preservation of masculinist genealogies, in which whitened mothers precariously reproduce the whiteness of fathers. When Henry V does eventually set out for France, he does so in pursuit of a racial bloodline designed to re-establish England's 'teeming womb' by neutralizing the danger of foreign women. Henry's innovative thinking about racial whiteness emerges out of the tetralogy's earlier conflicts, when his own identity is forged in opposition to an apparently indistinguishable Henry Percy. Following the cartographic machinations of Act III, Scene 1, the rebels of *Henry IV, Part 1* are joined by their wives, including Mortimer's Welsh wife, Catrin Glendower, who speaks and sings entirely in Welsh. '[T]hy tongue', Mortimer exclaims, 'Makes Welsh as sweet as ditties highly penn'd, / Sung by a fair queen in a summer's bow'r, / With ravishing division, to her lute' (3.1.205–8). At once ordering and destabilizing, Catrin's voice manages to evoke both the 'highly penn'd' structure of poetry and the disintegrative 'summer's bow'r', its 'ravishing division' a gendered uncoupling which upends Mortimer's rapine fantasies with the assistance of Catrin's 'lute'. The generative power of Catrin's singing is dangerously fertile, conjuring a bower of unbounded biological multiplication that leaves no room for Mortimer, who is ravished through division, taken apart by Catrin's voice, piece by piece, down to his constituent elements. Mortimer's description of his wife therefore constricts her, penning her in with metonymy and simile. Catrin's empowerment is restricted metonymically to her tongue, then removed by simile to an imagined 'fair queen'. Catrin is blurred at the margins of the play, portrayed and embodied by a Welsh-speaking actor but rendered virtually invisible within the text of the play itself.[22]

Highlighting the linguistic alterity of a woman whose marriage enforces diplomatic ties between erstwhile warring kingdoms, the appearance of Catrin anticipates Henry V's marriage to the French princess, Katherine. But whereas Catrin remains untranslated, Katherine's foreignness is absorbed into a newly articulated racial whiteness. The Welsh Catrin provides a template of division, a tilling of soil, and in *Henry V* the divisions are reincorporated in the novel generation of a white Katherine, as her self-blazoning attempt to learn the language of her conqueror translates her anatomy into English, reassembling the organs of her body into an appropriate vessel for advancing the English line. Katherine of France provides a formal structure for mapping the future, a scaffold upon which the newly racialized content of English identity might be hoisted. Between her epithet, 'fair Katherine', and the somatic language lessons, the play establishes the legibility of Katherine's fair, white body.

Henry V's centring of Katherine constitutes an important racial innovation developed over the course of the *Henriad*. Recognizing the importance of racial succession but wary of foreign biology, Hal transforms his French bride into a white one: 'An angel is like you Kate, and you are like an angel' (5.2.110–11). In the English theatre, representations of women necessitated the use of theatrical props, and modified skin colour offered one visible mechanism by which audiences could be informed about the presence of women onstage. Dympna Callaghan has suggested the visibility of racial whiteness emerges out of the use of whitening prosthetics to depict femininity onstage: 'whiteness becomes visible in an exaggerated white and, crucially, feminine identity'.[23] The emergence of a specific racial epistemology becomes evident in the coupling of visual theatrical materials with linguistic markers that establish whiteness as feminine and conquerable, characteristics defined by and through masculinist force. Shakespeare's audiences would likely find no quarrel with a conjunction of whiteness and royal power; Katherine's constructed angelic whiteness recalls Queen Elizabeth's mask of whiteness, and these closing moments heighten the theatrical resonances between women who were, in fact, blood relations. But despite a direct line between Shakespeare's Katherine and his Queen Elizabeth, the play rejects strictly genealogical connections to the past, opting instead to create a connection based on the maintenance of racial whiteness.

So the end of *Henry V* establishes racial succession but abandons the strictures of biology. Henry imagines his union with Katherine as an innovative racial 'compound': 'Shall not thou and I, between Saint Denis and Saint George, compound a boy, half French, half English, that shall go to Constantinople and take the Turk by the beard?' (5.2.204–8). Henry's 'compound' suggests an incomplete union, a combination that leaves visible and separable the discrete elements that make up the heir to England and France, and lays bare the extent to which biological reproduction alone is inadequate for the task of maintaining racial whiteness. But so too does Henry compound a newly discovered whiteness into a precarious composite of sameness. As with the ravishing division of Catrin's summer's bower, potential for separation and multiplication generates a fertile space of whiteness. By asserting Katherine's fairness and placing their future son in opposition to 'the Turk', Henry reminds his audience of the manifold threats to English whiteness, and the importance of racial purity. The play reimagines the conditions of racial genealogy, crafting a racial identity whereby inclusions and exclusions reshape past and future alike, and in which uncertainties of biology are no longer relied upon. Another mode of engaging with history appears, a mode in which the linearity of genealogy is replaced with a theatrical staging of England's origin, which is then made available to future generations of English readers.

* * *

Just as Hotspur moves a river, and Katherine is made white before her marriage, the Chorus of *Henry V* creates an originary whiteness through which it gazes upon past, present and future. Repeatedly interested in establishing traceable lines of descent, the Chorus appears to instil in King Henry V an inevitable and reiterating historical legitimacy. In the choric interlude that precedes the fifth act, the audience of *Henry V* hears what sounds like a linear account of history:

> The mayor and all his brethren in best sort,
> Like to the senators of th'antique Rome
> With plebeians swarming at their heels,
> Go forth and fetch their conquering Caesar in;
> As, by a lower but as loving likelihood,
> Were now the General of our gracious Empress,
> As in good time he may, from Ireland coming,
> Bringing rebellion broached on his sword,
> How many would the peaceful city quit
> To welcome him!
>
> —H5, 5.0.25–35

Shakespeare casts Henry in his triumphant return as a conquering Caesar and connects the exploits of both Henry and Caesar with Essex's not yet unsuccessful campaign into Ireland. But what appears sequential is rather a mode of repetition, a repeated return to the origin of a society 'founded on an act of violence by exclusion, while history is the chain of repetitive imitations of this act'.[24] Caesar conquers the Goths; Henry conquers the French; Essex conquers the Irish, and in distant anticipation of an act not yet performed, English whiteness conquers lands as yet unknown. History folds back on itself, having already anticipated what is yet to come, an operation evoking Sara Ahmed's claim that 'what appears in front of us, racism as what we have to confront, is already behind us'.[25] What the *Henriad* establishes is the foundation of a racial genealogy, a founding act out of which history itself emerges. When John Harris reads Shakespeare, his own understanding of English whiteness participates in this manipulation of historical time. Whiteness includes itself within a chosen lineage and originates a future.

Naming and singling out London's mayor, the Chorus recalls a configuration of race, land and royal power contemporaneous to Shakespeare's writing of *Henry V*. In 1596, Elizabeth I delivered '[a]n open letter to the Lord Mayor of London' concerning

> late diverse blackamoors brought into this realm, of which kind of people there are already too many, considering how God hath blessed this land with great increase of people of our own nation as any country in the world, whereof many for want of service and means to set them on work fall on idleness and to great extremity.[26]

Elizabeth's letter offers racial expulsion as a means to eliminating idleness, an invigorating exclusion of otherness which promises to aid the starving English. But despite the suggestion of 'great extremity', Elizabeth's language is generative, full of birth and growth; gone are Henry's concerns about an unfurnished kingdom. Elizabeth here imagines an England teeming with people, littering the countryside, idle without work. A decade later, some of those very English would begin tearing down enclosures separating them from workable land. But in this moment, the soil of England is covered over, fertile and overflowing with English bodies.

This overabundance of English bodies coincides with the articulation of white, English culture, the open-ended possibilities of racial whiteness convoluted with the fecundity of soil. Elizabeth's expulsion of blackamoors stages England's white racial origin, and constitutes a kind of clearing away, an exclusion that evokes what Michel Serres describes as the origin of agricultural society:

> The invention of an empty space, its discovery under floodwaters or its continuation by the sweat of our brow, open a gap in the world's tissue, produce a catastrophe, a distance, a fault through which rush, not the excluded multiplicity, but rather the mad multiplication of the most random or the best adapted single unit. The previous equilibrium was sewn with differences. But in the local whiteness that we produce, homogeneity appears.[27]

Nonwhite figures are not merely excluded from the city of whiteness, but the city is created in their exclusion. The *Henriad* creates empty, racial space, an invention realized in the Chorus of *Henry V*, and maintained by the sweat of English brows. The 'vasty fields of France' are crammed '[w]ithin this wooden O', and we 'attest in little place a million', multiplying the English actors onstage into the French, Welsh, Irish and Scottish portrayed therein (1.Pro.16). The Chorus is tediously concerned with imagining division amidst persistent sameness. Dissolution and agglomeration: the work of whiteness. The play's opening 'O' is not only an expanding physical border around England, but also a graphical representation of the scrubbing the play performs, of the white spot of homogeneity, a ring that persists and expands despite Henry VI's loss of the 'infant bands' into which he was crowned king (5.Epi.9). The play's depictions of white Englishness within an agriculturally violent milieu conjure the furrowing divisions of the plough, destruction and reconstruction, decay and growth, the commingling of blood and soil which weaves itself throughout the entire sequence, from Gloucester's sluiced blood to the 'famine, sword, and fire' and 'narrow ocean' cut 'asunder' in *Henry V*'s prologue (1.Pro.7, 22).

The *Henriad* cuts sacrificially. The creation of racial whiteness calls for a victim, and the *Henriad* offers them several, from Gloucester and Richard II to the unnamed English dead of *Henry V*. 'The ploughshare is a sacrificial knife', writes Serres,

> frenetically manipulated at the height of murdering fury. The knife kills a man or an animal. Abel or the lamb, Isaac or the scapegoat. [. . .] It marks a closed line: inside, the sacred; outside, the profane; inside, the temple; outside, the vague area filled with evil. Inside, the city, surrounded by walls, and the country outside. The ploughshare founded the city, and in the hollow of a furrow, a brother killed his twin.[28]

The Chorus creates enclosures and divisions, a wall between audience and performer, city and country, the voice of the people which compels the participation it receives, marking the partitions of the play, beginning and end, and every stage of Henry's journey along the way. The Chorus, or *chōra* – 'place occupied by someone, country, inhabited space, marked place, rank, post, assigned position, territory, or region' – calls our attention to the *Henriad*'s sustained interest in the space of borders.[29] Crucially, the Chorus makes portable its demarcations of space, the climactic effect of its racializing operations. One particular effect of the Chorus is to make sense of *Henry V*'s movement between France and England, and it does so in ways that place the English 'both at the centre and in the periphery' of their land.[30] Near the end of the entire dramatic sequence, in the prologue to the fifth act of *Henry V*, the Chorus will call attention to the English as a natural feature fencing in the unruly sea: 'Behold, the English beach / Pales in the flood with men, wives and boys' (5.Pro.10–11). English whiteness is in this final arrangement indistinguishable from the water for which it provides form; the pale skin of the English, the pale waves of the sea and the boundary – the 'pale' – formed in the juxtaposition blend into each other, a culminating, naturalized image of English whiteness.

The *Henriad*'s engagements with historiography provide form to inchoate epistemologies of race through the manipulation of inheritable cultural legacies, creating racial myths that operate as such insofar as they are 'distinguished by a high degree of constancy in their narrative core and by an equally pronounced capacity for marginal variation'.[31] The *Henriad* reshapes the story of Cain and Abel, recasting a narrative of primal fratricide as a myth of purity, soil, and genealogy. The history plays borrow freely from the libraries of myth, and Shakespeare's recourse to the figure of Mercury attests to the tetralogy's investment in modes of cultural transmission. Mercury first appears in the *Henriad* during Act 4, Scene 1 of *Henry IV, Part 1*, when Vernon arrives to report to an expectant Hotspur on Hal's performance in battle:

I saw young Harry with his beaver on,
His cushes on his thighs, gallantly arm'd,
Rise from the ground like feathered Mercury,
And vaulted with such ease into his seat
As if an angel dropp'd down from the clouds
To turn and wind a fiery Pegasus

—*1H4*, 4.1.104–9

The soil generates, in its abundant fecundity, a Hal who has not yet cast away his base, contagious clouds, and who assumes the likeness of an angel he will later confer upon Katherine. *Henry V* will conjure the earlier moment when the Chorus describes the 'youth of England' who 'sell the pasture now to buy a horse', and who follow Henry 'With winged heels, as English Mercuries' (2.Pro.1, 5–7). Like Henry's St. Crispin's Day speech in miniature, Mercury's transference from Hal to the youth of England creates Shakespeare's audience as fully realized individuals whose descendants might number themselves among Shakespeare's readers, and whose own personal histories become intertwined with the history of a white nation unfolded in the scenes and pages of the *Henriad*. One such reader was John Harris, the Leveller printer whose concern with the debasement of the English monarchy was felt personally across the pages of *Mercurius Militaris*. John Harris identifies in the *Henriad* a novel articulation of racial whiteness, a Shakespearean justification of dynastic power. For Harris, however, the power of whiteness is fully separable from the English monarchy. An astute and racist reader of Shakespeare, Harris locates the corruption of whiteness at the very moment of its consolidation. Harris finds rot beneath the mask, revealing under 'English habits' a genealogy contaminated by 'Boars of France and Negroes in Barbary'. Harris repairs racial and literary genealogies, learning from Shakespeare's plays how to initiate history through exclusion, forming a whiter England out of the muck of Shakespeare's past.

The story told here attests both to the need for a stabilizing framework at the turn of the seventeenth century, but also the dangerous unpredictability of racial whiteness as a mode of reading and writing history. An inevitable but unpredictable outcome of that racial generativity, John Harris wields the historiographical apparatus of the *Henriad* to dismantle its constructions of whiteness. Harris excludes and expels, slicing the impure roots of the monarchy away from the branch of whiteness. The precarious termination of the *Henriad* – its inconclusive final gesture toward the failures of Henry VI – anticipates the work of John Harris, and the acts of expulsion upon which the cultural legacy of racial whiteness rests.

NOTES

1. John Rees, *The Leveller Revolution: Radical Political Organisation in England, 1640-1650* (London: Verso Books, 2016), Kindle edition, ch. 12.
2. Steve Hindle, 'Imagining Insurrection in Seventeenth-Century England: Representations of the Midland Rising of 1607', *History Workshop Journal* 66 (2008): 21.
3. John Harris, *Mercurius Candidus. Communicating the Weekely Newes to the Kingdome of England. From Wednesday, Novemb. 11 to Friday, Novemb 20th. 1646. Published according to Order* (London, 1646), 2.
4. Nigel Smith, 'Soapboilers speak Shakespeare Rudely: Masquerade and Leveller Pamphleteering', *Critical Survey* 5.3 (1993): 242.
5. John Harris, *The true Informer, or Monthly Mercury. Being The certain Intelligence of Mercurius Militaris or the Armies Scout, from Tuesday October 7th, to Tuesday November 8th 1648. Communicating from all parts of England, Scotland and Ireland, all marshall enterprises, designes and successes; and particularly the actions, humours and qualities of the Army under the command of his Excellency THOMAS Lord FAIRFAX. Corrected and revised by the Author, at the earnest request of many wel-affected persons* (London, 1648), 9.
6. Ibid. Cf. Portia asking, 'Which is the merchant here? and which the Jew?" in William Shakespeare's The Merchant of Venice (4.1.172): all Shakespeare quotes are from The Arden Shakespeare, eds. Richard Proudfoot, Ann Thompson and David Scott Kastan (London: Bloomsbury, 2011).
7. Harris, *The true Informer*, 15.
8. Ibid., 9.
9. Steve Garner, *Whiteness: An Introduction* (New York: Routledge, 2007), 22.

10. Michael B. Levy, 'Freedom, Property and the Levellers: The Case of John Lilburne', *The Western Political Quarterly* 36.1 (1983): 116.

11. Joseph Valente, 'From Whiteboys to White Nationalism: Joyce and Modern Irish Populism', in *A History of Irish Modernism*, ed. Gregory Castle and Patrick Bixby (Cambridge: Cambridge University Press, 2019), 209–10.

12. Charles W. Mills, 'Racial Liberalism', *PMLA* 123.5 (2008): 1381.

13. 'William Camden's *Brittania* (1590) traced the origins of the Britons back to Brute, the great-grandson of Aeneas, who thus linked Britain to Troy, then stretched back further to Old Testament history, linking all Europeans to Japhet: son of Noah. Readers of the Bible genealogies could then calculate the ultimate link to Adam: Noah – Lamech – Methusaleh – Henoch – Jared – Mahalaleel – Kenan – Enosh – Sheth – Adam (Gen. 5).' Hannibal Hamlin, *The Bible in Shakespeare* (Oxford: Oxford University Press, 2013), 133–4.

14. Ricardo J. Quinones, *The Changes of Cain: Violence and the Lost Brother in Cain and Abel Literature* (Princeton, NJ: Princeton University Press, 1991), 39.

15. Garner, *Whiteness*, 11–12.

16. Lisa Hopkins, *Shakespeare on the Edge: Border-Crossing in the Tragedies and the Henriad* (Aldershot: Ashgate, 2005), 17.

17. William Harrison, *Harrison's Description of England in Shakespeare's Youth, Being The Second and Third Books of His Description of Britain and England*. Ed. from the *First Two Editions of Holinshed's* Chronicle, *A.D. 1577, 1587*, by Frederick J. Furnivall. Part I, Bk. 2 (London: New Shakspere Society, 1877), 332.

18. All supposed qualities of foreign waters detailed in Harrison, *Description of England*, 332–4.

19. Harrison, *Description of England*, 334.

20. Urszula Kizelbach, '"I Am Richard II, Know Ye Not That?": Queen Elizabeth and Her Political Role Playing', in *The Pragmatics of Early Modern Politics: Power and Kingship in Shakespeare's History Plays* (Boston: Brill, 2014), 113–43.

21. Stuart M. Kurland, 'Hamlet and the Scottish Succession?' *Studies in English Literature, 1500-1900* 34.2 (1994): 281.

22. As Terence Hawkes puts it, '[h]er powers are clearly located in a language that Shakespeare never attempts to transliterate, but presumably hands over to the invention of Welsh-speaking actors working within the company', Hawkes, 'Bryn Glas', in *Post-Colonial Shakespeares*, ed. Ania Loomba and Martin Orkin (New York: Routledge, 1998), 124.

23. Dympna Callaghan, *Shakespeare Without Women: Representing Gender and Race on the Renaissance Stage* (London: Routledge, 2000), 78.

24. Maria Assad, *Reading with Michel Serres: An Encounter with Time* (Albany, NY: SUNY Press, 1999), 11, qtd. in Cary Wolfe, 'Introduction to the New Edition', *The Parasite*, by Michel Serres (Minneapolis: University of Minnesota Press, 2007), xvi–xvii.

25. Sara Ahmed, 'Race as Sedimented History', *postmedieval: a journal of medieval cultural studies* 6 (2015): 96.

26. Queen Elizabeth I of England, 'An Open Letter to the Lord Maiour of London and th'Aldermen his brethren' (1596), in *Race in Early Modern England: A Documentary Companion*, ed. Ania Loomba and Jonathan Burton (New York: Palgrave Macmillan, 2007), 136.
27. Michel Serres, *The Parasite*, trans. Lawrence R. Schehr (Minneapolis: University of Minnesota Press, 1982), 178.
28. Ibid., 177.
29. Jacques Derrida, 'Khōra', trans. Ian Mcleod, in *On the Name* (Stanford, CA: Stanford University Press, 1995), 109.
30. Pierre Vidal-Naquet, *The Black Hunter: Forms of Thought and Forms of Society in the Greek World*, trans. Andrew Szegedy-Maszak (Baltimore: The Johns Hopkins University Press, 1986), 7.
31. Hans Blumenberg, *Work on Myth*, trans. Robert M. Wallace (Cambridge, MA: The MIT Press, 1985), 34.

CHAPTER EIGHT

Disrupting White Genealogies in *Cymbeline*

JOYCE MACDONALD

Cymbeline opens under the shadow of a crisis in the British royal succession. The fact that the king's daughter Innogen defied her father's right to choose her husband for her by marrying Posthumus Leonatus, the man she loves, instead of the partner he had chosen for her, is enough in itself to suggest his patriarchal weakness. But a further indication of Cymbeline's paternal inability to control his daughter and thereby direct the future of his dynasty might lie in the partner he preferred for her, the choice she spurned. His plan was for her to marry 'his wife's sole son'[1] Cloten – a marriage that would have proclaimed the bloodline of the anonymous 'widow / That late he married' (1.1.5–6) equal to his own, and which, if it produced sons, would effectively result in erasing him from the line of British kings. He had had two sons before the birth of Innogen, but they were kidnapped and, as the play opens, have not been seen in twenty years. His daughter's marriage is his last chance to project his own authority into a reproductive future.

The succession crisis the king now faces, in addition to demonstrating his lack of control over his daughter's will and his own poor judgement – since Cloten and Innogen are stepbrother and stepsister, could they really be expected to marry, as her father and the queen both plan? – may even be his own fault. We find out Cymbeline's once-trusted councillor Belarius was the one who kidnapped the two young princes and raised them in the woods for years, angry that the king readily believed malicious lies about his disloyalty and banished him. Arbitrarily turning on a supporter who had earned his trust and now planning to marry his surviving child off to a man who is both unworthy of her status and ineligible by the rules of consanguinity indicate, at the very least, that the king misunderstands his authority. More than ignorant, he may also be undeserving of the power he wields and unworthy of the glory of his descent from Cassibelan, a king of Britain during Julius Caesar's conquest, and his standing as grandson of King Lud, the founder of London. Belarius kidnapped Cymbeline's sons in a deliberate effort 'to bar [him] of succession' (3.3.102), destroying the king's royal posterity as Cymbeline had destroyed his good name.

The questions of succession, descent and lineage that drive *Cymbeline* are some of the same preoccupations that dominated one important early modern strand of racial thinking. George Best's fascinated anecdote about 'an Ethiopian as blacke as a cole' who married a 'faire Englishe woman' and fathered a son with her who was 'in all respectes as blacke as the father' demonstrates the masculinist bias of such racial thinking; this black father's genetic contribution was so strong that neither the milder English climate nor the mother's 'good complexion' could mitigate its influence over their son's physical appearance.[2] The romance, of course, does not share Best's concern with the origins and nature of blackness. Rather, *Cymbeline* reserves its racial anxiety for the fortunes of British whiteness, mapping its concerns with lineage and inheritance over its persistent sense of women's innate unworthiness. Posthumus, who has loved Innogen deeply, immediately believes Iachimo's lies about her infidelity (as Cymbeline immediately believed the lies about Belarius's disloyalty):

> Is there no way for men to be, but women
> Must be half-workers? We are all bastards,
> And that most venerable man which I
> Did call my father was I know not where
> When I was stamped.
>
> —*Cym* 2.4.153–7

In *Titus Andronicus*, Shakespeare's first Roman play, Aaron the Moor is far less anguished about women's capacity for reproductive deceit. Meeting his son by Tamora for the first time, he dismisses her older sons' horror that their mother will be shamed for having given birth to an obviously black baby. He explains to them that whether they want to accept it or not, the infant is manifestly their 'brother by the surer side', (4.2.128) as attested by the dark skin he shares with him: Aaron and Tamora's son is as black as the half-'Ethiopian', half-English baby in Best's anecdote. The remark is striking. Obviously, Chiron and Demetrius are white, and Aaron is not biologically related to them even though they and the baby have the same mother. Here, though, Aaron seems to be implying that their shared masculinity is what unites them all and that Tamora's older sons should recognize the baby as their 'brother' because his masculine bloodline is so clear, in a move that renders Posthumus's disgust with women's ability to conceal true paternity irrelevant. He fantasizes a future entirely without women for himself and the baby; he'll raise him alone in the wilderness, and teach him '[t]o be a warrior and command a camp' (4.2.182) – just as Belarius raised Cymbeline's sons in mountain caves in 'honest freedom' (3.3.71).

Titus Andronicus subsumes race within patriarchal prerogative, as Aaron insists that his son and Tamora's are really 'brothers'. Women are only uncertain and disposable biological instruments; families truly secure their posterity through sustaining their masculine primacy through every generation. Unfortunately, some men are incapable of doing so. Cymbeline has been reduced to meekly following the lead of his second wife, who 'most desir'd the match' (1.1.12) between Innogen and Cloten, and has thus surrendered what Aaron believes and Best feared was the decisive masculine role in establishing a family's future. A weak patriarch, he seems to have colluded with his bloodline's erasure from British history.

Cymbeline's status as a romance and not a tragedy, with romance's commitment to seeing male-female relations reconciled – reuniting fathers with their daughters, and then letting these fathers preside over their daughters' loving marriages – ultimately bypasses Posthumus and Aaron's misogyny. But because *Cymbeline* is a kind of history play as well as a romance, Innogen's reunion with Posthumus will do more than rehabilitate her relationship with her father or – along with her brothers' return – restore her family to wholeness. Her return and marriage will also be instrumental in reconciling Britain's mixed bloodline, combining her native British origins with Posthumus's apparently Roman ones and, through the reproductive contributions that Aaron dismisses and Best finds too weak, laying the foundation for a new kind of racially hybrid national future.

George Best's observations were animated in large part by the attempt to understand 'the first originall of these blacke men, and how by lineall discente they have hitherto continued thus black',[3] despite their reproductive congress with white Englishwomen. He seems troubled by the possibility that even despite the intimate connections of intermarriage, 'these blacke men' will never be truly assimilated by (white) Englishness. *Cymbeline*, on the other hand, is not concerned with invasive blackness. Rather, it begins by trying to reject the possibility that race-mixing – in the form of Britain's mixed native and Roman ancestry – matters at all to the nation's identity. The evil nameless Queen, of all people, is the one who patriotically asserts that Britain is a nation whose special place in the world guarantees its freedom from any merely political considerations; it

> stands
> As Neptune's park, ribbèd and pal'd in
> With rocks unscalable and roaring waters,
> With sands that will not bear your enemies' boats
> But suck them up to th' topmast.
>
> —*Cym* 3.1.20–3

She calls on Britons' descent from noble founders – Cassibelan, Lud, 'Mulmutius which / Ordained our laws' (3.1.56–7) – and urges them to fight to prove themselves worthy of their ancestors' accomplishments, denying any Roman contribution to the nation's identity. But the suspicion that the nation stands at the edge of crisis, despite such assurances of its immunity from harm, still rumbles through *Cymbeline*'s first two acts. The king's desire to prove himself worthy of his British ancestors' example is perhaps all the more urgent because he understands that his island's Roman history offers a compelling counter-vision of imperial origins and destiny, especially at a moment when his own succession seems so insecure. Both the Roman invasion and Innogen's romantic, sexual choice challenge the king's notions of descent, posterity and status. The play's concern with the authority of its competing bloodlines – British or Roman, Cloten or Posthumus – is an example of the operations of race, as it unfolds the competition between two competing stories of white origins.

This chapter's interest in reading historical whiteness in *Cymbeline* takes place in an historical moment that has seen whiteness claimed as a property of the classical past. Recently, for example, white supremacist organizations have appropriated the marmoreal whiteness of Roman statuary to their claims of foundational links between whiteness and Western civilization.[4] Scholarly organizations dedicated to the study of the ancient and early medieval worlds have had to come to grips with the ways in which their fields have been used to inscribe white supremacy into public understandings of the distant past, as Western civilization has been asserted by racist reactionaries to be an implicitly white project.[5] As we saw in the example from *Titus Andronicus*, conceptions of whiteness in early Shakespeare can be subsumed into representations of patriarchal bias in ways that can work to racialize conceptions of the classical past, and to define masculine descent as a foundation of the state. Carrying his dead father from the battlefield at Saint Albans in *2 Henry VI*, for example, Young Clifford finds a model for his grief in the *Aeneid*:

> As did Aeneas old Anchises bear,
> So bear I thee upon my manly shoulders.
> But then Aeneas bare a living load,
> Nothing so heavy as these woes of mine.
>
> —*2H6* 5.2.62–5

Losing his father, Young Clifford also loses his moral self: 'Henceforth I will not have to do with pity . . . In cruelty will I seek out my fame' (5.3.62–5, 56, 60). But when Aeneas carried his father away from Troy's burning ruins toward an uncertain future, the shade of his wife Creusa assured him that glory – 'happy days, kingship, and a royal wife' – awaited him, if he could only endure the hardships he would first have to face.[6] A royal posterity would be his reward.

Inflecting its tragic account of usurpation and failure of political will through Virgil's inscription of fatherhood into the origins of nations, *Henry VI* anticipates *Cymbeline*'s own interest in blood inheritance and in how family can become a bulwark of the state. But, again, *Cymbeline* is an English history play and a romance at the same time. The play shares Shakespearean romance's interest in daughters' chaste loves as a key to reuniting families and reforming fathers' authority within families. As it unfolds Innogen's journey back to Posthumus, we can also see it rethinking the patrilineal drama of an English history play or of the experimental Roman play by emphasizing women's role – instead of only the place of fathers and sons – in guaranteeing families' continuance, and families' connection to the nation. In this way, Innogen's sexuality, her marriage and their importance to the play's subject of a combined British-Roman history become instrumental to *Cymbeline*'s status as a play about the transmission of racial identity.

As it works toward dramatizing a balance between its British and Roman origins, the play echoes its sources, which are also deeply concerned with the nation's double past.[7] Following Holinshed by bringing Britain's Roman and native histories into relation, it incorporates Holinshed's close reliance on Geoffrey of Monmouth's twelfth-century *Historia regum Britanniae*, which first acknowledged the traditionally (and allegedly) Roman elements of the British past while insisting that the tradition of the nation's Celtic roots mattered just as much to its formation.

In Geoffrey, Brutus is Aeneas's great-grandson who was banished from Italy for accidentally killing his father. Travelling to Greece, he discovers a group of Trojan survivors whom he liberates from slavery and leads on a path of warfare and conquest across Europe until they arrive at an island called Albion, which in those days 'was inhabited by none but a few giants'.[8] Brutus and his men kill the giants and found a new permanent settlement. He decides to call his followers Britons and to rename the island Britain, in lasting memorial to himself. In Geoffrey's account, Brutus's followers rally to him because of his boldness, generosity, and military daring. Uninterested in material honours for himself, he distributes the spoils of war to his men, binding them to himself and to their new nation through acts of brotherhood and self-sacrifice, and through the call of their shared blood. Geoffrey's later emphasis on the Welsh origins of King Arthur would prove especially ideologically valuable to the Tudor dynasty, which identified their own relatively modest Welsh blood with the fulfilment of ancient prophecies of Arthur's return; King Henry VII named his first son Arthur.

In *Cymbeline*'s own time, James I boldly mined the symbolic implications of his Tudor ancestry in articulating his own right to power.[9] *The Speeches at Prince Henries Barriers*, a 1610 Twelfth Night court entertainment, is thoroughly Arthurian, climaxing with the revived Merlin delivering a long speech on British history to the Saxon king Meliadus (played by Henry, James's elder son), and finally presenting him with Arthur's shield, which he uses to defend himself in an interval of stage combat. Samuel Daniel's *Tethys Festival*, written to celebrate Henry's investiture as Prince of Wales in June of 1610, is even more explicit in its invocation of the Stuarts as the fulfilment of an ancient prophecy of Welsh-born kings who will augment Britain's greatness, as I'll return to later.[10]

Any contemporary ideological advantage that might rise from James and his son's appropriation of Celtic myth to their own plans, however, existed alongside the grave doubts that historians had long raised about the validity of Geoffrey's story of Britain's origins. By the end of the twelfth century, rival chronicler William of Newburgh was already denigrating Geoffrey's work for promulgating a 'laughable web of fiction' about the ancient Britons' descent from the Trojans, and for its effrontery in cloaking its unverifiable tales about the deeds of the Welsh King Arthur in the dignity of Latin.[11] This dismissal continued, amplified by new understandings of what it meant to write history, into *Cymbeline*'s own time, when William Camden gently but firmly cast final doubt on Geoffrey's 'Britain' etymology.[12] Citing the historical unverifiability of anything alleged to have happened 770 years before the birth of Christ, Camden names source after classical source who never mention Brutus at all – implying that the available facts of Britain's Roman history must take precedence over Geoffrey's British mythography. Protesting that he is only 'a plaine meaning man, and an ingenuous student of the truth', he insists that undermining the Brutus story is not his primary interest (although he plainly thinks it's nonsense). 'Let Antiquitie . . . be pardoned', he generously allows, 'if by entermingling falsities and truthes, humane matters and divine together, it make the first beginnings of nations and cities more noble, sacred, and of greater majestie [.]'.[13]

Even though he believes that Geoffrey's story of the British nation's origins is at best unprovable and at worst completely untrue, Camden also believes that it doesn't really matter if Geoffrey's story is true or not. He understands that reaching for 'greater majestie' may not always be compatible with recounting simple facts. History, he implies, consists of more than a mere record of events, even if it must acknowledge and seek facts on which to base its narrative. The myths of a classically descended British race, with its own record of heroic deeds and its own semi-divine origins, stand among those majestic stories that Camden sees as being instrumental to a nation's account of its standing in the world. Even if race – whether as lineage or in the more modern terms of skin colour – is a myth, Camden believes it is a necessary one.

That we can find concentrated theatrical examples of attempts to reframe the historical improbabilities that Camden politely pointed out in Geoffrey's account of how Britain became Britain points to the ways in which a healthy modern scepticism could peacefully exist alongside the mystery and majesty that even Camden acknowledged could inhere in such stories. That is to say that re-enactments of racial myths of a British past were understood to be capable of communicating powerful cultural and political values, even when shorn of their classical elements. Anthony Munday, for example, produced his 1605 Lord Mayor's show, *The Triumphs of Re-United Britania*, early in a new reign marked by the desire to augment the public sense of what 'Britain' might mean. Especially engaged with the history and glory of his native London, and also obligated to flatter the new Lord Mayor Sir Leonard Holliday, Munday aims for the sweet spot between 'humane matters and divine' as he attempts to contextualize the city's modern energy and enterprise within the events of its legendary past.[14] In contrast with Camden, who rejected Geoffrey's Celtic fantasies in favour of better documented classical sources, Munday keeps Geoffrey's Celtic elements but frames them Biblically, so as to render questions of the historicity of Geoffrey's contributions beside the point of a common modern Christian understanding. Munday first establishes that all of Europe, including the British Isles, had originally been under the control of Noah's third son Japhet after the floodwaters receded. After Japhet's death, his sixth son, Samothes, received a vast territory which he named 'Celtica', and whose inhabitants were known as 'Celtæ' – a name which, according to John Bale, 'was indifferent to them of Gallia, and us of this Isle of Britaine'.[15] He then proceeds to graft the core of Geoffrey's narrative onto these new, nonpagan roots, as he recounts how Brute slaughtered giants, built a city called Troynovant on the banks of the Thames, married Innogen, the daughter of the Greek king, and fathered three sons who divided the British Isles between them.

As Munday asserts that Britain's origins are Christian and Celtic and not Roman, he also makes the explicitly commercial and economic celebrations typical of a Lord Mayor's pageant flow smoothly into the equally important acknowledgement of the new reign. A ship called the Royall Exchange, 'Laden with *Spices*, *Silkes*, and *Indico*', (Aiv verso) has arrived in London. Part of the enterprise controlled by Sir Leonard – a member of the Merchant Taylors' Company and a founder of the East India Company – the ship and its crew become witnesses of the civic celebration of how the various districts of Britain, with their ancient Biblical origins, have now been reunited under the rule of 'that second Brute James our dread king . . . / Whose verie name did heavenlie comfort bring / When in despaire our hopes lay drooping dead' (Ciii). Rescued from the 'despair' that followed the death of Elizabeth, Britain enjoys a 'happy Holi-day' (Biii verso) on the day of James's arrival in his capital, as the ship's company scatters its rich load of exotic spices to the city crowd.

Munday's pretty pun manages both to compliment Sir Leonard, the locus of the day's celebrations, and to identify Britain's bright future of political reunification as an implicit return to the good old days when Brutus ruled over the whole land, despite the modernity of the global economy manifesting itself in the Royall Exchange's load of eastern goods. Indeed, the celebration of the 'Holyday' (Ciii verso) repeatedly invoked in the pageant's climax may even outweigh the attention it gives to the planned reunification of the nation under its new king: much more insistently than James's plans for Great Britain, the pageant identifies Sir Leonard's economic triumph with the conquests and prosperity of the nation's ancient roots. *The Triumphes of Re-United Britania* moves backwards and forwards in national time: reimagining Brutus's labour and bounty in modern terms, narrating the new century's political goals, interracial contacts and commercial possibilities through tropes derived from Britain's ancient origins.

So the old British stories could, with a little creativity, be made to serve new conditions, even if everyone knew such stories were not literally true, and even if civic poets like Munday had to balance the public and patronage occasions of their work with their audience's pleasurable familiarity with the old traditions. To cloak 'the first beginnings of nations' in majestic nobility through the process of elevating the deeds and qualities of a particular bloodline or a particular historical moment is more of an ideological process than what Camden would recognize as a purely historical one. In preserving even a modified notion of Britons' heroic deeds stretching along an historical continuum from the founding of Lud's Town into the global mercantilism of the city's present, Munday advances a new notion of the nobility of the British race.

Munday's discreet erasure of the classical elements of his nation's origin story is only one way of trying to make the British past more purely native, and thus to purify and simplify its racial inheritance. In *Cymbeline*, Shakespeare returns to the problem of how to approach the relative value of the native and Roman threads of the nation's imaginary past, but Munday's simple solution – erasing the Roman element altogether – isn't possible for him.[16] The Roman ambassador Lucius's attempt to make Cymbeline pay his tribute to Rome and the Queen's patriotic rejection of his request is only one example of the play's persistent awareness of multiple and sometimes contradictory kinds of historical and cultural difference, sometimes within a single character. Despite their rough edges, for example, Belarius's sturdy Welsh sons – who are, of course, actually British princes – express their delight in Fidele's civilized delicacy through classical reference. They marvel at how, when he cooked for them, Fidele 'cut our roots in characters / And sauced our broths as Juno had been sick / And he her dieter' (4.2.49–51).

What seems more aggressively odd, though, are the places where *Cymbeline* points us to its classical consciousness as it brings up Roman histories of how familial and racial integrity are reproductively transmitted, and then makes nothing of them. Iachimo, for example, is an English Renaissance Italian – subtle, malicious and false – who is as completely different from an ancient Roman like Lucius as he is from the Britons. Yet, he compares his nighttime incursion into Innogen's bedroom with Tarquin's secret observation of the sleeping Lucrece's beauty. Of course, Tarquin did more than merely observe Lucrece; he raped her, and her subsequent anguished suicide caused the overthrow of the Tarquins's rule and a revolution in the form of Roman government. Attempting to force Lucrece into submission and into keeping quiet about his crime, Shakespeare's Tarquin tells her that if she gets pregnant by him, any public accusation that he had raped her would only result in having her 'issue blurr'd with nameless bastardy' (*The Rape of Lucrece*, 522). Somehow, if sex with a man other than her husband became known, the effect would be so catastrophic that it would retroactively call into doubt the paternity of sons that have apparently not even yet been born to her and Collatine. Suicide seems preferable to the possibility of giving birth to Tarquin's child, because of the social damage such a birth would do to her husband and his line:

> Well, well dear Collatine, thou shalt not know
> The stainèd taste of violated troth.
> I will not wrong thy true affection so
> To flatter thee with an infringèd oath.
> This bastard graft shall never come to growth.
> > He shall not boast, who did thy stock pollute,
> > That thou art doting father of his fruit[.]
>
> —*Luc* 1058–64

Lucrece's horror at the thought of giving birth to her rapist's child is as fully available to her as Tamora's shame is to her in *Titus*. Both texts depict these women's shame and panic as racial crises, with *Lucrece*'s Petrarchan colour vocabulary associating her beauty and chastity with her whiteness and characterizing her rape as a 'black payment' (576) for her husband's generosity in inviting Tarquin to visit his home. After her suicide, Lucrece's blood drains out of her body in two streams: one 'still pure and red', and the one 'that false Tarquin stained', black (1742, 1743).

In contrast, Iachimo doesn't kiss or even touch the sleeping Innogen. Instead, he busies himself writing down the details of her bedroom in his handy pocket notebook, so as to be able to tell Posthumus a more convincing lie about having slept with her when he gets back to Rome.

Iachimo's discovery that Innogen apparently fell asleep reading about Tereus's rape of his sister-in-law Philomel in the *Metamorphoses* similarly goes nowhere. In Ovid, this brutal crime both breaks Tereus's faith with his father-in-law, who trusted him to take care of both his daughters, and destroys his own family when his outraged wife Procne kills their son to avenge her sister's violation. 'Behold thou hast confounded all', Philomel tells Tereus:

> > My sister through mee
> Is made a Cucqueane: and thyself through this offense of thee
> Art made a husband to us both, and unto me a foe,
> A just deserved punishment for lewdly doing so.[17]

Iachimo, however, just notes what she was reading, decides he has enough persuasive detail to hurt Posthumus, and climbs back into his trunk. When he tells Posthumus about what he saw in Innogen's bedchamber, he piles on yet another damning allusion to how illegitimate sexual connection can rock the foundations of empire: one of the wall hangings depicted the story of 'Proud Cleopatra when she met her

Roman' (2.4.70). In *Antony of Cleopatra*, Octavius is disgusted not only by Antony's unseemly subjection to the Egyptian queen, but by his plan to abandon his marriage of state with Octavia, seize power for himself in the east, and set up his 'unlawful issue' (3.6.7) with Cleopatra as his heirs.

In its strange bedchamber scene, *Cymbeline* runs right up to the edge of classical histories that tell how marriage and reproduction can transmit or undermine rulers' authority (perhaps especially when they cross colour lines, as they do in the case of Antony and the tawny Cleopatra), only to walk away without comment. What is equally noteworthy is that the play does the same thing with its treatment of British origins, thus undercutting the authority of the myth of modern British kings' Welsh descent at the same time as it declines to make use of its tales of Roman ancestry. Milford Haven in Wales, where Innogen intends to meet the exiled Posthumus, carried tremendous symbolic weight in Tudor history – it was where Henry Tudor gathered his army to march against Richard III – and Wales was the country that Geoffrey indelibly associated with legends of King Arthur's rise. Milford Haven is also a powerful symbolic location in Samuel Daniel's *Tethys' Festival*, one of the elaborate Welsh-themed celebrations of Prince Henry's investiture as Prince of Wales the year of *Cymbeline*'s premiere.[18] In Daniel's masque, Queen Anne played the goddess Tethys, who, presiding over all the generative waters of the earth, calls her rivers to Milford Haven, '[t]he happy Port of Union', to celebrate Meliadus's investiture. She gives him Astraea's sword and a fine scarf embroidered with 'All the spacious Emperie / That he is borne unto' (E4). He need not venture farther than the Pillars of Hercules, for within the borders of her 'waves, and watry Governement' lie '[m]ore treasure, and more certaine riches . . . / then all the Indies to Iberus brought' (F). Daniel's language here recalls the sturdy insistence of the Queen in *Cymbeline* that Britain stands apart as 'Neptune's park'. Queen Anne's motherhood figured centrally in the performance, in which she was joined by both her sons and by her thirteen-year-old daughter Elizabeth, who would be married to the Elector Palatine two years later.[19] The queen's identity as mother of James's heirs blurred smoothly into Tethys's standing as the mother of British waters; as her children contracted dynastic marriages of their own, she and her husband would gracefully preside over an augmentation of Britain's standing in the world, although its borders would remain the same. As in Munday, despite Britain's new international engagements, the nation would retain an unchanging national and racial identity, standing as 'world enough to yeeld / All workes of glory ever can be wrought' (E4, F).

Innogen's sense of Britain's place in the world markedly departs from that of her evil but patriotic stepmother. For her, instead of Neptune's enclosed self-generating realm, Britain is only one possible location out of a nearly infinite range: 'Hath Britain all the sun that shines? Day, night, / Are they not but in Britain?' (3.4.135–6). Willing to go to the ends of the earth to be with Posthumus again, she only goes to Milford Haven, hoping to find him and convince him he is wrong about her infidelity. It can't be an accident that Shakespeare's Innogen shares the name of the legendary princess who became the mother of the British race through her marriage to Brutus, or that of all places she travels to Milford's 'happy Port of Union'. Or can it?

Uninterested in reading Roman myth or Roman history in Innogen's bedchamber, in a moment of maritally-based British racial crisis *Cymbeline* also denies the reproductive and dynastic tropes of British history – Welsh ancestry, dreams of self-sufficiency, reunion and augmentation, the foundation of new political orders. 'Poor I am stale', Innogen grieves, 'a garment out of fashion, / And for I am richer than to hang by th'walls / I must be ripped' (3.4.51–3). As she reels from learning of Posthumus's hate for her, Innogen questions Rome's founding myth: 'True honest men being heard like false Aeneas / Were in his time thought false' (3.4.58–9). Here, Aeneas is presumably 'false' because he left Dido after telling her that he reciprocated her passion. For Innogen, any role he might have played as a founder of a new empire to the west of Troy – the role that makes him significant as Brutus's ancestor and to all the British history that will follow – disappears, subsumed within his romantic cruelty.[20] We know that Aeneas broke African Dido's heart because he knew he couldn't abandon his divine imperial mission, we know that he never stopped loving her or hoping for her understanding and forgiveness, and we know that he eventually made a sanctioned marriage to Lavinia, daughter of the king who ruled the lands at the mouth of the Tiber – but if Innogen knows about Aeneas's ultimate fulfilment of his imperial mission she doesn't care. What brings him to her mind is his refusal of love with Dido, even if their romantic future must stem from his defiance of his dynastic duty. She separates nationalistic formulations of the British race from reproduction.

Innogen's shock and anger at Posthumus' rejection bring belief in those stories of Britain's descent from Troy and Rome into doubt. But the place where the play seems most firmly to doubt its Roman history, as well as to refuse any kind of British genealogy that might be initiated by the lovers' reunion at Milford Haven, is in 4.2, where with increasing horror Innogen 'recognizes' the headless corpse next to her as Posthumus.

Except, of course, that it's not. That the headless corpse is in bed with Innogen gestures at the sexual and reproductive elements of British myths of origin: the playful engagement with Queen Anne's fecundity that *Tethys Festival* conducts at Milford Haven, for example, or Brutus's marriage to Holinshed's Innogen as the foundation of the British race. But the image of a headless corpse occurring in a play that understands so much about the bodily, familial origins of dynasties and nations doesn't invoke beginnings as much as it does endings and collapse, inevitably recalling Aeneas's anguished account of Priam's death in Book Two of the *Aeneid*. After invading the sacred structure that was both a royal palace and a temple of the Trojan gods and killing Priam and Hecuba's young son Polites 'before the eyes and faces of his parents', Achilles' son Pyrrhus then turned his rage on the king himself. '[S]lipping' in Polites' 'streaming blood', Pyrrhus drags the aged Priam to the altar and fatally stabs him with his 'flashing sword'. Even though he has found love and safe haven in Carthage, Aeneas is still stunned as he recalls the horror of Priam's fate: 'he who was once lord of so many tribes and lands, the monarch of Asia. He lies, a huge trunk upon the shore, a head severed from the neck, a corpse without a name!' (Fairclough, 353). The king's death confirmed the passing of a civilization: 'At once both Troy and Priam fell'.[21]

Innogen's anger at Posthumus and her horror at what she believes is his death blur together in her recollections of the *Aeneid*. He is a second faithless Aeneas, abandoning her as Virgil's hero abandoned Dido; he is a second fallen patriarch, although he and she do not yet have children, or a nation, of their own. (Lucrece's fear of what people will say about the paternity of her yet-unborn children faintly echoes here, as their proper paternity contributes to a properly patriarchal view of Rome.) Her assumption that the headless corpse is her husband invites us to compare Posthumus's death with the catastrophe of Troy's fall, even as Innogen also remembers how much Priam's death also marked a catastrophe for his surviving family. She pleads that 'All curses madded Hecuba gave the Greeks, / And mine to boot', (4.2.315–16) will land on Pisanio's head for leading her husband into ambush.

In another early engagement with Virgilian material, alongside the one we see in *2 Henry VI*, Tamora's sons rape and mutilate a young Roman woman who shares a name with Lavinia, Aeneas's eventual wife. From the beginning to nearly the end of his career, Shakespeare is thinking about how founding narratives of Roman and British history might overlap with, echo, anticipate each other, and how they might depend on daughters' fates. Like Queen Anne's daughter Elizabeth, Virgil's Lavinia is the destined 'Mother' of a nation, but early on Shakespeare experiments with Virgil by imagining what would happen if this female progenitor were violated by barbarians and any children thus 'blurred with ... bastardy'. Tarquin and Tereus, who figure in Iachimo's nighttime visit to Innogen's bedchamber, do actually succeed in committing sex crimes that destroy families and overturn states. Tamora believes that the evidence her black baby provides of her infidelity will not only shame her, but bring about 'stately Rome's disgrace' (4.2.60); her and Rome's shared whiteness ultimately matters more than her rage at Titus for sacrificing Alarbus. But in *Cymbeline*, at the end of his thinking about the Roman origins of British history and the relevance of bloodline to nation, Shakespeare rejects these connections. In contrast with Lavinia, whose chastity belongs to her father Titus, or Lucrece, whose reproductive capacity belongs to her husband, Innogen dares to criticize the Roman founder Aeneas's rejection of Dido, and all the inscription of patriarchal duty into the proper direction of nations that his rejection enshrines.

This haunting by the *Aeneid* and by other Roman stories of rape's power to break the proper bond between civic and familial order by 'contaminating' shared blood's capacity to transmit identity do cast a sombre light over *Cymbeline*. Innogen strikingly comes forward to reject the inevitable rightness of patriarchal authority but, deeply aware of its debts to British history, and of the places where British and Roman history (or myth) cross, the play still reaches an impasse where neither Roman nor British resources seem capable of reuniting the lovers, restoring the lost princes, or resetting the nation's deeply confused familial politics. We immediately grasp all the epic weight associated with civilizations' fall and new nations' rise when Innogen mistakenly assumes that the headless corpse is her husband, but neither epic nor the British myths of rise and triumph concentrated at Milford Haven offer a clear way forward.

If Posthumus and Innogen are going to be reunited, if Britain is going to be rescued from Roman invasion, and if this history/romance hybrid is going to accomplish its genres' work of restoring and increasing what has been destroyed, *Cymbeline* needs a miracle. It gets one when Posthumus's dead family appear to him in a dream and, in response to their prayers, Jupiter comes to reassure them and promise him a way forward. Roman gods perform this last spectacular service in the play, but in fact the work of affirming the value of family as the foundation of the state begins before Posthumus's liberation, when he, Guiderius, and Arviragus (still unrecognized as Innogen's lost brothers) fight the Romans together at Milford Haven's 'narrow lane' (5.5.52).

Coppélia Kahn points us to the symbolic weight of this masculine last stand. It anticipates the 'martial triad'[22] of Posthumus's dead father and brothers in the dream vision he will experience in prison, and repeats other moments from the Roman plays where men forge new bonds of male unity, as Aaron first intimated, across generations through competition and struggle. What is new about the powerful image of Posthumus and Innogen's brothers standing to fight together – we both see their battle onstage as it happens, and hear about it as Posthumus describes it for us in the next scene – Kahn suggests, is that it can be read in sexual as well as homosocial terms. Not only does the fight happen at that vaguely vaginal-sounding 'narrow lane', but Posthumus recalls seeing 'an ancient soldier' (5.5.15) – Belarius – repeatedly urging the younger fighters to 'Stand ... Stand, stand' (5.5.25, 28).[23] Men will 'stand' together, at a place sacred to the nation's mythological origins and celebrated as the fount of its female generativity, to defend the narrow path to Britain's future. The scene adds an historical, national dimension to the gender solidarity Aaron implies with Chiron and Demetrius when he urges them to accept their mother's new baby as their 'brother', even though he is black.

The shade of Posthumus's dead father Sicilius asks that Jupiter 'No longer exercise / Upon a valiant race thy harsh / And potent injuries' (5.5.176–8). For him, 'race' means the Leonati, perhaps especially he and his sons – two dead, only one still living. (Posthumus's mother died in childbirth, so that until he fell in love with Innogen, his family had always been composed only of men.) But the new kind of family the play has been moving toward insists as fully on its feminine as on its masculine parentage. As we saw in the court masques produced to celebrate Prince Henry's investiture, the women of the royal family were associated with Great Britain's history and its future: Queen Anne as Tethys, Princess Elizabeth as a future 'Mother of Nations'. *Cymbeline* raises the spectre of the abuse of women's sexual bodies – Lucrece, Philomela – only to reject it, just as it rejects the history of Aeneas's inconstant love. The troubled Britain in the play finds its way toward peace and fulfilment in the reunion of Posthumus and Innogen, 'lion's whelp' and 'tender air' (5.6.436, 438). The king is also reunited with his lost sons, so that both kinds of posterity – originating from the bonds between fathers and sons, as well as from the bonds between men and women – become possible. The 'old stock' (5.6.441) of paternal destiny and masculine connection inherent in Roman myth and British legend are grafted onto romance's conviction of the power of feminine chastity and virtue, and the hybrid result is a new sense of the reproductive origins of the British race.

NOTES

1. I take all Shakespeare quotations from *The Arden Shakespeare Complete Works*, ed. Richard Proudfoot, Ann Thompson and David Scott Kastan (London: The Arden Shakespeare, 2001), here 1.1.5, and will provide subsequent quotations parenthetically in my text.

2. George Best, *A True Discourse of the Late Voyages of Discoverie, for the Finding of a Passage to Cathaya, for the Northwest, Under the Conduct of Martin Frobisher* (London, 1584), 29.
3. Ibid., 30.
4. Stating that she was 'really sick of alt-right groups appropriating classical antiquities for nefarious reasons', classicist Sarah Bond wrote a 2017 blog post discussing how much ancient sculpture was originally painted and how the physical whiteness of classical statuary from which in many cases the coloured paint has faded away over time became associated with modern efforts to establish white male bodies as cultural and racial ideals. Bond was inundated with online threats, as described in 'For One Scholar, an Online Stoning Tests the Limits of Public Scholarship', *Chronicle of Higher Education*, 16 June 2017. See also 'White Supremacist Propaganda Surges on Campus', https://www.adl.org/resources/reports/white-supremacist-propaganda-surges-on-campus.
5. See '"It's All White People": Allegations of White Supremacy are Tearing Apart a Prestigious Medieval Studies Group', *Washington Post*, 19 September 2019. The article discusses racial tensions in the International Association of Anglo-Saxonists, which came to a head at their 2019 biennial meeting, at which a vote was taken that will change the organization's name in recognition of the extent to which 'Anglo-Saxon' has become a 'code for whiteness, a phrase that is co-opted today by white supremacists around the world to advance a false version of white-dominated history'.
6. *Eclogues, Georgics, Aeneid 1-6*, trans. H. Rushton Fairclough, rev. edn G. P. Goold (Cambridge, MA: Harvard University Press, 1999), 369. I'll provide subsequent citations parenthetically in my text.
7. Here, we can see Shakespeare mixing different kinds of historical materials together as well as following tradition in questioning the absoluteness of Caesar's success in Britain. See Homer Nearing, Jr., 'The Legend of Julius Caesar's British Conquest', *PMLA* 64.4 (1949): 889–929.
8. Geoffrey was first translated into English by Aaron Thompson in 1718 and revised by J. A. Giles in 1848. I cite the online edition of Thompson published in the Medieval Latin Series (Cambridge, Ontario: In Parentheses Publications, 1999), 20.
9. Paul Raffield, 'Common Law, *Cymbeline*, and the Jacobean *Aeneid*', *Law and Literature*, 27.3 (2015): 313–42, discusses links between the play's use of legends of national origin and foundation and James's desire to reform ancient notions of the relationship between the nation and the monarch. Also see Emrys Jones, 'Stuart *Cymbeline*', *Essays in Criticism* 11 (1961): 84–99.
10. Both Martin Butler's New Cambridge Shakespeare edition of the play (Cambridge: Cambridge University Press, 2005), 3–6, and Roger Warren's Oxford Shakespeare edition in Oxford World Classics (Oxford: Oxford University Press, 1998), 63–7, date the play in 1610, placing its concerns with Britishness in line with the mood of such court performances as Jonson's and Daniel's masques.
11. P. G. Walsh and M. J. Kennedy, ed. and trans., *The History of English Affairs* (Warminster, PA: Aris and Phillips Classical Texts, 2008), 29.

12. F. Smith Fussner, *The Historical Revolution: English Historical Writing and Thought, 1580-1640* (London: Routledge and Kegan Paul, 1962) discusses the emergence of a modern historiography in the sixteenth and seventeenth centuries, driven by new reliance on verified sources, evidence, and coherent narrative. Graham Parry, *The Trophies of Time: English Antiquarians of the Seventeenth Century* (Oxford: Oxford University Press, 1995), is among those pointing to the prominence of dismissing Geoffrey's work in this new British historiography, 70–129.

13. *Britain, or a Chorographicall Description of the Most Flourishing Kingdomes, England. Scotland and Ireland, and the Ilands Adjoyning, out of the Depth of Antiquitie*, trans. Philemon Holland (London, 1610), 8, 9. Camden's first edition of *Britannia*, written in Latin, was published in 1586.

14. As well as a polemicist and composer of public entertainments, Munday was also known for writing the 1618 continuation of John Stow's 1598 *Survay of London*. Both Stow and Munday begin their histories with the foundation of 'Lud's Town' (*Cymbeline*, 3.1.32) by a descendant of Brute, and Munday cribs from Camden (without attribution) as he notes that 'Antiquity . . . hath an especiall priviledge, by interlacing divine matters with humane, to make the first foundation of cities more honourable, more sacred, and as it were of greater majestie' (B).

15. Aii, Aiiv. I'll provide subsequent references parenthetically in my text.

16. G. Wilson Knight's influential discussion in *The Crown of Life: Essays in Interpretation of Shakespeare's Final Plays* (London: Oxford University Press, 1947) identifies the tension between Roman and British identities in the play, 129–202, a tension he believes is ultimately resolved. Jodi Mikalachki, 'The Masculine Romance of Roman Britain: *Cymbeline* and Early Modern English Nationalism', *SQ* 46.3 (1995): 301–22, complicates Knight's analysis by pointing to early modern historiographical conflict between accurately recovering the records of the past yet also rejecting the savagery of British (not Roman) antiquity. Leah S. Marcus, *Puzzling Shakespeare: Local Reading and Its Discontents* (Berkeley: University of California Press, 1990), argues that the play is actually much more intensely concerned with Jacobean politics and ideology than with its Roman materials.

17. Arthur Golding, trans., *The .xv. Bookes of P. Ovidius Naso, Entytuled Metamorphosis*, ed. John Frederick Nims (Philadelphia: Paul Dry Books, 2000), 6: 682–5. I will provide subsequent references parenthetically in my text.

18. *Tethys Festival: Or, The Queenes Wake* appears in *The Order and Solemnitie of the Creation of the High and Mightie Prince Henrie, Eldest Son to our Sacred Sovereaigne, Prince of Wales* (London, 1610).

19. *Speeches at Prince Henries Barriers*, in *The Workes of Benjamin Jonson* (London, 1616), had already predicted that Princess Elizabeth, following her mother's example, 'shall bee / Mother of Nations', 974.

20. For more detailed discussion of the likenesses between Aeneas and Posthumus, see Heather James, *Shakespeare's Troy: Drama, Politics, and the Translation of Empire* (Cambridge: Cambridge University Press, 2007), 160–2, and Patricia Parker, 'Romance and Empire: Anachronistic *Cymbeline*', in *Unfolded Tales: Essays on*

Renaissance Romance, ed. George M. Logan and Gordon Teskey (Ithaca, NY: Cornell University Press, 1989), 190–5.
21. Arthur Golding, trans., *The .XV. Bookes of P. Ovidius Naso, Entytuled Metamorphosis* (London, 1567), p. 164.
22. *Roman Shakespeare: Warriors, Wounds, and Women* (London: Routledge, 1997), 105.
23. Kahn discusses the sexual puns of the play's second half; ibid., 105–9.

CHAPTER NINE

White Freedom, White Property, and White Tears

Classical Racial Paradigms and the Construction of Whiteness in Julius Caesar

KATHERINE GILLEN

When John Wilkes Booth shot Abraham Lincoln in Ford's Theatre, he was driven by the fear that the President would grant suffrage to formerly enslaved Black Americans. As such the assassination constitutes a dramatic example of what Carol Anderson calls white rage, a backlash against Black advancement.[1] A Shakespearean actor and son of actor Junius Brutus Booth, Booth framed the assassination in terms provided by *Julius Caesar*, referring to the plot as 'Ides' and shouting 'Sic semper tyrannis', meaning 'Thus always to tyrants', after killing Lincoln.[2] Booth's invocation of *Julius Caesar* reflects not only his theatrical training, but also the common Confederate depiction of Lincoln as a Caesar figure who had destroyed the Republic and had tyrannically infringed upon the rights of enslavers. In a letter justifying the assassination, Booth wrote, 'When Caesar had conquered the enemies of Rome and the power that was his menaced the liberties of the people, Brutus arose and slew him.'[3] By killing Lincoln, Booth imagines himself in the role of Brutus, vanquishing a tyrant who, as he saw it, had rendered white people 'all slaves now' by granting Black people a degree of freedom.[4]

This anecdote points to the particular whiteness of Shakespeare's most famous Roman play, especially as it was interpreted within an American tradition seeking to affirm the Greco-Roman roots of its democracy and to cast these roots as racially white. As Nell Irvin Painter writes in *The History of White People*, 'not a few Westerners have attempted to racialize antiquity, making ancient history into white race history and classics into a lily-white field complete with pictures of blond ancient Greeks'.[5] Shakespeare, and particularly *Julius Caesar*, performs significant racial work within this paradigm, serving as a white, Anglo conduit of classicism that could be adapted to US racial politics. As Jason Demeter demonstrates, white American interpretations of the play often cast its class divisions in racial terms that present Black Americans as an unruly and irrational mob, incapable of participation in a democratic tradition 'that views whites of European ancestry as singularly capable of living up to the challenges of effective self-governance'.[6] Drawing on this tradition, American racists such as Booth depicted Black enfranchisement as destabilizing the foundation of the racial republic.

The appropriation of *Julius Caesar* in the interests of American white supremacy, I suggest, is not simply a misreading of the play, as it is often characterized, but is rather an extension of the play's racial ideologies. In contrast to plays such as *Titus Andronicus* and *Antony and Cleopatra*, in which Roman whiteness is explicitly defined in contrast to the blackness of conquered and/or enslaved subjects, *Julius Caesar* does not feature characters marked as nonwhite – an absence that has caused critics to overlook the play's racial ideologies. The play, however, is itself deeply concerned with the production of whiteness, as it negotiates and revises competing models of Roman racial formation, with the effect of aligning England with a transhistorial vision of whiteness that is simultaneously classicized and Christianized. In particular, I contend, *Julius Caesar* dramatizes a shift away from the Republican view that racial superiority should be accessible only to patricians and toward a vision of whiteness in which even common Romans are granted racial superiority in exchange for their submission to the imperial state. The triumph of imperial whiteness, I suggest, is accomplished in the play largely through Antony's transfiguration of Caesar's body from that of a deposed tyrant, often racialized as dark and foreign in Republican discourse, to that of a Christ-like martyr, whose whiteness and wealth are conferred upon the body politic. This whitened body politic is bound through the fruits of colonial exploitation and through Caesar's sacrificial blood, imagined as a conduit of racial material, which in turn inspires cleansing cathartic tears – a dynamic that points to the power of theatrical catharsis in fostering white affects and cementing racial solidarity.

SLAVERY, BARBARISM AND TYRANNY, AND THE CONSTRUCTION OF WHITENESS IN *JULIUS CAESAR*

The classical world informs visions of early modern English national and racial identity, with Rome in particular serving as what Coppélia Kahn terms a 'cultural parent' to England.[7] The English sought to bolster their somewhat marginal status in Europe by appealing to a mythical lineage in which Britain was founded by Brutus of Troy and by applying the model of *translatio imperii*, in which Britain would take on Rome's mantel as the world's next great empire.[8] As Ian Smith argues, Shakespeare and his contemporaries also adopted Greek and Roman racial paradigms, revising them so as to endow Englishness with racial normativity and displacing England's purported barbarity onto Africans, whom they defined as racially inferior.[9] Furthermore, Urvashi Chakravarty demonstrates that the figure of the Roman slave, found frequently in pedagogical texts and in comic drama, influenced English thinking about race, slavery, and service.[10] The English were attracted to classical political models and to their attendant ideals of liberty and virtue. These ideals, however, were imbricated in Greek and Roman systems of slavery and imperialism, as the liberty and virtue of the citizen were defined against the purported servility of the 'slave' and the 'barbarian', categories that were linked materially as well as discursively. Such frameworks were adapted in early modern England, which was embarking on its own colonial projects and pursuing involvement in the transatlantic slave trade.

Particularly illuminating in this regard is Aristotle's *Politics*, which, as Debora Shuger observes, functioned as 'a normative, central text for political theory' in early modern England.[11] Central to Aristotle's political thinking was his theory of natural slavery, which attributes innate servility to enslaved and colonialized people. Just as men were innately superior to women, in Aristotle's view, free men were superior to the enslaved, who were associated with the body rather than with the mind and who supposedly lacked the ability to govern themselves. The purportedly natural division of men into masters and slaves, Aristotle argues, is 'not only necessary, but expedient; from the hour of their birth, some are marked out for subjection, others for rule'.[12] Aristotle further attributes this subjection to foreigners whom he positions as deficient in comparison to the racial superiority of Mediterranean people. In particular, Aristotle contrasts the freedom-loving Greeks – and their Republican form of government – with those in Asia and Africa whom, he alleges, 'do not rebel against a despotic government' and are therefore readily conquerable and enslavable.[13] The discourse of slavery thus shapes both personal and colonial subjugation in Aristotle's thought. As Benjamin Isaac maintains, 'The justification of individual slavery . . . becomes applicable also to collective subjugation and thus becomes part of imperialist ideology', a dynamic that also works in the reverse, with the subjugation of colonized people justifying the enslavement of individuals.[14] Similar thinking was prevalent in Rome and was reinforced by the hereditary basis of Roman slavery.[15] Therefore, while enslaved people did not share a common origin or phenotype, there remains a strong racial dimension to classical slavery, especially if we understand race in the biopolitical sense advocated by Alexander G. Weheliye in which race functions 'not as a biological or cultural descriptor but as a conglomerate of sociopolitical relations that discipline humanity into full humans, not-quite-humans and nonhumans'.[16] Actively constructing racial categories, Greek and Roman slavery gathered disparate people, mostly from colonized communities, into a common 'not-quite-human' substratum of society.

The theory of natural slavery, moreover, is central to Aristotle's distinction between just and unjust – or tyrannous – rule. Although slavery itself is natural for Aristotle, he deems it the height of injustice to enslave someone who is 'unworthy to be a slave', and doing so constitutes the essence of tyranny.[17] As Mary Nyquist observes, antityranny ideology reifies the superiority of free citizens by 'represent[ing] the tyrant's subjects as figuratively enslaved – enslavement that seeks to dishonour and disenfranchise citizens who are meant to be "free"'.[18] Within this framework, tyranny amounts to treating free citizens, coded as racially superior, in a manner reserved for enslaved and colonized people. Central to the ideological foundation of the Roman Republic, this paradigm frames the central conflict in Shakespeare's *Julius Caesar*, as the characters debate the extent to which Caesar's consolidation of power constitutes tyranny. This conflict also concerns the constitution and the reach of racial whiteness. As Arthur L. Little, Jr. observes, 'To the extent that Rome was "a cultural parent", part of what it infused in or passed on to [the English] was a classically derived and historically fixed whiteness deeply embedded in human freedom'.[19] *Julius Caesar* explores this intersection of freedom and whiteness, illuminating the limitations of Republican whiteness in the context of an expanding empire and dramatizing the formation of an alternate mode of whiteness that is at once more imperial and more Christian.

Julius Caesar's conspirators largely embrace the racial, class-based and gendered epistemologies central to Republican ideology, which defined the patrician's liberty and personhood in contrast to the servility of enslaved people and women. As Kahn outlines, 'the Roman republic is built on a profound distinction between *polis* and *oikos*, between *politics* as the freely willed action of rational men and *household* as the realm of mere physical necessity, of women, children and slaves'.[20] Free male citizens are invested in the '*res publica*', the 'public thing', whereas women and the enslaved remain in the private realm that sustains the Republic, deprived of access to it and perceived as lacking the virtue to succeed within it.[21] In addition to its investment in masculinity, which Kahn and other feminist critics have shown, Roman citizenship has a strong racial component and is often coded as white in its early modern applications. Brutus points to this racial component of Roman citizenship when he prepares the conspirators for action, stating that they need not take an oath

>   when every drop of blood
> That every Roman bears, and nobly bears,
> Is guilty of a several bastardy
> If he do break the smallest particle
> Of any promise that hath passed from him.
>
> —*JC* 2.1.135–9[22]

Brutus suggests that virtue adheres in Roman citizenship, which is imagined in ethno-nationalist terms of blood. Any rejection of 'the virtue of their enterprise' – that is, killing Caesar – would indicate that Roman blood has been adulterated with something low class, servile, or foreign, thus signalling bastard origins. The conspirators must therefore perform their possession of racially pure, virtuous blood in order to, as Brutus directs, 'show yourselves true Romans' (2.1.222). Cassius also applies this logic of racial purity and degeneration in his complaint against Caesar's sycophantic admirers, lamenting that Rome has 'lost the breed of noble bloods' (1.2.150).

The racial component of Roman citizenship is especially prominent within Republican antitryanny discourse. When a citizen succumbs to tyrannous mastery deemed appropriate only for women, the enslaved and the colonized, he is accused of exhibiting the effeminacy, servility and racial debasement associated with these oppressed groups. Cassius opines, for example, that 'our fathers' minds are dead, / And we are governed with our mother's spirits: / Our yoke and sufferance show us womanish' (1.3.81–4). The common use of the word 'yoke' in Republican discourse evokes not just the yoke of marriage but, more literally, the yoke of the chattel animals with which enslaved people were often associated. Reflecting a similarly objectifying impulse, those 'willing bondmen' (1.3.113) who submit to Caesar are referred to as animals – in particular docile animals such as sheep and hinds – and as refuse, constituting the 'trash', 'rubbish', and 'offal' that make Rome 'base matter to illuminate / So vile a thing as Caesar' (1.3.108–11). Tyranny, which is defined in Thomas Thomas's *Dictionarium Linguae Latinae et Anglicanae* (1587) as 'gouernment for a priuate commoditie and not the publike weale', removes Roman men from the public realm and treats them as though they are subjugated members of a household, that is, as possessions. For this reason, tyranny threatens the self-possession integral to Roman racial citizenship, a quality understood literally as the capacity to own oneself.[23]

In the play's first scene, the Republicans take offence at Caesar's military triumph because they believe that Caesar is treating Roman citizens in a manner suited to foreigners and the enslaved. As Plutarch notes in his account of Caesar's life, the people resented Caesar's triumph after vanquishing Pompey's sons in Spain 'because he had not overcome Captaines that were strangers, nor barbarous kings, but had destroyed the sons of the noblest man in Rome, whom fortune had overthrown'.[24] Caesar inflicts upon Pompey's sons humiliation that does not befit their station. Castigating the workers planning 'to rejoice in his triumph' (1.1.32), Murellus asks,

> Wherefore rejoice? What conquest brings he home?
> What tributaries follow him to Rome
> To grace in captive bonds his chariot wheels?
> You blocks, you stones, you worse than senseless things!
>
> —*JC* 1.1.33–6

Caesar, Murellus maintains, has failed to augment the Republic through foreign conquest, as he has not brought home 'tributaries . . . in captive bonds'. Rather, Caesar oppresses fellow Romans and, in the process, compromises their racial citizenship. Those Romans who support Caesar's actions, according to Republican ideology, are depicted as complicit in their own transformation into 'blocks, stones . . . worse than senseless things', objectifying terms indicative of their metaphorical enslavement. This objectification of the enslaved is underscored in the bizarre event, recounted by Caska in the prelude to Caesar's murder, of a 'common slave' with his hand ablaze 'which did flame and burn / Like twenty torches joined' (1.3.15–17). Although the enslaved man's hand miraculously 'remained unscorched' (1.3.18), this image points to violence inflicted upon enslaved Romans, who had little legal recourse.

REWRITING LUCRETIA: SACRIFICE AND THE FORMULATION OF WHITE, IMPERIAL AFFECTS

Julius Caesar's conspirators are particularly invested in the racial logics surrounding the foundational antityrannical act of the Roman Republic: the overthrow of Lucius Tarquinius, the last king of Rome, following the rape of the noblewoman Lucretia in a rebellion led by Marcus Brutus's ancestor Junius Brutus. As Shakespeare's Brutus himself states, 'his ancestors did from the streets of Rome / The Tarquin drive, when he was called a king' (2.1.53–4), recalling the events that followed Lucretia's suicide after she was raped by the king's son Sextus Tarquinius. As Little maintains, this

Republican origin story, which was retold frequently in early modern England, has significant racial stakes. In it, freedom is associated with whiteness, which is imbued in Lucretia's chaste body and is transmitted to the body politic through the revolution that Brutus leads in her name.[25] Tyrannical power is depicted as racially other in this framework, as the Etruscan king Tarquinius is depicted as a foreign contagion that must be expunged from the body politic and, as Little observes, Tarquin the rapist is often linked discursively with the slave to whom he threatens to bind Lucretia if she resists him.[26] Lucretia's suicide ostensibly purifies her body of Tarquin's racial stain, causing her tainted blood to stream from her wound; as Shakespeare writes in his rendition of the myth, some blood 'still pure and red remained, / And some looked black, and that false Tarquin stained' (ll.1742–3).[27] Analogously, the revolution cleanses Rome of the tyranny of King Tarquinius. Killing the tyrant, in this framework, thus purifies – and whitens – the state and returns self-possession to Roman citizens.

In the Lucretia myth, purgation is effected through stoic resistance to the tyrant. As Stephanie Jed notes, Junius Brutus serves as a *castigator lacrimarum* who transforms lamentation over Lucretia's death into political action, thus suppressing emotional and ethical considerations in the interests of revolution (a tendency subsequently evident in his willingness to execute his sons for treason against the Republic). As such, Jed contends, Brutus facilitates the Lucretia myth's lasting humanist dynamic of 'chaste thinking', which denies complex material and affective contexts in favour of purportedly rational abstractions and fantasies of purity.[28] As Little argues, moreover, chaste thinking is white thinking.[29] This white thinking cordons off rationality from embodiment, which is displaced largely onto women and the enslaved, and it abstracts ideals of liberty and citizenship from their material basis in slavery and colonialism. From this perspective, white subjectivity is expressed not only through the fair chastity of Lucretia but also through the impenetrable stoic masculinity of Brutus and his fellow Republicans.

Although Cassius and Caska expect Marcus Brutus to uphold the legacy of Junius Brutus, he diverges from his ancestor's model in several respects. As Plutarch explains, Marcus Brutus differs significantly from his famous ancestor:

> ... that *Junius Brutus* being of a slower stearn nature, not softened by reason, being like unto sword blades of too hard a temper: was so subject to his choler and malice he bare unto the tyrants, that for their sakes he caused his owne sonnes to be executed. But this *Marcus Brutus* in contrary maner, whose like we presently write, having framed his manners of life by the rules of virtue and study of Philosophy, and having imployed his wit, which was gentle and constant, in attempting great things: me thinks he was rightly made and framed unto vertue.[30]

In both Plutarch and Shakespeare, Marcus Brutus is characterized by exceptional virtue and by a kindness to his subordinates that contrasts with the tendency of his fellow Romans to dehumanize and demean commoners, the enslaved and the colonized.

In Shakespeare's play, this liberal quality is reflected in Brutus's humane treatment of his servant Lucius, who is distinctly not depicted as enslaved. It is also evident in Brutus's political rhetoric, especially in his refusal to demonize Caesar through racializing and effeminizing antityranny discourse. Cassius and Caska emphasize Caesar's physical weakness and epilepsy, suggesting that his debased presence enervates the state, causing 'the vile contagion of the night' and 'the rheumy and unpurged air' (2.1.264–5). But while Brutus uses the language of political slavery, asking the public, for example, 'Who is here so base, that would be a bondman?' (3.2.29) and 'Had you rather Caesar were living, and die all slaves, than that Caesar were dead, to live all freeman?' (3.2.22–4), he stops short of depicting Caesar himself as a contaminant to be exterminated. Instead, Brutus casts Caesar's murder as a cleansing sacrifice. As Naomi Conn Liebler demonstrates, Brutus's desire to 'be sacrificers but not butchers' (2.1.165) and 'purgers, not murders' (2.1.179) reflects the rejuvenating framework of the Lupercalia, the fertility and purgation rite celebrated contemporaneously with the play's action. Harkening back to the founding of Rome, when Romulus and Remus were suckled by the wolf, the Lupercalia involves the sacrifice of goats and dogs to 'purify the community, cleanse it of disease and restore its health'.[31] Brutus's insistence that the conspirators 'bathe [their] hands in Caesar's blood / Up to the elbows and besmear our swords' (3.1.106–8), Liebler contends, can be read in this context, in which 'the cutting up of the *pharmakos*, whose blood is then smeared upon the flesh of the priestly celebrants, is one of the central rites'.[32] Following in this vein, Brutus instructs the conspirators, 'Let's carve him as a dish fit for the gods, / Not hew him as a carcass fit for hounds' (2.1.172–3). Brutus thus presents Caesar's death as an unfortunate but necessary bloodletting that will restore health to the community, 'A piece of work that will make sick men whole' (2.1.326). Rather than demonizing Caesar, therefore, Brutus weeps for him, insisting that he killed him not because 'I loved Caesar less, but that I loved Rome more' (3.2.21–2).

In an influential essay, René Girard contends that the murder of Caesar 'has become the *fundamental violence* of the Roman Empire', functioning as an 'original sacrifice' in which the community 'unite[s] *around* some transfigured victim'.[33] For Girard, Caesar's murder replicates the murder of Tarquin, which served a similar function for the Republic.[34] There are, however, significant differences between the two murders, particularly in their racial dimensions. In the Lucretia myth, it is Lucretia's body – not King Tarquinius's – that is sacrificed, displayed and mobilized in the interest of whiteness. In *Julius Caesar*, though, it is the erstwhile tyrant's sovereign body that is redeemed and whitened, but ultimately to an anti-Republican end. By refusing to position Caesar as a debased source of adulterating corruption, Brutus allows for the recuperation of Caesar's body and blood within an alternate framework – at once Christian, monarchal and imperial – in which the whiteness of the sacrificed sovereign, concentrated in his blood, is extended to the Roman citizenry, including to those commoners generally excluded from racial superiority within Republican racial frameworks.

Whereas Brutus regrets that 'Caesar must bleed' (2.1.170) to save Rome, Caesar's blood – like Christ's blood, Lucretia's blood and the blood of the Lupercalian sacrifice – becomes central to the redemption both of Caesar's sovereign whiteness and of Roman whiteness more generally. Blood imagery first appears in Calphurnia's dream, in which Caesar's statue, 'like a fountain with an hundred spouts, / Did run pure blood; and many lusty Romans / Came smiling and did bathe their hands in it'

(2.2.77–9). Hoping to convince Caesar to come to the Capitol, Decius recodes this violent portent to emphasize Caesar's status as the heart of the body politic, nourishing the city with his lifeblood:

> Your statue spouting blood in many pipes
> In which so many smiling Romans bathed
> Signifies that from you great Rome shall suck
> Reviving blood, and that great men shall press
> For tinctures, stains, relics and cognizance.
>
> —*JC* 2.2.85–9

As Gail Kern Paster points out, this image of Rome 'suck[ing] / Reviving blood' from Caesar relies on medieval Christian iconography, in which the lactating Christ sustains the community of believers.[35] In this Christian physiology, all bodily fluid is reduced to blood, thus linking Christ's sacrificial blood with both breast milk and menstrual fluid.[36] As such, it reflects Christianity's debt to pagan traditions that associate bleeding women with purgation, a trope also evident in the Lucretia myth. In Decius's image, then, Caesar will provide the salubrious menstrual cleansing that, Calphurnia's barrenness indicates, is lacking in the body politic. Caesar's 'pure blood' also has a strong racial component, reflecting blood's significance in the early modern period as 'a repository of sacred principles and properties'.[37] The image of the fountain thus presents Caesar's sacrificial blood as binding the community together into one racial body, the valuable whiteness of which can be reified and possessed in relics and consumable tinctures.

In his funeral oration, Antony exploits the racial possibilities of this framework. In particular, he evokes a sense of racial solidarity by appealing to the iconographic tradition in which the community is bound together by witnessing Christ's martyred body. As Dennis Austin Britton argues, the affective power of martyred bodies relies on a semiotics of colour in which 'Whiteness signifies both purity and wholeness, both of which are sacrificed in order to redeem sinful, black humanity'. Depictions of desecrated white bodies, sullied by red blood or black and blue bruises, thus recall 'the desecration of Christ's divine whiteness' in the crucifixion, and produce a racialized pathos in the Christian witness.[38] Antony casts the 'bloody spectacle' (3.2.198) of the martyred Caesar in these terms, emphasizing the wounds that 'like dumb mouths do ope their ruby lips' (3.1.260). Caesar's soft and white skin, noted in Plutarch as an indication of physical weakness, is transfigured within this martyrological framework to signal the feminized purity emblematized by both Lucretia and Christ.[39] Antony, moreover, employs Petrarchan tropes in relation to Caesar, drawing on a gendered and racial discourse that, as Kim F. Hall demonstrates, employs 'a poetics of colour in which whiteness is established as a valued goal'.[40] In so doing, Antony emphasizes the whiteness that can be conveyed through the martyr's feminized blood, when Romans, fulfilling their sexual/racial fantasies, 'put a tongue / In every wound of Caesar.'

In contrast to Junius Brutus's rejection of lamentation in the Lucretia myth, Antony stokes the cathartic pathos inspired by the martyred body, recruiting white affects in the interests of imperial power. Connecting cleansing tears to sacrificial blood, Antony laments,

> Had I as many eyes as thou hast wounds,
> Weeping as fast as they stream forth thy blood,
> It would become me better than to close
> In terms of friendship with thine enemies.
>
> —*JC* 3.1.200–3

Antony figures his tears, rendered virtuous rather than effeminate, as possessing a cleansing, purgative power, and he encourages a similar response in his audience during his funeral oration. Caesar's bleeding body, he implores, should cause the public to reject Brutus's 'bloody treason' (3.2.190), and to weep penitent tears, 'gracious drops' (3.2.191) that Antony casts as a sign of 'pity' (3.2.192) and thus of humanity. These cathartic tears perform a whitening function, purging not just personal sin from the individual witness but also racialized contaminants from the community. Antony's audience is therefore united through their collective response to Caesar's desecrated whiteness, forging affective bonds imagined in terms of the corporeal transmission of bodily fluids: blood, tears, breast milk and semen.

By extending Caesar's corporeal and spiritual whiteness to the community, Antony crafts a populist alternative to Republican racial discourse, which restricts full racial normativity to patricians and regards plebeians as 'tag-rag people' (1.2.256), 'idle creatures' (1.1.1), and 'rabblement' (1.2.242). In place of class hierarchies, Daniel Juan Gil suggests, 'Antony teaches Rome a grammar of interpersonal bonding that defines connections between bodies (via emotions conceived as fluids), and these connections are meant to replace any politically mediated public life.'[41] This shift, however, is not emancipatory. Rather, it is central to Antony's populist extension of whiteness to all free Romans in exchange for submission to a state with the power not only to oppress colonized and enslaved subjects but also to condemn citizens with the sweep of a pen, a power Antony demonstrates when, recalling the callousness of Junius Brutus, he commits to executing his nephew Publius with the chilling comment, 'Look, with a spot I damn him' (4.1.6).

ANTONY'S RACIAL CONTRACT AND THE PRODUCTION OF WHITENESS AS PROPERTY

This racial contract depends upon Antony's promise that Roman citizens will benefit, both materially and psychologically, from the imperialist projects of the state. In contrast to the Republican discourse alleging that citizens would be treated *like slaves* in imperial Rome, Antony insists that Roman citizens benefit from intertwined systems of colonialism and slavery and that they should therefore submit to the authority of the empire rather than resist it. He reminds the people that Caesar 'hath brought many captives home to Rome, / Whose ransoms did the general coffers fill' (3.2.89). Rather than presaging tyranny, he contends, Caesar's great wealth, amassed through conquest, redeems the humanity of the Roman people. This redemption is most evident in the bestowal of Caesar's will, which provides a parallel means through which the public may share in Caesar's lineage. Preparing the public for its contents, Antony exclaims: 'You are not wood, you are not stones, but men; / And being men, hearing the will of Caesar / It will inflame you, it will make you mad' (3.2.143–5). It is not tyranny, Antony insists, that has rendered Romans bestial but rather their own lack of pity for Caesar, as 'judgment [has] fled to brutish beasts / And men have lost their reason' (3.2.105–6). Caesar's will, which disburses money and land to the people, will make them repent, causing them to 'kiss dead Caesar's wounds, / And dip their napkins in his sacred blood' (3.2.133–4). Humanity, in Antony's vision, is redeemed through submission to imperial power, symbolized by Caesar's body, which in turn rewards the community with both racial whiteness and the profits of conquest.

In the process of 'Produc[ing]' Caesar's 'body to the market-place' (3.1.228), Antony literally renders whiteness property, a framework Cheryl I. Harris uses to describe the ways in which 'the set of assumptions, privileges, and benefits that accompany the status of being white have become a valuable asset'.[42] In *Julius Caesar*, white property is imbued in Caesar's body and in the economic and legal systems he authorizes. Antony imagines that the people will 'beg a hair of him for memory' (3.2.138), which they will include in their own wills, 'Bequeathing it as a rich legacy / Unto their issue' (3.2.137–8). Caesar's reified whiteness, passed through generations of Romans, thus compounds the land and money gifted to the people in Caesar's will. As such, Antony interpolates Caesar's legacy into a capitalistic and imperialist marketplace that is governed largely by private interests rather than the public ethos of the Republic. In this, Antony naturalizes tyranny, in the sense defined by Thomas, as 'gouernment for a priuate commoditie and not the publike weale'. Republican stoicism is ill equipped to accommodate this market economy, and Brutus resists its mercenary logics (even as he succumbs to them), claiming that he would

> . . . rather coin my heart
> And drop my blood for drachmas, than to wring
> From the hard hands of peasants their vile trash
> By any indirection.
>
> —*JC* 4.3.72–5

Such commercial behaviour constitutes an affront to stoic Roman subjectivity, commoditizing it as Antony does to Caesar's corpse and as traffickers do to the bodies of the enslaved. Catalysed by Antony, who has no qualms about stealing from 'the hard hands of peasants', Republican racial normativity thus gives way to something more closely resembling imperialist, capitalist whiteness. In this paradigm, commoners are seduced by the promise of whiteness as property, submitting to a violent and oppressive state in exchange for the oversold privileges – both material and psychological – accrued from colonial expansion and enslavement.

The final scenes of *Julius Caesar* work to recuperate aspects of stoic virtue as a feature of Rome's racial supremacy, but only in an elegiac mode in which embattled Republicanism no longer constitutes a threat to the imperial state. Both Cassius and Brutus commit suicide, though not without assistance from subordinates, thus approximating but not fully accomplishing the ultimate stoic act of self-mastery, that which differentiates the free Roman from the enslaved. Cassius's death, ironically, depends upon the coerced labour of his own 'bondman' (5.3. 56), and he dies seeking bodily union with Caesar, asking Pindarus to 'with this good sword / That ran through Caesar's bowels, search this bosom' (5.3.41–2). Cassius's compromised but still noble stoic virtue is thus incorporated into the racial community inaugurated by Antony, constituted through bodily connection to the imperial martyr. Caesar more literally haunts Brutus's death, reminding audiences of his victory in the play's ideological war. In the presence of Caesar's ghost, Brutus cannot maintain his stoic self-control; instead, the 'noble vessel' (5.5.13) overflows and 'runs over even at his eyes' (5.5.14), thus releasing the pathos – the white tears – expected in the presence of the sacrificed sovereign. These tears unite him with the broader Roman racial community, in which racial normativity is no longer the exclusive domain of the stoic patrician but rather the shared property of Roman citizens. Thus integrated into Antony's imperial regime, Brutus's legacy is honoured, with Antony proclaiming him 'the noblest Roman of them all' (5.5.69). Ultimately, Brutus's legacy is folded into Antony's vision of imperial whiteness – which shares with Republicanism an interest in suppressing the enslaved and the colonized. Although the political regime changes, the essential whiteness of the Roman state does not.

In these concluding moments, then, disparate models of racial formation are reconciled in a manner that naturalizes the link between Roman virtue and racial whiteness in the early modern English imagination. Rather than representing stark ideological divisions that could have created an irreparable rift in the community, the conflict among the play's major characters is presented as little more than an unfortunate disagreement among noble white men who have known one another since boyhood. The play's relative embrace of both Brutus's and Antony's racial visions, therefore, contributes to the sense that the play itself, like Shakespeare more broadly, is white property.[43] This quality, I believe, coupled with the absence of marked characters of colour, lends *Julius Caesar* to theatrical, educational and political projects that celebrate racial whiteness. As such, the play's racist uses have been remarkably varied. John Wilkes Booth, with whose act of white rage I opened this essay, sided with Brutus, as he was influenced by an American tradition that aligned Republican values with the rights of enslavers. But other racists, notably from fascist traditions, have found allies in Caesar and Antony, strong men who use their rhetorical skill to seduce the populace with fantasies of racial power.

RACIAL PURGATION: SHAKESPEAREAN CATHARSIS AND WHITE HUMANISM

In addition to negotiating ideologies of whiteness, *Julius Caesar* taps into the roots of the humanist tradition that finds its fullest expression in Shakespeare's theatre, as it explores the power of theatre to manufacture white affects and bonds of racial solidarity. In particular, *Julius Caesar* illuminates the desire for racial purification at the heart of Western tragedy, a form born from Athens's colonial, slave-holding society.[44] Girard famously argues that *Julius Caesar* reveals tragedy's ritual roots, showing that 'Tragedy is a by-product of sacrifice; it is sacrifice without the immolation of the victim.'[45] The sacrificial ritual – central to the Lupercalia, to Lucretia's suicide, and to the crucifixion – is rooted in a desire to cleanse and to purify, and this purgation is also racial, depicted as whitening in the early modern period. Such catharsis, stemming from the Greek *kathairein*, to cleanse or purge, is the aim of Aristotelian tragedy, in which audience members emote in response to aestheticized violence, purifying themselves and their community. Such purgation, too, is the aim of tyrannicide. For Aristotle, the goal of tragedy is to refine the individual elite citizen, and tragedy's value and potency rests not in vulgar spectacle but in its finely crafted poetry. The theatre that Antony calls into being, however, like Shakespeare's theatre, depends upon embodied spectacle and encourages *collective* bonding and *communal* purification, incorporating plebeians into a sense of shared whiteness, though one still defined against those deemed 'less than human'.

In *Julius Caesar*, Shakespeare reflexively theorizes and critiques this process, but he is also complicit with it, offering a cathartic ending that produces its own white affects and conjures a sense of racial solidarity imaged in terms of corporeal interpenetration and shared blood. These racial affects bind English audience members not just to Caesar but also to Brutus and Antony and to one another, thus interpolating them into a broader, transhistorical humanist lineage of classicized whiteness. In its focus on white men, *Julius Caesar* largely occludes the systemic racial and colonial violence undergirding this ritual production of white tears, white property and ultimately white humanity. For evidence of the actual victims of this purgation, we might look not to the sacrificed Caesar but instead to the end of *Titus Andronicus* – not coincidentally, a play long disparaged in the humanist tradition. There Aaron, deemed a 'barbarous Moor' and an 'inhuman dog, unhallowed slave', is buried alive outside the city walls, reminding audiences of the enslaved, colonized people upon whose oppression Roman subjectivity depends.[46]

NOTES

1. Carol Anderson, *White Rage: The Unspoken Truth of Our Racial Divide* (New York: Bloomsbury, 2017), 3.
2. James Shapiro, *Shakespeare in a Divided America* (London: Faber & Faber, 2020), 130; Maria Wyke, *Caesar in the USA* (Berkeley: University of California Press, 2012), 4–5.
3. Ibid., 133.
4. Ibid., 132.
5. Nell Irvin Painter, *History of White People* (New York: W.W. Norton, 2010), x.
6. Jason Demeter, '"The Soul of a Great White Poet": Shakespearean Educations and the Civil Rights Era', in this volume, 235–52.
7. Coppélia Kahn, *Roman Shakespeare: Warriors, Wounds, Women* (New York: Routledge, 1997), 3.
8. For the influence of this framework, see Heather James, *Shakespeare's Troy: Drama, Politics, and the Translation of Empire* (New York: Cambridge University Press, 1999).
9. Ian Smith, *Race and Rhetoric in the Renaissance: Barbarian Errors* (New York: Palgrave, 2009).
10. Urvashi Chakravarty, *Fictions of Consent: Slavery, Servitude, and Free Service in Early Modern England* (Philadelphia: University of Pennsylvania Press, 2022).

11. Debora K. Shuger, 'Review', *Shakespeare Quarterly* 44.4 (1993): 488–93, qtd. in Kahn 82.
12. Aristotle, *Politics*, trans. Benjamin Jowett, in *The Basic Works of Aristotle*, ed. Richard McKeon (New York: The Modern Library), 1114–1316, esp. 1.5.1254b (p. 1132).
13. Ibid., 3.14.1285a (p. 1198).
14. Benjamin Isaac, *The Invention of Racism in Classical Antiquity* (Princeton, NJ: Princeton University Press, 2004), 172.
15. Contrary to dominant impressions, the majority of enslaved people in Rome were not captured in war but were born into slavery, with slave status passed through the mother (a legal precedent adopted by the American colonies in contradistinction to English common law). See Walter Scheidel, 'Quantifying the Sources of Slaves in the Early Roman Empire', *Journal of Roman Studies* 87 (1997): 156–69.
16. Alexander G. Weheliye, *Habeas Viscus: Racializing Assemblages, Biopolitics, and Black Feminist Theories of the Human* (Durham, NC: Duke University Press, 2014), 3.
17. Aristotle, *Politics*, 1.6.1255a (p. 1143).
18. Mary Nyquist, *Arbitrary Rule: Slavery, Tyranny, and the Power of Life and Death* (Chicago: University of Chicago Press, 2013), 1.
19. Arthur L. Little, Jr., 'Re-Historicizing Race, White Melancholia, and the Shakespearean Property', *Shakespeare Quarterly* 67.1 (2016): 84–103, esp. 102–3.
20. Kahn, *Roman Shakespeare*, 77–8.
21. Ibid., 83.
22. William Shakespeare, *Julius Caesar*, ed. David Daniel (New York: The Arden Shakespeare, 1998), 2.1.135–9, hereafter cited parenthetically.
23. 'Tyrannis', in Thomas Thomas, *Dictionarium Linguae Latinae et Anglicanae* (1587), LEME: Lexicons of Early Modern English.
24. Plutarch, *The Lives of the Noble Grecians and Romanes*, trans. Thomas North (Richard Field for Thomas Wight, 1595), 784.
25. Arthur L. Little, Jr., *Shakespeare Jungle Fever: National-Imperial Re-Visions of Race, Rape, and Sacrifice*, (Palo Alto, CA: Stanford University Press, 2000), 44–8.
26. Ibid., 4, 44–5.
27. William Shakespeare, *The Rape of Lucrece*, in *The Arden Shakespeare Complete Works*, ed. Richard Proudfoot, Ann Thompson and David Scott Kastan (London: The Arden Shakespeare, 2011).
28. Stephanie H. Jed, *Chaste Thinking: The Rape of Lucretia and the Birth of Humanism* (Bloomington: Indiana University Press, 1989), 18–50.
29. Little, *Shakespeare Jungle Fever*, 17.
30. Plutarch, *Lives*, 1053.
31. Naomi Conn Liebler, '"Thou bleeding piece of earth": The Ritual Ground of *Julius Caesar*', in *Julius Caesar: New Casebooks*, ed. Richard Wilson (New York: Palgrave, 2002), 128–48, esp. 133.
32. Liebler, '"Thou bleeding piece of earth"', 137.

33. René Girard, 'Collective Violence and Sacrifice in *Julius Caesar*', in *Julius Caesar: New Casebooks*, ed. Richard Wilson (New York: Palgrave, 2002), 108–27, esp. 120, 131.
34. Ibid., 121.
35. Gail Kern Paster, '"In the spirit of men there is no blood": Blood as Trope of Gender in *Julius Caesar*', in *Julius Caesar: New Casebooks*, ed. Richard Wilson (New York: Palgrave, 2002), 149–69, esp. 162.
36. Ibid., 162.
37. Jean E. Feerick, *Strangers in Blood: Relocating Race in the Renaissance* (Toronto: University of Toronto Press, 2010), 14.
38. Dennis Austin Britton, 'Red Blood on White Saints: Affective Piety, Racial Violence, and *Measure for Measure*', in this volume, 65–76.
39. Plutarch, *Lives*, 766. For a discussion of the ways in which Antony constructs Caesar as an icon, see Lisa S. Starks-Estes, *Violence, Trauma, and Virtus in Shakespeare's Roman Poems and Plays: Transforming Ovid* (New York: Palgrave, 2014), 137–8.
40. Kim F. Hall, *Things of Darkness: Economies of Race and Gender in Early Modern England* (Ithaca, NY: Cornell University Press, 1995), 66.
41. Daniel Juan Gil, '"Bare Life": Political Order and the Specter of Antisocial Being in Shakespeare's *Julius Caesar*', *Common Knowledge* 13.1 (2007): 67–79, reprinted in Harold Bloom, ed., *Bloom's Modern Critical Interpretations* (New York: Bloom's Literary Criticism, 2010), 147–61, esp. 149.
42. Cheryl I. Harris, 'Whiteness as Property', *Harvard Law Review* 106.8 (1993): 1707–91, esp. 1713.
43. For a discussion of Shakespeare as white property, see Little, 'Re-Historicizing Race', 88.
44. For the role of Athenian drama in the construction of Greek racial identity, see Edith Hall, *Inventing the Barbarian: Greek Self-Definition through Tragedy* (New York: Oxford University Press, 1989)
45. Girard, 'Collective Violence', 124.
46. William Shakespeare, *Titus Andronicus*, ed. Jonathan Bate, Arden Shakespeare, 3rd Series (London: Thompson Learning, 2006), 5.3.4; 5.3.14.

CHAPTER TEN

Hamlet and the Education of the White Self

ERIC DE BARROS

By the racist logic of *Hamlet*, King Hamlet was an N-word and deserved to die. At best, this statement seems to strain beyond even the most liberal conventions of textual interpretations, and, at worst, its offensive evocation of the logic of modern racism seems grossly, if not ridiculously, anachronistic. Indeed, thinking it and writing it goes against the most basic tenets of my training as a literary critic. And because of that training, that training as a 'good' historicist[1] committed to responsible, evidence-based textual analysis, I now fully expect that there will be a considerable army of similarly trained and committed early modern critics ready to attack.

I have nevertheless insisted on thinking it and writing it, because the fight over its underlying interpretive and political implications remains necessary, perhaps now more urgently so than ever with social media amplifying various disorienting forms of bigotry along with the often fragmented and simplistic social justice responses to them. Therefore, in the spirit of Hamlet's initial insistence that his actual internal blackness – his 'within which passes show' (1.2.85)[2] – is truly blacker than the seeming or superficial blackness of 'customary suits of solemn black' (1.2.78), I am declaring it as a provocative invitation for us to think seriously about both the limits of customary interpretive seeming and the 'real' interpretive possibilities of a presentist, transhistorical reorientation to our early modern past. In other words, I am not just inviting us to think about the racial-historical implications of colour symbolism in *Hamlet*; as I will reference, several critics have already done or are in the process of doing that important work. Rather, I am inviting us also to think about race/racism in terms of the habits of thought that have developed to protect and perpetuate it.

In that regard, my thinking is deeply influenced by Arthur L. Little Jr.'s understanding of white melancholia. As Little explains, white melancholia results from the spectre of racial histories haunting white people as and after they engage in forgetful processes of fashioning their identities – their whiteness – as a kind of unmarked, non-property. This self-fashioning, as Little emphasizes, is not 'so much about the self-fashioning of the [racialized] Other as it is about the self-fashioning of the [white] self'.[3] And through that process, as Little continues, 'The *white* melancholic subject – one may think of Hamlet, "Renaissance England's most renowned case of melancholia" – becomes the modern subject, abstracted and universalized, the end and the beginning of a *historical*, humanist teleology.'[4] As a vulnerably constituted Black Shakespearean, Little is particularly concerned with how this unmarking continues today in early modern studies. Indeed, as he rhetorically asks, 'Is there something of a *working* assumption in early modern studies that the early modern period . . . is a field for . . . 'white' scholars and those who can unmark themselves?'[5] Importantly, Little follows this question by warning those scholars that by 'signing onto a raceless Renaissance [they are repeating] some of the foundational principles of whiteness – its claims of being . . . both the arbiter of history and outside of it, outside of any legitimately humanistic critical frame'.[6]

In what follows, I will make more of Little's passing reference to Hamlet by arguing that Hamlet's white melancholia results from a similar process of racial marking and unmarking. That is, in light of Little's emphasis on the self-fashioning of the white self, I will argue that Hamlet's racial unmarking – his self-fashioning of an abstracted and universalized self – is strictly a family affair in that it develops out of a process of racializing the questionable legacy of his father in an attempt to forget it. In other words, as I began, King Hamlet was an N-word and deserved to die, because I see in Hamlet's struggle to think about or remember his father – that is, his need to forget about the worst qualities of a father he loved and so desperately wants to avenge – the inchoate elements of present-day selective white racial memory. Stated differently, I see in Hamlet the ability of white people variously and perpetually to forget their racist histories – their King Hamlets – so as to protect and perpetuate their right to act decisively as if morally in the present.

In the play, this politics of forgetting begins as a generic struggle with the Ghost and Hamlet refusing to play along with Claudius's hasty attempt to cycle the tragedy of King Hamlet's sudden death into the political comedy of his ascension to the throne. In his specific appeal to Hamlet, as David Scott Kastan explains, Claudius grounds that attempt in Protestant doctrine by depicting 'Hamlet's grief as somehow Catholic, ostentatiously opposed to the dignified Protestant forms of "moderate" sorrow, which were themselves ameliorations of an extreme Calvinist providentialism . . . uncomfortable with any forms of mourning at all'.[7] In that light, by rejecting Hamlet's 'intent / In going back to school in Wittenberg' (1.2.113), the birthplace of Protestantism, Claudius ironically misses its suggestion of Hamlet's own desire to escape to a place conducive to forgetting.

But although the environs of Denmark, with the offensive reminder of an uncle-father and a mother-aunt, will not allow him to let go of the mournful memory of his father, his promise to avenge that father is also curiously marked by a need to forget. After the Ghost reveals Claudius's villainy and exits the scene with the haunting 'Adieu, adieu, adieu: remember me' (1.5.9), Hamlet responds,

> Remember thee?
> Ay, thou poor ghost, whiles memory holds a seat
> In this distracted globe, Remember thee?
> Yea, from the table of my memory
> I'll wipe away all trivial fond records,
> All saws of books, all forms, all pressures past

That youth and observation copied there,
And thy commandment all alone shall live
Within the book and volume of my brain
Unmixed with baser matter. Yes, by heaven!

—*Ham* 1.5.95–104

As reflected in Horatio's opening failure to speak to or understand the Ghost and Hamlet's subsequent conclusion that 'There are more things in heaven and earth Horatio, / Than are dreamt of in your [or our] philosophy' (2.1.174–5), Hamlet is differently expressing the play's scepticism about formal education vis-à-vis the supernatural. However, this insistence on dismissing the sum total of his formative education as 'trivial fond records' and 'baser matter' also suggests that something else, something more radical, is going on. It is my contention that the inconsistency between this promise of vengeful simplicity and his life-long educational investment ironically reveals Hamlet as the product of a relatively recent ethically and culturally conflicted educational history. In other words, it reveals him as one of the first, first-generation students. Specifically, with the bureaucratic complexities that came along with the consolidation of power in monarchical courts and the advances in military technology that rendered the martial skills of the feudal knight-warrior obsolete, early modern educational theorists and practitioners enthusiastically attempted to persuade uneducated – in some cases, proudly uneducated – aristocratic men that their survival as a ruling class depended on providing their children, especially their male children, a humanistic or liberal education.[8] The problem for children like Hamlet is that those educators, as Mary Thomas Crane explains, sought to instil an 'opposition to aristocratic codes of honour, violence, and frivolous display'.[9]

Although there is no explicit representation of this generational transition in the play, everything about the contrast between King Hamlet's celebrated militarism and Prince Hamlet's bookish deliberativeness suggests something like it. Therefore, it would not be unreasonable to imagine for the play a backstory comparable to the history between pacifistic humanists like Erasmus and defenders of the militaristic honour code of the nobility throughout the sixteenth century. In short, as documented throughout his political and pedagogical writings, Erasmus hated war, and, along with the humanists of his circle, believed that their 'first and foremost concern must be for training the prince in skills relevant to wise administration in time of peace, because with them he must strive to his utmost end: that the devices of war may never be needed'.[10] As I am imagining, Hamlet is the product of a comparable education, one that began at home under Erasmian-inspired humanists before continuing, as Suzanne Stein suggests, at Melanchthon's pacifistic Wittenberg.[11]

In that regard, the appearance of the armoured Ghost and the references to the king it disturbingly represents are defined by and against the oppositional voice of Erasmian pacifism echoing throughout the play. Indeed, within this interpretive echo chamber, we immediately hear Erasmus in the exchange between Horatio and Marcellus after the Ghost makes its first appearance. Left, as Marcellus describes, 'trembl[ing] and look[ing] pale' (1.1.56), Horatio answers Marcellus's question about the Ghost's resemblance to the late king by agreeing that he had the same armour on when he combated 'the ambitious Norway' (1.1.60) and that 'So frowned he once, when in an angry parle / He smote the sledded Polacks' (1.161–2). In response to Marcellus's next question about Denmark's toilsome and feverish preparation for war, Horatio continues that the 'emulate pride' (1.1.82) that 'pricked on' (1.1.82) the late king against the elder Fortinbras is to blame for the impending war with the 'hot and full' (1.1.95) younger Fortinbras, who has now 'sharked up' a 'lawless' (1.1.97) band of soldiers to reclaim the 'lands / So by his father lost' (1.1.102–3). Although, within this exchange, Horatio praises the late king as 'our valiant Hamlet' (1.1.83), he immediately qualifies that praise with, 'For so this side of our known world esteemed him.' (1.1.84). While subtle, that qualification opens the door to another side of the known world – an Erasmian side – that sees nothing distinguishing or praiseworthy about the king that Horatio has just described. On the contrary, from that side, the king was an angry, competitive and proud man in a world of angry, competitive and proud men selfishly advancing those un-Christian qualities against the interests of his subjects.

In that way, the Ghost perfectly represents the immoral spirit of the king as he lived. As Eleanor Prosser pointed in her intuitively motivated, historically supported argument against the critical acceptance of revenge as a moral given in the play, 'The Ghost . . . fails the test that every member of Shakespeare's audience undoubtedly would have recognized as the crucial one, a failure that scholars have been trying to rationalize for two centuries: its command violates Christian teaching.'[12] My point is that his audience might have also recognized that the Ghost's violation merely reflects and attempts to extend that of the late king, and that Hamlet, much like the scholarly tradition Prosser intuitively doubts and historically challenges, struggles to rationalize beyond his own recognition of that connection. For instance, although triggered by the sound of Claudius's drunken, late-night revelling, a shameful custom which 'Makes [Denmark] traduced and taxed of other nations' (1.4.18), Hamlet's general cultural criticism quickly develops into an oddly focused, sympathetic reflection on the minor flaws of otherwise virtuous men (1.4.23–37). In that light, it is unlikely that such a reflection could possibly apply to the 'satyr' (1.2.140), 'incestuous', and 'adulterous' (1.5.42) uncle triggering it, an unlikelihood that might explain the omission of the passage from the First Folio. But whatever the reason, in that omission, the First Folio fails to appreciate the important functioning of the passage as an anticipatory, indirect moral rationalization right before Hamlet encounters the Ghost for the first time. In other words, as Hamlet waits, it is significant that we see him lovingly and desperately attempting to rationalize and thereby forget the complex legacy of a father 'Cut off even in the blossoms of [his] sin' (1.5.76).

While the play emphasizes that sinfulness with the Ghost immediately explaining its purgatorial status for 'the foul crimes done in my days of nature' (1.5.12) and with Hamlet later recalling that his uncle 'took [his] father grossly full of bread, / With all his crimes broad blown' (3.4.81), there is strangely nothing but silence on the specific connection between that sin and those crimes. Effectively allowing or encouraging a conflation of big political crimes with smaller personal sins, this paucity of expression in Shakespeare's most expressive play strategically distances and thereby protects the memory of the late king from those impossible-to-answer Erasmian questions about his militarism.

By way of contrast, about a year earlier in *Henry V*, Shakespeare represents just how potentially dangerous saying too much can be to the illusion of morally based monarchical legitimacy. In the 4.1 dialogue between the common soldiers Court, Bates and Williams on the eve of the battle at Agincourt, after Bates expresses doubt about the King's desire to suffer and possibly die on the battlefields of France as well as his own desire to be safely back in England, the disguised king makes the mistake of defending their ostensibly suicidal presence in France on conditional, moral grounds: 'Methinks I could not die anywhere so contented as in the /King's company, *his cause being just and his quarrel honour-/able.*' (H5 4.1.120-2; my italics). It is as if the King forgets to strategically forget all the questions about his legitimacy and specifically Canterbury's convoluted and therefore questionable justification for the French campaign that opened the play. And, as if present for and commenting on that disorienting disquisition on Salic Law, Williams first responds, 'That's more than we know' (4.1.123), before he and Bates reflect profoundly on the moral consequences to the King of the 'if not just and honourable' possibility. After Bates distinguishes the big political of the King from the smaller personal of his common soldiers with, 'If his cause be wrong, our obedience to the King wipes the crime of it out of us' (4.1.125-6), Williams adds,

> But if the cause be not good, the King himself hath a heavy reckoning to make when all those legs and arms and heads chopped off in a battle shall join together at the latter day, and cry all, 'We died at such a place' – some swearing, some crying for a surgeon, some upon their wives left poor behind them, some upon the debts they owe, some upon their children rawly left. I am afeard there are few die well that die in a battle, for how can they charitably dispose of anything, when blood is their argument? Now, if these men do not die well, it will be a black matter for the King that led them to it – who to disobey were against all proportion of subjection.
>
> —H5 4.1.128-38

This long and grotesquely vivid reflection on the moral responsibility of the 'the King himself' builds to an Erasmian question against the 'blood argument' of militarism. As I have suggested with *Hamlet*, there is no good answer to it. Indeed, the best that Henry can do, as he does at key moments of exposure throughout the play, is distance and thereby protect himself from it with a disorienting, verbally dexterous display of choplogic. And while that rhetorical strategy indeed drives the plot all the way to and beyond the victory that seemingly endorses Henry as a legitimate and moral king, the unanswered-because-unanswerable question haunts the play and anyone unable or unwilling to forget that it was asked.

In *Hamlet*, the same kind of Erasmian question haunts the legacy of the late king haunting the play. However, instead of equipping Hamlet with disorienting choplogic, Shakespeare gives him more-difficult-to-evade educational memories of the colour black. In his 2.2 meeting with the travelling players, after his initial struggle to remember 'Aeneas's tale to Dido', Hamlet recites with disturbing clarity,

> 'The rugged Pyrrhus, he whose *sable* arms,
> *Black* as his purpose, did the *night* resemble

> When he lay couchèd in the ominous horse,
> Hath now this dread and *black complexion* smeared
> With heraldry more dismal. Head to foot
> Now is he total gules, horridly tricked
> With blood of fathers, mothers, daughters, sons,
> Baked and impasted with the parching streets,
> That lend a tyrannous and damnèd light
> To their vile murders. Roasted in wrath and fire,
> And thus o'er-sizèd with coagulate gore,
> With eyes like carbuncles the hellish Pyrrhus
> Old grandsire Priam seeks.'
>
> —*Ham* 2.2.432–44; my italics

An avenging son driven by his father's angry ghost, Pyrrhus models for Hamlet a parallel journey through the gruesome immorality of war and revenge. While comparable to the examples Shakespeare found in his likely source texts, the Pyrrhus that Hamlet recalls significantly goes beyond them in one key respect.[13] That is, it is not enough to describe Pyrrhus as 'crazed with carnage' (*Aeneid*, 2: 620), as Virgil does; or as an enraged, bloody-minded, fierce, unbridled, cursed, and tyrannous butcher,[14] as George Peele does; or finally, as a butcher 'fell and full of ire',[15] as Marlowe does. Shakespeare initially and repeatedly adds the colour black to that already thoroughly damning catalogue of descriptive terms.

While it is perfectly reasonable to explain this addition of the colour black in terms of 'a long-standing ethical association of blackness with evil',[16] that Shakespeare adds it to a character already thoroughly marked as such suggests perhaps some other distinguishing association; perhaps it suggests, as Peter Erickson invites us to consider, the emergence of a period-specific consciousness of racial difference. That is, as Erickson concludes, 'Though lacking racial specificity, [*Hamlet*'s] general preoccupation with a vocabulary of black and white imagery conveys a symbolic world . . . [with] racially toned anxieties appear[ing] just under the surface.'[17] Beyond that, as Erickson importantly argues, the play's white-black colour scheme participates in an ethical (re-)fashioning of white identity through the representation of 'whiteness . . . as an ideal lost beyond recovery'.[18]

In this understanding of the play's symbolic world, King Hamlet represents the ideal of a vulnerable and innocent whiteness disfigured and destroyed by the racial opposite of Claudius's blackened villainy. However, as I have indicated, the Pyrrhus passage, which is Erickson's second and perhaps most pivotal example, subverts and thereby destabilizes the moral simplicity of Hamlet's black-white idealization. While one might argue, as Erickson does, that Pyrrhus's murderous blackness belongs to Claudius, it is also true, as I have indicated, that it extends to Hamlet through the comparable haunting of a father demanding revenge.[19] In that regard, the ghost of King Hamlet is not simply defined by the idealized, innocent whiteness of Priam; it is also simultaneously defined by the ghost of the father 'entycing',[20] as Peele describes it, Pyrrhus to smear his 'dread and black complexion. . . . / With blood of fathers, mothers, daughters, sons.' That is, it is also already simultaneously defined by the ghost of Achilles.

For Shakespeare, there is nothing good about this association. Indeed, written and performed at around the same time as *Hamlet*, his *Troilus and Cressida* represents Achilles as the least virtuous character in a play cynically focused on representing the immorality of war as so irrational it borders on generically confused, tragic stupidity. That is, despite a general awareness of Thersites's characteristically bitter assessment that 'All the argument [of the Trojan War] is a whore and a cuckold. / A good quarrel to draw emulous factions and bleed to death upon' (*TC* 2.3.65–6), the men foolishly and deceptively manage to convince themselves that it makes sense to continue to fight, bleed and die. A curious mode of consciousness defined by what Linda Charnes describes as 'cynically essentialism',[21] this specific instance of reason's failure links the two plays, for Hamlet uses the notorious verbalization of Pandarus's name during the 3.3 bedroom scene to condemn Gertrude's remarriage as what happens when love fails 'And reason panders will' (*Ham*, 3.4.78). In short, with reason serving rather than restraining will in this way, love devolves into lust, and military honour comparably devolves into murderous pride. And, as Harold Goddard usefully identifies, in *Troilus and Cressida*, 'Achilles' Achilles heel is pride'.[22]

Arguably a precursor to the cunning with which Iago targets Othello's racial insecurity,[23] Ulysses targets the insecurity of Achilles' pride in an effort to draw him back into the war. After Agamemnon and the Grecian lords play along with his elaborate scheme by 'pass[ing] strangely by [Achilles], / As if he were forgot' (*TC* 3.3.39–40), Ulysses comes last as if reading a letter from a 'strange fellow' (3.3.90), who, as Ulysses later reveals to an inquiring Achilles, has shared with him a conveniently applicable reflection on the nature of reputation. Specifically, as soon as the thoroughly baffled Achilles asks what he is reading, Ulysses slyly administers the 'derision medicinable' (3.3.44) of the letter's argument that, no matter one's material possessions or past noble exploits, it is only through the continued acknowledgement of others that one's reputation counts at all. Therefore, as he extrapolates, unless a renowned person continuously works against being forgotten, a lesser person will steal that renown through nothing more than a willingness to act boldly. For Achilles, Ajax is that lesser, 'unknown' (3.3.120) and 'lubber' (3.3.134) person playing out what Ulysses vividly describes as, 'How one man eats into another's pride / While pride is fasting in his wantonness' (3.3.131–2).

It is with this and other images of pride, honour, reputation, or renown as a horrifying, zero-sum game against oblivion that Ulysses persuades Achilles 'not to entomb thyself alive / And case thy reputation in thy tent' (3.3.180–1). However, as I am suggesting, this same nightmarish image of inaction as a status-erasing, death-in-life also tragically pushes him past the opportunity for a loving peace created by the familial reconciliation between Hector and Ajax as well as his own love for Polyxena and his promise to her and Hecuba not to fight. Furthermore, and most tragically, that fear of oblivion pushes his cowardly ordering of his Myrmidons to kill an unarmoured and unarmed Hector, whose body he dishonourably reduces to a 'dainty bait' (5.9.20) to be 'dragged through the shameful field' (5.11.5). Indeed, as the ghosts of Achilles and King Hamlet illustrate, that push is so strong that not even death can stop it.

These are the moral lessons – the educational memories – forcing Hamlet, however indirectly, to re-fashion, mark, or other his white father as the black-as-

Pyrrhus N-word deserving to die. However, as I have suggested, what enables him to avenge that blackened father is his eventual, ironic ability to fashion himself as an unmarked, abstracted, universal, and therefore innocent white self. While indicated throughout the play in Hamlet's tortured rationalizations, the pivotal moment in this process comes in 5.2, when he settles down with Horatio to fill in the details of the 4.6 letter reporting his return to Denmark. As he explains,

> Sir, in my heart there was a kind of fighting
> That would not let me sleep. Methought I lay
> Worse than the mutines in the bilboes. Rashly –
> And praised be rashness for it: let us know
> Our indiscretion sometimes serves us well
> When our dear plots do pall, and that should teach us
> There's a divinity that shapes our ends,
> Rough-hew them how we will –
>
> —*Ham* 5.2.4–11

It is on that never-completed trip to England that Hamlet figures out how, at once, to forget and carry out the charge of his inherited blackness. Beyond the impossible promise of complete erasure or even a Claudian rationalization between discretion and nature, the simple and complex answer for Hamlet is to ignore his morally based education through a convenient, self-serving endorsement of providential impulsiveness. Indeed, just a little later, after Horatio encourages him to think twice about the wager to duel Laertes 'If your mind dislike anything' (5.2.155), Hamlet rejects this advice with 'There's a special providence in the fall of a sparrow' (5.2.157), before simply concluding 'The readiness is all' (5.2.160) and 'Let be.' (5.2.161. [Q2]).

In this new impulsive or forgetful theory of action, moral education remains, but only in a de-moralized technical-bureaucratic form. Further illustrating the intuitiveness of that process as he groped his way through the dark of the ship to find the sealed commission ordering his execution, which his 'fears forgetting manners' (5.2.18) enables him to boldly unseal, Hamlet concludes,

> Being thus benetted with villainies –
> Ere I could make a prologue to my brains,
> They had begun to play – I sat me down,
> Devised a new commission, wrote it *fair*.
> I once did hold it, as our statists do,
> A baseness to write *fair*, and laboured much
> How to forget that learning; but, sir, now
> It did me yeoman's service.
>
> —*Ham* 5.2.30–8; my italics

With no moral guard against impulsiveness, with impulsiveness embraced as part of a divine plan beyond human comprehension, Hamlet is now intuitively able to engage in the self-fashioning of his white self. In other words, it is that intuitiveness that now thoughtlessly drives his hand through a homicidal act of writing himself 'fair' – that is, writing himself white and therefore innocent – against the darkness of the ship as well as his father's black legacy.[24]

From an Erasmian perspective, this ability – the ability of a *fear*-driven thoughtlessness to reduce learning to the political instrumentality of *fair* writing – is the tragedy of the play. And in that sense, *Hamlet* ironically and sadly amounts to a deeply intellectual anti-intellectual play, illustrating the historical process whereby humanistic ideals faded or were forgotten in favour of the technical skills essential to the functioning of early modern bureaucracies.[25] As Hannah Arendt infamously concludes, Adolf Eichmann was the logical, tragic consequence of this kind of bureaucratic thoughtlessness. But, for Arendt, there was nothing Shakespearean about this thoroughly unimpressive man. Indeed, as she insists, he 'was not Iago and not Macbeth, and nothing would have been farther from his mind than to determine with Richard III "to prove a villain"'.[26] However, what Arendt misses and, by contrast, what I am arguing is that the banality of Eichmann's evil – characterized as it was by 'the sheer thoughtlessness . . . that predisposed him to become one of the greatest criminals of the [twentieth century]'[27] – can ironically be traced to this pivotal moment of Hamlet's white self-fashioning.

Therefore, it is not, as several critics have argued, simply that King Hamlet has been forgotten by the end of the play and that Hamlet's killing of Claudius amounts to little more than an 'instinctive retaliation for his own and Gertrude's death'.[28] Instead, the late king has only, more complexly been blackened or obscured as if forgotten in the fairness – that is, the whiteness – of Hamlet's bureaucratic activities. That is what's going on, for instance, when he answers Horatio's question about the practical matter of sealing the commission with,

> Why, even in that was heaven ordinant
> I had my father's signet in my purse,
> Which was the model of that Danish seal;
> Folded the writ up in the form of th'other,
> Subscribed it, gave't th'impression, placed it safely,
> The changeling never known.
>
> —*Ham* 5.2.49–54

Despite concluding as others that Hamlet ultimately forgets his father, Stephen Greenblatt's reading of the signet as 'oddly conjoin[ing] memory – an impression stamped in wax – and bureaucracy'[29] similarly suggests a different, more insidious form of remembering. That is, with his father's memory sealed within the legitimating seal of his signet ring, Hamlet is now free to move with a kind of thoughtless detail-oriented bureaucratic pleasure – a kind of white bureaucratic pleasure – through that homicidal process of writing, folding, signing and sealing the commission. And by obscuring the moral questions raised by the questionable evidence against his friends, that ring and that process also prepare Hamlet to walk with and as his N-word father into the bloodbath that ends the play.

In the final analysis, as I have already referenced Little as saying, white self-fashioning is never really about the Other. And in that regard, what I have tried to do by illustrating that King Hamlet is Hamlet's N-word is give back to Hamlet (and by extension Shakespeare and the early modern world) the problem that James Baldwin gave back to white America at the end of the 1964 documentary film 'Take This Hammer'.[30] In the process of repeatedly refusing that the concept of 'the Nigger' has anything to do with him – that it is unnecessary to him, that he has always known this, and that he is not the victim, Baldwin argues that the concept of 'the Nigger' is a uniquely white American invention and, as such, a projection of the needs, fears, and desires of white people. Therefore, as he concludes to his white American audience in 1964 and as I am extending back to Hamlet and ahead to all those unmarked, innocent self-fashioning white people today, 'You're 'the Nigger', Baby; it isn't me.'[31]

NOTES

1. Eric L. De Barros, 'The Gatekeeping Politics of "Good" Historicism: Early Modern Orientalism and "The Diary of Master Thomas Dallam"'. *College Literature: A Journal of Critical Literary Studies* 43.4 (Fall 2016): 619–44.

2. William Shakespeare, *Hamlet*, in *The Arden Shakespeare Complete Works*, ed. Richard Proudfoot, Ann Thompson, and David Scott Kastan (Thomas Nelson and Sons, 1998. All Shakespeare quotations are from this edition, and citations will appear parenthetically in the essay.

3. Arthur Little Jr., 'Re-Historicizing Race, White Melancholia, and the Shakespearean Property'. *Shakespeare Quarterly* 67.1 (2016), 92.

4. Ibid., 93

5. Ibid., 88.

6. Ibid., 93

7. David Scott Kastan, 'Forgetting Hamlet', in *A Will to Believe: Shakespeare and Religion* (New York: Oxford University Press, 2014), 125.

8. For analyses of this history, see Lawrence Stone, 'Education and Culture', in *The Crisis of the Aristocracy, 1558–1641* (Oxford: Clarendon Press, 1965), 672–83; Ruth Kelso, 'The Education of the Gentleman – In General', *The Doctrine of the English Gentleman in the Sixteenth Century* (Urbana: University of Illinois Press, 1929), 111–29; and Mary Thomas Crane, 'Pastime or Profit: Aristocratic and Humanist Ideology, 1520–1550', in *Framing Authority: Saying, Self, and Society in Sixteenth Century England*. (Princeton, NJ: Princeton University Press, 1993), 93–115.

9. Crane, ibid., 94.

10. Desiderius Erasmus, *The Education of a Christian Prince* (1516). *Collected Works of Erasmus*. Vol. 26. (Buffalo, NY: University of Toronto Press, 1985), 253.

11. Suzanne Stein, 'Hamlet in Melanchthon's Wittenberg'. *Notes and Queries* (March 2009): 55–57.

12. Eleanor Prosser, *Hamlet and Revenge* 2nd edn (Stanford, CA: Stanford University Press, 1971), 136.

13. For an assessment of those sources, see Prosser, *Hamlet and Revenge*, 154.

14. George Peele, *A [H]farewell Entituled to the famous and fortunate generalls of our English forces: Sir Iohn Norris & Syr Frauncis Drake Knights, and all theyr braue and resolute followers. VVhereunto is annexed: a tale of Troy*. (At London : Printed by I[ohn] C[harlewood] and are to bee solde by William Wright, at his shop adioyning to S. Mildreds Church in the Poultrie, Anno. 1589), 20. [STC (2nd edn) / 19537]

15. Christopher Marlowe, *Dido, Queen of Carthage*, in *The Complete Plays*, ed. J. B. Steane (New York: Penguin Books, 1969), 2.1.213.

16. Walter Cohen, *Othello* ('Introduction'), in *The Norton Shakespeare*, 1st edn, ed. Stephen Greenblatt, Walter Cohen, Jean E. Howard, and Katherine Eisaman Maus (New York: W.W. Norton, 1997), 2091.

17. Peter Erickson, 'Can We Talk about Race in Hamlet?' in *Hamlet: New Critical Essays*, ed. Arthur F. Kinney (New York: Routledge, 2002), 212.

18. Ibid., 210.

19. For a similar argument, see Patricia Parker, 'Black Hamlet: Battening on the Moor'. *Shakespeare Studies* 31 (2003): 127–64. In particular, Parker considers the early texts of *Hamlet* in relationship 'to the "tropical" reversibility or indistinguishability of white and black, angel and devil', 129.

20. Peele, *A [H]farewell Entituled*, 20.

21. Linda Charnes, 'The Two Party System in *Troilus and Cressida*', in *A Companion to Shakespeare's Works, Volume IV: The Poems, Problem Comedies, Late Plays*, ed. Richard Burton and Jean E. Howard. (Malden, MA: Blackwell, 2003), 306.

22. Harold C. Goddard, 'Troilus and Cressida', in *The Meaning of Shakespeare*, Volume II. (Chicago: The University of Chicago Press, 1951), 17.

23. Specifically, I have in mind that pivotal moment in 3.3, when Iago seizes on Othello's expression of doubt about the naturalness Desdemona's love for him: 'And yet how nature, erring from itself –' (*Oth* 3.3.232).

24. Shakespeare makes this racialization of 'fair' writing explicit in *The Merchant of Venice*, when Lorenzo identifies a letter from Jessica with 'I know the hand. In faith, 'tis a fair hand / And whiter than the paper it writ on / Is the fair hand that writ' (2.4.12–14). Also, for an important reading of the racialization of white hands in *Antony and Cleopatra*, see David Sterling Brown, 'White Hands: Gesturing Toward Shakespeare's "Other Race Plays"', Shakespeare Association of America 47th Annual Meeting, Washington DC, 19 April 2019. Available at https://youtu.be/szUlxHjUCOg?t=2589.

25. For this history, see Anthony Grafton and Lisa Jardine, *From Humanism to the Humanities: The Institutionalizing of the Liberal Arts in Fifteenth- and Sixteenth-Century Europe* (Cambridge, MA: Harvard University Press, 1986).

26. Hannah Arendt, 'Postscript', in *Eichmann in Jerusalem: A Report on the Banality of Evil* (New York: Penguin Books, [1963] 1977), 287.

27. Ibid., 287–8.

28. Prosser, *Hamlet and Revenge*, 236; Kastan, 'Forgetting Hamlet', 140–1; and Stephen Greenblatt, *Hamlet in Purgatory* (Princeton, NJ: Princeton University Press, 2001), 227.

29. Greenblatt, *Hamlet in Purgatory*, 226.
30. 'Take This Hammer', produced by KQED (National Educational Television [NET]), first aired February 4, 1964. < https://diva.sfsu.edu/bundles/187041> (accessed January 3, 2020).
31. Ibid., 40:3–43:48.

CHAPTER ELEVEN

'The Blank of What He Was'

Dryden, Newton, and the Discipline of Shakespeare's White People

JUSTIN P. SHAW

Unlike in Shakespeare's *Antony and Cleopatra*, John Dryden's *All for Love* treads into dangerous territory when it has Antony's white Roman wife publicly confront the Black Egyptian queen. 'Is all perfection confined to her?' asks Cleopatra of Octavia (3.1.402–3).[1] Dryden's method in revising Shakespeare is invested in the perfection of Shakespeare's white characters. For England's first Poet Laureate, the project of revising Shakespeare to suit the tastes of his modern audience involved refining the corruptible whiteness of Shakespeare's characters. Dryden's pioneering of what might be called Shakespearean nationalism, or England's cultural dependence on Shakespeare to fashion a racialized litmus test for civility and exceptionalism, is defined and augmented by both the expanding transatlantic slave trade and rising influence of the Royal Society in the late-17th Century. This push in the English Restoration to perfect whiteness as a science to cohere or confine racial power depends on melancholy and anxiety about backsliding into a political, intellectual and racial obsolescence that Dryden's tragedy, *All for Love*, calls blankness. In the two hundred years following this play's first production, the legibility of *Antony and Cleopatra* and its dynamic representation of racial difference was eclipsed such that virtually all Shakespeare on English and American stages was influenced by Dryden's Shakespeare. Thus this Shakespeare – indeed our Shakespeare – became inescapably white.

In his first publication for *Philosophical Transactions*, the journal for the Royal Society, a young Isaac Newton challenged the orthodoxy and sparked debate that would last for decades on the theory for the production of light and colour.[2] The essay and its sequels most famously outline his work with prisms but is also invested in the reproduction and superiority of the colour white. In his experiment, he finds that the quality of the colour white is 'the most surprising and wonderful composition' and that 'the usual colour of Light' is 'entirely and perfectly white', much like that of the Sun, which illuminates and gives life. For Newton, 'whiteness is most perfect' when it is physically separated from other colours, especially from black.³ As scientific language was often employed to justify racial norms, Newton's ideas about colour and light could thus be employed to portray whiteness as the superior norm, as something desirable, illuminating, and fragile to be protected.

Four years after Newton's original essay appeared, fellow Royal Society member John Dryden produced the play *All for Love, or the World Well Lost* (1676), the most successful of the stream of his Shakespeare rehabilitations in the late seventeenth century.⁴ While the play is based on *Antony and Cleopatra*, Dryden makes clear that his take is not simply a footnote to the former. Instead, he attempts to improve Shakespeare by adapting emergent ideas about light and colour to form the theoretical basis for his theatrical representations of political allegiance and racial betrayal. Leaning on Newton's work, Dryden crafts a play that examines the efficacy of whiteness as a matter of racial and scientific perfection. However, the play undermines its efforts to curate social power in such a white supremacy in that it projects that whiteness is in constant need of discipline and surveillance. Ever on the verge of insignificance, whiteness risks becoming not Black but blank. Here on the Restoration stage, the racist concern of degeneration is not the Renaissance anxiety of Shakespeare's white people 'turning Turk', but is rather represented in Dryden's struggle to reify Shakespeare's white people, to use Newton's words, as 'entirely and perfectly white'.

All for Love experiments with solutions to the fragility of the ever-evolving category of whiteness in early modern England. In the climate of imperialism and radical political change accumulating in the 1660s–1680s, the fragility of a stable English racial identity was being laid bare such that the notion of white was becoming blank. Dryden provides his fraught solution to the problem by appropriating Shakespeare as a means to reaffirm the supremacy of the monarchy and of a supposedly incorrigible white race. However, he resists adapting Shakespearewholesale. In his essay, *Of Dramatick Poesie* (1668), he elevates himself above the more 'naturally learn'd' Bard and describes the scope of *Antony and Cleopatra* as too broad to successfully assert the authority and hegemony of a coherent Englishness.⁵ As such, *All for Love* emerges as Dryden's attempt to correct what he sees as Shakespeare's insufficient representation of whiteness. In his most obvious correction to the earlier play, Dryden places Shakespeare into a prism, confining or regularizing the expansive earlier drama into the three classical unities. This move imagines a fantasy of whiteness that is equally confined or disciplined and thus guarded against the anxieties of fragility. Much like how Newton's experiment employs a prism to produce an extremely focused ray of white light, the play aims to project a highly focused representation of white racial power for its audience. Put simply, Dryden's tragedy of the doomed lovers suggests that Shakespeare's white characters are not white enough – a notion that reveals a fissure in the very notion of a stable, secure and centralized white identity.

The earlier *Antony and Cleopatra* functions for Dryden, not as sacred, but as a blank canvas available for a refined vision of white English identity in line with the refined tastes of the Restoration. As he revises Shakespeare, he demonstrates a new conduct of whiteness that exposes the problem of blankness. The play both introduces new characters and magnifies the melancholic and erratic behaviour of familiar ones. Often these characters discipline each other under the guide of love and duty. In one of her opening speeches, Cleopatra herself laments that 'Antony is lost' (2.1.11). What Dryden's Antony risks is not simply becoming Black – or what Shakespeare's audiences might have termed 'turning Turk' – but rather becoming blank, which is to say being insufficiently white, a potential race traitor. Consider also Ventidius, a new addition, who criticizes Antony and nostalgically reflects upon how Cleopatra's influence has made him 'the blank of what he was' (1.1.173). While for contemporaneous writers like John Locke, the term 'blank' might have connoted both 'empty' and 'impressionable', Dryden delves further, using Shakespeare's well-studied linking of Egypt with Blackness, and connects blankness to Blackness, weakness, inferiority and corruption.[6] Dryden ennobles whiteness in his play as superior to and distinct from the relative blankness of the undisciplined white people both in Shakespeare's play as well as in his own.

Writing about Shakespeare's play, Arthur L. Little, Jr. writes, 'England's nostalgia for an imperial Rome also tells a story . . . about Antony's lost racial whiteness.'[7] What was true in Shakespeare's time is even more evident in Dryden's. Fifty years after Shakespeare's death, this imperial nostalgia had evolved into a colonial promise that was being exercised with force across the Atlantic with that same racial story at its core, here mapped out across characters in the ancient Mediterranean. While he claims whiteness is the perfection of all colours, and set apart from all else, Newton also views whiteness as the 'confused aggregate' of colour as well, perfected by its relation to and purity among the others.[8] This reflects the tenuous system emerging in the Atlantic where England was defined in relation to and set apart from its colonies, or of the monarch who was both human and divine, a member of and superior to the people. For Newton, white is colour, but also colour without corruption and dilution. Dryden tests this theory of the 'confused aggregate' in the play through the relationship of Rome to Egypt and Caesar to everyone else. But while Shakespeare negotiates these dynamics through visible bodies on the stage, Dryden sees whiteness as a system that organizes and governs all bodies, spaces and relations in the play. Rather than linger on Antony's lost whiteness, *All for Love* conflates Black Egyptians with blank Romans who unsuccessfully contest an inevitable submission to the dominating and disembodied force of white racial power circulating around an almost mythical sovereign. Free from the corruption of bodies and actors, the power of whiteness in the play operates almost entirely through nostalgia and promise, complicating the notion of blankness and making whiteness even more insidious.

Because whiteness is obsessed with and often defined by Blackness, Dryden's play cannot simply be said to be about whiteness. His interest in colour comes not just from studying Newton but also his other colleague Robert Boyle, who was a much more established theorist at the time. Boyle dedicates one third of his *Experiments and Considerations touching Colours* (1664) to a study of skin colour where he assumes scientific authority in longstanding debates about darkness and lightness.[9] The dark/light binary constructs the colonial boundaries of the 'known', as Kim F. Hall has argued, and is especially pertinent for a late Restoration play that reflects empirical enterprise of not just separating the 'unknown' – in some ways Egypt, but in other ways Caesar, too – from the 'known' but rather subsuming one into the other.[10] In Dryden's play, Roman whiteness is an unseen inevitability for the literal and metaphorical dark Egypt, conflating both what is known and unknown about racial identification. The science of *All for Love*, then, explores how darkness entangles lightness, literally, and how blankness gets conflated with Blackness.

Writing before Newton, Boyle intentionally uses science to make assumptions about racial difference. These ideas also find a home on Dryden's stage. Understood as antithetical to whiteness, Blackness for Boyle is only a 'particular kind of Texture' that reflects like 'as it were Dead'.[11] But, as if anticipating Ventidius's claim to have 'wash'd an *Aethiope*' (2.1.226), Boyle asserts, somewhat theatrically, that 'by a Change of Position in the Parts, a Body that is not White, may be made White'.[12] Eliding connotations of 'flesh' and 'object' into 'Body', Boyle provides the blueprint for what Dryden imagines as 'fair hands' and 'white arms' for the discursively Black and 'tawny' Cleopatra (2.1.223; 3.1.1). Shakespeare's Cleopatra, in whose 'infinite variety' was with 'Phoebus' amorous pinches black', is indicative of what Boyle calls 'a Body that is not White' (2.2.277; 1.5.33).[13] But on Dryden's stage, this characterization is neutralized and aggressively transformed into a lustrous white object that reproduces the 'mythical norm' of white racial power. But Boyle cautions that, 'by a Slight change of the Texture of its Surface, a White Body may be Depriv'd of its Whiteness'.[14] As with Newton's unstable attempt at reproducing light through a prism, Boyle's notion of whitening must attend to its own fragility and vulnerability to change. While it may seem that Dryden imagines a fully white Cleopatra, 'arms' and 'hands' are merely appendages, particularities that reflect Boyle's concern about the precarity and malleability of an already fragile whiteness. *All for Love* thus dramatizes this science of perfected whiteness that repeatedly undermines itself by presenting changeable white bodies 'depriv'd of whiteness', and susceptible to their own undoing.

In his renovation of Shakespeare's play, Dryden experiments with a 'perfect whiteness' that is protected from and succumbs to the realities of its own vulnerability. As mentioned, he limits the vastness of Shakespeare's play by confining it to the classical unities. This formal disciplining of the earlier drama anticipates a disciplining of categories of racial difference. The racial power exhibited by whiteness in *Antony and Cleopatra* is perfected against its own fragility and elusiveness in *All for Love*. In addition to this disciplining, Dryden excises Caesar from the action of the play entirely. He becomes an agent of power and surveillance to which the whole play must respond. By removing Caesar, Dryden excuses whiteness from both the possibility of encountering Blackness and from the risk of blankness – both being the failures of Shakespeare's Antony. But Caesar is named and remembered in the play; he is invisible, not imaginary. His reality presupposes the presence of whiteness to those who feel its pressure, rendering it and him ultimately and inevitably examinable. Moreover, in an era when female actors drove theatrical profits, the play stages a confrontation unseen in Shakespeare between Octavia and Cleopatra. In making such an addition, it is no longer Caesar but rather Octavia, his 'Ambassadress', who becomes the most visible arbitrator of 'perfect whiteness' and the most immediate harbinger of Black loss in the play (3.1.272).

While Mary Nyquist has considered *All for Love* a domestic tragedy about a household and the internal 'moral crisis' of its 'hero', Antony, we must remember that the domestic is a political sphere in which the more public discourses of science, race and racism are embedded.[15] Joyce Green MacDonald argues that the 'consistently organized' play binds together notions of propriety and impropriety with nation and region and sexuality. I would suggest further that the play doesn't just approach a racial consciousness; its success in the period fuels a national and colonial consciousness that interweaves sexuality with racial concerns that imagined whiteness at its centre.[16] The late Charles W. Mills acknowledges that white supremacy is 'the unnamed political system' that has shaped the modern world.[17] The play is not simply 'all for love' but is embedded in debates about politics, science and early modern notions of racial difference. It is precisely because of this that Dryden's domestic-appearing tragedy about love cannot be relegated safely to the realm of the domestic and private. The division itself into such spheres assumes the presence and operation of a larger political system.

In the 1670s, Dryden had models besides Shakespeare on which he could rely for his grand dramatic experiment. Most notably was Charles Sedley's *Antony and Cleopatra*, produced earlier in 1676 as a theatrical veneration of English republicanism.[18] By challenging Shakespeare through Sedley, Dryden can attempt to disassociate white power from Caesar's body and refashion that power as a force, a system, a relation whereby all actors are made into docile bodies, constituents and participants. Dryden whitewashes all his characters, making them beneficiaries of Caesar's power and influence, even if they seek to resist it. As Mills writes, 'All whites are *beneficiaries* of the Contract, though some whites are not *signatories* to it.'[19] Thus, while a 'blank' Antony calls attention to the inconsistency of a white identity, it also renders him white and vulnerable to its influence. The play renders Romanness, or whiteness, for Antony, Cleopatra and their allies, on a spectrum from innate to inevitable. Moreover, as passive beneficiaries of the racial contract structuring the play, Dryden's characters undermine any hope in the success of republicanism or democracy over absolutism. Contributing to debates in the 1670s about the fragile and contested authority of the English monarchy, *All for Love* presents a fantasy where any rebellion is fruitless, disloyalty is a farce, and all subjects are domesticated under one omnipotent force.

The subtitle of Dryden's play, *The World Well Lost*, indicates both a state of being and a problem needing correction. Using Shakespeare as a foundation, Dryden's solution to this problem of white betrayal and fragility is found in fashioning Shakespeare's characters and play into a 'perfect whiteness' fit for the modern world. Like many dramatists and readers in the Restoration, Dryden's relationship to Shakespeare was tenuous and evolving. The generation of spectators who would have experienced *Antony and Cleopatra* first-hand was coming to an end. More likely, by Dryden's time, people of a certain class had read the play in one of the Folios, where *Antony and Cleopatra* had first appeared in print in 1623. By the Restoration, as Tiffany Stern notes, 'all Shakespeare was adapted Shakespeare'. As audiences only indirectly knew Shakespeare through writers like Dryden, the adapters were free to 'tame and regularize' the originals into current ideologies, contexts and formats.[20] Although Dryden turned away from Shakespeare in 1679 with his version of *Troilus and Cressida*, I would suggest that the earlier *All for Love* initiates his experiment of honouring 'the beauties of [Shakespeare's] thoughts' while replacing the insufficiencies of Shakespeare's language.[21] To 'disencumber' himself from his own heroic formula and from the 'Divine *Shakespeare*', Dryden claims that 'Words and Phrases must of necessity receive a Change in succeeding Ages'. Of his own play, he writes that, 'The Fabrick of the Play is regular enough, as to the inferior parts of it; and the Unities of Time, Place and Action, more exactly observ'd, than, perhaps, the English Theatre requires.'[22]

By regularizing of the 'fabric of the play', Dryden responds to and anticipates a 'change in succeeding Ages' where whiteness reflects the formal unity of the play's poetry and provides a basis for the structure of the drama itself. This regularizing, or 'taming' is a response to what sociologist Robin DiAngelo describes as white fragility, or the state in which any amount of 'racial stress' becomes intolerable, triggering a set of defensive moves to reconstitute a state of 'white racial equilibrium'.[23] Renovating Shakespeare requires some addition and subtraction, and Dryden does this by domesticating a political tragedy and eliminating the predominant marker of race, Blackness. His play seeks to counteract fragility by removing Octavius and thus the possibility of a corrosive inter-racial encounter between the truest Roman and Africans. White supremacy is protected and reaffirmed when it does not have to encounter Blackness, nor come to terms with its own raced-ness. Egypt, to this end, becomes a pseudo-African liminal space where Roman bodies can invade and occupy without fear of real contact with Africa. Moreover, when Cleopatra's body is whitened, Roman characters like Octavia and Dolabella, and dissenters like Ventidius and Antony, can interact with 'real' Black bodies without fear of corruption.

Dryden's renovation of Shakespeare might be understood in terms of what George Yancy refers to as 'suturing' which comes from the Latin word *sutura*, meaning a 'seam' or a 'sewing together', and is 'the process whereby whites install forms of closure, forms of protection from counter-white axiological and embodied iterations, epistemic fissure and white normative disruption. . . . the concept of suture functions as a site of keeping pure, preserving what is unsullied'.[24] By regularizing the formal structure of the play, and attempting to re-order Shakespeare's bodies, Dryden invests in a process of suturing. It is the mechanism for Dryden's project of enforcing a fantasy of solidarity and cohesion against realities, histories and anxieties of white fragility. While he does look backward for models, Dryden finds that Shakespeare's characters are not white enough, and Sedley's characters are not disciplined royal subjects. He thus sews together the 'fabric of the play' to preserve and keep pure an idealized whiteness – not unlike what Newton does in his condensed dark room – and to illuminate a politicized racial way of being in the world.

All for Love demonstrates how white fragility enforces one manifestation of whiteness over another and then sustains the anxious positioning of white people between fidelity to either collective identity or individual autonomy. This plays out between Caesar, who exists in the play merely as an idea – but one to which all characters must submit and around which they circulate – and Antony, who acknowledges his Romanness but struggles with this complete submission to the collective. Shakespeare's play also dramatizes a conflict between Caesar and Antony, but there, Caesar is a character seen moving and speaking on the stage. There is nothing different between the two other than behaviour and ideology, perhaps. But

Dryden takes the idea further. By removing Caesar from the stage but not necessarily the play, the locus of white racial power manifests differently from what Shakespeare allows. Whiteness, in the later text, becomes a matter not just about skin colour, or physiology, but rather a relationship of power and surveillance negotiated between bodies and systems, individuals and collectives.

The fact of surveillance by the absent but virtually omnipotent Octavius, and later by his physical envoy, Octavia, effectively racializes every single character on stage as Black or blank, which, to stretch the Lockean connotations of blank as 'impressionable' and 'empty', here comes to mean 'available for surveillance'. What is meant by 'all for love' subsumes or subordinates 'all' individuals into a collective principle and the disciplining power of Caesar, and of whiteness. The play examines the parameters of whiteness itself through the surveillance of Blackness and blankness. As Simone Browne argues, surveillance is an integral part of the fact and disciplining of Black life and of anti-Blackness.[25] Surveillance creates whiteness as much as it marks out what whiteness is not. Blankness in this play becomes a racial marker indicating the inaccessibility of whiteness and the shift from Roman sociality to Egyptian social death. Whiteness tends to escape surveillance by removing itself from the purview of race, thus becoming valorised in its presumed absence.

Boyle and Newton both, ultimately, understand whiteness as exceptional because it is the absence of colour. Therefore, it escapes examinability in their science. But none of this is consistent in Dryden's play. The naming, memory and anticipation of Caesar conflicts with Dryden's intention of Caesar as purely an idea. He is examinable even in his absence. Little argues that to name or 'narrativize' whiteness, as the characters do, is 'to erase it'.[26] Dryden attempts to prevent this loss or erasure by regularizing the design of the play, by unmarking Caesar's whiteness, by turning away from the subject of racial difference and distributing racial sameness throughout the 'fabric of the play'. Unlike Shakespeare, his white people are made to confront what appears to them as other white people. Dryden's carefully structured Restoration tragedy intends to be all about love but must necessarily be all about racial discipline.

When Ventidius describes Caesar as having 'all the World, / And, at his back, Nations come pouring in, / To fill the gaps' Antony has made, he illustrates how whiteness as a racial category is inherently fragile and fears its own vulnerability (3.1.77–9). Dryden's solution to the problem DiAngelo outlines comes in the form of a seemingly omnipotent Caesar coming to 'pour in' and 'fill the gaps', to make whiteness less susceptible to early modern racial stress. But these gaps are caused neither by interactions with Black people nor, in the play, Egyptians. Ventidius compares Caesar's force with Antony's reliance on 'one poor Town / And of *Aegyptians*' (3.1.76–7). Antony 'made' the gaps by turning away from his responsibilities to Rome, and as such, complicates what DiAngelo sees as 'racial stress' or 'interruptions to the racially familiar'.[27] Moreover, Newton does not necessarily say that Blackness corrupts white light. In fact, in his experiment, whiteness *needs* Blackness to reflect most fully. For 'the composition of whiteness to be perfect, care must be taken' to protect the lens from the corrupting exposure of other colours.[28] Thus what dilutes the experience of true light is presence of adjacent colours, things closer to the more 'perfect Whiteness'. The problem is local.

Blackness is always marked for scientific and political examination, and, as Boyle and Newton have it, proves the authority of whiteness over it. Taking up these ideas, Dryden conveys the disciplining power of whiteness through both the relative darkness or blankness of Antony and the unmarkedness of Caesar. As the Epilogue of the play states, 'Let Caesar's Pow'r the Mens ambition move', the focus is less on Caesar than it is on his power (l. 22). Ambition moves nothing; imperial power does. In a play that resists productive action for fear of exposing the vulnerability of whiteness, Caesar promises to move ambition and give the characters purpose beyond themselves. Like Newton's white light, Dryden's enigmatic version of Caesar represents a purified aggregation of all other characters physically and visually within the play, on stage. As power is tied up with knowledge, he can know and be known yet be invisible and unheard. Caesar is the Rome that is absent from the setting of the play and a representation of how whiteness operates in the abstract, excusing itself from the bounds and consequences of race. Race, in this way, is conveniently attached to Blackness and Black bodies, which are in turn marked as objects of white consumption. Dryden subjects all the characters and spaces of the play to the authority, the 'unnamed political system', of Caesar surrounding the play.

Dryden's characters are consumed with anxieties about the inevitable push toward empire, and fantasies about racial solidarity, but their attempts at resistance are rendered null at the outset. Early in the play, the priest Serapion explains how, regardless of what Antony does, Egypt is 'doom'd' to become a Roman province, whether he 'be vanquished, / Or make his peace' (1.1.63–4). As the entirety of the play takes place at court in Alexandria, Egypt appears as a nostalgic colony that itself could be the 'world well lost' indicated by the play's subtitle. Blackness is forced into a blank past, 'doom'd' to Roman and white rewriting just as much as Shakespeare is subject to Dryden's rewriting. Serapion's lamentation here further suggests that rebellion or resistance against Rome is futile since everything in the play is, even here at the beginning, subsumed into or under the surveillance of Roman authority. In the restricted space of the stage where the drama is confined to one setting and a cast of characters who are all supposedly factions of the same sort, there is nothing against which the characters can rebel or resist effectively. Dryden relegates any sense of rebellion against Rome to the realm of fantasy and nostalgia, or even a melancholic pathology, of the Shakespearean past rather than the present. He even removes the names of the potential rebels from the title of the play, opting instead for a focus on 'love', the engrossing concept to which all must strive. After all, who could possibly rebel against love?

Love is rhetorically positioned against loss both in the title and in the main plot of the drama, which depicts the final day in the lives of Cleopatra VII and Mark Antony. However, where Shakespeare covers several years of the torrid romance between the two figures, Dryden focuses on the melancholic final day of their lives, a day where loss seems to supersede and/or govern love. Moreover, love – or fidelity – also figures as the primary aspirational object in the play and is necessarily associated with whiteness. Thus, as all the characters must contend with their inevitable movement toward Rome and toward whiteness, they are struggling with a compulsion for political and racial fidelity. This movement is fraught, however, because it is always informed by a lament, a counterpoint that pulls away from such forced fidelity and seeks comfort in the 'world well lost'. This is where the drama of

Dryden's play manifests. Antony begins the play, not sailing the Mediterranean, but rather quarantined within Isis' temple, hiding from Cleopatra, making his 'Heart a Prey to Black despair' (1.1.60–1). By constructing Egypt as 'doom'd' and as the 'world well lost', each of the characters positioned within that space – including Octavia, temporarily – becomes Black and lost. Lostness here could mean blankness, which then could mean a loss of fidelity, Antony's 'Black despair'. As white characters spend time in Egypt, Dryden constructs that time spent as time lost, as racial loss and marginality. Characters like Antony are no longer Roman but are also not fully Black, or Egyptian; they are blank or lost, which approximates the loss that actual Black characters like Cleopatra and her Egyptian subjects experience throughout the play. Black loss, then, is the backdrop against which – or Newtonian prism through which – white fantasies of power are exercised on Dryden's stage.

Extending what Shakespeare began, Dryden constructs his Egypt as an eroding African space at the precipice of white conquest and Roman assimilation. Antony explains to Ventidius, who replaces Enobarbus in some ways, that accepting Cleopatra's bracelet won't corrupt him: 'You fear too soon. / I'm constant to myself: I know my strength; / And yet she shall not think me barbarous neither, / Born in the depths of *Afric*: I'm a *Roman*, / Bred to the rules of soft humanity' (1.1.228–32). Where Antony draws contrasts between birth and breeding, and depth and height here, he also aligns himself with constructions of Roman civility, constancy, and humanity against ideas surrounding the baseness of an Africanized Egypt. Francesca T. Royster has pointed out how England's developing racial identity has long depended on a tense relationship to its barbaric past.[29] Antony's claim plays into centuries of racist stereotypes, as Carol Mejia LaPerle reminds us, about migrant Roma masquerading as the more 'lawful race' of Egyptians, or ethnic and religious minorities disguised and passing as Protestant English subjects.[30] In response, Ventidius complains that the whole world, that consists of '*Europe, Africk, Asia*', has been 'put in balance' and is 'weigh'd down by one light worthless Woman!' He claims that Antony has given the world away 'to none but wasteful hands' (1.1.369–75). Ventidius, who is described in terms of 'the plainness, fierceness, rugged virtue / Of an old true-stamped *Roman*', does not wish to see a balanced world, but rather Antony on top of that world (1.1.107–8). Neither does Newton – who sees whiteness as the transcendent 'aggregate' of colour – find a balance of colours useful.

Antony's rejection of and flight from Rome and whiteness may in fact work against his intentions. He is not any less 'white' because of his ambivalent allegiance to Egypt because, as Dryden portrays, this flight from Rome is well within the privilege of his native Romanness. Shannon Sullivan explains that 'white people's flight from their whiteness is not necessarily the opposite of white narcissism. It instead tends to be another manifestation of it', and that assuming a distance from racial identification is a key point of white privilege. She terms it 'ontological expansiveness' where 'good white people' unconsciously imagine themselves free to invade or interrupt nonwhite spaces.[31] In occupying and conquering both the space of Egypt and the body of its queen, Antony has simply done what Julius Caesar had done before him and what Caesar will do after. Antony reminds Cleopatra of this when he explains how he saw her in Egypt where Caesar had first seen her, and 'stept in' with 'a greedy hand' to 'enjoy' her (2.1.267–71). Hoping to assuage

Antony's anxiety, Cleopatra then counters this narrative to explain how Caesar only 'possess'd [her] Person' and Antony possesses her love (2.1.352–5).

The terms 'ontological expansiveness' and 'white fragility' may be too passive to describe the phenomena around Antony and Cleopatra in *All for Love*. The progressive erasure of Cleopatra, for example, continues through the end of the play when, after she dies, Charmion explains that she was 'the last of her great Race' (5.1.504–5). This could point to the historical end of a lineage of Egyptian monarchs, and to the success of the anti-Black project of Roman domination and white supremacy in the tragedy. Dryden's dramatic experiment appears to be a matter of direct aggression against Black bodies and spaces, an act of violence that renders both them and their allies insignificant and blank. Historian Carol Anderson names this phenomenon 'white rage', a phenomenon triggered not just by Black presence, but by 'blackness with ambition'.[32] White rage is present in every historical era of the Western tradition as it works against advancement, modernity, and progress even as whiteness imagines itself invested in these activities. *All for Love* shows how white rage not only responds to Black ambition but to white approximations and support of Black ambition. Just as white light both cancels out and subsumes darkness in Newton's experiment, white rage challenges anything that does not end in Black loss, or blankness. By centring the play in Egypt, Rome does not completely disappear, but moves into the background. The space and characters of what was Shakespeare's play become racially white and politically Roman. For Dryden, both Antony's racial fluctuations and Cleopatra's political ambitions are not only met with rage but are constructed as 'blank'.

White rage and fragility operate in tandem. One is a manifestation, or perhaps an instigator, of the other. Ian Smith argues that early modern English writers increasingly sought to displace classical rhetoric of barbarity – originally attributed to them and their ancestors – onto racialized and ethnic others.[33] Likewise, Elliott Visconsi suggests that intellectuals like Dryden understood literature to counteract native barbarism and 'saw the Restoration as a liberating remedy for the lawless and sullen qualities of the English people'.[34] It is impossible to separate this uncertainty or fear and fragility occurring within the category of whiteness from acts of violence directed against darker skinned people in Africa and the Americas. But Dryden also uses the anxiety around being white – between histories of barbarity, present realities of betrayal, and the mysteries of forthcoming modernity – to license acts of violence that enforce certain performances of whiteness in early modern England. Defending the monarchy in his dedicatory letter to the Earl of Danby, Dryden writes, 'if he be a true Englishmen, he must at the same time be fir'd with Indignation, and revenge himself as he can on the Disturbers of his Country'.[35] Thus, enforcing white solidarity against 'Disturbers' like Antony is entirely dependent on anxiety about white racial collapse.

Dryden's contribution to the stage history of *Antony and Cleopatra* offers a compelling critique of the white people in the Shakespeare play. However 'regularized' Dryden envisions his play, he cannot completely erase the Blackness of Egypt and of Cleopatra. He may actually highlight its efficacy and resilience by centring so much of his play on Black spaces and bodies. Newton's white light could not permanently get rid of darkness, and in fact required it to make sense of the other colours. Mills suggests that 'the hypocrisy of the racial polity is most transparent to its victims'.[36] Dryden brings the false conflict between 'good whites' and 'bad whites' to the forefront while rendering racial power systemic and unseen. By removing Caesar, the white power evident in Shakespeare becomes invisible and dispersed among those active participants and passive beneficiaries of the racial contract. However, in rendering Antony blank, the play seems to offer an ironic counter-reading that makes the operations of white racial power transparent and vulnerable to those it most seeks to erase.

NOTES

My thanks to Patricia Cahill, George Yancy, Paul Kelleher, and Arthur L. Little, Jr. for generous feedback on early drafts of this essay, and to my former students at Emory for encouraging me to revisit Isaac Newton's work. Research for this essay was made possible with funding from the James Weldon Johnson Institute for the Study of Race and Difference at Emory University.

1. All references to the play and prefatory material refer to *All for Love, or The World Well Lost*, in *The Works of John Dryden*, vol. XIII, ed. Maximillian E. Novak, et al. (Berkeley: University of California Press, 1984), 1–111.
2. Isaac Newton, 'A Letter of Mr. Isaac Newton, Professor of the Mathematicks in the University of Cambridge; Containing His New Theory about Light and Colors'. *Philosophical Transactions* 6 (1671-2): 3075–87. Newton uses the term 'perfect Whiteness' no fewer than ten times in the later *Opticks* (1704). He was elected to the Royal Society in 1672; Dryden in 1663, but only remained a member for a short period.
3. Ibid., 3083, 3086.
4. John Dryden, *All for Love, or The World Well Lost*, in *The Works of John Dryden*, Volume XIII, 1–111, ed. Maximillian E. Novak, et al. (Berkeley: University of California Press, 1984).
5. John Dryden, *Of Dramatick Poesie, An Essay* (London: Henry Herringman, 1668), 47.
6. Locke, I.3.25, II.1.37. Locke used the term 'blank' as such in early drafts of the *Essay Concerning Human Understanding* where it became 'white' in the 1689 first edition. It served as a generalized ethnic term for Englishmen, while blank, 'white paper' signified a child's 'yet unprejudiced understanding'. For more on Locke, see Gary Taylor, *Buying Whiteness: Race, Culture, and Identity from Columbus to Hip Hop* (New York: Palgrave Macmillan, 2005), 314–16.
7. Arthur L. Little, Jr., *Shakespeare Jungle Fever: Nation-Imperial Re-Visions of Race, Rape, and Sacrifice* (Palo Alto, CA: Stanford University Press, 2000), 122.
8. Newton, 'A Letter', 3083.
9. Robert Boyle, *Experiments and Considerations Touching Colours* (London: Henry Herringman, 1664), 151–67.
10. Kim F. Hall, *Things of Darkness: Economies of Race and Gender in Early Modern England* (Ithaca, NY: Cornell University Press, 1995), 2–10, 48.
11. Boyle, *Experiments*, 118.
12. Ibid., 115.

13. William Shakespeare, *The Tragedy of Antony and Cleopatra*, ed. Michael Neill (New York: Oxford University Press, 1994).
14. Boyle, *Experiments*, 115.
15. Mary Nyquist, '"Profuse, proud Cleopatra": "Barbarism" and Female Rule in Early Modern English Republicanism', *Women's Studies: An Interdisciplinary Journal* 24.1–2 (1994): 109.
16. Joyce Green MacDonald, *Women and Race in Early Modern Texts* (Cambridge: Cambridge University Press, 2002), 48–9.
17. Charles W. Mills, *The Racial Contract* (Ithaca, NY: Cornell University Press, 1997), 1.
18. Nyquist, "Profuse, proud Cleopatra", 108.
19. Mills, *Racial Contract*, 11.
20. Tiffany Stern, 'Shakespeare in Drama', in *Shakespeare in the Eighteenth Century*, ed. Fiona Ritchie and Peter Sabor, 141–59 (Cambridge: Cambridge University Press, 2012), 142.
21. See Maximillian Novak, 'Commentary', in *Works*, 370.
22. Dryden, *All for Love*, 18, 10.
23. Robin DiAngelo, *White Fragility: Why It's So Hard for White People to Talk About Racism* (Boston: Beacon Press, 2018), 103.
24. George Yancy, 'Introduction: Un-Sutured', in *White Self-Criticality beyond Anti-Racism: How Does It Feel to be a White Problem?*, ed. George Yancy, xi–xxvii (Lanham, MD: Lexington Books, 2015), xv–xvi.
25. Simone Browne, *Dark Matters: On the Surveillance of Blackness* (Durham, NC: Duke University Press, 2015), 7–10.
26. Little, *Shakespeare Jungle Fever*, 123.
27. DiAngelo, *White Fragility*, 103.
28. Newton, 'A Letter', 3086.
29. Francesca T. Royster, *Becoming Cleopatra: The Shifting Image of an Icon* (New York: Palgrave Macmillan, 2003), 45.
30. Carol Mejia LaPerle, 'An Unlawful Race: Shakespeare's Cleopatra and the Crimes of Early Modern Gypsies'. *Shakespeare* 13.3 (2017): 232.
31. Shannon Sullivan, *Good White People: The Problem with Middle-Class White Anti-Racism* (Albany, NY: SUNY Press, 2014), 145, 20.
32. Carol Anderson, *White Rage: The Unspoken Truth of Our Racial Divide* (New York: Bloomsbury, 2016), 3.
33. Ian Smith, *Race and Rhetoric in the Renaissance: Barbarian Errors* (New York: Palgrave Macmillan, 2009), 14.
34. Elliott Visconsi, *Lines of Equity: Literature and the Origins of Law in Later Stuart Literature* (Ithaca, NY: Cornell University Press, 2008), 18.
35. Dryden, *All for Love*, 8.
36. Mills, *Racial Contract*, 110.

PART TWO

White People's Shakespeare

CHAPTER TWELVE

'I Saw Them in My Visage'

Whiteness, Early Modern Race Studies, and Me

MARGO HENDRICKS

Johannesburg South Africa
August 1996
Dear William,
1996 was my first, and, as of this epistolary essay, only visit to Africa's continent. It was a historic moment for me, coming two years after Nelson Mandela's election to the presidency. However, it took a politically charged question about Shakespeare from a Black South African student to set into motion most of the reflections I've voiced over my career. It was a simple query: given the uses to which Shakespearean texts have functioned as an imperialist/colonialist weapon, why would (or should) Black people engage with Shakespeare? What could a tool of settler colonizers and imperialists have to say to the millions and millions of non-white people across the globe?

So much of who you are, William Shakespeare, despite being quite dead, and what you wrote are instrumental to the celebration of whiteness and the advancement of an ideology of white supremacy. Ah, sweet William, your texts have been used to 'charm [our] eyes against' the questions that surface. As we, the Black American Shakespeareans present in Johannesburg (Professor Kim Hall, Professor Arthur Little and myself), endeavoured to answer 'why Shakespeare' we recognized our complicated relationship with whiteness and white supremacy by our political and professional positions within Shakespeare studies. Had you been there, you would have listened as we spoke of the history of white supremacist attitudes about Black Americans and Shakespearean theatrical performances. Perhaps you might have been moved as we reflected on the long history of white privilege that denies non-whites access to literacy in the United States.

The student questioned the notion of 'universality', long attendant on the cloak of whiteness that wraps your creativity – an expectation about a person's relationship, historical, individual and cultural, to a literary icon. However, as the student's query suggested, there is a lethal dichotomy in the idea of Shakespearean universality. Unstated in the belief in Shakespeare's universality is an assumption about a shared culture; that 'universal Shakespeare' overrides all other cultural iterations. The

South African student's question highlighted an implicit code of awareness that certain groups cannot assume de facto, despite Shakespeare's much-touted universality. That awareness is the link between universality, male 'genius', and 'whiteness'. What is more striking are the lengths cultural institutions have gone to hide their role in fostering what Arthur L. Little, Jr. describes as 'the ideologies and hegemonies that often insist on defining and assessing the worth of people of colour through the prism of race, press[ing] even more arduously (and at times, religiously) to define white peoples as nonraced or, more tacitly and chillingly, as "the human race itself"'.[1]

In unexpected ways, reading, teaching and writing about your texts created a dissonant chord. This jarring refrain occluded the possibility of seeing whiteness as racial and aligned with black, brown, yellow, or red as labels to somatically mark difference among human beings. In 1996 Johannesburg, in the auditorium of the University of Witwatersrand, a Black South African student asked why should Black peoples, or any peoples of colour, study the plays and poems of William Shakespeare. What could Blacks and peoples of colour possibly glean except how perfectly situated whiteness has become as the universal signifier of humanity? If I have learned your lessons well, dearest Shakespeare, I must acknowledge the subtle deflections away from whiteness that your 'universality' enacts. I have trained countless readers and students to scour your writings for inky signs of race-making but never to search for the erasures. My research attended to the state of *race* and the presence of the 'black body' as you wrote them, as your cultural peers wrote them, and as your world covered itself in whiteness to instantiate a global and hegemonic economic system.

Seattle, Washington
April 2011
Dearest Will,
'Parting is such sweet sorrow.' You wrote these words and set them in one of the most dangerous white-centric plays in your corpus, *Romeo and Juliet*. The only good that came of this troubling depiction of 'love' is that a twentieth-century filmmaker, Baz Luhrmann, made it palatable for me. I whisper these words to you now as I reflect on a past decision to sever our relationship. The place was Seattle, Washington. The event, the annual gathering of your academic acolytes, aka the Shakespeare Association of America. The year, 2011. My words:

> *What if the black scholars working within Shakespeare Studies and their entire corpus of writings suddenly disappeared and all traces of their existence vanished at the same time?*

The inspiration behind these words was the systemic white supremacist thinking that defined 'Shakespeare Studies'. In answer to my question, I suggested that an immediate effect would be the vanishing of significant references to 'Shakespeare and race' on Google, generating a slight dip in bibliographic citations for already over-burdened undergraduate and graduate students. However, I did observe the disappearance of the eight to ten Black American scholars whose scholarly and critical work focused on 'Shakespeare and race' was a different matter. These individuals collectively pushed for a radical reassessment of the politics of race in both Renaissance/early modern England and Shakespeare Studies. The theoretical and archival lens that these scholars deployed in their insistence on the study of 'blackness' and 'whiteness' as somatic markers of 'race' and the displacement of 'race-making' onto the non-European body (especially those of African origins) redefined a field of academic study.

But, I murmured, 'there is a disturbance in the force'. An emerging presence that is smoothing the ripples our disappeared scholars generated. It seemed the discourse on race bore an unmistakable sameness in terms of scripts or texts studied and arguments made. Yet, beneath the surface of this sameness was a problematic trend. Works celebrated as 'groundbreaking' or 'pivotal' turned away from what is best defined as a political conception of race as linked to geographic groups and skin colour and the politics of subjectivity to a more benign and diffuse notion that allowed race to be whatever 'we want' (race as 'blood' or 'social status' or lineage).

As one author wrote, the 'variability of racial ideology and experience may mean that no stable or simple account of race is available for casual theoretical application'.[2] The author then proceeds to make what I even acknowledged in my review of the book as an 'insightful, nuanced and a persuasive contribution to ongoing debates about race' but one where race functions as a metaphor for gender – a disservice to both gender studies and critical race theory.[3] Even with its limitations, the book and others like it 'heard' the call for more rigorous scholarly engagements with race in early modern English culture. And, dear Will, therein lies the problem. For the past decade, we have seen studies where race functions ornamentally in service to academic publication and career trajectories. In these instances, the use of race functions similarly to the term 'like' in everyday speech. Invoke it and, de facto, all is well. In particular, it is the focus on 'blood' and humoral theory as constitutive of race that most disturbs. Not because, at least with blood, there is inaccuracy in historical significance but because an emphasis on blood or humoral aspects allows for a devaluation of the physical body that gave materiality to race studies in Shakespeare. In addition, such thinking silently legitimates notions of socially defined hierarchies (gender and class in particular) under the guise of reading blood. At the end of that farewell to academic Shakespeare, I invoked a Black Shakespearean moment and recast Helena's words to Hermia, 'It is not friendly, 'tis not maidenly: / Our [blackness], as well as I, may chide you for it.'[4]

My initial enthusiasm ended with a nagging sense of disquiet about what goes unsaid behind this new brand of new 'race' and early modern cultural studies: an apprehension made even more complicated because the underlying premise of a number of these publications – race as 'blood' or genealogy or lineage or gender – builds on and even, in some instances, celebrate the body of work generated by our 'disappeared' Black scholars while at the same time dismissing the black or dark-skinned bodies that gave rise to that scholarship. This intriguing turn to negation (or should I say a return) has served to skew the politics of race in Shakespeare studies (and, by extension, early modern studies). What I mean by this statement is that the black body becomes a shifting literary signifier (a metaphor, if you will) rather than a historical subject in the ever-flowing articles and books that take race as the subject of their inquiry. Now that wouldn't be a problem if our Black scholars had truly disappeared. They have not, nor has the critical discussion about race that their research has engendered.

I still hadn't figured out what was needed, so I went into academic exile. It was not entirely by choice. The vagaries of being Black in academia, of being Black in Shakespeare Studies, of being a Black woman in Shakespeare Studies in academia in the twenty-first century's imperial centre of white supremacy took its toll.

In the end I was replaced by a white man.

Nevada
Early December 2020
Dear William Shakespeare,
A revised stage direction for your 'canon': *Exit stage left and stage right: 'white people'*.
Imagine a world without 'white' people, yet a diverse society. A newly graduated scholar/director discovers an obscure script written by someone named William Shakespeare. After reading the script, our director is determined to mount a production. They search for historical information on the obscure playwright and his wildly strange, and to their mind, comical text. Despite their academic background, our director quickly realizes they have no historical, epistemological, or theoretical context for the ideas depicted in the script. Their world has no social or cultural framework for the peculiar ideologies in Shakespeare's script. The notion of race as a marker of subjectivity doesn't exist in our director's societal vocabulary. More importantly, the opposition at the centre of the script, 'black' skin versus 'white' skin, would make no sense to their audience since 'whiteness' and 'white people' as signifiers of identity do not exist (which in turn means skin colour has no cultural currency). To produce Shakespeare's script on the stage, our director will have to make believable the existence of 'white' people and an entire society that defines itself in terms of a colour-based dichotomy.

So what does our brilliantly intrepid director choose to do?

Introduce Shakespeare's *Othello* to their world. The actors appear in white face except for Othello. Programme notes attempt to explain the peculiar ideas that inform the script. The staging has Desdemona declare 'I saw his visage in my mind' as a lens for the audience to imagine a world alien to them, a world of 'whiteness' that marks 'blackness' as its opposite and inferior. *Othello*'s run is a smashing success, despite voices that question the director's purpose in staging such a fantastical script. The production wins several major performance awards and, with the end of its theatrical run, the script *Othello* and its author are returned to the forgotten vaults of history to languish once more; that is, until the day a strange vessel founders on the beach where the director lives and its passengers disembark.

Late December 2020
Dear W.S.,
I write to you once again. I would love to say I empathize with Desdemona, to see beyond the colour of Othello's skin, to first whisper and then shout, 'I saw his visage in my mind.' It would be consistent with sympathetic readings of her declaration that 'love is colour-blind' and that it's only Othello's inner qualities that she sees. As

a romance fiction author (my current career), I definitely see advantages to this potential 'happily ever after' moment. As a Shakespearean, what looms large for me is the suggestive possibility that her mind can disappear Othello's 'blackness' and replace it with a colour acceptable to her world, 'whiteness'. Has Desdemona got the right of things: is the only way to mitigate the centrality of Blackness and the invisibility of whiteness in racial logic is to see its 'visage in [our] minds?'[5] That is, to pretend not to see colour. In a world construed by white supremacy,

I think not.

Evelynn Hammonds asked, 'how do you deduce the presence of a black hole? And, second, what is it like inside of a black hole?'[6] The 'existence of the black hole', she explains, 'is inferred from the fact that the visible star is in orbit and its shape is distorted in some way or it is detected by the energy emanating from the region in space around the visible star that could not be produced by the visible star alone'.[7] In physics, one is trained to be attentive to the energy and distortions generated around the visible star under scrutiny rather than merely focusing on the star itself. In premodern critical race studies, we must train ourselves to similar forms of attentiveness except instead of 'black (wholes)', it is the invisibility of whiteness, as the collection of essays in this volume illustrates, that must be subject to scrutiny. As my example of a theatrical staging of *Othello* is intended to show, even in a world where 'whiteness' would be unavailable as a social construct, whiteness in Shakespeare's play would make its presence felt. In the decision to stage the 'newly discovered' script, the director was forced to engage the imagined community at the heart of *Othello*. In doing so, the director would have to make 'blackness' invisible to render 'whiteness' visible. To make the play legible the director would have to introduce the idea of race into the audience's world-view.

In a world where notions of 'Shakespeare's universality' are present, it is easier to study the emanations of race by focusing on Shakespeare's 'Black holes' rather than the energetic distortions of whiteness at play, to expose the gravitational pull towards an unquestioned template for future generations of 'white people'. This template perpetuates systemic marginalization, devaluation, exploitation, and, as is routinely taking place across the globe, the sanctioned murder of Black, people of colour and native peoples. Because you are dead, we can't hold you responsible for how your writings have been weaponized but, and this is a very significant 'but', scholar/activists can challenge their using them to further white supremacy. As individuals and a collective, what we Shakespeareans can do is resist the idea that whiteness is a non-racialized category and teach it as such. We must find ways to negotiate the terms of whiteness you helped to create, the whiteness that makes your texts a mark of white supremacy.

To ignore the systemic legacies that tie 'whiteness', Shakespeare, and US culture together does no one any good. We must choose, like Shakespeare's 'other Moor' Aaron, to speak out, to reject the idea of universality when Muslims are murdered while they worship; when schools are closed because, in the name of whiteness, someone threatens the lives and promise of non-white children; when people opposed to racism put their lives on the line and those in power dismiss their deaths as regrettable; when trans people of colour are brutally assaulted or murdered simply because of who they are. No one can remain unaccountable in the face of racial hatred and violence that white supremacy has unleashed on our world. Not even you, William Shakespeare.

Postscripts: In My Visage
January 2021
Dear Early Modern Studies Beloved White Cousins,
Shakespeare didn't invent whiteness, but he and his writings are used to further it along. Academia aids and abets white supremacy's deployment of William Shakespeare, and to expect that to end without critical and political intervention would be foolish. William Shakespeare, as humanist doctrine, doesn't have that capacity.

He can't.

White supremacy can only end when white people take the burden of dismantling the naturalness and invisibility of whiteness. Beloved cousins, many of you have made careers on premodern analyses of anti-blackness without attending to the hegemony of whiteness. 'Tis time whiteness is subject to microscopic scrutiny as it enables your privileges, cements the ideologies of racial capitalism, and invigorates a presumptive natural hierarchy of colourism. What does it mean to reflect on Shakespeare scholarship through such a lens? What would it look like for white people to examine whiteness as a racial construct in Shakespeare through a lens unfiltered by Blackness?

Conversely, what does it mean to perform whiteness through a filtered lens? When you pen another scholarly essay on *Othello* or Aaron the Moor or Morocco, you are not writing about Blackness but whiteness. When you witness the implosion of a monarchy (the history plays), 'tis the fracturing of whiteness. Why aren't you writing about white people? It wasn't Blackness that destroyed Desdemona – it was whiteness that consumed her existence. Had she not been white, she would not have mattered.

February 2021
Dear Academic Cousins,
'Tis not difficult to undertake a critical study of whiteness in Shakespeare Studies. This brief missive is illustrative of that fact. There is no need to raise a hue and cry for premodern white studies as an academic field. There is an epistemological need to study the ways whiteness and white people become ghosted in academic analyses of premodern cultures. As so much of this volume attests, the embodiment of whiteness, of 'white-world-making', is central to 'race-making' in early modern English culture and our twenty-first century.[8] Where, then, does the 'blindness' come in? Why are English sixteenth- and seventeenth-centuries' constructions of whiteness elided and constructions of blackness/anti-blackness foregrounded in contemporary Shakespeare scholarship? Is it formed in the idea of William Shakespeare as cultural capital – commodities to be circulated and re-circulated where whiteness becomes strategically ghosted yet ever-present?

Is it the fear that the devaluation of whiteness inherently brings with it the loss of white profitability within racial capitalism? Is it the fear of a humanity that doesn't require violence to afford privilege? Wherein, oh cousin, lies your anxiety, your sense of fear of what our world might look like without colourism where whiteness is the baseline of positivity and all other hues sites of negativity? What is the source of your trepidation, your rage? The source of your unspoken abjection and negation? Do you gaze in the mirror and see the pale ghosts, like Hamlet's father, beckoning you to reckon with your complicity in the brutal exploitation of non-white people? Will you, can you, confront the privilege your whiteness has 'battened' on for centuries? The privilege that Shakespeare's clever mind and hands have had a role in making?

Today
Dearest White People,
This is my lament to and for you as you trip over the rubble of white supremacy, over the pits of Shakespearean violence perfected on the bodies of non-white peoples – you will not be remembered well.

NOTES

1. Arthur L. Little, Jr. 'Is It Possible to Read Shakespeare Through Critical White Studies', *The Cambridge Companion To Shakespeare and Race*, ed. Ayanna Thompson (Cambridge: Cambridge University Press 2021), 268–80, esp. 268.
2. Lara Bovilsky, *Barbarous Play: Race on the English Renaissance Stage* (Minneapolis: University of Minnesota 2008).
3. Margo Hendricks, 'Review: *Barbarous Play: Race on the English Renaissance Stage*', *Shakespeare Bulletin*, 27.3 (Fall 2009), 527–30.
4. William Shakespeare, 'A Midsummer Night's Dream', *The Arden Shakespeare Complete Works*, ed. Richard Proudfoot, Ann Thompson and David Scott Kastan (London: The Arden Shakespeare, 2001), 3.2.217–18.
5. William Shakespeare, 'Othello', *The Arden Shakespeare Complete Works*, 1.3.254.
6. Evelynn Hammonds, 'Black (W)holes and the Geometry of Black Female Sexuality', *differences: A Journal of Feminist Cultural Studies*, 6.2–3 (Summer-Fall 1994), 126.
7. Ibid., 139.
8. Little, 'Is It Possible', 269.

CHAPTER THIRTEEN

A Theatre Practice against the Unbearable Whiteness of Shakespeare

In Conversation

KEITH HAMILTON COBB, ANCHULI FELICIA KING, AND ROBIN ALFRIEND KELLO

Keith Hamilton Cobb is a Black American actor, playwright, and author of *American Moor*, in which he performs the lead role in a dramatic onstage collision with Shakespeare and national legacies of racial violence and exclusion. Anchuli Felicia King is a Thai-Australian playwright, screenwriter, multidisciplinary artist, and author of *Keene*, a satirical take on the predominantly white milieu of Shakespeare in the academy. Both plays make use of *Othello*, the play as well as its long cultural afterlife, to indict the whiteness of the Shakespeare industry, and readings of both works were included in Red Bull Theater's *Othello 2020* series. This conversation occurred via Zoom in the late autumn of 2021.

Kello We're here to talk about how you think whiteness does or doesn't operate as an institutional or artistic force in your engagements with Shakespeare.

King Shakespeare is one of those continuums in the history of colonization. Because Shakespeare is supposed to symbolize a British white excellence that brings distinction to academia and theatre, it's fairly impossible for me to be a theatre artist of colour and not engage with Shakespeare and whiteness in scholarship and in practice. At this historical juncture, both theatres and academic institutions are grappling with the legacy of racism and Shakespeare and saying, 'Oh, we want new voices. We want more diverse voices to engage with the canon.' But within the boundaries of what they find palatable and acceptable so that they don't have to dismantle their love of Shakespeare. Because to dismantle their bardolatry is to dismantle the elevation of whiteness and white culture over the cultures that whiteness has erased. That's where I feel like we are right now as a culture. We want interruptions in the canon but we're not willing to dismantle the canon.

Cobb   *American Moor* has been policed because it is honestly and directly indicting that structure. It's not a thing that you could sit to the left or the right of. You're in the firing line of that character's righteous anger and truth. It's hard to escape it, and that's very unsettling. It also creates a bad business model because you're handing this white structure a play about its indictment and saying, 'Please produce this.' And the structure is either overtly or covertly saying, 'Well, nah, nah, dude. Write something else.' Or: 'Change this. Write something else or change this in a way that doesn't make us feel indicted.'

Whiteness in America is, for all intents and purposes, America, and we are all going to be affected by it, by its inception, its growth, and the articulation and perpetuation of structures of control that descend from great wealth and therefore great power. Everything we do as a culture, not just brown people but as a culture, is going to be affected in one way or another by that overarching structure.

Kello   Felicia, I'm curious what this looks like to you coming from an Australian context and having worked both in the UK and the US. How do you navigate an industry that is constantly reminding us that it wants to support diversity, but also wants to make sure that the diverse voices brought in are kept in check and don't overstep certain boundaries?

King   I would say that my experience working in different English-speaking Western countries has been that we're dealing with different shades of the legacy of colonization, specifically British colonization, in these three different cultural contexts, three different indigenous genocides, and three different histories of slavery, for which there is a historical continuum, but there are different cultural implications.

Kello   Keith, this makes me think of the scene in *American Moor* in which you talk about being drawn to Shakespeare, not as a symbol of cultural capital and white excellence, but because of the beauty of the language. How do you balance this attraction to the richness of Shakespearean verse against these layered histories of racial violence and exclusion, especially with *Othello*, which is a core text for how ideas about race have been constructed, particularly in the United States?

Cobb   There are a couple of things going on here. There's this growing family of brown Shakespeare and race scholars who have become very adept at going back to the source and saying: 'You can no longer gaslight me. I can point to where these racial paradigms and tropes existed and show you the line of progression up until now. I can show you the place in the text that this meant this thing at that moment. When it was said, this is what it meant and what an early modern audience heard.' I appreciate that scholarship. It's essential that it continues to be nurtured. At the same time, as a theatre maker, I am interested only in what is performable.

I'm interested in what I can perform. By the time I started community college and was looking at English as a direction to go, it was becoming easier [to appreciate the language]. I was fortunate enough to see a couple of really strong productions where the performers really knew what they were doing and, more important, saying. All of a sudden, I realized, 'Oh, this can be performed. This is how you perform this,' and I wanted to do that. I can go through the canon and find a great deal of dross. But then there's language that's just so sublime, and I don't have a problem idolizing this white playwright for having said that.

Kello Felicia, what's your relationship to the language in the plays? Do you like Shakespeare, or is he just a tool for you to use because of his cultural presence? Also, Keith's point about the cultural capital of Shakespeare reminds me of how *Keene* sets Shakespeare against modern pop music.

King I agree with Keith that no one would try to make the argument that he's not a great poet or whatever bastardized transcription that we've received is great poetry. I have a strong affinity for early modern theatre in general, not just Shakespeare. I like how early modern theatre lends itself to shocking theatricality, and I love that early modern theatre is so grotesque. I love a lot of early seventeenth-century English theatre. I am less invested in the culture around Shakespeare, the culture of veneration surrounding him.

What I was trying to do with the various silly, inter-textual interventions in *Keene* – Ariana Grande and various other things – was to conflate high and low culture in a playful way, so that we don't have to elevate one over the other. The play is also invested in poking fun at the sanctimonious, self-aggrandizing, serious way that academics get into these hermetically sealed conversations about Shakespeare. It's exactly what Keith was saying: it takes it out of the realm of what it is on stage, what's performable, and into this more abstract, esoteric realm of critical theory.

Kello Yes. It makes me think about the immediacy of the theatre experience. Keith, this reminds me how in *American Moor*, the Black Actor basically puts the play's mostly white audience in the same position as the self-assured white Director guy in his mid-thirties, well-intentioned but a bit cocky and so very naïve.[1] His whiteness and my own become impossible to ignore. How did you decide that that device was going to work for the story you wanted to tell?

Cobb I had originally used a recording. There was somebody in the booth just hitting a button when it was time for him to talk. Then that became a person in the booth doing it live, which added a greater moment-to-moment reality in the piece. But in both those instances, it was only the voice, this omnipresent voice that the text describes as 'answerable to and impossible to ignore'. When we were in London, at the Sam Wanamaker Playhouse, they had no sound producing equipment, so we had to put a person in the house. That's where that started. We were suddenly privy to how the audience reacted to discovering that this person was amongst them – *was* them. They were in one way or another being conflated with this white Director, this arbiter of everything, and there were an array of feelings attached to that discovery that they were eager to voice in post-performance discussions. So, it was kind of by accident that we created that in the evolution of the piece, but truly significant.

King That device feels key to *American Moor*. The decision to have that character in the audience is driven by theatrical demands, much like early modern theatre makers were usually driven by practical stagecraft demands. Some of the best Shakespearean decisions are like – they needed to make a banquet disappear because they needed to use this new magic stagecraft device that they had.

Kello By putting the audience in the Director's position in the theatre, *American Moor* makes us face the racial dynamics that influence the audition. And in *Keene*, I remember the prefatory section where the characters say that the definition of whiteness is a three-day Shakespeare conference. It's incredibly funny, but it also pierces this industry that we are all a part of in different ways. From the beginning, we see that whiteness is not unraced, that everything we experience in both these plays is conditioned by race and no one can pretend that we're in some magical colour-blind world. You complicate the context even further by having the character of Kai, who is not just of a presumed different racial category, but also a different linguistic and cultural background.

King Similarly, the decision to foreground whiteness by having an all-white chorus in *Keene* was a practical theatrical decision to begin with. I knew I wanted the play to be choric and to make the audience feel like they were having the information about what was going on at that Shakespeare conference given to them in sort of an early modern way, where nothing was visually depicted on stage, but it was all in the minds of the audience.

Because I think a lot about racializing characters, I didn't want to have a neutral chorus. It felt important to signpost the lived reality of these two academics of colour at this Shakespeare conference. They would be in a sea of whiteness. I wanted to depict that onstage. It was primarily a theatrical decision that then became a very political decision in the act of writing the play.

Kello Keith, can you talk about this overlap between the performance aspects and the political aspects of the work? At what point does what the Actor character in *American Moor* says to the Director on a dramatic level become something that you want to get across to the audience in terms of the whiteness of professional theatre in the United States? Particularly Shakespeare?

Cobb Everything is riding upon the audience's view of this character's emotional journey, upon them embracing him as very human. Which I think the prologue in the piece before the Director comes into it allows them to do. They are disarmed to a certain extent. He's made them laugh. He has talked about how there's this wealth of emotion in all of them that needs to come out and should be given egress. Once he has succeeded in creating that affinity, it is much easier to load all these myriad elements. People say: 'I had never been presented that idea before. I had to go home and think about that. I came back to see it again because this thing had never occurred to me.' In the post performance discussions, you'll hear people say things like: 'I'm a white, middle-class woman. I'm aware of my privilege. Your play made me aware, and I'm still shaking. I understand my complicity. I want to help, but I don't know how.'

I'll say: 'You want to know the truth? You're not going to sell your house that you got because of a structure that has allowed you that position of wealth or at least access to it. You're not going to sell it and give it to brown people whose ancestors' bodies fed these structures of white wealth and power for generations. You're not going to dismantle this thing that you are the beneficiary of. So, there's nothing for you to do, right? You can listen, but until we tear all this down and rebuild it . . .' That's the frightening part. I can indict it and indict it and indict it, but the political reality is that it's not going to change in any kind of significant way, not in my lifetime. It doesn't mean I should stop talking about it, and making you feel uncomfortable that it exists because complacency has no value.

Kello Right. We're forced to think about all kinds of racial legacies. Felicia, you do this in *Keene*, where you blend the history of Ira Aldridge with these other characters, including Kai, a Japanese woman, who at least in the US and the UK often has no visible 'place' in the institutionalized, racialized structure of academia.

FIGURE 3: Ira Aldridge (1807–1867) in Whiteface as King Lear from the collection of the State Central Theatre Museum (Moscow) via The New York Public Library.

King I was interested in exploring the legacies of Aldridge's career as a Black Shakespearean actor. Certainly, our notions of racialized performance have radically shifted. I wanted to underline the fact that both minstrelsy and 'powdering up' were huge parts of his career, performances of racialized identity that would be unthinkable to us as a contemporary audience (Figure 3). But equally, I saw Aldridge's career as part of a historical continuum – that people of colour have for centuries been trying to reclaim and insert themselves into this canon of plays that either stereotyped or erased them.

Kello I can't help but be reminded of the Actor in *American Moor*: this history of the Black Shakespeare actor making his way in what culture thinks of as Shakespeare's white world is very much his legacy, and, of course, the cockiness and naïveté of the play's white audience shares that legacy, too.

King What I found inspiring about Aldridge is how much acclaim he garnered for his virtuosity as an actor, in spite of these overwhelming commercial and cultural forces that should've made it impossible for him to succeed. But equally, one of the things I tried to do with *Keene* is to thoroughly dispense with the myth that genius can somehow allow people to transcend bigotry. In spite of his overwhelming talent, Aldridge remained fetishized for his entire career – he was only ever allowed to achieve success as a Black actor within the lines of a white supremacist culture.

About Kai: because I'm a necessarily globalized citizen, I'm always trying to write from a global perspective. It felt important that the play looked at the current climate of Shakespeare scholarship, not just in an American context, but in a global context. It was largely informed by my experiences at a Shakespeare conference, of watching how the global hegemony of the English language has been so oppressive on a global scale, particularly for scholars who love Shakespeare but don't speak English as their first language. It's a very different kind of struggle from that of a scholar of colour in the United States, Britain, or Australia. So, it felt important for me to have these two characters grappling with two separate legacies of colonization through Shakespeare. One of the things that I heard articulated from audience members was that they had emotional access to the struggle of trying to occupy a space where you don't speak the language. Which for a lot of Americans and English speakers, is a struggle that you've never had to experience because it's the world language.

The cultural capital of English is something that people don't necessarily interrogate on a global scale. And that the cultural capital of English and the cultural capital of Shakespeare, which is of 'speaking well', basically, in a colonized global society, is one and the same. That's something that audiences responded to when we did talk-backs. But similarly, I think they only responded because they empathized with the characters. It's a poison pill: you have to get them to really love and identify with your protagonists for them to feel sufficiently indicted. If you just had an angry screed about Shakespearean scholarship, white audiences in particular would feel alienated, but because you give them emotional access to these people that they like and whose emotional crises they understand, they come away feeling like they're complicit in the system that's led to the oppression of these two characters.

Kello I think of how vicious the white scholars in your play are. The Director in *American Moor* has a lot of blind spots, but he's not conniving and vicious in a conscious way, as your characters seem to be. How did audiences relate to somebody like Ian, who very consciously seems to sabotage Tyler, a Black scholar, so as to maintain white ownership over Shakespeare?[2] It's an indictment – we keep using this word, but that is what's going on.

King I don't think that they are that vicious. Ian is certainly an incredibly vicious, Iago-like, Machiavellian villain – there's no denying that. But other characters: Dana, who fetishizes male Blackness and has complicated blind spots and a lot of white fragility, and the Shakespearean scholar who recruits Kai only because he wants more diversity in his journal – none of those feel like caricatures of white academia to me. They feel very true to things I have witnessed and experienced, so they don't feel like vicious satires. When we had an audience of Shakespeare scholars watching the reading at the American Shakespeare Center, they laughed the loudest because they self-identified with these characters. There's a kernel of truth in the play's critique of Shakespearean scholarship that makes them feel both attacked and seen.

Cobb There is this portion of the structure that feels so terribly indicted by *American Moor*. At the end of performances of *American Moor*, there are those people asking me, 'How can I help? I get it. I saw myself represented, and that has changed me or moved me, thank you.' Then are others that say, 'Let's talk about *Othello*. Let's talk about this Director . . . Why did you write him that way?' And that line of questioning always seemed to me to be about deflecting complicity, about changing the subject. And then the questions would turn to Shakespeare's play: 'Are you going to do it? Are you going to direct it?' And the answer was always, 'No, we don't have the tools. We can't work past a racial divide.' You can't work past your privilege. Generally speaking, in most any regional theatre in the country, we'd have three weeks and limited funds to try and unpack this play, not only to unpack it, but to build a world out of it, and to discover a set of fully dimensionalized human beings to people that world and, with our inability to communicate across these barriers to begin with, the best to ever hope for would be a mediocre recycling of Shakespeare's play.

But then I thought, 'Let me see if I can create something that at least seems plausible to me.' As you know, I love the language. I'm not about rewriting Shakespeare, but I'm about taking away things that people in his plays say that I would just as readily be able to see them do if they were human beings. Othello blathers on about revenge in his heart and all this bullshit and does nothing. He kills his wife eventually, perhaps the least able to fight back, but he takes no proactive stance on any of the data that he is being assaulted with. The playwright seems to want me to believe that Othello is a complete psycho-emotional cripple. I don't know how real that is. I don't think it's real at all, and I think it depends upon several holes in Shakespeare's overall narrative that might have been totally acceptable for his audience, but that American audiences have been trained to just leap over. We come and watch and say, 'We've seen Shakespeare. We've seen *Othello*.' I'd like to disrupt that. If we get to the end of six months, or a year, or eighteen months of interrogation and realize that we haven't plumbed any new ground, then we can all put it down, go home, and say we should never perform this play again. It's a perfectly valid idea. I just want to be free to have the time and the wherewithal to discover whether it's true for myself. That's where the work of the *Untitled Othello Project* begins.[3] I want people to leave *Othello*, saying, 'Yeah, well, he did that, but I understand why. Now it makes sense. Now I see several human beings conspiring to create tragedy. It's just like us. It's not just because somebody whispered some shit in his ear and he was crazy jealous.'

Kello Felicia, what drew you to *Othello*?

King The American Shakespeare Center invites playwrights to respond to something in the canon from a specific tranche of plays, and *Othello* was in the tranche.[4] I decided that I wanted to respond to *Othello* for two reasons: I was interested in the life of Ira Aldridge, but I was also interested in how, as this weird Asian-Australian theatre maker who has been dancing around Shakespeare for a lot of my scholarship and my practice as a theatre maker, I fit into the complicated, thorny discussion that is *Othello*. Can I even approach that play or write about it? Should I, as a non-Black writer? Does my voice have any value there? The play in some ways is only tangentially about, or a response to, *Othello*, and far more about the structures of scholarship around *Othello*. I didn't feel like I had anything valuable to contribute to any sort of post-colonial or even racial discussion of *Othello*, as that's not my play to write and I would never try to write that play. I was far more interested in how we talk about *Othello* in Shakespeare scholarship.

Kello I look at the Red Bull *Othello 2020* series, books like *Shakespeare and Social Justice* and *Teaching Social Justice through Shakespeare*,[5] and I see a trend in Shakespeare studies away from 'just' thinking about blackness to really interrogating whiteness. Just this past year there was a plenary panel at the Shakespeare of America Association conference focused on 'Shakespeare and White-World-Making'.[6] How optimistic should we be about these changes in the Shakespeare industry? I know you're both very attentive to the material reality behind the symbolic gesture and how it's all wrapped up in capitalism. Do you think institutions are really becoming more critically attuned to the legacies of racial and colonial violence in Shakespeare? And isn't this gesture or whatever it is in real conflict with the ways Shakespeare continues to stand for universality and at the same time for white excellence?

King I had a great Early Modern Studies professor who was a person of colour at Melbourne Uni. I think maybe he was the only professor of colour in my entire undergraduate experience because Australian academia is this whole other racist clusterfuck. But he gave me a nuanced perspective on the canon and its historical context, and he tried to engage with the complexities of canonicity and not whitewash it. That was my real academic introduction to Shakespeare.

I've always clung to the hope that there is innate value in encouraging critical thought around Shakespeare. I wouldn't be an artist if I didn't believe that you could move the conversation a little bit further just by using theatre as an empathy machine.

So, this reframing of the conversation around Shakespeare in the academic context? Here's what I'll say – it's better than nothing. In an ideal world, we would dismantle all the systems of power that have led to Shakespeare becoming a bastion of white excellence and dismantle the Anglocentric colonial structures within our academic institutions. But that would take a lot of power and money, and it's a much bigger project. I think that we push the envelope a little by reframing the discussion and interrupting what we used to teach about Shakespeare. My hope is that I'm contributing a tiny piece to that reframing.

Cobb I think Felicia is right. It boots us nothing not to continue to do our little pushes of the envelope. If that's all we've got, that's what is incumbent upon us to continue, because we teach by example. People are inspired by the work we do, certainly in academia. If your students respect the work that you are doing and the things that you're putting in their mind, if they're beginning to spark to the ideas that you are not only telling them but embodying in the work that they see you do, there is change. That doesn't let academia off the hook. We're all inside this structure, which is beholden to capitalist American business practices.

If you're asking me about the work that I do, I continue to do it because I have no other choice. I'm committed to it and I'm optimistic, because I have no other choice. I'm optimistic right now, because the first generation of twenty-first-century intellectuals is happening right now. Maybe what you're asking is: can we actually create anything that transcends this capitalist machine descended from chattel slavery? How do you answer the question? There's no stopping us from trying, even as we acknowledge the fact that capitalism is everywhere. It's deep. But in the end, we're still theatre makers. We're still artists. We still create.

Kello This talk about global capital makes me very conscious of how we are having this Zoom conversation right now in LA, New York, London, these centres of the arts that are really centres of capital. Keith's point about the next generation of intellectuals also makes me think optimistically about *White People in Shakespeare*. It will be scholars, probably younger scholars, theatre makers, and students who will be reading this interview – who I hope will be assigned to read this interview in their Shakespeare classes.

King What I continue to find valuable about studying early modern theatre – I keep stressing early modern theatre because I don't care just specifically about Shakespeare – is that theatre makers from that period had a radically communal model for making theatre, that arguably was far less capitalist than the way that we make it now. The specific structure that they had to make theatre as shared actor managers, as shared playwrights, who all had a stake in the business, led to the kinds of plays that they created. I think it's a useful model for radically reshaping the way that we make and study theatre to look at the plays that they produced from the commercial models that they employed. Having said that, you can't separate the xenophobia and the racial stereotyping in those early modern plays from the system of global commercial trade that they existed in, in this central hub of chattel slavery. It's both of those things simultaneously. They were collaborative theatre makers and artisans that existed outside of society, but they were still incumbent on the structures that that society imposed upon them.

Insofar as 'whiteness' exists as this mythological category that denotes a hermetically sealed, superior Western culture (in direct opposition to an inferior racialized Other), I think that bardolatry – the idea that this white (cis male) genius is the single most pre-eminent poet and playwright to have ever existed, and that through his work he has somehow encapsulated the universal human condition – it's just another narrative of white supremacy. And by that, I'm not saying that everyone who loves Shakespeare is a swastika-wearing, lynch-mobbing racist – it's just that any uncritical valorisation of Shakespeare inevitably bolsters a white supremacist narrative. Which is why, I'd posit, the study and performance of Shakespeare remains such a white field – because that narrative fits comfortably within the extant white supremacist power structures of both academia and theatre. My goal in *Keene* is to disrupt both the idea of Shakespeare's singular genius and his universality. I want to look at who is erased in and precluded from Shakespeare, both in the actual content of his plays but also in who gets to claim ownership of Shakespeare as a cultural property.

Cobb   If the country is predicated upon structures of white dominance, cultures of slavery, and capitalism, which is slavery in another form, then Shakespeare is just another part of that structure. To speak of 'white people in Shakespeare' is to speak of Shakespeare in America because of the ancient and insidious designs of white entitlement that position whiteness as arbiter and owner of everything of worth that exists here. White people in Shakespeare *is* American Shakespeare, and neither Shakespeare nor America is the better for it.

Kello   Thank you, Keith. Thank you, Felicia. Thank you for being so generous with your time.

NOTES

1. *American Moor* is structured by an audition in which the character of the Actor, played by Keith, is performing for the Director, who sits in the audience. The Actor's second-person address to the Director regarding race in general and whiteness in particular becomes a direct address to the audience as well.
2. Spoiler alert: the character of Ian in *Keene* ensures Tyler's failure at the conference by getting him very drunk the night before. Tyler oversleeps and fails to present his essay on Aldridge; Ian's paper is given an offer of publication.
3. The *Untitled Othello Project*, an ensemble of artists doing an in-depth interrogation of Shakespeare's play, was about to begin a two-week residency at Sacred Heart University when this interview was conducted.
4. *Keene* won the American Shakespeare Center's Shakespeare's New Contemporaries prize. Red Bull Theater's *Red Bull 2020* initiative offered staged readings of both plays as well as a reading of the play with other artists and scholars: https://www.redbulltheater.com/othello-2020.

5. See *The Arden Research Handbook of Shakespeare and Social Justice*, ed. David Ruiter (London: The Arden Shakespeare, 2020), and *Teaching Social Justice through Shakespeare: Why Renaissance Literature Matters Now*, ed. Hillary Eklund and Wendy Beth Hyman (Edinburgh: Edinburgh University Press, 2019).
6. The panel took place in April 2021, and was organized by Arthur L. Little, Jr., who presented alongside Matthieu Chapman, Peter Erickson, and Katherine Gillen, and was chaired by Ruben Espinosa.

CHAPTER FOURTEEN

White Lies

In Conversation

PETER SELLARS AND AYANNA THOMPSON

Peter Sellars is a MacArthur Fellow and Distinguished Professor in UCLA's Department of World Arts and Cultures/Dance. His work as a theatre director and visionary has gained worldwide widespread recognition over the past few decades for his transformative stagings of classical and contemporary works. Sellars is also the founding director of the Boethius Institute at UCLA, which invites scholars, activists, and artists to work together to explore radical ways of rethinking communities and complex issues in and through the arts. Ayanna Thompson is a Regents Professor of English at Arizona State University and the Director of the Arizona Center for Medieval & Renaissance Studies. She is the author of several books, most recently, *Blackface* (2021). She has recently served as president of the Shakespeare Association of America and is a recent inductee to the American Academy of Arts and Sciences. Thompson is also a Shakespeare Scholar in Residence at The Public Theatre in New York and chairs the Council of Scholars at Theatre for a New Audience. The following is a conversation between them in the autumn of 2020.

Thompson Today we're talking about 'white people in Shakespeare' for Arthur L. Little Jr.'s book, thinking through it together. Actually, this is probably the perfect moment to think about white people in Shakespeare with what's happening in Shakespeare companies right now. To start with Little's big question: can white people move along as white people without Shakespeare, and can Shakespeare move along about his business without white people?

Sellars Well, I love Little's use of the word 'people' because, you know, Shakespeare starts with that. And as soon as you start with Shakespeare's people, then the adjective is not necessarily the main issue. In what way are people *people* is, I think, Shakespeare's primary question. Then, of course, he problematizes that in various ways, particularly in two plays that I'm obsessed with, *Merchant of Venice* and *Othello*, by saying, 'In what ways are people not allowed to be people?' And in what ways are people treated as less than human, in what ways are people's ability to flourish and live fulfilling lives being deliberately circumscribed by power structures? Those power structures are first and foremost economic and political.

Then, of course, they're organized, very organized – it's a very organized situation that keeps white power and white financial power in place, and the only way you can actually *do* that ... is to cheat.

[Laughs] Shakespeare's up front about it: watch these people cheat, watch these people lie. If you're going to treat another human being as less than human, that is going to require an enormous amount of dishonesty. Shakespeare just constantly shows you these people lying to hold onto power.

Thompson I have never thought of the plays in that way, but I think you're right. I feel like you could go from the comedies, the histories, tragedies, romances ... and at the end, it is all about systemic lying, microscale and macroscale.

Sellars Yes, and because they're busy keeping track of their lies, or elaborating them, or embroidering them, or whatever – they lose track of whether that was a macro lie or a micro lie. They can't keep track. And gradually they are the ones infected by their own dishonesty. To actually watch these Shakespeare characters, you know, fall sick of their own dishonesty is *very* incredible: they, these so-called white people, these purveyors of humanness, have been spreading [lies] virally, and they are the ones actually dying of the virus. It's very very intense. Meanwhile, you watch the stunted growth of the brilliant people around them, who have not been permitted to fulfil their promise, whose reason they're on earth has been suddenly circumscribed. Shakespeare's just aware of the disappointment of not fully empowering all people and is super alert to what it means that if lies are told about you, and then they spread and people believe them, you doubt yourself.

Thompson [Sighs] Yeah. All those lies burrowing into people's being who are not *the* people (as you were talking about) has done this to the humanity of all of us.

Sellars There's a beautiful line from Simone Weil in her essay on affliction that just stunned me the other day. She was writing once World War II was underway, and she said it was no surprise that there are concentration camps, genocide, torture, mass starvation – because you can always find people to do that stuff.[1] Which is like, what? Shocking. But then she says, what is *deeply* a surprise is to realize how many people feel themselves to be less than human.

You're standing next to somebody who has the mark of the slave imprinted on them. You don't know that, but *they* feel that they're not fully human. You just think they're behaving strangely, and you don't know what to say to them. So ... you don't say anything. This is what makes the picture of Jessica [*The Merchant of Venice*] so heartbreaking. She actually *sees* human beings internalize lies about them[selves], and it was never true, but everybody's looking at you as if it is. Then you start looking for something in yourself. And all of that hurt is so deeply, deeply pictured in Shakespeare – but frequently in tiny little asides.

I think that's one of the big things about Shakespeare: very little of that official content arrives in giant speeches. It's just these tiny little asides when you realize what people are carrying with them.

Thompson It's true, and those are always the lines that are cut out because they don't lend themselves to a smooth narrative. But those are the moments that can actually be more telling. I think about the importance of those moments in life where we rarely know what's happening or going on, where you feel like you're not in control of your own story or how people perceive you or hear you.

Sellars You and I have gone on about the nightmare of these plays being cut so that there's an absolutely slick narrative, and the Shakespeare play is over painlessly in, you know, whatever the two-hour traffic is. But the weird thing is, when you're in a giant structure composed of lies, the truth *only* shows in the cracks. So that's why it's so important not to cut the cracks – to actually show that Shakespeare *knows* this thing is hollow. All these tiny little cracks are the most profound human moments in these plays, over and over again.

Thompson Yes. So, I'm wondering if we could talk [about] this moment, in 2020 and 2021, as theatres across the world are in crisis because we cannot commune. Shakespeare theatres, in particular, are in crisis because they are having a reckoning with how inclusive, or not, they've been in the past, and where they're going to go in the future. So, if Shakespeare's plays, as you have articulated, are about – I love the Simone Weil-way into thinking about this, people who are damaged, feeling that they're less than human, and you don't even understand how that's impacted the interaction – so, if Shakespeare's interested in that, I don't know that that's what Shakespeare *companies* have been interested in.

I think that Shakespeare companies have been interested in a kind of whiteness-as-universal, presenting Shakespeare's plays as being white *and* as being representative of the universal experience. But now they're realizing that that may be problematic. So, I'm wondering if you could speak to that, because I love the fact that you have not been involved in a Shakespeare company.

Sellars [Laughs]

Thompson You've been Shakespeare-company adjacent.

Sellars You know, it's hard because obviously Shakespeare was used for centuries as the proof of white supremacy. [Moreover,] the proof of greatness is, 'I understand this,' which is a problem with Shakespeare interpretation. So much of Shakespeare interpretation, until you and your generation came along, was about the commentator showing *their* superiority and mastery, and Shakespeare was the place where everybody who wanted to demonstrate their mastery [would] demonstrate it. Which is just such a *drag*. An unpleasant thing to be is the master of everything, for god's sake. You want to say, 'Wouldn't you just be curious if there was something you *didn't* know, wouldn't that interest you?' [But] they want to say, no, 'I am the master of all I survey, and I survey Shakespeare with complete authority.' These claims of authority have always been what Shakespeare has been used for, even though Shakespeare undercuts every power structure in every play. Even though Shakespeare takes that behaviour and shows you how doomed it is. You watch the collapse of that authority in every damn Shakespeare play.

So, it's *bizarre* that Shakespeare was taken hostage by nightmare authority figures, by 'white' people looking for domination. It does mean, and this is across the world, that Shakespeare represents a certain 'I am cultivated' thing, which can't be separated from how whiteness works in so many global contexts. The plays don't ever represent that; they challenge that in every way. They challenge, you know, all is that the appearances you're judging – those are, as they say, mistaken identities. How many mistaken identities is this world made up of? And you're still judging somebody by what they look like? This delusional way you're looking at them, you're unable to see who they are. Shakespeare repeats that over and over and over again, shows you dialogues that are not fully present – or where one person's present and the other person goes, 'Are you sure'? The plays themselves are so challenging, and the presentation of the plays has been to say 'there's no challenge here, this is easy. You can understand this, I understand this, and it's very straightforward' – which it isn't.

We now have to get Shakespeare away from the sense of the feel-good, or the feel-good for certain people, and move into a place where Shakespeare is feel-good in the sense that it feels better to deal with your issues than to avoid them. And it is in *that* sense that Shakespeare is feel-good. Shakespeare is interested in confronting all of this. These plays are fantastic, I mean *thrilling*, battlefields to actually move into and challenge all of these structures of self-importance and structures of domination. So, I don't want to just say that all Shakespeare has been is bad. But, if I could say, even when the Royal Shakespeare Company had its halcyon days, in the Peter Brook and beyond field, most of the interest was formal.

Thompson Yes, I love the sense that this official Shakespeare, or formal Shakespeare, is a type of white supremacy. And that the contested and messy Shakespeare might actually do the anti-racist work that we'd like it to do moving forward. But that would mean, really . . . I mean, there are financial stakes for theatre companies. And, you know, the people who are giving the big bucks are invested in a type of official Shakespeare. So, I'm wondering if you have advice, for if we wanted to make it something different.

Sellars I think, as always, in life, if you're just following the money, you're sad. Shakespeare wasn't looking at wealth. What he was looking at was so raw and weirdly in your face. Accumulating stuff didn't make you a person, didn't give you an identity. Shakespeare's right there on both the environmental and also spiritual question of what it means not to accumulate stuff, not to make everything based on stuff. That is a genuine motivator in every Shakespeare play. And to talk about the people who fund *official* Shakespeare, Shakespeare shows you very important white people realizing they need to find new identities. That's very powerful and actually the message to corporate America, the message to a sense of wealth and privilege, of white wealth and white privilege. Shakespeare in every case creates a crisis. And it's not just Shakespeare creating an identity crisis for individuals but for America itself, and we see the rawness of this in nineteenth-century American Shakespeare theatre. My favourite!

Thompson That's exactly right. You can see it in the 1821–1830 New York theatre scene. Going through those records and really thinking about what Shakespeare was doing in that moment in America! In one night, in one theatre you would see a pantomime, a melodrama, *and* a Shakespeare play.

Sellars And some little girl giving a temperance talk in a song.

Thompson And Native Americans in the audience invited on stage to do what white recollections referred to as a 'war dance'. This was the moment Andrew Jackson was ordering Native Americans whom he defeated in the war to go to theatres in New York so that they could see the splendour of 'culture'. I think we really were working out what our nation was going to be, but it wasn't necessarily that theatre was going to be the place of progress.

Sellars All of that is alive, very alive. Again, the debate in theatre was, in those decades, 'What kind of country do you want to have' – that was, truly, the debate. Theatre was the mirror. And that's the Shakespeare thing: 'just please look at yourself, please, please. I have a mirror right here.' And what you look like is not the story. Shakespeare goes out of his way to say, '*How* are you living? *How* are you treating other people? Are you lying to them?'

Thompson 'Are you lying to yourself?'

Sellars I was about to say! And then, 'Now who are you really lying to?' And that would be you. Shakespeare is absolutely laser sharp with that. Something most of the Shakespeare business wants is to make everything affirmative, but I want to say Shakespeare is the saddest playwright in history.

Of course, I know Shakespeare company after Shakespeare company wants that standing ovation, but that's not the mood of any Shakespeare play that I know. That's too often the Shakespeare of white wealth and white privilege. That's that 'official' Shakespeare.

The ending is always the question. I think, like Octavia Butler or Dostoyevsky, he is genuinely asking the audience, 'Is this the world you wanted? Do you want this world to continue or should this world be stopped now?' You rarely get that impact in most Shakespeare performances – you're being literally asked, 'Will we continue this?' So, I think this era in which we're in – which is being called an era of reckoning, and I hope it is an era of reckoning – means we have to be more honest with Shakespeare, and let Shakespeare be very honest with us. Which is what I think Shakespeare has in mind. And I guess this goes back to Arthur's question in a way: how honest can white people be with Shakespeare if they're committed to keeping their 'official' Shakespeare outside this reckoning?

Thompson If you were invited – which I'm sure you are and you turned them down – but if you were invited, and you accepted, to put on the first Shakespeare play in a reopened theatre sometime in the future, in this moment of reckoning, what would you stage?

Sellars [Pause]. You know, there's no wrong answer. There just is no wrong answer. I, of course, am always drawn to the 'problem plays' because at least people acknowledge that they don't know what they are, and that's a relief. You don't have the tradition of triumphalism, and that's very helpful. On the other hand, it's always great to take on one of the famous ones because then there's a shock on the way for people of, 'This isn't the play I love,' and 'you're saying you're right, and you're not.' But of course, our system means the theatre critics also say that, which is a drag for the box office. Because the theatre critic particularly is invested in the plays they love. So, it's a tricky one in terms of the finances of a company. A 'my sense of wellbeing and self-possessiveness is based on this play being the play that *I* know! Because I am a cultivated person, and I know that *I* understand this!' Of course, as soon as you problematize the play, which is problematic, then people feel personally – personally – like you're saying they're stupid or that their place in the world or above the world isn't what they think it is.

Thompson Yes, you're challenging their authority and, of course, white supremacy.

Sellars You are right in every way. It's a very hard thing. Of course, the other thing is the education system which we are in now that is teaching toward the test. You're getting generations for whom Shakespeare is either a drag or is this official thing that comes pre-packaged. It's a weird moment. But there's not one play that doesn't do everything that we need to have done now in the twenty-first century.

Thompson I was thinking that I would love to see your *Hamlet*, and I would love to see your *Shrew*. And I would love to see your *Cymbeline*. So, I think you should do them all! [Laughs].

Sellars The other thing that you saw was a *Midsummer Night's Dream*, where I have to do the opposite. I have to cut them so radically because people have a shorter attention span; nobody wants a four-hour thing. Everybody wants a nugget that fits in your pocket, and you can take it home. Sometimes, as in *Midsummer Night's Dream*, I have to cut it so deeply – but cut the lines you know and leave the lines you didn't know to create a sense of, 'Wait a minute, what *is* this thing?' Also, for me, I'm very much into doing it with a handful of people. Again, just the economics – the idea of a full panoply of a full Shakespeare company is hard to muster in these economic times. So, the other thing that interests me a lot is doing Shakespeare with a small group of people. By doubling and tripling the roles, it already plays into Shakespeare's thing about identity. But with the cultural world on the skids economically, it's no longer about this panoply of spectacle and thirty people on stage. All of that, we just can't do it.

For me, this rawness . . . I just want to touch the rawness again. I just want to touch something raw and experimental and open-ended where Shakespeare's audiences *didn't* know how it would end, and get to that place again with Shakespeare. Where you really are hanging on every line, like 'Is this what's happening? What? Oh! Hold it! He's with – with her? Really?' I just want to get it so you don't already know the play inside and out as you sit down. Where the play itself is alive line-by-line, and you say, 'Is this the plot?' That would be very exciting, so that's, of course, on my mind. And then larger than the Shakespeare question is for me, what you've written about beautifully: where does Shakespeare belong in prisons? Where does Shakespeare belong in high schools and bad neighbourhoods? Shakespeare belongs wherever people have issues, painful issues, that they have to work through. *Not* where 'people' want to applaud their own success.

But genuinely where you have this heartrending reality where the absence of justice is so vivid, and people walk in *knowing* that and can actually testify to that. It's then that this play becomes a useful tool in reshaping your reality and refocusing your commitment, your sense of purpose, and your sense of worthiness to engage in the serious structural changes that we have to engage with. And you're worthy to do that, you're motivated, because now you have stood up to the public and wrestled with these things. Because Shakespeare's always wrestled with those things in society but also wrestled with these things in the self.

That's why, you know, Shakespeare in prison is so overwhelming. *At its best*, it's not played from a position of pride, it's played from a position of humility and hurt, and a sense of wrong – layers of wrong. That is, how many layers of wrong are there in you and in what's around you? Suddenly, those plays are so alive and so urgent. So, the Shakespeare tradition that I'm particularly interested in at this moment is Shakespeare for people who need to change their situation. Suddenly, Shakespeare is powerful and urgent and red hot and is the tool we need to move forward in our century.

Thompson   All the baggage that we have in professional theatre companies, that's not what the emphasis is inside prisons. [Instead,] it's about personal growth, development, exploration, contestation – all the things that traditional, official Shakespeare does not allow you to do predominately in theatre companies, where you're paying, whatever, $150 to see the play.

Sellars   And in a prison, you don't have to worry about diversity of casting. That is happening; you actually get a representative cross-section of our society.

Thompson   And they talk about it!

Sellars   Yes, it's right there. You can't miss it. Oh my god, and Shakespeare's improvisatory casting – anyway. Let's just include that. I think that's a beautiful place to stop.

Sellars   You were such a thrill.

Thompson   *You* were such a thrill!

NOTES

1. See Simone Weil's essays, '*Human Personality*', 9–34, and '*The Great Beast: Reflections on the Origins of Hilterism*', 89–144, in "Selected Essays, 1934–1943: *Historical, Political, and Moral Writings*," ed. Richard Rees (Oxford: Oxford University Press, 1962).

CHAPTER FIFTEEN

Can You Be White and Hear This?

The Racial Art of Listening in American Moor *and* Desdemona

KIM F. HALL

> The white man wants the world; he wants it for himself. He discovers he is the predestined master of the world. He enslaves it. His relationship with the world is one of appropriation.
>
> – Franz Fanon, *Black Skin, White Masks*[1]

Othello, it turns out, is the perfect play for talking about white people and sound. In his introduction to *Desdemona*, a collaboration with Toni Morrison and Rokia Traoré, Peter Sellars reminds us, 'Shakespeare's *Othello* is a permanent provocation, for four centuries the most visible portrayal of a black man in Western Art.'[2] This singular place in the canon means that *Othello* has also become a canonical text for race studies. The play in performance often becomes Iago's play: he beguiles the audience, and in many contemporary productions it can be difficult to tell whether audiences eventually feel complicit in his laughter or share his position of white omniscience.[3] Exploring race and Shakespeare of necessity poses a problem of representing whiteness as both a property [4] and a structure of power. Othello's most remembered speeches are those where he faces white judgement, thus, part of the play's provocation is the fact that he is a Black man in the midst of whiteness: 'This black man is performing in front of white people and we have very few clues about his inner life.'[5] Alone amongst Shakespeare's eponymous tragedies, the villain has as much stage time as the eponymous hero. Perhaps in response to this, several Black 'respeakings' of Othello leave out Iago almost entirely. [6] However, even the near excision of Iago leaves the uneasy conundrum of whiteness with the related problem of Black 'speech'. Is Black speech actually heard in the whiteness of contemporary theatre? While much has been made about amplifying women's voices in the play, *American Moor* points out the many ways the theatre silences Black men's voices as well, even (or especially) in *Othello*.

This essay focuses primarily on Keith Hamilton Cobb's play, *American Moor*, in which Cobb attempts to 'speak of me as I am,' to tell the story of how his blackness and his love of Shakespeare collide with various facets of the Shakespeare industry – teachers, acting coaches, agents and directors – who subtly maintain Shakespeare as white property; however, as I turn to questions of listening, I draw in Toni Morrison/Rokia Traoré's *Desdemona*. Both *Desdemona* and *American Moor* are pieces about speaking over the colour line, they perform conversations that highlight the missed readings and over-readings replete in *Othello*, asking, what does it mean to listen and what does it mean to be heard?

BLACK ACTORS AS WHITE PROPERTY

In *American Moor*, The Actor, a 50-ish Black man, auditions for a younger, less-experienced white director, who is only a voice that comes from either the audience or from behind a sound booth.[7] The asymmetry of the actor/director relationship mirrors the performative asymmetry of white supremacy:

> existentially speaking, the Black person's ever-present Black skin is always visible to the panopticism of the white gaze. Bodily proximity, whether to make eye contact, what vocal inflections ought to be used – such mundane actions, which never occur to the white person, become questions over which the Black person must labour.[8]

This moment of the audition thus reflects much of our reality: 'I began to think about how we are all always auditioning for the role of ourselves, or for the role that someone expects of us. So much of American culture is predicated on the idea of selling one's self.'[9] Throughout the play Cobb speaks both to the director and to the audience, a device that allows him to deconstruct the power relations of theatre and of the US. This parallel between Othello before the Senate and the Black actor auditioning for Othello offers pointed counterpart to actor Hugh Quarshie's early contention that 'being a black actor gives me no greater insight into *Othello*, the play, than being Danish would into *Hamlet*'.[10] However, as The Actor insists on his unique vantage point, he faces the problem of white appropriation, pointedly articulated in my epigraph from Frantz Fanon's *Black Skin, White Masks*.

If the original Othello is the primal appropriation of a Black man in Western art, white conversations about *Othello* are replete with this sense of mastery: white actors covet playing the wily Iago and some strain against the twentieth century concession that the role should belong to men of colour.[11] Even in *Othello* performances Black actors with opinions are interlopers. A similar sense of the Black subject piercing the cocoon of the white-owned world is pervasive in *Black Skin/White Masks*. Strikingly, Fanon depicts the colonized Black man's attempt to reclaim subjectivity with a performance metaphor:

> So here we have the Negro rehabilitated, 'standing at the helm,' governing the world with his intuition, rediscovered, reappropriated, in demand, accepted; and it's not a Negro, oh, no, but the Negro, alerting the prolific antennae of the world, standing in the spotlight of the world, spraying the world with his poetical power, 'porous to every breath in the world'.[12]

As Edwin Hill notes, racial alienation in Fanon 'is less a loss of self than a public hammering of the self into its assigned subject position'.[13] This moment in the spotlight only takes place after the Black subject has already been subjected to relentless blows to the psyche. Concurrent with these blows is the constant disciplining of and appropriation of Black voices to speak the perspectives of the white world.[14] *American Moor* is this moment in the spotlight; Cobb reappropriates and makes sense of these years of white disciplining and appropriation.

Cobb begins by resisting the inevitability of *Othello* for the Black actor. However, once he moves to a kinship with Othello based on what he knows about *Othello* from being a Black man in a white elite world, he realizes he is made a mouthpiece for how white people understand blackness or race. The Actor/Director at the audition is emblematic of dozens of other Black encounters with the Shakespeare world – and for Othello in Venice. The Black actor, like Fanon's Black subject, releases his energies into a world of white judgement. The Actor's love of Shakespeare – his sense that Shakespeare speaks to him and can help him reach the world in profound ways – is inextricably tied to reinforcement of Shakespeare as a white property. Starting with school, he is disciplined into his relationship with Shakespeare: only allowed access as decided by white people. He performs this disciplining as a series of nudges and assumptions from his drama teacher as The Actor attempts various soliloquys: 'Pick something you might realistically play! Something befitting your age, and experience! . . . 'Hamlet is hardly your experience . . .'[15] The teacher advances through the 'Black' roles, but the script imposes a temporal shift that refuses the speaking of the inevitable conclusion: 'They're both probably about your age . . . And . . . well, now you *would* be playing older, but I might even be interested in having you *try* to do something with –'[16] The performance then shifts back to The Actor, now grown, being greeted by the Director, showing the continuity of the pressure, but also revealing that the issues with age are pretextual.

As The Actor ages and accumulates more experiences of a Black man performing for the white world, Othello becomes 'kinfolk', a family constructed from shared experiences of blackness and of oppression: 'my sense of self-assessment matured healthily, presided over by the doting ghosts of my brilliant Black progenitors. . . . And, in that moment, that sacred moment, I suddenly could not *not* care for Othello. I began rather to feel like I have a brother who can't defend himself. And you been slappin' him around for four hundred years.'[17]

The Actor and the Director fundamentally struggle over the meanings of the play. The disembodied director insists that his instincts about the Venetians should hold sway over the actor's experience or even the cues in the text. For example, he proposes the story of astronaut Lisa Nowak, who drove hundreds of miles in an adult diaper to confront a romantic rival, as a way that one can understand Othello's jealousy – but it really becomes a way of substituting a white woman's story for that of a Black man.[18] The dialogue is one-sided. It is not a conversation between people about the meanings of the text, it is a conversation with a white man awarded privilege of authority who speaks *for* Shakespeare to the Black man directed to perform that limited understanding.

This substitution of white experience/perspective comes to a head with The Director's suggestion that The Actor play Othello as someone who needs to 'ingratiate himself a little more to them, I mean, the senate thrives on . . . uh . . . obeisance . . . Right'?[19] The layers of power and judgement are made clear here: Othello is The Actor and The Actor is Othello:

> You think that he thinks that he needs to do . . . 'a number' for these guys, in order to succeed in getting from them the thing that *you* think he wants . . . in order to succeed in getting from *you* the thing that *you* think *I* want . . . you're implying that *I* need to do 'a number . . . for *you*.[20]

The Director's power, however, is not simply the ability to offer a gig, it is a specifically white power, a whiteness based on assumptions of white ownership of Shakespeare.

In her influential essay, 'Whiteness as Property,' Cheryl Harris details the ways in which American society has created whiteness both as a structure of power and a valuable asset:

> My grandmother's story illustrates the valorisation of whiteness as treasured property in a society structured on racial caste . . . . the set of assumptions, privileges, and benefits that accompany the status of being white have become a valuable asset that whites sought to protect and that those who passed sought to attain – by fraud if necessary. Whites have come to expect and rely on these benefits, and over time these expectations have been affirmed, legitimated, and protected by the law.[21]

American Moor reveals two aspects of the creation of whiteness's value: the power of definition and the power of exclusion. The Actor's asides demonstrate that exclusion begins well before any audition. His burgeoning love of Shakespeare and desire to perform are intertwined with multiple acts of exclusion, from the professor who eventually refuses to entertain his enthusiastic questions about the plays, to the acting teacher who derides his requests to perform Titania, Hamlet and other characters, to the well-meaning agent who steers him to stereotypical 'Black' roles. Harris notes that 'The fundamental precept of whiteness – the core of its value – is its exclusivity';[22] certainly despite democratizing efforts, Shakespeare retains this aura of exclusivity, a high-culture currency at times offered as mass entertainment in various forms, but more often promoted as the gateway to social advancement and acceptance.[23]

Although Harris focuses on how the law controls the meaning and definition of whiteness, 'Whiteness as a property is also constituted through the reification of expectations in the continued right of white-dominated institutions to control the legal meaning of group identity',[24] her descriptions of how whiteness is defined applies to discursive, extra-legal realms. If one substitutes 'Shakespeare' for 'group identity' in her passage, one has a pretty accurate description of the state of Shakespeare scholarship, performance and pedagogy. The United States culture wars and debates over cross-racial casting in the UK and US are all symptoms of the struggle over the Shakespearean property, over the right of institutions to control the meanings of Shakespeare and to police or relegate to the margins groups or individuals who assert the right to define the meanings and uses of the Shakespeare text. The much younger Director brings with him, not only the power of his position, but the power of his whiteness, rendered as lineage: 'And he's as scared shitless of Shakespeare as most people, but he studied with somebody who studied with somebody who was British, so he's runnin' with it.'[25] The Black Actor fights, not the Shakespeare text, but the accumulated power of definition over Shakespeare and his plays, an inherited white property passed down from one generation to the next.

As The Actor's biography unfolds, the various older white male interlocutors (the agent and the teacher) have the presumed authority of experience, but the conversations with the young Director, show that the through-line is the power of whiteness. Both the power of definition (seen in the interactions between The Actor and the teacher) and the power of exclusion are attributes of whiteness: 'The possessors of whiteness were granted the legal right to exclude others from the privileges inhering in whiteness; whiteness became an exclusive club whose membership was closely and grudgingly regarded.'[26] The 'audition' as the centrepiece of Cobb's performance brings to the fore the power of exclusion, making it literal and conceptual: The Actor appeals to the director for inclusion in the projected performance, but there is a deeper appeal to the audience for understanding and inclusion in the circle of humanity.

When the director asks The Actor to play Othello as someone who wants to 'please' and 'entertain' the Venetian Senate (minimizing the fact that Othello is a warrior who is in fact needed by the Venetians), The Actor's questions make it clear that this is a move to emasculate the character, make his performance a modern-day version of minstrelsy. Harris uses Andrew Hacker's description of minstrelsy to introduce blackness's role in inviting or excluding immigrant groups from the circle of whiteness:

> Through minstrel shows in which white actors masquerading in blackface played out racist stereotypes, the popular culture put the black at a 'solo spot centre stage, providing a relational model in contrast to which masses of Americans could establish a positive and superior sense of identity . . . established by infinitely manipulable negation comparing whites with a construct of a socially defenceless group'.[27]

Hacker's image of the minstrel actor given 'a solo spot centre stage' eerily resonates against Cobb's central spot in his performance. The Actor in the spotlight, for Fanon an image of expansive manhood and connection, is too often in American theatre an avenue for Blacks to be used to create white identity through exclusivity. It is not coincidental that *American Moor* focuses almost entirely on Act I. The dialogue with the Director is about 1.3, that moment of debate over Othello's fate, when he is most clearly centre stage, but when white judgement will settle his fate. With each encounter over Othello's 'her father loved me' speech, the Director asks The Actor to interpret the lines through Brabantio, the Senate, or through his, the Director's, interpretation of a Black man's feelings:

> . . . First up, a little white man is asking me if I have any questions about being a large Black man, enacting the role of a large Black man in a famous Shakespeare play about a large Black man which, for the last fifty, sixty years or so, has been more or less wholly the province of large Black men . . .[28]

The truncated space of the audition (and of theatre in general) leaves no room for The Actor to offer insights based on his experience. The Black actor is never able to fully inhabit this 'Black' role, but is instead doomed to inhabit the director's imagination of blackness, one shaped by a long history of caricature and misrecognition. If part of appropriating 'is to extend the solitary self out towards the broader world of Shakespeare and what Shakespeare touches',[29] Black appropriation has to work around the whiteness of Shakespeare and its disciplining force to accomplish this expansiveness.

The extended 'asides' in *American Moor* reveal the conversations that theatre has no time or capacity for.[30] Its power lies not just in its critique of whiteness in American theatre but in its profound plea for mutual recognition and for real conversation about race in Shakespeare, American theatre and American life. In this it shares much with Toni Morrison/Rokia Traoré's *Desdemona*, which is also a demand for a listening space. Set in the play's afterlife, *Desdemona* centres women's perspectives, reflecting Morrison's wish to 'reveal interior lives and characters' motives unexamined in *Othello*'.[31] *Desdemona* posits that Desdemona's love for Othello is prepared for by an earlier childhood love in her relationship with Barbary, the African maid who has died before the play begins, but whose story and Willow song carries the pathos of 4.3. In death, 'Barbary' appears with her 'original' name Sa'ran (meaning Joy) to tell her own story. Although *Desdemona* suggests a certain universality in women's experiences, particularly in the silencing of women's experiences across patriarchal cultures,[32] it is important to see how the play models the difficulty and complexity of listening, even amongst women. When Desdemona confronts Emilia's sardonic greeting by opining of the afterlife, 'All is known here, though not always understood,'[33] she ironically prepares the audience for her own education in the blindness of elite white womanhood.

Not only does Sa'ran voice her own love story, she makes clear the power relations that shaped her relationship with Desdemona. In perhaps the play's most jarring moment, she cuts through Desdemona's nostalgia:

> **Desdemona** ... How I have missed you. Remember the days we spent by the canal? We ate sweets and you saved the honey for me eating none yourself. We shared so much.
> **Barbary** We shared nothing.
> **Desdemona** What do you mean?
> **Sa'ran** I mean you don't even know my name. Barbary? Barbary is what you call Africa. Barbary is the geography of the foreigner, the savage. Barbary? ...
> Barbary is the name of those without whom you could neither live nor prosper.
> **Desdemona** So tell me. What is your name?
> **Sa'ran** Sa'ran.
> **Desdemona** Well, Sa'ran, whatever your name, you were my best friend.
> **Sa'ran** I was your slave.[34]

Desdemona has to unlearn her ignorance and colour-blindness in order to get beyond an appropriative relationship to Barbary to a complicated bond with Sa'ran that yields greater understanding in both.[35] Before Desdemona can hear, she must learn and unlearn. Tara N. Meister notes that this unpacking of whiteness necessarily involves just such jarring dissonance: 'Spaces and moments of dissonance push against taken-for-granted ideas to see beyond our *particular* realities to consider other realities inscribed historically.'[36]

SONIC WHITENESS

Both *American Moor* and *Desdemona* point to issues of sound, silence, listening and whiteness at the heart of *Othello*. Bruce R. Smith beautifully renders the many dimensions of sound:

> Sound immerses me in the world: it is there and here, in front of me and behind me, above and below me. Sound moves into presence and moves out of presence: it gives me reference points for situating myself in space and time. Sound subsumes me: it is continually present, pulsing within my body, penetrating my body from without, filling my perceptual world to the very horizons of hearing.[37]

Smith strikingly points us to sound's embodiedness and its expansiveness. It stabilizes the self, but it also enlarges: we open out beyond body's limits into realms almost unmeasurable. Like beautiful sounds, one wants to lose oneself in this description, but to do so is to forget that, if sound is a fact of the natural world, what we hear and how we understand what we hear is culturally constructed.

Both *American Moor* and *Desdemona* point us beyond whiteness and race as visual regimes to the politics of sound. To examine their engagement with sound and listening, I turn to Jennifer Lynn Stoever's *Sonic Color Line*, which asks that we reconsider 'racialization as a sonic practice,' an intervention she argues began with W. E. B. Du Bois's *Dusk of Dawn*.[38] Here, Du Bois questions the fundamental strategies of *The Souls of Black Folk*, which was based on the idea that 'The world was thinking wrong about race, because it did not know.'[39] *Dusk* questions *Souls*' attempt to overcome white supremacy with assaults on its flawed logic: 'Any literary, artistic, or political project challenging race, *Dusk of Dawn* warns, will be gravely complicated by the fact that whites not only have been conditioned to see *and* hear the world differently but also have labelled and propagated this sensory configuration as universal, objective truth.'[40] Du Bois depicts this problem of white sensory perception substituting for truth using an image of a glass vacuum chamber where Black people, trapped inside are 'screaming in the vacuum, unheard'.[41] In this image, the problem is neither Black eloquence nor Black intellectual capacity, but white refusal to hear. Stoever theorizes this dimension of race as 'the sonic colour line' which 'produces, codes, and polices racial differences through the ear, enabling us to hear race as well as see it'.[42]

The instrument of the sonic colour line is the 'listening ear,' a powerful disciplining force that narrows 'the individual's myriad, fine-grained embodied listening experiences by shunting them into narrow, conditioned and "correct" responses that are politically, culturally, economically, legally and socially advantageous to whites'.[43] Whites cannot hear, it turns out, because they control the registers of what can be heard. In line with Stoever's analysis, I suggest that Morrison, Traoré and Cobb are 'theorists of listening'.[44] *American Moor* and *Desdemona* demonstrate how Black speech and articulated Black experience are continually conditioned for white consumption. While Cobb stages the ways the Black actor's verbal and emotional exuberance is channelled and shaped by whites, Morrison, by resituating Desdemona, is able to work around the disciplining ear to create an 'intimate listening space'.[45] Both pieces hold out hope for generative conversations across racial and historical divides, but make clear that true change will take both Black decolonization and white unlearning.

Cobb theorizes the American theatre as a disciplining sonic space, which codes Black exuberance, particularly in relationship to Shakespeare, as 'noise' both unwelcome and unShakespearean. It is the sonic dimension of the words that attracted The Actor to Shakespeare: 'You know it was never written to be read. It was written to be seen, *and heard*' (emphasis added).[46] In fact, The Actor sees a kinship between the richness of Shakespeare's language and Black male emotional life:

> ... young American men of African descent, whether they voice it or not, have a great deal of external stimuli to react to, all the time. ... Then, Willy walked in ... I realized that *these* characters, each had this depthless reservoir of emotion already roiling around within them.[47]

He sees in Shakespeare's range of emotion the opportunity to overcome a lifetime of psychological trauma and repression and the possibility of enlivening the Shakespearean text: 'I, my intellect, my instrument, and my crazy-ass African American emotionality could serve the words well, *and* be served well by them.'[48]

Sound is a way of projecting oneself beyond the body, something that is policed in Black men, Cobb says, almost from birth – not just what we say, but how we say things. The Actor's evocation of Trayvon Martin, who refused to be silent in the face of provocation, into this sense of kinship is a reminder that the listening ear means the difference between justice and injustice, life and death.[49] Mastery of Shakespeare can be a safe way of becoming expansive as a Black man, of using Shakespeare's words to reach other people, for this Fanonian connection: 'I could say that, as well as anyone, and infused with every ounce of my glorious African American emotional arrogance, it would sing.'[50] But between Shakespeare's words and The Actor's infusion of emotion lies the problem of the white listening ear, which in fact recoils from Black emotionality. In the white dominated world, this depth of feeling is continually repressed. For theatre, which depends on emotion and sound, the imposition of the white listening ear is particularly fraught and subtle, 'noise and loudness frequently function as aural substitutes for and markers of race and form key contours of the sonic colour line'.[51]

In earlier *American Moor* performances, the Director was performed acousmatically (that is a recorded voice without a clear origin) or from the control booth.[52] That voice was technically amplified and omnipresent, a configuration literally referred to as 'the voice of god' in theatre. It is a young masculine voice that is also almost studiously emotionless, a flatness that becomes more and more noticeable in the face of Cobb's code switching between various forms of Blackness, Shakespearean prose and the accents of his interlocutors. Whiteness as a sonic presence then mirrors the attributes and power of whiteness itself: invisible, all encompassing, and yet almost unlocatable. On one hand, The Director is a person who is both entirely flawed and human and thus someone one can hope to persuade or move into recognition: 'He's just a guy who lives by these American rules, and he wants me to live by them too.'⁵³ On the other hand, the Director is a figuration of Stoever's listening ear – powerful and disciplining: 'A disembodied voice interrupts. It will remain only a voice throughout the play. But it is omnipresent, answerable to and impossible to ignore. It always has been.'⁵⁴ It interrupts The Actor, redirecting towards white comfort: 'But look, this is not the time or place to have this discussion.'⁵⁵

Elsewhere, Cobb makes it clear that the Director is the form of the white 'listening ear', a force Black men experience almost from birth:

> The voice of that director, he is invisible for a reason. It is the omniscient voice that we hear in the world. I walk out of my house and there is voice that says, 'You watch how you behave.' And young Black men hear this from the time they are babies. You take that bass out of your voice. You don't respond, they are not going to get you. You're going to get yourself shot. They do not get you. [Interviewer interrupts]. That voice is everywhere . . . that voice is saying 'we will accept this, this, this and this from you, but not this, this and this.'⁵⁶

Cobb also implies that awareness of the listening ear is necessary for Black self-protection. The Director's voice is connected to the listening ears that Othello/The Actor is 'answerable to': it speaks for Brabantio and the Venetian Senate. Furthermore, because Cobb himself performs the variety of white characters who speak with the certainty of white supremacy, the sonic, intermittent presence of the Director is complemented with the variety of white figures that stand in for 'Shakespeare' and continually reinforce Shakespeare as white property. The audience ('whatever portion of the audience will, or can, listen')⁵⁷ is that space of possibility between.

A deep-voiced actor, Cobb is exquisitely attuned to the subtleties of the sonic colour line that 'produces, codes, and polices racial difference through the ear, enabling us to hear race as well as see it. Within this socially constructed boundary that racially codes sonic phenomena such as vocal timbre, accents, and musical tones',⁵⁸ the much-admired deep timbre of some Black voices is seen as a potential source of danger:

> I learned . . . that people in our American culture, who are not Black like me, they do not respond in the same manner to Black men, like me, raising their voices, even slightly, as they do with one another . . . or even changing tone. They do not respond well to my adamance.⁵⁹

When The Actor claims the expansive right to identify and express the canon regardless of gender and race, his acting teacher relies on the 'commonsense' of whiteness to shrink his horizons. Reducing his identifications with a range of Shakespeare's characters – from Titania to Hamlet – to the roles he deems properly suited to The Actor's blackness, insisting that he 'pick something you might realistically play' (from a dramatic corpus full of witches, fairies and ghosts that no one can 'realistically' play). The Actor's attempted performances of Titania provokes one of many white interruptions:

I said I'd like to do Titania (the middle 'a' pronounced like Vanya), from *A Midsummer Night's Dream*. And he said to me,
 'The Fairie Queen?'
I said,
 'Yeah, sure.'
He said,
 'Titania' (the middle 'a' pronounced like canyon).
I said,
 'Huh?'
 'The correct pronunciation . . . is Titania.'
I said,
 You want I should give you a slap?'
Okay, I didn't really say that. I mean, of course I didn't, right? But I wanted to. I mean, he needed to hear it.[60]

Instead of a teaching moment, this is an enforcement of the listening ear, a moment of disciplining and alienation, performed again when he interrupts The Actor's 'forgeries of jealousy' speech: 'The poetry trips up the best of them.'[61]

Although whiteness in *Desdemona* appears in an array of performance registers, here, I am interested in *Desdemona*'s sonic dimensions. Peter Sellars notes the perversities of both speech/silence in *Othello* ('*Othello* is a loud play, men are yelling a lot')[62] and the centrality of listening to *Desdemona*. Desdemona's silence, epitomized by Othello's choice to strangle her, is key to the play's characterization. Morrison, following Desdemona into the afterlife, forces a reversal of women's silencing. To complement Morrison's project of unleashing women's voices, the costume and set design took a backseat to acoustics: 'We invested the set budget in . . . extremely high quality microphones. Because if Toni was going to have these women finally speak, then I really wanted to hear them.'[63] However, it is not enough to give voice to and amplify unspoken truths, those truths must be understood. Both the process of creating *Desdemona* and the text/performance itself reveals the pain and labour of actually hearing.

In *Desdemona*, one sees that the listening ear's capacity for discipline doesn't just apply to people of colour, nor is it just applied by men. Desdemona's childhood memories are of being disciplined into codes of conduct that are highly gendered:[64] 'Constraint was the theme of behaviour. / Duty was its plot.'[65] When she is punished, ostensibly for soaking her clothes, laughter is key to her disobedience: 'My unleashed laughter was long and loud. The unseemliness of such behaviour in a girl of less than one decade brought my mother's attention.'[66] Laughter is the auditory dimension of Desdemona's desires and wilfulness: silence and stillness the lesson. Not coincidentally, it is in this zone of punishment and stillness that Desdemona first 'hears' Barbary the maid: 'Barbary alone conspired with me to let my imagination run free. She told me stories of other lives, other countries. Places where gods speak in thundering silence.'[67] 'To hear Barbary sing was to wonder at the mediocrity of flutes and pipes,' suggests that Desdemona as a child becomes attuned to another dimension beyond the cloistered life of a rich Venetian woman: 'I yearned for talk, for meaning.'[68]

Desdemona only achieves true talk and meaning in the afterlife, after learning to listen. She suggests that she can actually hear the African notes of *Othello* (and we presume, the Malian sounds composed by Traoré) in distinction to the European travellers for whom the singing of African women was 'Full ill to our ears.'[69] Nonetheless, Desdemona's relationship to the Willow Song is as appropriative as her relationship to Sa'ran. In Desdemona's telling, Sa'ran's death is about Sa'ran's abandonment and her loss: 'When I needed her most, she stumbled under the spell of her lover.'[70] Although she speaks of mourning, her sense of Barbary is an object lesson in womanhood, 'And yet even in grief I questioned: were we women so frail in the wake of men who swore they cherished us?'[71] The confrontation over their power differences seems to come to a stalemate:

Desdemona Was I ever cruel to you? Ever?
Sa'ran No. You never hurt or abused me.
Desdemona Who did?
Sa'ran You know who did. But I have thought long and hard about my sorrow.[72]

Remembering they were both abused by men is not enough. Desdemona has to give up her sentimental attachment to the Willow Song and hear Sa'ran's African song, sung by Traoré: 'No more "willow". Afterlife is time and with time there is change. My song is new.'[73] Desdemona must then sit in silence during the African performance. Reconciliation comes only when Desdemona is able to sing Sa'ran's song of the afterlife: 'What bliss to know / I will never die again.' Desdemona: 'We will never die again.'[74]

DISRUPTING *OTHELLO*

If we consider the theatre as an acoustic space, à la Bruce R. Smith, then we must hear it as a white, male space. *Othello* in particular is loud, as Sellars notes. Sound is cacophonous and untrustworthy. (White) women's speech, by its very nature condemns them. Black speech is limited to performative speech, which is to say that we rarely have moments of intimacy with Othello: Shakespeare doesn't pretend to let us into Othello's inner life. Iago's 'inner life' as offered to the audience is full of deception, false intimacy and jealousy. Peter Erickson's *Citing Shakespeare* reminds us, 'much of the play's final scene hinges on the drama of speaking'[75] and calls attention to how many of the characters define themselves using the term 'speak'. Emilia, he notes, 'insists on this word repeatedly . . .' while 'the previously loquacious Iago . . . adopts silence'.[76] Having framed speech as a problem, '[Othello] transfers to us the responsibility for speaking'.[77] In this sense Othello starts a conversation in which he can only *hope* to be known or heard. He can hope that the audience can love him with more faith and less ownership than he loved Desdemona. *Desdemona*, too, holds out Othello's hope: the dialogue in the scene where he confesses to rape and murder ends with his wish 'I pray that I am more.'[78] More than Shakespeare's Moor and more than the orphan and former child soldier who has done the unspeakable.

Many Black appropriations speak to that inner life. *American Moor* in particular suggests that the Black actor's experience can replace Othello's presumed inner life at least more fully than can the white director's incomplete understanding of race. However, the whiteness that uplifts and claims Shakespeare poses a conundrum. These plays are less interested in individual white racism than in whiteness as an institution.[79] Thus they draw our attention to the fact that US theatrical spaces are primarily 'white' – both composed of mostly white audiences and also historically designed to either discourage 'black sound' or to enact Stoever's 'listening ear' (for example, to insist that black performance be heard through the laughter of minstrelsy). Certainly Black Shakespeareans and female Shakespeareans have been 'disciplined' by dirty looks or shushing when laughing at points a white person deems inappropriate. This is the silence that accompanies gentrification.[80]

Returning to Du Bois's image of the glass vacuum with screaming Blacks inside and indifferent whites outside, Stoever reminds us of the necessity of changing our listening practices: 'For the glass to be removed, fundamental shifts in listening must occur on either side – a dismantling of the listening ear outside the glass and a decolonizing of listening on the inside.[81] Both *American Moor* & *Desdemona* disrupt the listening ear by filling the theatre with (and interleaving the Shakespeare text with) sounds from Africa and the diaspora, from the code-switching of Keith Hamilton Cobb's Actor to Toni Morrison's script to Rokia Traoré's music and the Morrison/Traoré lyrics that weave Malian and African folktales with snippets of Shakespearean text.[82] These texts suggest that, in attempting to hear these other sounds, we can break through the whiteness, but only if we hear some 'noise' for the music it is, accept dissonance over convention and experience the Shakespearean text differently. As we continue to read, teach, watch and perform Shakespeare in a world with heightened tensions over race, religion, ethnicity and nation, it seems incumbent on us to help students and audiences hear voices beyond the white noise of the Shakespeare industry.

NOTES

1. Frantz Fanon, *Black Skin, White Masks*, trans. Richard Philcox (New York: Grove Press, 2008), 107.

2. Peter Sellars, 'Forward' in Toni Morrison and Rokia Traoré, *Desdemona* (London: Oberon Books, 2012), 9.

3. Perhaps it's not just contemporary productions. Sheila Rose Bland's 'How I would Direct *Othello*' insists that the play reads as a minstrel show and that, 'when you make Othello a white male actor in blackface makeup . . . instead of laughing with the character Othello, the audience will tend to laugh at him. In fact, much of the seemingly "tragic" dissipates'. Sheila Rose Bland, 'How I Would Direct *Othello*', in *Othello: New Essays by Black Writers*, ed. Mythili Kaul (Washington, DC: Howard University Press, 1997), 33.

4. Cheryl I. Harris, 'Whiteness as Property', *Harvard Law Review* 106.8 (1 June 1993): 1707–91, https://doi.org/10.2307/1341787. I'm particularly grateful for Keith Hamilton Cobb's generosity with the academic community and to Hannah Ehrenberg for indispensable research that contributed to this essay. Some of my analysis of *American Moor* goes back to my early review of the play in *Shakespeare Bulletin* 34.35 (2016): 524–8.

5. Sellars, 'Forward', 9.
6. In addition to *Desdemona* and *American Moor* (early versions of *American Moor* have scenes with a Desdemona-character), see, for example, Alice Childress's unpublished TV adaptation of *Othello* and Curley Holden's *Othello in Sepia*. Although Ambereen Dadabhoy powerfully reads the Director as a figuration of Iago, I think it is important to see him as a broader embodiment of whiteness. See Dadabhoy, 'Wincing at Shakespeare: Looking B(l)ack at the Bard', *The Journal of American Studies*, 54 (2020): 82. I borrow the term 'respeakings' from Peter Erickson, who uses it in his reading of Fred Wilson's Venice Biennale installation, *Speak of Me As I Am* because 'so much of the play's final scene hinges on the drama of speaking'. Peter Erickson, *Citing Shakespeare: The Reinterpretation of Race in Contemporary Literature and Art* (Basingstoke: Palgrave Macmillan, 2007), 9.
7. Although the Director refers to the actor once as 'Keith', the script uses 'The Actor' for the dialogue. This essay uses 'The Actor' to refer to the character and 'Cobb' when referring to the author and performer. Keith Hamilton Cobb, *American Moor* (London: Methuen Drama, 2020), 10.
8. Cynthia R. Nielsen, 'Frantz Fanon and the Négritude Movement: How Strategic Essentialism Subverts Manichean Binaries', *Callaloo* 36.2 (2013): 350.
9. Keith Hamilton Cobb, 'American Moor: An Overview | Keith Hamilton Cobb', accessed 2 August 2017, http://keithhamiltoncobb.com/site/american-moor-an-overview/.
10. Hugh Quarshie, 'Second Thoughts About Othello', in *International Shakespeare Association Occasional Papers*, vol. 7, Hudson Strode Lectures on Race and Class in the Renaissance, University of Alabama, Tuscaloosa (Chipping Camden, UK: Clouds Hill Printers, 1999), 3.
11. Shakespeare, Sebastian, 'Sir Patrick Stewart: I'm Going to Play Othello as a White Man', *Mail Online*, accessed 22 July 2015, http://www.dailymail.co.uk/tvshowbiz/article-3163224/Sir-Patrick-Stewart-m-going-play-Othello-white-man.html.
12. Fanon, *Black Skin, White Masks*, 106–7.
13. Hill, Edwin C., Jr. *Black Soundscapes White Stages: The Meaning of Francophone Sound in the Black Atlantic* (Baltimore: Johns Hopkins University Press, 2013), 107.
14. Although Fanon, throughout the chapter 'The Lived Experience of the Black Man', is searingly critical of Negritude, his quote from Cesaire in this passage suggests that he agrees with Negritude's sense that Blacks must claim and create Black spaces to resist and heal from the trauma of centuries of colonization.
15. Cobb, *American Moor*, 9.
16. Ibid., 10.
17. Ibid., 27–8.
18. I witnessed something similar during a talkback after a 2015 performance of *Rasheeda Speaking* starring Tonya Pinkins and Dianne Wiest. When asked what discussions the cast had about race, Director Cynthia Nixon responded that she brought in an article about Korea airlines executive Heather Cho's infamous 'nut rage' incident for the cast to discuss –for an American play about tensions between a white office manager and a black employee.

19. Cobb, *American Moor*, 17.
20. Ibid., 17.
21. Harris, 'Whiteness as Property', 1713.
22. Ibid., 1789.
23. Harris goes on to note the role of people of colour in this production of exclusivity: 'but exclusivity is predicated not on any intrinsic characteristic, but on the existence of the symbolic Other, which functions to "create an illusion of unity" among whites' (Ibid., 1789).
24. Ibid., 1761.
25. Cobb, *American Moor*, 12.
26. Harris, 'Whiteness as Property', 1736.
27. Ibid., 1743.
28. Cobb, *American Moor*, 13.
29. Christie Desmet and Sujata Iyengar, 'Adaptation, Appropriation, or What You Will', *Shakespeare* 11.1 (2 January 2015), 5.
30. In dialogue cut from the final script, Cobb points to the economics of modern theatre that exacerbate the inability to dig into the play. 'Your two weeks and change in the rehearsal hall is analogous to your five minutes lookin' at me in this room. Othello on the page, or the Black man in front of you; in that short space you can't do nothing but fucking pretend to know shit about either' (*American Moor*, 47).
31. Lenore Kitts, 'The Sound of Change: A Musical Transit Through the Wounded Modernity of *Desdemona*', in *Toni Morrison: Memory and Meaning*, ed. Adrienne Lanier Seward and Justine Tally (Jackson, MS: University Press of Mississippi, 2014), 258.
32. Ibid., 260ff.
33. Toni Morrison and Rokia Traoré, *Desdemona* (London: Oberon Books, 2012), 42.
34. Ibid., 45.
35. By 'colorblindness', I am not referring to a willful neoconservative project, but to the general refusal/inability to see 'the immense sociohistorical weight of race'. See Michael Omi and Howard Winant, *Racial Formation in the United States* (New York: Routledge, 2015), 220; and Kyle Grady, 'Othello, Colin Powell, and Post-Racial Anachronisms', *Shakespeare Quarterly* 67.1 (2016): 68–83.
36. Tara N. Meister, 'From Interior to Dialogue and Deconstruction: Dismantling Ideologies of Whiteness with Stories', *Journal of Critical Thought and Praxis* 6.3 (2017): 86. https://doi.org/10.31274/jctp-180810-86.
37. Bruce R. Smith, *The Acoustic World of Early Modern England : Attending to the O-Factor* (Chicago: University of Chicago Press, 1999), 9–10.
38. Jennifer Lynn Stoever, *The Sonic Color Line: Race and the Cultural Politics of Listening* (New York: New York University Press, 2016), 10.
39. W. E. B. Du Bois, *Dusk of Dawn: An Essay toward an Autobiography of a Race Concept* (New York: Oxford University Press, 2007), 30. See also, W. E. B. Du Bois, *The Souls of Black Folk: Essays and Sketches* (Chicago: A. C. McClurg, 1903).

40. Stoever, *The Sonic Color Line*, 10.
41. Du Bois, *Dusk of Dawn*, 66; and Stoever, *The Sonic Color Line*, 10.
42. Stoever, *The Sonic Color Line*, 11.
43. Ibid., 15.
44. Ibid., 17.
45. Peter Sellars, 'Desdemona Takes The Microphone: Toni Morrison and Shakespeare's Hidden Women' (University of California–Berkeley, 28 October 2011), https://www.youtube.com/watch?v=G73AhP7Sfpg (accessed 17 October 2015).
46. Cobb, *American Moor*, 4.
47. Ibid., 5.
48. Ibid., 5.
49. Ibid., 32. Brittney Cooper was one of the first to point out the American Judicial system's (and media's) inability to hear Jeantel Martin, the only witness to Trayvon's murder, because of her darkness, her size and her vernacular speaking style that resisted the aural codes of the white male dominated courtroom. See Brittney Cooper, 'Dark-Skinned and Plus-Sized: The Real Rachel Jeantel Story', *Salon*, 28 June, 2013, https://www.salon.com/2013/06/28/did_anyone_really_hear_rachel_jeantel/. See also Stoever, *The Sonic Color Line*, 278–9.
50. Cobb, *American Moor*, 6.
51. Stoever, *The Sonic Color Line*, 13.
52. *American Moor*'s 2018 performance in London at the Sam Wanamaker Playhouse at Shakespeare's Globe was the first where the Director, played by Josh Tyson, appears in person. There, and in subsequent performances, he sits amidst the audience.
53. Cobb, *American Moor*, 8.
54. Ibid., 10.
55. Ibid., 40.
56. Barbara Bogaev, *American Moor*, *Shakespeare Unlimited* (accessed 9 August, 2016), https://www.folger.edu/shakespeare-unlimited/american-moor.
57. Cobb, *American Moor*, 11.
58. Stoever, *Sonic Color Line*, 11.
59. Cobb, *American Moor*, 8.
60. Ibid., 6.
61. Ibid., 7. You can hear Barbara Bogaev discuss this moment with Cobb on the *Shakespeare Unlimited* podcast. *American Moor*, Shakespeare Unlimited (accessed 9 August, 2016), https://www.folger.edu/shakespeare-unlimited/american-moor.
62. Sellars, 'Desdemona Takes The Microphone'.
63. Ibid. Although there is not the space to elaborate in this essay, it is worth noting that even the microphone, a seemingly objective piece of technology, was in America constructed around race and the sonic colour line, with black people somewhat equated with the 'microphone's mute utility, which, while fundamental to

broadcasting, can only amplify others' voices'. See Stoever, *The Sonic Color Line*, 240.

64. For more on the links between Renaissance codes of conduct, class and race, see Patricia Akhimie, *Shakespeare and the Cultivation of Difference: Race and Conduct in the Early Modern World* (London: Routledge, 2018).
65. Morrison and Traoré, *Desdemona*, 17.
66. Ibid., 17.
67. Ibid., 18.
68. Ibid., 22.
69. Merchant William Towerson's description from his 1555 voyage to Guinea, quoted in Anthony Gerard Barthelemy, *Black Face, Maligned Race: The Representation of Blacks in English Drama from Shakespeare to Southerne* (Baton Rouge: Louisiana State University Press, 1987), 59.
70. Morrison and Traoré, *Desdemona*, 18.
71. Ibid., 18.
72. Ibid., 49.
73. Ibid., 49.
74. Ibid., 49.
75. Erickson, *Citing Shakespeare*, 9.
76. Ibid., 10.
77. Ibid., 10.
78. Morrison and Rokia Traoré, *Desdemona*, 39.
79. Errol Hill, *Shakespeare in Sable: A History of Black Shakespearean Actors* (Amherst: University of Massachusetts Press, 1984), 40–1.
80. See, for example, the controversy over the 30-year-old African drum circle in Harlem's Mount Morris Park, Timothy Williams, 'An Old Sound in Harlem Draws New Neighbors' Ire', *The New York Times*, 6 July, 2008, sec. N.Y. / Region, https://www.nytimes.com/2008/07/06/nyregion/06drummers.html.
81. Stoever, *The Sonic Color Line*, 261–2.
82. Teaching *Desdemona* suggests that this aural disruption is very incomplete. Since the text does not come with a soundtrack, one mostly experiences Traoré's voice and her musical text in snippets. Even in live performance, it is unclear if the audience invests as much in experiencing the music and movement of the black women performers as they do in the text.

CHAPTER SIXTEEN

'The Soul of a Great White Poet'

Shakespearean Educations and the Civil Rights Era

JASON M. DEMETER

SHAKESPEARE AND WHITE AMERICA

In the opening paragraphs of a widely syndicated newspaper column published in 1970, President of San Francisco State College S. I. Hayakawa describes a remarkable scene:

> A Negro professor of English is giving a lecture on Shakespeare to a mostly white class. He is a well-qualified literary scholar, held in high esteem by his colleagues. The students listen respectfully.
>
> Suddenly a group of 40 or more white youths break into the classroom. They shout and scream racist obscenities at the black professor. They say the class must be dismissed at once. The professor, they say, is incompetent, because how can a black man understand the soul of a great white poet like Shakespeare? Having broken up the classroom with threats of physical violence, the band of white youths stomp out.[1]

Shocking as it is, Hayakawa soon makes clear that the above incident of racial terrorism was a fiction – a rhetorical device used to demonstrate what the author views as a pervasive double standard within higher education. With that, readers learn that a comparable situation had played out at his university in 1968 when a group of Black students, 'some of them carrying lead pipes', infiltrated a classroom to disrupt a course on African American history, demanding the white instructor be replaced by one who was Black.[2] Hayakawa imagines an outraged response to the hypothetical white protesters, contrasting it with the sympathetic one with which the university community met the Black protesters, arguing ultimately that, on college campuses throughout the nation, 'there is a law for white hoodlums, but a different one for blacks'.[3]

Notable of Hayakawa's rhetoric is how it equates Black students' investment in African American history with white students' presumed ownership of Shakespeare.

Contradicting popular narratives of Shakespeare's universality – narratives invoked frequently within educational discourse to justify the Bard's privileged place within the Western cultural canon – Hayakawa's editorial, written in the twilight of the civil rights/Black Power era, presents a counter-narrative, framing Shakespeare instead as an avatar of white European values and aesthetics.

In what follows, I examine how the racist assumptions underpinning Hayakawa's rhetoric – specifically the notion that Shakespeare exists as white property – are rehearsed and recirculated throughout early- and mid-twentieth-century American scholastic culture. It is my contention herein that the nation's system of compulsory mass education plays an important role in revising the poet's racial signification moving forward. Though he was used to bolster myths of America's Anglo-Saxon cultural heritage throughout the eighteenth and nineteenth centuries, the mid-twentieth century finds Shakespeare imagined no longer as an avatar for English identity, but rather as a broader representation of undifferentiated whiteness defined in direct opposition to an imagined Black antithesis. This reconfiguration of Shakespeare's racial signification, I argue, is tied to his mounting prominence within American mass education. With the rise of compulsory schooling in the early-twentieth century, along with Shakespeare's increasingly central role within a developing English curriculum, the poet is implicated within a segregated educational system.[4] Thus the playwright, once perceived as an object of popular entertainment, is reconfigured throughout the early- and mid-twentieth century into an object of mandatory study, compulsory veneration and racial division.

One site where we can see with clarity Shakespeare's functionality within the white supremacist American educational programme is in the editorial apparatuses and educational para-texts that accompany what is – by any measure – the dominant work within the postwar curriculum: *Julius Caesar*.[5] Depicted in the pages of popular textbooks, Caesar becomes a proto-fascist dictator, the conspirators, champions of democratic values and the citizenry, a thoughtless, easily manipulated rabble incapable of effective self-governance; the play is thus made to pose questions of identity and citizenship similar to those underpinning racist laws used to disenfranchise Black Americans since Reconstruction. In this way, *Julius Caesar*'s systematic dissemination among tenth-grade students throughout American public and private schools helps predicate Shakespeare's racially charged signification moving forward. In an analysis of the casually white supremacist editorial content accompanying the play within the pages of the nation's popular textbooks, I show how Shakespeare was reimagined in the early-twentieth century as a path to enculturation for European immigrants – a way to homogenize a melting pot of disparate European races within a uniquely English cultural paradigm – all while implicitly excluding Black Americans from Shakespeare and, crucially, the cultural capital he might impart. Especially in their construction of what is framed as America's classically inspired democratic heritage – a tradition that views whites of European ancestry as singularly capable of living up to the challenges of effective self-governance – the period's anthologies employ a racial logic consonant with Hayakawa's construction of Shakespeare as the quintessence of white American history and culture. Perhaps more revealing is the way Black people are portrayed as symbolic threats whose presence is evidence of a decadent and rapidly declining

Republic. Shakespeare's play, I argue finally, is thus made instrumental in the construction of a monolithic whiteness – a project that reconfigured the heterogeneous ethno-racial divisions of eighteenth- and early-nineteenth-century America into a blunt, mutually constitutive, two-tiered hierarchy in which a freshly reincorporated white race is imagined as always superior to the largely undifferentiated Black population against which it is defined.

WHITENESS AND CITIZENSHIP IN THE US

For most of the nation's history, race was instrumental in delineating who was eligible for American citizenship. Racial exclusion was codified under the Naturalization Law of 1790, which extended citizenship to 'free white' immigrants of 'good moral character' who had lived in the country for at least two full years.[6] Despite the egalitarian ideals put forth in the nation's founding documents, race-based exclusion was built into the legal system even before colonists had secured their independence from England. While revisions to the law would redefine periodically the criteria for who might be eligible for citizenship, America's immigration policy was overtly discriminatory until after the conclusion of the Second World War.[7] Yet even as early immigration laws sought to limit the extension of citizenship to white immigrants, the radical instability of whiteness as a racial category made implementing such policies complicated. As the work of numerous contemporary social historians concerned with racial formation in the United States has shown, constructions of whiteness have varied significantly throughout American history, and ethnic groups who are perceived as non-white in one epoch might come to be categorized as white in another.[8]

Perhaps *because* of the variability of whiteness over time, it would become increasingly salient, both socially and politically, during the nineteenth century, as greater numbers of non-English European immigrants crossed the Atlantic. Rather than assimilating freely into the American citizenry, many of these early immigrants found their opportunities limited by the stereotypical ethno-racial categories into which they were made to fit. While Irish, Italian, Jewish, Greek, Slavic, and other non-English ethnic groups might be viewed as morally, intellectually, and constitutionally superior to Black, Asian, and indigenous Americans, so too were they considered racially inferior to the imagined Anglo-Saxon ideal. As members of numerous ethnic factions struggled for prosperity in their newly adopted nation, they would frequently find their lineage an impediment to social and economic advancement. Rather than being embraced by native-born white Americans of supposedly Anglo-Saxon derivation in light of their shared European ancestry, immigrants were viewed as subordinate in their assumed position within an ethnically determined racial order. In this way, the wave of mass European immigration spanning from the 1840s to the early 1920s resulted in the splintering of whiteness into a hierarchical plurality of distinct white races. Though members of most European ethnic groups were considered to be nominally white, so too was their whiteness viewed as incomplete due to their distinctly non-English, non-Anglo-Saxon heritage. While the multi-tiered racial matrix into which immigrants were positioned was never fully stable, Anglo-Saxons were always understood as superior to their Greek, Irish and Italian counterparts. Thus European ethnic minorities found themselves consigned to a liminal space within American society; while they might be white for legal purposes, they were deemed neither fully white nor fully Black within the broader socio-racial schema. Reginald Horsman's study of American Anglo-Saxonism traces its rise through the Revolutionary period until its peak in the 1850s, by which time he argues that Americans had thoroughly internalized its racist presuppositions, including the belief that 'the peoples of large parts of the world were incapable of creating efficient, democratic and prosperous governments'.[9] Given the English origins of American jurisprudence, it became a highly debated question in the nineteenth century as to whether or not individuals of non-English extraction were deserving of the rights and responsibilities of self-government under the nation's political system.

Adding urgency to these matters were the increasing numbers of Europeans immigrating to the US throughout the nineteenth century. These numbers would swell throughout the 1800s, peaking in the first decade of the twentieth century. Even after its apex in 1907, when the US would admit more than one and a quarter million European settlers as permanent residents, immigration would continue at a relatively steady pace until 1921.[10] The passage of the so-called Emergency Quota Act and the even-more-restrictive Johnson-Reed act of 1924 had the effect of reducing immigration to its lowest rates in a century. As immigration slowed, there was a gradual abatement of anti-immigrant anxiety. Yet this new regime of protectionist immigration policies, coupled with the subsequent enactment of discriminatory New Deal programmes effectively precluding Black Americans from receiving proportional governmental benefits, had the effect of massively reconfiguring the racial dynamics of the American body politic.[11] As distinct ethno-racial categories that had been well-defined in earlier decades were eventually subsumed under a broad umbrella of undifferentiated whiteness, racial tensions in the US would become centred on a dualistic paradigm that pitted a freshly congealed white majority against a long-oppressed Black minority. The historian Matthew Frye Jacobson, describes this phenomenon, noting that: '[a]s the "Negro Question" steadily eclipsed every other race question on the national agenda between the 1930s and the 1950s, the interracial coalitions that formed ... increasingly assumed a racially unvariegated group of whites to be ... a preexisting, static, and self-evident entity'.[12] The reconsolidation of whiteness in the period was so complete and successful that, according to Jacobson, 'by the 1950s ... [it] was "forgotten" ... that [non-English immigrants] had ever *been* distinct races in the first place'.[13] The effects of this massive reconfiguration of racial apprehension in America would be profound, especially as members of ethnic groups that were previously held in slight regard were able gradually to work their way into the majority white culture.

Unsurprisingly, one means through which members of European ethnic minorities were able to integrate themselves within the wider white population was through their involvement in America's burgeoning mass education system. In this regard, the study of language and literature was particularly useful, and Shakespeare, already established as the preeminent English author, was viewed as an essential tool for use in the Americanization of non-English immigrants. One of the clearest expressions of the poet's perceived value as a means of enculturation can be seen in Joseph Quincy Adams's 1932 address upon the dedication of the Folger Shakespeare Library, wherein the esteemed professor describes thousands of 'Italians, Poles, Slavs, Hungarians, Czechs, Greeks, Lithuanians, Rumanians, [and] Armenians . . . swarm[ing] into [the United States] like the locust in Egypt'.[14] Noting a tendency among these populations to remain insular and self-segregating, Adams gives voice to fears about the splintering of American culture. 'Foreign in their background and alien in their outlook upon life', he writes, '[immigrants] exhibited varied racial characteristics, varied ideals, and varied types of civilization'.[15] Adams laments how 'America seemed destined to become a babel of tongues and cultures'.[16] And it is here where Shakespeare emerges as a solution. 'Fortunately', he argues:

> about the time that the forces of immigration became a menace to the preservation of our long-established English civilization, there was initiated throughout the country a system of free and compulsory education for youth. . . . And here Shakespeare, the object of general idolatry, was . . . called upon to play a part in American national life. . . . [H]e was made the corner-stone of cultural discipline. A study of his works was required in successive grades extending over a period of years. . . . Everywhere pupils were set to the task of memorizing his lines, of reciting on platforms his more eloquent passages, of composing innumerable essays on his art, his technique, [and] his ideals of life. . . . The great English dramatist was held up as the supreme thinker, artist, [and] poet . . . . If out of America, unwieldy in size, and commonly called the melting pot of races, there has been evolved a homogeneous nation, with a culture that is still essentially English, we must acknowledge that in the process Shakespeare has played a major part.[17]

Yet amidst all of his exhortations regarding Shakespeare's functionality at uniting a racially disparate American citizenry, nowhere does he mention non-Europeans. Especially since Black people made up almost ten per cent of the population at the time of the speech, and that that so-called 'Negro Question' had loomed large in the American consciousness since Reconstruction, it is unlikely that their omission was an oversight.[18] More likely, the speech is illustrative of the gradual reconsolidation of whiteness that occurred following the enactment of immigration restrictions in the early 1920s. What is implicit in Adams's framing of Shakespeare as a means for 'the child of foreign parentage' to become American is the idea that to be American is to be white.[19] While white Europeans might be permitted access to American citizenship under the freshly reconfigured racial paradigm of the early-twentieth century, it remained theretofore inconceivable that such inclusion might be extended to those whose appearance remained the standard against which whiteness defined itself. While Adams's use of Shakespeare in this regard is notable for its direct engagement with questions of education, assimilation, and exclusion, his address is by no means the only instance in which Shakespeare is employed to suggest that American citizenship is the explicit province of a white majority. Indeed, and as we shall see, the poet is often used within educational materials of the early- and mid-twentieth century to reinforce contemporary ideologies of white supremacy.

SHAKESPEARE IN AMERICAN EDUCATION

The story of Shakespeare's position within American life is long and varied. The poet and his work had been present in the so-called New World since even before the War of American Independence, and his popularity, particularly on American stages, would continue through the eighteenth and nineteenth centuries.[20] While the playwright would remain a significant presence in American entertainment, especially as a means of imparting a veneer of prestige upon newly developing media technologies like film and radio, the early years of the twentieth century saw Shakespeare consigned to a decidedly contrastive sphere of mass culture, as his plays became aligned with an increasingly high-cultural, rather than recreational, agenda. While Shakespeare would continue to be disseminated through print, stage, and new media platforms, his works were frequently seen in terms of their importance as reminders of America's English heritage rather than heralded for their commercial appeal. Shakespeare's continued evolution from an object of mass entertainment to a high-cultural icon would be intensified by his prominence within America's burgeoning mass educational project. Indeed, by the early-twentieth century, American secondary schools would come to function as a primary site for the dissemination of Shakespeare among a broad swath of the American public. Once Shakespeare comes to be associated with a pedagogical agenda in the early-twentieth century, the poet becomes inextricable from popular associations with mass education in the years that follow. This situation persists even into the twenty-first century, and Shakespeare's continued implication with America's educational programme helps to account for the poet's sustained association with good taste, cultivation, and refinement within the contemporary imagination.[21] As Denise Albanese asserts, within contemporary American culture 'the social fact [is] that Shakespeare is, above all, schoolroom matter'.[22]

This is not to say that Shakespeare was absent from schools before the 1900s. To be sure, the poet had long been a presence within American pre-collegiate education, especially in the service of oratorical instruction. While antebellum schools varied widely in quality and curricular-focus, their primary instructional mission served generally to reinforce already existing social hierarchies, and the schools of the day catered almost exclusively to white males. Consequently, speeches from Shakespeare were employed with some frequency in rhetorical instruction, being used to prepare young pupils for the eventual demands of public and political life.[23] It was only in the decades immediately preceding the civil war that educational opportunities were extended sporadically to growing numbers of women, free Blacks and recent European immigrants. After the War's conclusion, as the American mass educational project took further hold, curricula became progressively regimented and standardized. Schools in the immediate postbellum period also began erecting the framework for what would become English studies in their use of literature in the instruction of spelling, reading and grammar; by the 1890s literary studies had emerged as a nascent discipline at both the collegiate and high school levels.[24] Based on a model of classical instruction that had thrived for centuries and then outfitted with a newfound methodological rigour borrowed from German philologists of the Romantic period, English literary studies gradually obtained its perceived curricular legitimacy and was ultimately accepted as a subject capable of imparting 'discipline, moral value, . . . and even patriotism' to American students.[25]

Given his longstanding use within rhetorical and oratorical instruction, Shakespeare was made to fit easily into the developing English curriculum. Though excerpts from Shakespeare's plays had long been fixtures of popular elocutionary manuals of the nineteenth century, what students encountered in anthologies such as the wildly popular series of *McGuffey Readers* were decontextualized, expurgated and heavily edited passages taken from Shakespeare's works that were intended for memorization and declamation; very few early- and mid-nineteenth century students would have engaged in the formal study of Shakespeare's plays in their entirety.[26] All of this began to change in the 1870s when American universities, beginning with Harvard, inaugurated entrance examinations that asked students to compose essays related to prominent works of English literature. These requirements were refined and expanded in the years that followed, and by 1874 candidates for admission were being made to 'write a short English composition . . . taken from works of standard authors'.[27] In addition to texts by Oliver Goldsmith and Sir Walter Scott, the 1874 Harvard entrance exam demanded students demonstrate familiarity with three plays from Shakespeare: *The Tempest*, *The Merchant of Venice* and *Julius Caesar*.[28] Following Harvard, similar requirements soon were adopted by universities across the US. While the particular plays that appeared on college entrance exams would vary slightly, even after attempts to formalize reading lists via the National Conference on Uniform Entrance Requirements in English in 1894, Shakespeare was a continuous presence on university entrance exams until the eventual diminution of their influence in the 1920s and 1930s.[29]

JULIUS CAESAR AND THE TWENTIETH-CENTURY LITERARY ANTHOLOGY

One of the more far-reaching effects resulting from the codification of specifically prescribed College Board reading lists was the solidification of a relatively stable group of works and authors who would come to comprise the high school literary canon. These selections were first disseminated in the form of heavily annotated editions of popular works conceived explicitly with college entrance lists in mind.[30] By the 1920s, under the influence of progressive educators who favoured fewer constraints on the curriculum and a greater number of texts from which teachers might choose, the College Board gradually loosened its hold on the programme of study within secondary education, eventually doing away with its uniform lists in the 1930s. This, along with increased budgetary restrictions on schools during the Depression, helped precipitate the rise of the high school literary anthology. While some publishing houses adopted a relatively conservative approach, simply importing many works directly from the uniform lists into their newly developed anthologies, others opened up their textbooks to a greater number of contemporary writers and genres. In general, most anthologies strove for moderation, employing a balanced approach that included both modern and so-called classic texts in their selections.[31]

By the 1930s, literary anthologies had evolved from their initial role in supplementing traditional, separately bound literary works, into a far more central place in the classroom. As the twentieth century wore on, the literary anthology would become the primary means through which canonical texts would be transmitted within schools. While anthologies of the period varied widely in their selection of modern literature, the choice of classic texts was far more homogeneous. This is particularly the case of Shakespeare; by the time James J. Lynch and Bertrand Evans had published their monumental 1963 study of every high school literary anthology in wide use during the previous fifteen years, Shakespeare's oeuvre, as represented in secondary school textbooks, had been distilled to just five works, three of which were anthologized relatively anomalously. Laidlaw Brothers' *Exploring Literary Trails* (1957) included *As You Like It*, while Scribner's *Exploring Literature Old and New* (1953) featured an excerpt of *The Taming of the Shrew*. Two texts from the period, Macmillan's *Interpreting Literature* (1955) and Scott, Foresman, and Company's *Good Times Through Literature* (1951) contained *A Midsummer Night's Dream*.[32] Still, these anthologies were outliers. By far, the most popularly anthologized Shakespeare plays in the period covered by Lynch and Evan's study were *Julius Caesar*, which was included in eleven separate tenth-grade anthologies (as well as one ninth-grade reader), and *Macbeth*, which appeared in eleven twelfth-grade textbooks. While data as to each play's inclusion in anthologies before the period covered by Lynch and Evans is unavailable, a survey of earlier editions of the texts in question reveals that anthologies from the 1930s and 1940s included *Julius Caesar* and *Macbeth* with similar frequency as these later editions. So prevalent were these two tragedies that, upon the publication of a 1968 National Council of Teachers of English (NCTE) backed study, it could be said that only two works, *Macbeth* and *Julius Caesar*, were required in over half of the college preparatory classes in the schools surveyed.[33] In addition to their prominence within classroom instruction and between the covers of the popular anthologies of the day, so too is the centrality of these plays attested to by students themselves; in the aforementioned NTCE study, students rated Shakespeare, as exemplified by *Macbeth*, *Julius Caesar*, and, to a lesser extent, *Hamlet*, as the most significant author that they had read as a part of their formal education.[34] And there is every reason to believe that these works enjoyed similar curricular prominence well before the 1960s. As the 1933 National Survey of Secondary Education attests, it was not uncommon for classes to devote a great deal of class time to the study of a single Shakespearean text; many instructors would spend four or more weeks working through *Julius Caesar*, *Macbeth*, or *As You Like It*.[35]

CAESAR, CITIZENSHIP AND THE WHITE IDEAL

Julius Caesar is commonly framed within the pages of tenth-grade literary anthologies from the 1930s, 1940s and 1950s as a meditation on democracy as well as an anti-dictatorial polemic. Parallels between the play's ancient Roman setting and the concerns of twentieth-century America are stressed as Caesar is portrayed as a tyrannical dictator while those who conspire against him are seen as idealistic, if not a bit naïve, in their principled stand against a would-be despot. As might be expected, this is especially the case for anthologies published during and after the Second World War. A representative example of such anti-dictatorial boilerplate appears in the 1944 edition of *Adventures in Appreciation*, whose preface to *Caesar* emphasizes the tragedy's modern implications. 'Every age adapts Shakespeare to its own taste', readers are informed, 'and ours is an age of radio orators, dictators, and shouting crowds'.³⁶ Using Orson Welles's 1938 modern-dress production of the play, subtitled 'The Death of a Dictator', as a touchstone, the editors describe how '[t]he audience who watched this version ... learned that propaganda was not a new method for controlling people's minds'.³⁷ They go on to note that '[d]ictators find their strength in masses of dissatisfied, unhappy young people', and they give voice to anxieties regarding how America might continue to 'allow organizations like the Nazi Bund the freedom to meet without losing to their ranks all our unemployed youth'.³⁸ In a related vein, 1954's *Types of Literature* invites students to draw connections between the world of the play and modern geopolitics by way of a series of post-unit study questions, one of which asks them to consider: '[w]hat conditions lead to the rise of such a dictator as Caesar – or Mussolini – or Hitler?'³⁹ Harcourt, Brace, and Company's *People in Literature* (1948) asks a similar question in pictorial form. A photograph of a proud, defiant Benito Mussolini standing atop a tank and flanked by Italian soldiers is paired with a caption asking, simply, '[a] modern Caesar?'⁴⁰

What is most significant about the anthologies' repeated condemnations of dictatorial rule, as well as their representation of America and its allies' ideological and martial resistance thereto, is that the tensions that would lead to the Second World War are reduced to a simple clash between two contesting political systems, both European, and therefore white, in their derivations. While fascism is always vilified, it is also represented as a worthy ideological adversary against whom the forces of democracy must periodically struggle. Couched in this dualistic opposition is the sense that, while strife among Western powers is inevitable, such is the burden that great European cultures and their descendants must bear in light of their globally dominant positions. The texts reduce the complexity of twentieth-century geopolitics to a broad fight between duelling factions that – while ideologically opposed – are united in their white European political heritage. All of this ignores how the West's longstanding imperial proclivities predicated the conflict as well as the prominent ethno-racial tensions underpinning what was a transnational, multi-ethnic conflict in which questions of race were anything but incidental.

One of the most legible threads of white supremacy found within several anthologies involves their construction of specific conceptual through-lines beginning in the Roman Republic, continuing – somewhat counterintuitively – through Elizabethan England, and arriving finally in the form of the democratic values codified within America's founding documents. Sometimes, these connections are implicit, as is the case within *Types of Literature* (1954) whose introduction to the play informs us that after the fall of Tarquin the Proud, '[t]he Romans bound themselves by solemn oath never again to tolerate a King'.⁴¹ After learning of their organization of an 'anti-king government', we are informed of Rome's choice to choose rulers electorally.⁴² Significantly, by the time we make our way to the play itself, these erstwhile democratic Romans have been transformed inexplicably into Elizabethans. In an extended stage direction before the play's first act, we are introduced to '[a] group of common workingmen, clad in their poor best attire ... looking expectantly down the street'.⁴³ Though we are told that the play's action is set precisely on 'February 15, 44 BC', this is followed by the puzzling assertion that, '[t]hese citizens are Londoners, not Romans'.[44] In this way, *Types of Literature*'s para-textual stage directions function to collapse ancient Rome and Elizabethan England into a single, undifferentiated political space, as direct connections are drawn between the ideals and values of these spatially, temporally and ideologically disparate cultures. These parallels are extended even further into twentieth-century America within the unit's follow-up questions, in which students are asked about the capricious nature of the citizenry within *Julius Caesar*.[45] Readers are directed to reflect upon the 'fickle, many-headed' qualities of the play's Roman/Elizabethan mobs and then made to consider '[w]hy the answer to this question [is] important to those who uphold a democratic form of government'.[46] The text works in this way to establish an imagined continuity between the political concerns of Shakespeare and those of modern-day, democratic America.

These connections are made even more explicit in *People in Literature*, whose prefatory materials inform us that '[i]n ancient Greece began the western world's idea of freedom'.[47] Readers are told that '[a]bout two thousand years ago, a few men began to say what many had thought: that human life was precious'.[48] 'Once this idea was clearly seen', it is explained, 'the ideal of freedom was invented'.[49] After a few centuries, we learn, 'the idea of freedom was lost to the world for more than a thousand years', only to reappear finally in northern Europe.[50] The takeaway from this brief history of an idea, according to the editors, is that '[i]t is important for Americans to know that freedom is not an American invention or an America possession', but rather 'a gift from our past'.[51] What is unstated but clear is that the past which is here being evoked is one that is created by whites and for whites.

Perhaps the whitewashing of American political values by way of Shakespeare's tragedy can most readily be seen in the 1955 edition of L. W. Singer's *Prose and Poetry for Appreciation*. Here, in addition to the standard associations between Caesar and the dictators of the twentieth century, readers are presented with extra-textual additions that impose a racialized subtext upon the play found nowhere in Shakespeare's text. In an extensive stage direction at the beginning of its second scene, readers are presented with descriptions of several of the drama's most prominent characters. 'Mark Antony', we are informed, 'wears the traditional goatskin tunic, his bronzed legs, arms, and breast bared for the race'.[52] 'No less handsome and brave is Brutus', who comes attired in 'the long, graceful, white tunic that marks the Roman nobleman'. In obvious contrast to the 'quiet, intelligent, [and] dignified' Brutus stands Cassius, characterized as 'lean and yellow-skinned, hot-tempered and jealous'.[53] One of the more remarkable features of this description lies in the varieties of whiteness on display. While Antony and Cassius are both described using chromatic signifiers that suggest deviation from a pure, white ideal, their whiteness is, nevertheless, to be understood. Antony's bronze skin, rather than suggesting Blackness, points to the numerous hues that were often subsumed under the rubric of whiteness within mid-twentieth-century America. Richard Dyer, in his study of white representation within Western visual culture, makes this point, contending that within certain bounds, whiteness is 'a matter of ascription'.[54] Put more simply: 'white people are who white people say'.[55] Thus the text's depiction of Antony's tawny complexion provides an example of Shakespeare's implication within an ongoing racial project in which the boundaries of whiteness were extended to allow for increasing phenotypic variety. While paleness had long been prized and cultivated by the upper classes in the West, tan skin had come by the 1920s to serve as a marker of vigour, athleticism and leisure. It is in keeping with the text's latent white supremacy that Antony is characterized in terms of his tan, healthy body. What is important to remember, however, is that it is precisely Antony's essential whiteness that allows him to capitalize on the positive connotations of his comparatively dark complexion. No matter how bronze Antony is imaged, he remains white.[56] His suntanned hue acts instead as a marker of the somatic diversity subsumed under the banner of whiteness. Antony's bronzed body, as well as the jaundiced physicality of Cassius, works to illustrate the infinite variety of whiteness as a social category.

Yet whiteness is not only seen here as an endlessly diverse grouping marked by its broad and unstable signification. Also present is the existence of an evaluative hierarchy within the broader taxonomy of whiteness. While it might be perceived as monolithic when compared to its Black antithesis, the fact remains that, within this broader heading, 'some people are whiter than others'.[57] If this is the case, it should come as no surprise to find that the play's eponymous centre is represented as the quintessence of white. After describing the complexions of Rome's political class, readers are at last introduced to the play's nominal protagonist: '[f]inally', we are told, 'and . . . in contrast to Antony and Brutus, comes Caesar, tall, thin, his face lean and chalk-white, his eyes dark and piercing'.[58] Significantly, while Antony and Cassius are characterized using terms that might accurately describe human skin colour, Caesar is portrayed as literally, rather than figuratively, white. But as Dyer helpfully reminds us: '[w]hite people are neither literally nor symbolically white. [They] are not the colour of snow or bleached linen, nor are [they] uniquely virtuous or pure'.[59] Shakespeare's *Caesar*, as a textual construct, can transcend the narrow somatic constraints that limit the expression of colour within actual human bodies. His whiteness is unconstrained by biological restrictions and thus he is made into a figure of absolute moral and aesthetic superiority – a blank slate that is capable of subtending all manner of available complexions while still embodying an unmatched and uncontestable white ideal. For this reason, it is no surprise that the 'chalk-white' Caesar is subsequently defined by an 'easy superiority in his manner that marks him as one born to rule and be obeyed'.[60] While many of the anthologies examined in this study avoid imposing a similar text-based racialized physiognomy upon the characters, Caesar's construction as the apotheosis of whiteness can be seen readily in several of the paintings, photographs, and line drawings that commonly accompany the play and often function subtly to depict Caesar's relative pallor, even in contrast to the physiognomy of other Romans in the frame (Figure 4).

In contrast to the conspicuous whiteness of both Caesar and the conspirators, non-Europeans are generally excluded from consideration within the anthologies of the day. Perhaps this should be expected given that the tragedy is more concerned with Rome's internal politics than it is with its relationship with the wider world.[61] It is for this reason that it is striking to find examples of anthologies whose editors chose to add explicit extra-textual references to personages of colour within their treatments of the play. Harcourt, Brace, and Company's *Adventures in Appreciation* (1944), for

FIGURE 4: Illustration of Roman figures by Muriel and Jim Collins from *Exploring Life Through Literature* (Glenview, IL: Scott, Foresman and Co, 1951). © 1951 by Savvas Learning Company LLC, or its affiliates. Used by permission. All Rights Reserved.

example, includes a historical anecdote describing Caesar's rise to power in Rome. In a description of a lavish parade held in celebration of Caesar's victories in Africa, we bear witness to '[c]rowds of Egyptian slaves, carrying sacks of wheat, paraded in the streets of Rome', accompanied by 'an Egyptian princess . . . her arms bound with golden chins'.[62] Black slaves appear again in Act 1, which opens with an extended direction asking students to 'bring to mind from reading about ancient Rome a narrow street lined with arched doorways and overhanging balconies, open booths and bright-coloured awnings'.[63] They are then asked to imagine 'men in togas – one perhaps, in a litter carried by dark-skinned slaves'.[64] In a similar vein, L.W. Singer's *Prose and Poetry for Appreciation* (1948) adds a narrator who acts as an announcer in 'a modern radio presentation'.[65] In an extended prefatory description, we are made witness to the 'glorious history of the Roman race from the days of Æneas'.[66] After the customary evocation of chariots and Roman soldiers, readers are asked then to imagine 'black Nubian slaves carry[ing] gilt and silk chairs in which recline the 'debutantes' and patrician ladies of Rome'.[67] Although non-Western peoples are almost universally excluded within the generally Eurocentric ideological province of Shakespeare's *Julius Caesar*, the occasional glimpses of racial alterity that are manifest are uniform in their depiction of non-whites strictly within positions of submission, disempowerment and servitude. Interestingly, many of the anthologies in this investigation show an interest in the practices of Roman slavery within their framing of the play. It is important to note, however, that slavery in Rome is considered by the vast majority of textbooks, not in terms of its enormity or inhumanity, but in terms of how the practice had an ultimately deleterious effect on Rome, as foreign slaves functioned to saturate the Roman economy with cheap labour, thereby displacing legitimate Romans and contributing to the decline of the empire.

Of course, the association of Black phenotypes with the practice of slavery is something that would resonate for tenth graders living less than a century after the ratification of the Thirteenth Amendment. And while it is clear that slavery in ancient Rome is distinct in numerous ways from the systematically enforced servitude of Black people in early America, these qualitative differences are erased within the texts' depictions of exotic, dark-skinned labourers, who, barred access to the vigorous political life of Rome, are made to function as scenery. While their inclusion gestures towards a world beyond the hegemonic whiteness of Shakespeare's imagined Rome, the larger importance of the anthologies' imposition of a non-white presence upon *Julius Caesar* lies in the gesture's contrastive signification. While the anthologies consistently celebrate Rome whose inhabitants are described in terms of their influence, intellect and endless variety, Black people, when visible at all, function as props whose monolithic servility exists to glorify and shed light upon the play's ideological white centre.

By way of conclusion, I would like to return briefly to *Julius Caesars*'s position within American rhetorics of race. I hope that my analysis has illustrated some of the more elusive ways that Shakespeare's Roman tragedy has influenced, and been influenced by, the evolving racial politics of mid-twentieth-century America. And I would like to suggest, finally, that perhaps *Julius Caesar*'s pedagogical prominence might help us better understand contentions such as those made by Black power icon Amiri Baraka, who reads the play as a meditation upon 'the relationship between government and the people . . . [that] deal[s] with the elimination of the whole aristocratic class in that period'.[68] It also might help us to uncover the larger racial subtext behind Eldridge Cleaver's comparison of Richard Wright and James Baldwin to Shakespeare's Caesar and Antony in *Soul on Ice*.[69] And even glancing evocations of the play, such as that in George Wallace's 1963 Inaugural Address, in which the incoming Governor accuses President Kennedy of 'tak[ing] up Caesar's pen' while issuing an executive order banning segregation, might seem a bit more meaningful when considered in tandem with the play's inveterate implication within schools as an instrument of white racial hegemony in postwar America.[70]

NOTES

1. Hayakawa, S.I. 1970. 'Prof Blasts Double Standard on Campus for Blacks, Whites'. *The Chicago Tribune*, April 19 1970, A4.
2. Ibid., A4.
3. Ibid., A4.
4. Catherine Prendergast's landmark analysis in *Literacy and Racial Justice* (2003) has influenced my thinking on the interplay between race, literacy, and citizenship in America. Of particular relevance is her description of the 'economy of literacy', that developed in the US following 1954's momentous *Brown v. Board of Education* decision ending legal segregation in schools. Prendergast argues that *Brown* functions to reinforce the longstanding notion in American life that literacy exists as white property, resulting in a system in which African-American access to an educational object works to lower its perceived value for all; Catherine Prendergast, *Literacy and*

Racial Justice: The Politics of Learning After Brown V. Board of Education (Carbondale: Southern Illinois University Press, 2003), 11. And if, as Prendergast suggests, Black educational access leads inevitably to the devaluation of said educational object, then my analysis can be viewed, in part, as a case study of one of the ways that whiteness responds to defend itself against what it perceives as a threat. Following the logic of Prendergast's economy of literacy, if Shakespeare is the quintessence of white literary achievement – the *sine qua non* of the English tradition – then it makes perfect sense to see him ardently defended from the (presumably Black) masses within whom lies the potential to divest Shakespeare of his significatory power.

5. The classicist Maria Wyke notes that, within the early- and mid-twentieth century, tenth grade was often known colloquially as 'the Caesar grade' since students frequently were asked to study Caesar's *De bello Gallico* (*The Gallic War*) in their second-year Latin courses while also being made to read *The Tragedy of Julius Caesar* in most English classes.

6. 'An Act to Establish a Uniform Rule of Naturalization'. 1845. 1 Stat 103–4. 26 March 1790. In *United States Statutes at Large* Vol. 1: 103.

7. The clause limiting citizenship to free whites persisted within revisions of the Act in 1795, 1798, 1802, and would remain in effect until 1870, at which time naturalization laws were extended to 'aliens of African nativity and to persons of African descent' ('An Act' 256). Even then discriminatory immigration policies persisted in the form of the Page Act (1875) and the Chinese Exclusion Act (1882) both of which restricted immigration from Asia and would remain in effect until 1943. Racial constraints on naturalization would persist in some form until their explicit prohibition under the Immigration and Nationality Act of 1952.

8. See Theodore Allen, *The Invention of the White Race: Racial Oppression and Social Control*, Vol. 1 (New York: Verso, 1994); Theodore Allen, *The Invention of the White Race: Racial Oppression and Social Control*, Vol. 2 (New York: Verso, 1997); Karen Brodkin, *How Jews Became White Folks and What That Says about Race in America* (New Brunswick, NJ: Rutgers University Press, 1998); Noel Ignatiev, *How the Irish Became White* (New York: Routledge, 1995); Matthew Frye Jacobson, *Whiteness of a Different Color: European Immigrants and the Alchemy of Race* (Cambridge, MA: Harvard University Press, Harvard University Press); David Roediger, *The Wages of Whiteness: Race and the Making of the American Working Class* (London: Verso, 1991); David Roediger, *Working Toward Whiteness: How America's Immigrants Became White* (New York: Basic Books, 2005).

9. Reginald, Horsman, *Race and Manifest Destiny: The Origins of American Anglo-Saxonism* (Cambridge, MA: Harvard University Press, 1981), 298.

10. Randall, Monger and James Yankay, 2012. *U.S. Legal Permanent Residents: 2012. A report prepared by the United States Office of Immigration Statistics*. Washington, DC: Department of Homeland Security.

11. See Katznelson for an examination of the discriminatory, anti-Black tenor of programmes implemented in the US during the 1930s and 1940s under both the New Deal and the Fair Deal; Ira Katznelson, *When Affirmative Action Was White: An Untold History of Racial Inequality in Twentieth-Century America* (New York: W.W. Norton,

2005).

12. Jacobson, *Whiteness of a Different Color*, p. 247.
13. Ibid., 246.
14. Adams, Joseph Quincy. 1993. 'The Folger Shakespeare Memorial Dedicated April 23, 1932'. *The Spinning Wheel* 12:9–10 (June–July): 230.
15. Ibid., 230.
16. Ibid., 230.
17. Ibid., 230–1.
18. Hobbs, Frank and Nicole Stoops. *Demographic Trends in the 20th Century* (Washington, DC: U.S. Dept. of Commerce, Economics and Statistics Administration, U.S. Census Bureau, 2002), 75.
19. Adams, 'The Folger Shakespeare Memorial', 231.
20. See Bristol, Levin, Sturgess, Teague, and, more recently, Vaughan and Vaughan regarding Shakespeare in America before the twentieth century; Michael D. Bristol, *Shakespeare's America, America's Shakespeare* (London: Routledge, 1990); Lawrence W. Levine, *Highbrow/Lowbrow: The Emergence of Cultural Hierarchy in America* (Cambridge, MA: Harvard University Press, 1988); Kim C. Sturgess, *Shakespeare and the American Nation* (Cambridge: Cambridge University Press, 2004); Frances Teague, *Shakespeare and the American Popular Stage* (Cambridge: Cambridge University Press, 2006); Alden T. and Vaughan and Virginia Mason Vaughan. *Shakespeare in America* (Oxford: Oxford University Press, 2012). While each approaches the question of his prominence and estimation from a unique perspective, a common thread that runs throughout all of their analyses involves the degree to which Shakespeare was very much a part of popular culture within nineteenth-century America. This is particularly true regarding iterations of Shakespeare's works within performance. While Bristol in particular shows that the poet was never entirely divorced from elite cultural associations in the US, it is abundantly clear from each of the aforementioned studies that Shakespeare, in some form or another, was also the province of mass culture, especially, though not exclusively among white Americans. See McAllister for more on Black performances of Shakespeare in nineteenth-century New York and Berkowitz for accounts of Shakespeare's presence on American Yiddish stages in the late-nineteenth and early-twentieth centuries; Marvin McAllister, *White People Do Not Know How to Behave at Entertainments Designed for Ladies and Gentleman of Colour: William Brown's African and American Theater* (Chapel Hill: University of North Carolina Press, 2003); Joel Berkowitz, *Shakespeare on the American Yiddish Stage* (Iowa City: University of Iowa Press, 2002).
21. Denise Albanese's *Extramural Shakespeare*, an invaluable study of the American public's relationship to Shakespeare in the early years of the twenty-first century, presents an extensive analysis of the playwright's use and implementation within America's twentieth century mass educational project; Denise Albanese, *Extramural Shakespeare* (New York: Palgrave, 2010). See 67–93 in particular for more on Shakespeare's institutional prominence in schools.
22. Ibid., 5.

23. Kahn, Coppélia and Heather S. Nathans. 'Introduction'. In *Shakespearean Educations: Power, Citizenship, and Performance*, ed. Coppélia Kahn, Heather S. Nathans, and Mimi Godfrey (Newark: University of Delaware Press, 2011), pp. 17–18.
24. Applebee, Arthur, N. *Tradition and Reform in the Teaching of English: A History* (Urbana, IL: National Council of Teachers of English, 1974), 1
25. Ibid., 25–29.
26. See Jonathan Burton for more on the misrepresentation of Shakespeare in the *McGuffey Readers*: Lay on, McGuffy: Excerpting Shakespeare in Nineteenth-Century Schoolbooks." *Shakespearean Educations: Power, Citizenship, and Performance*. Coppélia Kahn, Heather S. Nathans, and Mimi Godfrey eds. Newark: U of Delaware P, 2011. 95–111.
27. Qtd in Applebee, *Tradition and Reform*, 30.
28. Ibid., 30.
29. Ibid., 31, 125.
30. Ibid., 34.
31. Ibid., 129.
32. *Good Times through Literature*'s selection is limited to a seven-page edited excerpt from *MND*, titled 'A Midsummer Night's Play', featuring the Mechanical's performance of *Pyramus and Thisbe* from 5.1.
33. Squire, James R. and Roger Applebee, *The National Study of High School English Programs: High School English Instruction Today* (New York: Appleton-Century-Crofts, 1968), 100. Significantly, Squire and Applebee found that *Hamlet*, a work that seems to have resisted anthologizing in twentieth-century secondary school textbooks, was required in at least 40 per cent of the schools surveyed; ibid., 100.
34. Ibid., 101.
35. Smith, Dora V. *Instruction in English*. Bureau of Education Bulletin 1932, no. 17. National Survey of Secondary Education Monograph no. 20 (Washington DC: Government Printing Office, 1933), 53. *As You Like It* was the most commonly anthologized of Shakespeare's comedies in early-twentieth-century America. Since the 1920s, it was dropped by an increasing number of textbooks in favour of *Julius Caesar*, and it had disappeared almost entirely from anthologies by the 1960s.
36. Cook, Luella B., H.A. Miller, Jr., and Walter Loban, eds, *Adventures in Appreciation* (New York: Harcourt, Brace, and Co., 1944), 452.
37. Ibid., 452.
38. Ibid., 452. The German American Bund was an ethnonationalist organization established in 1936. Known for their embrace of Nazi ideology and symbolism, the Bund's visibility peaked at an infamous 1939 rally held in New York City at Madison Square Garden. See Leland V. Bell, 'The Failure of Nazism in America: The German American Bund, 1936–1941', *Political Science Quarterly* 85.4 (1970), 585–99, and Marshall Curry, director. *A Night at the Garden*, 2017, https://anightatthegarden.com/#post-67 (accessed 13 May 2022).
39. Cross, E.A. and Neal M. Cross, *Literature: A Series of Anthologies: Types of Literature* (New York: Macmillan, 1954), 580.

40. Cook, Luella B., Walter Loban, and Ruth M. Stauffer, eds, *People in Literature* (New York: Harcourt, Brace, and Co., 1948), 470.
41. Cross and Cross, *Types of Literature*, 507.
42. Ibid., 507.
43. Ibid., 509.
44. Ibid., 509.
45. Ibid., 580.
46. Ibid., 580.
47. Cook, Loban, and Stauffer, *People in Literature*, 415.
48. Ibid., 413.
49. Ibid., 413.
50. Ibid., 413.
51. Ibid., 413.
52. Agnew, J. Kenner and Agnes L. McCarthy, eds, *Prose and Poetry for Appreciation* (Syracuse, NY: Singer, 1955), p. 453.
53. Ibid., 453.
54. Dyer, Richard. *White* (London: Routledge, 1997), 48
55. Ibid.
56. Although Antony's whiteness in *Julius Caesar* is taken for granted in *Prose and Poetry*, his relative darkness among the Romans depicted here is notable in light of the ways that Antony's time in Egypt, as depicted in *Antony and Cleopatra*, works to complicate his racial signification. As Arthur L. Little, Jr. has argued, 'before Antony encounters Egypt, his body is presumably well completed, tall, strong, white, and courageous . . . , a body primed for imperial things': *Shakespeare Jungle Fever: National-Imperial Re-Visions of Race, Rape, and Sacrifice* (Stanford, CA: Stanford University Press, 2000), 103. Antony's time in Egypt and, especially, his romantic relationship with Cleopatra in this later play works to complicate his 'imperial and masculine identity', ultimately calling his civility into question, as Antony 'go[es] Egyptian [and] in effect African', ibid., 103. All of this is to observe that Antony's latent Blackness is in some ways hinted at in *Prose and Poetry*'s depiction of his bronze colouring.
57. Dyer, *White*, 12.
58. Agnew and McCarthy, *Prose and Poetry for Appreciation*, 453.
59. Dyer, *White*, 42.
60. Agnew and McCarthy, *Prose and Poetry for Appreciation*, 453.
61. While the play makes mention of Ceasar's global exploits, the narrative is inward-looking and its primary concern lies in what the consolidation of power under Caesar means to Rome and its citizenry.
62. Cook, Miller, and Loban, *Adventures in Appreciation*, 455.
63. Ibid., 457.

64. Ibid.
65. Maline, Julian L. and Wilfred M. Mallon, eds, *Prose and Poetry for Appreciation: The St. Thomas More Series* (Syracuse, NY: L.W. Singer, 1948), 574.
66. Ibid.
67. Ibid.
68. Udin, Sala. (2011), 'A Conversation with Amiri Baraka: Civil Rights, Black Arts, and Politics'. *Sampsonia Way*. 16 September 2011. https://web.archive.org/web/20111025005343/https://www.sampsoniaway.org/bi-monthly/2011/09/16/a-conversation-with-amiri-baraka-civil-rights-black-arts-and-politics/
69. Cleaver, Eldridge, *Soul On Ice* (New York: Ramparts Press Inc., 1968), 133.
70. Wallace, George. 'Inaugural Address', 14 January 1963.

CHAPTER SEVENTEEN

White Anger

Shakespeare's My Meat

RUBEN ESPINOSA

In considering the ease with which white people in Shakespeare are quick to anger, nowhere are the implications more menacing than when it comes to perceptions of white supremacy. When, in *Titus Andronicus*, the eponymous hero erupts in anger after Marcus has killed a fly, Marcus justifies his actions by saying, 'Pardon me, sir; it was a black ill-favoured fly, / Like to the empress' Moor', to which Titus responds, 'Oh, Oh, Oh, / Then pardon me for reprehending thee' (3.4.67–9).[1] Ultimately, Titus says, 'Yet, I think, we are not brought so low, / But that between us we can kill a fly / That comes in blackness of a coal-black Moor' (3.4.76–8). The vulnerable white people gathered in that room rationalize their value – and their racial superiority even within their lowly state – only through the imagined violation of Black people. These imaginings of baseless aggression speak to perceptions, in Shakespeare and in our present moment, of a white anger that is often understood as warranted, indeed legitimate, and used to bolster the belief in white supremacy.[2]

Irrational white anger is precisely what this chapter seeks to scrutinize by putting Shakespeare into conversation with contemporary figures and events that rely on rage to espouse views of white superiority, either implicitly or explicitly. How, this chapter asks, does Shakespeare speak to and even feed white anger – anger evinced by the likes of Boris Johnson and Steve Bannon? Shakespeare populates many of his plays with angry white men and women, and he also offers much in the way of imagining, and contributing to the idea of, white supremacy.[3] Without doubt, Shakespeare's iconic status and perceived universalism are often deployed to perpetuate narratives that advance what Ta-Nehisi Coates describes as the 'truculent and sanctimonious power' of white supremacy.[4] This chapter considers how the likes of Johnson and Bannon feed on Shakespeare's social capital to reinforce and justify feelings of white anger within their plural societies. More broadly, it engages cross-historical energies to consider what Shakespeare stands to teach us about the concurrent vulnerabilities and dangers of elevating whiteness in our present moment – a moment when white incivility desperately relies on the abiding civility of people of colour.

To arrive at a constructive examination of these issues, I first want to draw attention to specific elements behind white anger that I have in mind. Rather than gesturing only toward aggressive anger, I instead want to consider sustained dangers that a seemingly muted white anger poses to people of colour. Carol Anderson, who scrutinizes the media's dominant emphasis on 'black rage' when Black communities protest killings of unarmed Black men and women and/or take issue with paradigms of racism that lead to violent aggression against Black Americans, suggests that Black rage is not at all the issue, but instead it is white rage that is at work. She writes:

> White rage is not about visible violence, but rather it works its way through the courts, the legislatures, and a range of government bureaucracies. It wreaks havoc subtly, almost imperceptibly. Too imperceptibly, certainly, for a nation consistently drawn to the spectacular – to what it can see. It's not the Klan. White rage doesn't have to wear sheets, burn crosses, or take to the streets. Working the halls of power, it can achieve its ends far more effectively, far more destructively.[5]

The seeming subtleties at work here are rather nefarious, and Anderson offers an unambiguous reason for such sentiments. 'The trigger for white rage', she writes, 'inevitably, is black advancement. It is not the mere presence of black people that is the problem; rather, it is blackness with ambition, with drive, with purpose, with aspirations, and with demand for full and equal citizenship.'[6] This final point not only makes clear the stakes for people of colour, but also casts light on the enduring vulnerabilities of whiteness that are so often hidden behind the bravado of white supremacy. Equal citizenship threatens to undermine systems of white superiority, and the fear this triggers manifests into insidious rage.

SHAKESPEARE'S GENTLE WHITE JUSTICE

Examples of white anger abound, of course, across dramatic genres in Shakespeare. Be it Tybalt, Volumnia, Orsino, Isabella, Henry V, Hermione, Hamlet, Margaret, or Lear, there is no shortage of moments when white people lose it. When we consider the actors who undertake these roles in contemporary productions, what we witness on stage then is not necessarily identified as white anger but rather something closer to emotional outbursts that the moment in which they exist demands. This is to say, all of these characters come at this anger in their respective plays from a position of privilege, and this privilege extends into the space of the stage for white actors. Anchored in whiteness, it is an anger that is never really seen nor identified as rage. When this white anger is aimed at characters who are not white of skin – the many white men of *Titus Andronicus* expressing disdain for Aaron, Emilia lashing out at Othello, Prospero's grotesque treatment of Caliban, and even the muted white anger at Antony's relationship with the Black Cleopatra – the implications are much more dire. Indeed, this type of white anger comes closer to the white rage that Anderson explores. In this essay, though, I delimit my exploration of this issue to *The Merchant of Venice* because, in so many ways, that particular play illustrates the iniquitousness of whiteness at work throughout the judicial system.

From the onset of *The Merchant*, the fix is in. When Portia suggests that the easiest means to prevent the Duke of Saxony's nephew from choosing the correct casket is to 'set a deep glass of Rhenish whine on the contrary casket' (1.2.94)[7] because of his affinity for drinking, she admits that she does in fact possess the means to manipulate her father's will.[8] Given that she arrives at this line after revealing her deep disdain for foreigners, her role within a play firmly focused on antisemitism and xenophobia warrants scrutiny. It seems clear that the risk of an intercultural and/or interracial marriage is certainly present for Portia, and without this risk the happy marriage to Bassanio that celebrates homogeneity would not appear quite as fortuitous. But I want to sidestep that comedic resolution altogether to examine instead how Portia, who appeals to her audience by positioning herself as 'a little body ... aweary of this great world' (1.2.1), epitomizes Anderson's idea of white rage that, I argue, runs throughout *The Merchant*. Perhaps the 'little body' tired of the wider world was England's own *'little body with a mighty heart'* (*Henry V*, 2.0.17).[9]

Portia's racism is on full display when the Prince of Morocco chooses the incorrect casket. As he departs empty handed, Portia says, 'A gentle riddance, – draw the curtains, go – / Let all of his complexion choose me so' (2.7.78–9). Her initial declaration plays on the term 'gentle' insofar as she suggests that ridding herself of someone unwanted is benign while simultaneously alluding to the social degree she shares with the Prince of Morocco. I want to push on her use of 'gentle riddance' here because it echoes what Antonio says to Shylock earlier in the play. After Shylock and Antonio agree to the bond, and as Shylock exits, Antonio says, 'Hie thee, gentle Jew' (1.3.176). He then says, 'The Hebrew will turn Christian; he grows kind' (1.3.177). Kindness here not only plays off Antonio's use of 'gentle', but it also alludes both to altruism and alikeness. Antonio, of course, says this sardonically, as does – I suggest – Portia about Morocco. Within the belief in white supremacy, neither Shylock nor Morocco will ever belong, despite their social and economic standings. Demeaning them based on their difference, then, is a way for Portia and Antonio – whose grasp on control over their own situations is not so secure – to assert belief in their racial superiority. It also makes clear their vulnerabilities.

The air of superiority that surrounds Antonio and Portia in these encounters with empowered people of colour brings to mind George Lipsitz's sharp attention to cultural categories that perpetuate the 'fictions of whiteness'.[10] As Lipsitz suggests, 'whiteness is a matter of interests as well as attitudes ... it has more to do with property than pigment', and goes on to argue that 'the possessive investment in whiteness is a matter of behaviour as well as belief'.[11] For Antonio and Portia, then, it is not only their cultural attitudes surrounding race that infuse these encounters with the feeling of entitlement, but the sinister desire to make sure that investments in economic and social wellbeing are firmly fixed on bolstering white power. This paradigm materializes in very sinister ways once Portia secures Bassanio as her partner and Belmont becomes a site of white homogeneity. Once that facet of her instability is settled, she invests in securing whiteness beyond the borders of her own society.

Portia's arrival into Venice is grounded in duplicity on several levels. On the one hand, she is disguised as Balthazar, and on the other hand she attempts to give the impression of blind justice. When she arrives in the courtroom, she remarks, 'Which is the merchant here? And which the Jew?' (4.1.171).[12] The façade of impartiality frames a scene where we, as an audience, witness how the law, at every turn, favours those deemed legitimate members of the white citizenry.

It would be easy for me to detail the various injustices that Shylock encounters, but I want to focus specifically on the sabotaging of his autonomous existence as indicative of the ability of white rage to have the potent, destructive effects to which Anderson alludes. On some level, we need to look past the grotesque treatment of Shylock that he details early on – that is, the description of Antonio spitting on him (1.3.124). He endures this humiliation, but is still able to conduct his business, have a home, worship, eat, and exist with relative freedom. But the verdict in the courtroom altogether strips Shylock of any control and autonomy he might have had. Kim F. Hall explains, 'More than providing an object lesson for Shylock, "hitting him where it hurts", as it were, the punishment makes sure that the uneven balance of wealth in the economy is righted along racial and gender lines.'[13] As Hall goes on to argue, 'Portia does indeed drop manna (which she redistributes from the city's aliens) upon the males of Venice: she is the bearer of fortunes for Bassanio, Antonio and Lorenzo.'[14] The play's white, wealthy men, it seems, stand to gain everything from the subjugation of Shylock.

To consider what Shylock loses, and indeed what Morocco loses, is critical. When considering the 'exclusionary values of Belmont', Hall argues that in the process of risking all and choosing the incorrect casket, Morocco 'loses his right to reproduce his own bloodline'.[15] In both instances, what we find is a seeming erasure of these two characters because of the delimited control they have over their own futures. However 'little' Portia's body might feel, she wields a great deal of white anger as she minimizes and disparages foreigners. As I mentioned above, the fix is in, and at every turn it favours a 'gentle' whiteness.

BORIS JOHNSON SEEING RED

In our present moment, Shakespeare's capital has been deployed to explore a host of issues and to advance manifold agendas. While we, in our academy, have often sought to explore the potential for social justice through Shakespeare,[16] we also see in the public sphere the use of Shakespeare to advance ideas of white supremacy. Take, for example, Boris Johnson, Brexit champion and now former prime minister. While much of the current spotlight involving the intersection of Shakespeare and Johnson is focused on his forthcoming book, *Shakespeare: The Riddle of Genius*,[17] he has drawn on Shakespeare's cultural capital in the past to underscore his disdain for foreigners in England.

Johnson's attention to Shakespeare in a 2015 piece he penned for *The Telegraph* underscores his desire to align Englishness – and, more specifically, whiteness – with Shakespeare's iconic status, and he comes at this desire with unmistakable anger. Indeed, at one point in the essay Johnson writes, 'I am afraid I saw red.'[18] And what, exactly, made Johnson so utterly angry? It was the fact that a 'Lefty council' in London allowed certain individuals to put up satellite dishes to watch programming in foreign languages if they could demonstrate 'social needs', but not his friend, who wanted a satellite to watch programmes in English – 'cricket and so on'.[19] Johnson mocks those who are 'at risk of "social exclusion" unless [they are] able to watch a regular diet of Bangladeshi soaps or Turkish cookery shows or Blind Date in Serbo-Croat'.[20] In his myopic exploration of attitudes that take into account the cultural integrity of London's diverse population, Johnson diminishes the value of this multilingual and multicultural society. Indeed, he highlights a sport that originated in Shakespeare's England and juxtaposes it against what he undoubtedly considers inferior television programming. One is not like the other, and the other is simply much too trivial. What is his solution? Johnson writes, 'Helping people to speak English is not so much an act of cultural imperialism as of economic liberation.'[21] As a would-be white saviour, Johnson has only one thing in mind – erasure of cultural identity under the guise of economic stability for those individuals.

Ultimately, Johnson engages Shakespeare to justify this feeling of white rage when considering the intercultural and cross-racial dynamics of his plural society. For Johnson, Shakespeare is a cornerstone of Englishness, and he relies on the understood white affinities surrounding Shakespeare to articulate his views of an English nation that fosters white superiority. To do this, he draws on linguistic identity as the clear marker of English (linguistic and cultural) superiority: 'The question is: what sort of society do we want – a society that is integrated, or one that is balkanised? Do we let people live and work in mutually segregated sub-cultures? Or do we insist on the primacy of the English language?'[22] In his estimation, the 'answer is clear'.[23] Johnson thinks England 'should insist absolutely on English as the common language', and he goes on to explain why:

> But the final reason why I think we should insist on English is unashamedly emotional, atavistic, and culturally conservative. This is our language, the language of Shakespeare, the King James Bible, the language that has been spoken in London for centuries; and in the face of the vast migratory influx we have seen, we must insist on English if we are to have any hope of eupeptic absorption and assimilation.[24]

Shakespeare is deployed here to espouse and bolster Johnson's white anger. It is worth noting that Shakespeare is listed alongside the King James Bible, and in this way, Johnson seems to look backward to a historical period, the early seventeenth century, where a 'vast migratory influx' posed no threat to the integrity of England's linguistic identity.

The truth is, however, that large-scale immigration also defined the London of Shakespeare and King James.[25] In many ways, then, we can see how intercultural encounters influence the drama of Shakespeare – including *The Merchant* – and we can also see that where Johnson is concerned, what really matters is not the content of Shakespeare's works, but rather the mere idea of Shakespeare as a stand-in for a whiteness that is imagined as superior. It does not matter what his plays offer in the way of understanding cross-cultural dynamics, and the manifold racist actions that one can find within a work like *The Merchant*. What matters, in the eyes of Johnson, is that linguistic diversity – and, therefore, ethnic and racial diversity[26] – threaten to undermine the power behind homogenous whiteness. That his friend does not have the same access to satellite television as his 'foreign' neighbours is what has Johnson seeing red. That seemingly 'gentle' anger is one thing, but Johnson, we know, has been influential in the UK political and legislative landscape. His piece in *The Telegraph* is not merely an irascible white man griping, but that of a white man openly exploring his bigotry in an effort to kindle nationalistic sentiments pushed by a white rage that anticipated Brexit, which at the time of publication wasn't too far off. A similar bigotry was informing white nationalism on the opposite side of the Atlantic, of course.

RIOTING WITH STEPHEN BANNON

Given their shared interest in promoting white nationalism, the strange affinity that Boris Johnson and Stephen Bannon, cultural provocateur, share for Shakespeare is, perhaps, understandable. But where Johnson casually draws on Shakespeare in speeches and in print to promote his vision of white supremacy, Bannon appears to be invested in partaking in the ongoing making of Shakespeare. He is listed as an executive producer for Julie Taymor's *Titus* (1999), for example, and in the late 1990s, he co-authored, with Julia Jones, the rap musical *The Thing I Am*, an adaptation of *Coriolanus*. *The Thing I Am* was never produced, but its script exists. Excerpts from the script reveal Bannon's seeming infatuation not only with Shakespeare but also with racial tensions.

The Thing I Am is set during the 1992 L.A. riots, and it imagines *Coriolanus*' Romans and Volscians as Bloods and Crips in South Central Los Angeles.[27] Daniel Pollack-Pelzner notes that Bannon's script 'offers a vision of his Shakespeare-fuelled fantasy: a violent macho conflict to purge corrupt leaders and pave the way for a new strongman to emerge'.[28] This vision, Pollack-Pelzner suggests, offers an early glimpse of Bannon's views of populism that inform his later infatuation with Donald Trump. Given Bannon's penchant for white supremacy, Pollack-Pelzner recognizes how 'surprising' it is to read a screenplay that exalts Black gang leaders. I, however, am less convinced that exalting Black men and women is the impetus for the script. Indeed, when we think about the energies of Shakespeare's *Coriolanus*, we recognize within it the corrupt, violent, angry world that the eponymous hero inhabits. To map those qualities onto a Black community in contemporary Los Angeles (however incompetently that world is imagined via the script) does not infuse that community with the gravitas that Shakespeare's work often lends (or is imagined to lend), but rather renders Shakespeare's angry white men and women Black.

By envisioning the anger espoused in *Coriolanus* through the Black characters in *The Thing I Am*, Bannon situates civil unrest firmly in the laps of those he later deems lesser than when, from within the White House, he fosters views of white supremacy. It is difficult not to cringe at the narration within this script, as the descriptions set up the audience to behold Black anger as the catalyst for destruction. Take, for example, the narrator describing the riots: 'The National Guard rushes in followed by the LAPD with bully clubs, smashing skulls.'[29] Although the narration highlights police brutality, it is Black strength that emerges: 'The disheveled guards on the heels of Volumnia. In front, Virgilia tows a reluctant little Marcius. Behind her a defiant Volumnia holds off the guards with blows, boxing their ears. A drama-queen in black, a mighty warrior-mother intent on reclaiming her cub.'[30] When Coriolanus registers unease with disappointing his mother, she says to him, 'We're not here to save your homies and do in these Crips. This boy had a Crip for a mama; another wife, maybe; some bastard child by chance somewhere. No more words from me until our city is on fire. Then I'll speak a little.'[31] It would be all-too easy to scoff at the narration and dialogue here, but it delivers a familiar narrative about angry Black people intent on burning down their own communities. In no uncertain terms, it employs *Coriolanus* to imagine Black rage.

The truth, of course, is that Shakespeare posits this rage through the experiences and actions of white men and, significantly, women. Indeed, *Coriolanus*' Volumnia delivers her rather famous lines about the rage she feels regarding the tribune's dissenting views of Coriolanus: 'Anger's my meat: I sup upon myself, / And so shall starve with feeding' (4.2.50–1). The difference between a white woman and a Black woman delivering the very same lines is critical in understanding perceptions of unmitigated rage. The vilification of Black women who express their discontent is ubiquitous – Michelle Obama, Shonda Rhimes, Serena Williams and Oprah Winfrey all come to mind. It is, unequivocally, a racist trope meant to silence and diminish Black women. And yet, vocalized anger is precisely what makes Volumnia so magnetic in *Coriolanus* – she is not silenced. For Bannon to deploy this confidence and anger via a Black character, then, is in many ways an act that devitalizes that strength because it relies on the popular view of the angry Black woman trope. Even more unnerving, it points to the type of societal imaginings that Bannon brings with him, many years later, to Trump's White House.

Like Johnson, Bannon inhabited an influential role where policy at the highest national level in the US was being forged with white supremacy as a guiding principle. It is exactly this type of destructive white rage that Anderson articulates so thoughtfully. But I want to make clear that I am not situating Bannon, or Johnson for that matter, as would-be lone racists in their respective circles. Indeed, that would be like imagining that Iago is the sole racist in his imagined society.[32] So many are complicit in the racism of *Othello*, and in the racism of *The Merchant*, for that matter. In the same vein, then, Johnson and Bannon are mirroring back to their societies and making mainstream the brazen belief in white supremacy to which so many subscribe. As Anderson writes in regard to the 2016 US presidential election:

> The motivation in 2016 was equally nefarious and destructive. Trump tapped into an increasingly powerful conservative base that had been nurtured for decades on the Southern Strategy's politics of anti-Black resentment. Similar to George Wallace's run for the presidency in 1968, Trump's supporters bristled at the thought that public policies would provide any help to African Americans and were certain that blacks were getting much more than they deserved from the government while the 'average American' was getting much less. The message was clear: They weren't deserving and weren't really Americans.[33]

In so many ways, Johnson's admission to 'seeing red' speaks directly to the American sentiments that Anderson outlines here. If you can espouse, perpetuate, and reinforce resentment for Black ambition and belonging, then you can rely on that resentment to advance white supremacy. White rage manifests from the belief that whites are entitled while nonwhites – and I use that term deliberately here – are *always* undeserving.

For Johnson, then, aligning his vision of linguistic and cultural homogeneity with Shakespeare is a means of undergirding this xenophobic vision for a Brexit England that takes for granted English people's belief in a Shakespeare who also, promotes white supremacy. He draws on Shakespeare's cultural capital to promote his view of English superiority. From my estimation, this explains, on various levels, his attraction to Shakespeare – he wants to write about Shakespeare so as to give the appearance that he is more intimately connected to an imagined past of pristine linguistic similitude and cultural whiteness that never truly was. To be certain, many people, both then and now, would like that to be the case – but it simply isn't. Shakespeare's works engage intercultural and interracial tensions and often bring to bear on the stage the ugly face of racism. Always, it is white.

Bannon's motivations for connecting to Shakespeare are somewhat less clear. In his particular Shakespeare adaptation in the 1990s, Bannon appears to use Shakespeare as a vehicle to scrutinize a Black population defined by gang violence. He imagines Volumnia as a Black woman unrepentantly intent on burning her own city. This vision has concurrent energies because, on the one hand, he taps into perceptions of Black rage fuelling destruction while simultaneously engaging the potential behind populism. The implications, as Pollack-Pelzner notes, are far-reaching: 'As chief strategist to Mr Trump, Mr Bannon could see his vision of racial aggression, driven by a hammer-headed hero who doesn't have to pander to the craven media, gain an audience far beyond Shakespeare's Globe.'[34] And indeed, like Portia, who looks to extend her racist view of homogeneity beyond the parameters of Belmont, Bannon has taken his right-wing message of xenophobia across the Atlantic on a European speaking tour promoting fascism.[35]

Johnson and Bannon's actions reveal the frightening workings of white rage and register the role of influential figures advancing divisive policies, but – as I mention above – they are hardly alone. The narrative of dangerous Black men and women persists, and unsurprisingly we seldomly scrutinize how white rage propels such narratives. Take, for example, US Senator Lindsey Graham's relatively recent angry speech during the Bret Kavanaugh judicial confirmation hearings. These hearings, of course, were fraught because Dr. Christine Blasey Ford had accused Kavanaugh of attempted rape when they were high school classmates. Speaking to Kavanaugh, after shaking his finger at Diane Feinstein in the near distance, Graham says, 'This is not a job interview. This is hell. This is going to destroy the ability of good people to come forward because of this crap. Your high school yearbook – you have interacted with professional women all your life, not one accusation. You're supposed to be Bill Cosby when you're a junior and senior in high school. And all of a sudden, you got over it.'[36] The reference, of course, is to the fact that Bill Cosby had recently been found guilty of drugging and raping several women throughout his career (though his conviction would later be overturned on appeal). Graham, defending Kavanaugh, seeks to exculpate him, vilify Feinstein and other Democrats for bringing this accusation to light, and to suggest that Kavanaugh is no Bill Cosby. There is no shortage of men whom Graham could have employed as a point of comparison for Kavanaugh (Harvey Weinstein comes to mind), but the reference to Bill Cosby, a prominent and once-beloved Black actor, is – to my thinking – no coincidence. In one fell swoop, a very angry (indeed, his rage was palpable) Lindsey Graham sought to discredit Ford, chastise Feinstein, and supplant the accused white man with the image of a convicted Black man. Kavanaugh was confirmed.

To consider white rage and to scrutinize how this concept unearths meaningful understandings of Shakespeare's white characters is to trace the often-malignant efforts to organize community at the expense of dehumanizing people of colour. Like Titus, and like Portia perhaps, many people locate their sense of satisfaction and self-worth in the imagined and actual violation of Black men and women. It is a monstrous perspective that allows them to negotiate their own disempowered and sometimes vulnerable existence. That vulnerability, of course, pales in comparison to the vulnerability that Black people face – in the imaginings of Shakespeare, in the world he inhabited, and in our world today.

In recognizing the far-reaching destructiveness of white rage, we, too, can mobilize communities and allies that interrogate and undermine those who seek to oppress Black and brown people. As Anderson writes, 'This is the moment now when all of us – black, white, Latino, Native American, Asian American – must step out of the shadow of white rage, deny its power, understand its unseemly goals, and refuse to be seduced by its buzzwords, dog whistles, and sophistry, by its Shakespeare.'[37] For those of us in Shakespeare studies, it is an opportunity to scrutinize our own commitments and responsibilities in our scholarship, and to bring those discussions into our classrooms, into our conferences, and into the way we think about the future of our academy.[38] Constructive conversations about race do not begin and end by scrutinizing only the likes of Aaron, Shylock, Othello, Cleopatra and Caliban, but also by looking squarely at the whiteness and white anger abounding in Shakespeare. To unpack not only the motivations behind white anger but also the maliciously methodical strategies that protect and perpetuate the notion that white equates to legitimacy (while everything else does not) is to make this whiteness visible, which, in our present moment, is an urgency we cannot ignore.

NOTES

1. William Shakespeare, *Titus Andronicus*, ed. Richard Proudfoot, Ann Thompson and David Scott Kastan [The Arden Shakespeare Complete Works] (London: The Arden Shakespeare 2001). Shakespeare references are to this edition.
2. For studies that attend to the issue of white supremacy in early modern England, see Kim F. Hall, *Things of Darkness: Economies of Race and Gender in Early Modern England* (Ithaca, NY: Cornell University Press, 1995); Arthur L. Little, Jr., *Shakespeare Jungle Fever: National-Imperial Re-Visions of Race, Rape, and Sacrifice* (Stanford, CA: Stanford University Press, 2000).
3. For an excellent study that attends to the language of white supremacy in Shakespeare and his contemporaries, see Kim F. Hall, '"These Bastard Signs of Fair": Literary Whiteness in Shakespeare's Sonnets', *Postcolonial Shakespeares*, ed. Ania Loomba and Martin Orkin (New York: Routledge, 1998), 64–83.
4. Ta-Nehisi Coates, 'The First White President', *The Atlantic*, 1 October 2017, 3.
5. Carol Anderson, *White Rage: The Unspoken Truth of Our Racial Divide* (New York: Bloomsbury, 2016), 3.
6. Ibid.
7. It's worth seeing the whole of Act 1 (scene 2).
8. For an insightful reading of Portia's ability to manipulate the system, see Elizabeth Acosta, 'Open Doors, Secure Borders: The Paradoxical Immigration Policy of Belmont in *The Merchant of Venice*', in *Shakespeare and Immigration*, ed. Ruben Espinosa and David Ruiter (New York: Routledge, 2014).

9. The reader may find it worthwhile to take a closer look at the fuller description (2.0.17–20).

10. George Lipsitz, *The Possessive Investment in Whiteness: How White People Profit from Identity Politics* (Philadelphia: Temple University Press, 1998): 99.

11. Ibid., 233.

12. For a thoughtful reading of the way these lines register anxieties about Jewish difference/alikeness, see Ania Loomba, *Shakespeare, Race, and Colonialism* (Oxford: Oxford University Press), 149–51.

13. Kim F. Hall, 'Guess Who's Coming to Dinner? Colonization and Miscegenation in *The Merchant of Venice*', *Renaissance Drama* 23.1 (1992): 87–111, esp. 100.

14. Ibid., 100.

15. Ibid., 98.

16. I have in mind here not only the recently organized symposium on 'Shakespeare and Social Justice' in Cape Town, South Africa, sponsored by the Shakespeare Society of South Africa and organized by Chris Thurman and Sandra Young, but also the collection, *Teaching Social Justice Through Shakespeare: Why Renaissance Literature Matters Now*, ed. Hillary Eklund and Wendy Beth Hyman (Edinburgh: Edinburgh University Press, 2019).

17. To date, the book has not been published. Most recent reports suggest he was seeking someone to aid in the completion of his book. See: 'Boris Johnson Offered to Pay for Help Writing Shakespeare Biography, Says Scholar,' *The Guardian*, 2 July, 2021. https://www.theguardian.com/books/2021/jul/02/boris-johnson-offered-to-pay-for-help-writing-shakespeare-biography-says-scholar. https://www.theguardian.com/books/2019/apr/23/boris-johnsons-much-delayed-shakespeare-book-now-set-for-2020

18. Boris Johnson, 'For Their Sake, Immigrants Must Speak the Language of Shakespeare', *The Telegraph*, 8 March 2015.

19. Ibid.

20. Ibid.

21. Ibid.

22. Ibid.

23. Ibid.

24. Ibid.

25. For more on the issue of immigration in Shakespeare's England, see Ruben Espinosa and David Ruiter, eds, *Shakespeare and Immigration* (Burlington, VT: Ashgate, 2014); Scott Oldenburg, *Alien Albion: Literature and Immigration in Early Modern England* (Toronto: University of Toronto Press, 2014); and Laura H. Yungblut, *Strangers Settled Here Amongst Us: Policies, Perceptions, and the Presence of Aliens in Elizabethan England* (London: Routledge, 1996).

26. As Gloria Anzaldúa argues, 'Ethnic identity is twin skin to linguistic identity'; Gloria Anzaldúa, *Borderlands/La Frontera: The New Mestiza*, 2nd edn (San Francisco: Aunt Lute Books, 1999), 19.

27. For attention to this script, see: Daniel Pollack-Pelzner, 'Behold Steve Bannon's Hip-Hop Shakespeare Rewrite: "Coriolanus"', *The New York Times*, 7 December 2016; Yohana Desta, 'Steve Bannon's Hip-Hop Musical is as Horrifying as You Would Imagine', *Vanity Fair*, 1 May 2017; and Alyssa Rosenberg, 'Stephen Bannon Wrote a Movie About the 1992 L.A. Riots. Now You Can Finally Watch It', *The Washington Post*, 1 May 2017. The latter two articles include a link to a *NowThis* production where actors do a read through of an excerpt from the script.
28. Pollack-Pelzner, 'Behold Steven Bannon's Hip-Hop Shakespeare Rewrite'.
29. See, 'The Thing I Am: Table Read', *NowThis* https://www.facebook.com/NowThisNews/videos/1423744654382321
30. Ibid.
31. Ibid.
32. For more on this, see Peter Erickson, 'Race Words in *Othello*', in *Shakespeare and Immigration*, ed. Ruben Espinosa and David Ruiter (New York: Routledge, 2014), 159–76, esp. 170.
33. Anderson, *White Rage*, 169.
34. Pollack-Pelzner, 'Behold Steve Bannon's Hip-Hop Shakespeare Rewrite'.
35. See, for example, Natalie Nougayréde, 'Steven Bannon Is on a Far-Right Mission to Radicalise Europe', *The Guardian*, 6 June 6 2018.
36. https://www.lgraham.senate.gov/public/index.cfm/2018/9/transcript-of-graham-s-remarks-on-kavanaugh-nomination.
37. Anderson, *White Rage*, 178.
38. I am thinking here of the kind of work that Ian Smith and Ayanna Thompson offer. For example, see Ian Smith, 'We are Othello: Speaking of Race in Early Modern Studies', *Shakespeare Quarterly* 67.1 (2016), 104–24; and Ayanna Thompson, *Passing Strange: Shakespeare, Race, and Contemporary America* (Oxford: Oxford University Press, 2011).

CHAPTER EIGHTEEN

The White Shakespearean and Daily Practice

JEAN E. HOWARD

Making Shakespeare studies 'less white' – that is, less racially oppressive and less dominated by white assumptions, epistemologies and bodies – is the goal to which I hope my essay will contribute.[1] Even as the profession has opened some spaces for scholars of colour and their allies to examine race, Shakespeare studies is still dominated by white scholars and, more importantly, by white norms and deeply engrained assumptions. In this essay I will unpack what I mean by these statements and point to some of the daily practices that might begin to change the current power dynamics in Shakespeare studies. Overt racism is seldom the issue; inducing guilt is not the goal; breaking completely free of institutionalized, systematic racism is an impossibility both for white scholars and for those of colour. I see my job, instead, as the never-to-be-finished work of becoming 'less white' in my institutional practices. This means coming to terms with the privilege that has fostered white ignorance (discussed below) and overcoming the white reticence that inhibits direct discussions of race in pedagogical and institutional settings.[2] It also means being actively engaged in changing institutional practices on the ground where racism is an ordinary or quotidian matter.[3] Change begins where we live and work: classrooms, departments, professional organizations. I take to heart Miles Grier's observation that 'the great number of white people still have quite limited experience *doing something* to redistribute racial authority' in their institution and, he suggests, within Shakespeare studies broadly conceived.[4] So how will change happen?

I am a white female Shakespearean at an Ivy League institution. While the woman part has brought its difficulties through the decades, the white part has brought many privileges. Acknowledging that – what can I do, in collaboration with others, to redistribute racial authority and make Shakespeare studies 'less white'? What practices can be efficacious, what theory useful? I will suggest, first, that all early modern scholars should be familiar with and incorporate the complex body of early modern race scholarship into every aspect of their teaching, research and other professional work. That is a professional responsibility as much as a political imperative. Beyond that lies another challenge: through an explicitly anti-racist pedagogy thoughtfully to engage with the racial dynamics in our classrooms, in which whiteness is often a privileged but occluded and unexamined term and position.

EDITING

I begin at what I hope is an unexpected place: editing Shakespeare. We forget that most students get their first experience of Shakespeare through the editions we put in their hands. If there is nothing in the introductions, notes and glosses about race, then they will assume it is not relevant to Shakespeare studies. They will see Shakespeare as an author who bears no mark of race himself, but who, occasionally, gave us complex portraits of individual Moors (Aaron and Othello), Jews (Shylock), Egyptians (Cleopatra) and Indigenous figures (Caliban) and so could not have been 'racist'. Editorial work can help our students nuance this further, making them aware of how complicated were sixteenth and seventeenth century modes of racialization and how crucial these centuries were not just for the racialization of religious difference and the emergence of somatic difference as a key instrument in the justification of the Atlantic trade in Black slaves, but, importantly for this volume, how Shakespeare's works participated in the creation of a privileged whiteness (often using the white woman as vehicle), and the systematic denigration of Blackness through discourses characterizing Black people as demonic, deceitful, lascivious, and mentally deficient. Shakespeare was a raced subject, and his plays contribute to the construction and perpetuation of racial paradigms, often at the level of the word. Editing can elucidate this process.

This is why I begin with editing as a practice that can in consequential ways make Shakespeare studies 'less white'. In earlier decades scholars such as Valerie Wayne and Ann Thompson urged women to edit Shakespeare.[5] They urged this as a matter of equity, but also because they believed women editors by virtue of their social positions, training and lived experience would see things about Shakespearean texts that other editors had not seen. Their work affected many subsequent editions of Shakespeare, including *The Norton Shakespeare* I helped to edit. In the early 1990s I deliberately thinned out the number of received annotations having to do, for example, with political history so I could add fresh annotations dealing with social history, material culture, the household, sexuality and gender – topics that feminist literary and historical scholars had had a special role in elucidating. A feminist lens proved of positive value, expanding what the Shakespearean text could mean.

A race-conscious editing practice invites a similar expansion of the possible meanings of Shakespeare's plays by focusing on how they help forge racial categories and hierarchies at the level of the word. Kim F. Hall's pioneering work in the 1990s on the meaning of the word *fair* in Elizabethan beauty discourse reveals the usefulness of such an approach.[6] Glossing *fair* in its racialized opposition to *black* reveals how somatic difference begins to emerge as a paradigm for creating racial hierarchies. Such racializing discourse is present in the sonnets and in plays like *Othello*, but also wherever whiteness becomes the trope of a privileged group, whether that is the Nordic whiteness of the pale Hamlet or of the fair Helen in *Troilus and Cressida*. Glossing words like *fair*, *white*, *black*, *dark*, *dun* and *tawny* for their potentially racial meanings, alongside words like *kind*, *blood*, *barbarian*, *infidel*, *misbeliever*, *dog* and *Turk*, opens the door to discussions of the different registers in which racial difference was posited in the early modern period and of the global geographies across which, and the global power relations within which, such discourses took shape.[7]

Peter Erickson's incisive essay on three keywords in Othello – *slavery*, *Barbary*, *Mauritania* – shows the efficacy of drilling down on specific words as part of a race-conscious editorial or pedagogical practice.[8] Erickson argues that completely to absorb how a play like Othello references race requires lingering with these words while expanding the temporal and geographical coordinates through which Shakespeare's play is understood. A Black Atlantic that saw Africans transported to the New World as slaves was connected to and not entirely separable from a Black Mediterranean that saw Africans brought to Europe for various kinds of 'service'.[9] Understanding this, readers can grasp anew the precarity of Othello's position within Venice from the moment the play opens.

Toni Morrison likewise lingers on the word *Barbary* in her play, *Desdemona*. She uses the word's associations with North Africa to suggest that Barbary was a Black servant in Desdemona's household and functioned as her nurse.[10] In a sentimental reading, Desdemona could be seen as primed for love across the colour line because of childhood intimacy with a Black servant. Morrison eschews such sentimentality, however. *Her* Barbary rebuffs Desdemona's claims to friendship, pointing to the reality of her subordination to the white women in Desdemona's family and to the fact that Desdemona does not even know her name.

> I mean you don't even know my name. Barbary? Barbary is what you call Africa. Barbary is the geography of the foreigner, the savage. Barbary? Barbary equals the sly, vicious enemy who must be put down at any price; held down at any cost for the conquerors' pleasure. Barbary is the name of those without whom you could neither live or prosper.[11]

By tugging at the thread in Shakespeare's text that gives Desdemona's mother a maid named Barbary, Morrison plays out the possibility of giving the Black servant a powerful voice in re-imagining the Othello story, thus decentring the white woman, and exposes some of the ideological work done by the term in Shakespeare's text. Naming a servant Barbary suggests that servant's African Blackness and determines both her subordination to a white woman and silently authorizes Desdemona's appropriation of her song and story.

It should be the job of everyone who edits Shakespeare to provide a textual apparatus that takes full account of the new knowledge about race that has been accruing at least since the 1960s.[12] It will be great when more faculty of colour edit Shakespeare, but the work of making editions of Shakespeare less white is everyone's job.

TEACHING

Teaching, of course, is where the rubber hits the road for most of us attempting to become less white in our daily practices. Editions of Shakespeare alert to the racializing power of words can open the door to different reading experiences, but these opportunities have to be augmented by teaching strategies that make race a consistent through-line of a course. In my Shakespeare classes I have often talked about race only sporadically, and often in association with the famous 'race plays': *Titus Andronicus*, *Othello*, *Merchant of Venice*, and, sometimes,

The Tempest. Of course, it is better to address race in this set of texts than to shut down discussion by asserting that race is an anachronistic term in the early modern period or that Othello transcends race because of his status as a tragic hero or his inherent nobility, his exceptionality.[13] However, a more challenging practice would be to push a consideration of race through an entire Shakespeare course; to insist that early modern racial categories included much more than variations in skin colour; and to make the point that whiteness, as a colour designation and a position of privilege, is central to the early modern racial system.[14]

There are at least two ways to do such a course. One is to make race the designated subject. In constructing a 'Shakespeare and Race' syllabus, one can teach Shakespeare's plays in relation to such exciting scholarship as Habib on new archival discoveries about black inhabitants of early modern London; Loomba, Burton, Britton, and Kaplan on early modern race and religion; Floyd-Wilson on geohumoralism; Royster and Erickson on Northern European and Gothic whiteness and on *differences* within the category of whiteness; Minor and Thompson on the blackness of Poor Tom; Hendricks on race and *A Midsummer Night's Dream*; Smith on what happens to our understanding of *Othello* if Desdemona's lost handkerchief is read as black, not snow white.[15] Other examples abound. Such a course gives students invigorating competence in the latest scholarship on early modern race and raises crucial questions about evidence, the limits of the *OED*, the history of criticism, and claims of anachronism.

A second kind of course, probably more destabilizing to normative practices, infuses race inquiry throughout a regular Shakespeare survey rather than confining it to a special topics course on race. It may surprise students to encounter a sustained consideration of the early modern race system in a Shakespeare survey, and it may challenge professors to design such a course. At the 2018 Shakespeare Association of America (SAA) meeting, I received help with this task by participating in Holly Dugan, Dorothy Kim and Reginald Wilburn's workshop on Teaching the Premodern in a Time of White Supremacy. We read some race theory and practical criticism addressing race in early modern texts as a prelude to reconceiving an existing syllabus to make race integral to the design of the whole course. I worked on the second half of the Shakespeare survey that I regularly teach.

I want to highlight two important conversations that arose from the exchanges before and during the workshop. One was the extent to which the current moment demands a wholesale reorientation of our teaching around questions of race and white supremacy. Simply put: do we all need to become focused on race in our teaching and writing as opposed to addressing other intellectual concerns? Some argued, given both the whiteness of Shakespeare studies and the perdurance of racism in our culture, that this was indeed an urgent need. Others warned that untenured or part-time faculty might be put in jeopardy for foregrounding race in their Shakespeare classes if they were perceived to be 'distorting' the course from its traditional purpose. For those beyond tenure what felt most threatening was the anticipated disruption of established ways of managing their Shakespeare classrooms if race and the work of BIPOC scholars became central to the big Shakespeare lecture. But is such a disruption what it takes to make our classrooms 'less white'? We were also challenged to ask a different question: would a sustained consideration of race make for better, more interesting, more socially consequential Shakespeare classes? For many, the answer was yes, justifying the labour it would require.

A second particularly difficult and productive aspect of our conversations concerned whether and how to acknowledge and productively work with the different racial positions of class participants. Race, of course, is always in the early modern classroom because raced people are present there, but this fact often goes unacknowledged, the silence an expression of white privilege. As a result, we fail to explore how whiteness prevents us from seeing certain things, asking certain questions, and interacting with all our students in positive ways. In revising my Shakespeare syllabus I attempted to develop an intersectional approach to Shakespeare's post-1600 plays, foregrounding several modalities of social difference: race, gender and class. While these are familiar terms of analysis, relating them to the lived experience of people in the classroom is not, in my experience, common pedagogical practice.[16] Positionality, however, is key to understanding privilege and blindness. Openness about the positions from which each of us makes knowledge about Shakespeare opens the door to moving beyond a race-conscious to an anti-racist class. Such a class attends not just to early modern race, but actively attempts to mitigate racial harm in the classroom and to honour and utilize the various forms of knowledge and expertise that arise from social difference.[17]

For such a class, it is crucial to unpack what it means to see, in Charles Mills's term, from inside a white epistemology.[18] Mills suggests that a white vantage point selectively attends to the world, ignoring or designating as less important, less advanced, less worthy of attention whole continents and their people, as well as whole categories of others close at hand.

> Whites generally see black interests as opposed to their own. Inevitably, then, this will affect white social cognition – the concepts (e.g., today's 'colour blindness'), the refusal to perceive systemic discrimination, the convenient amnesia about the past and its legacy in the present, and the hostility to black testimony on continuing white privilege and the need to eliminate it to achieve racial justice.[19]

Implicitly assuming superior merit and the justified centrality of the white perspective, white epistemology ironically produces what Mills calls 'white ignorance'. In the domain of early modern studies this includes, for example, the common view that confines Shakespeare's 'race plays' to those containing non-white characters, or in some instances, non-Christian characters. It also includes the tacit assumption that Shakespeare naturally belongs to white people and so must be 'universal,' belonging to everyone, ignoring, for example, the blackface practices that for centuries made clear that Shakespeare did not belong to Black actors.[20] Keith Hamilton Cobb's *American Moor* shows that this history persists into the present.[21] In *American Moor* Cobb plays a black actor auditioning for a white director who repeatedly tells him what Othello must feel, know, and do, all the while oblivious to what the black actor might bring to the role.

Teaching in an anti-racist way involves more than having students read the latest early modern race scholarship; it also entails having them think about concepts like *positionality*, *epistemology*, *systematic* and *institutional racism* and *whiteness*, and to do so in relation to their own implication in such structures.[22] Theoretical readings can help students dig deep into these ideas. Essays by Mills and DiAngelo helped those of us in the SAA workshop do just that. Short reflection papers (not made public) that invite students to apply these terms to their own position in the class or in relation to Shakespeare as a cultural icon are another technique for raising awareness about one's relative racial privilege. If teachers are willing to share their own reflection essays, that will make it easier for students to do theirs, as will clear prompts that invite students to think in specific terms about how aspects of their social identity affect their reading practice in both positive and less enabling ways. Race and gender are social constructs – fictions – but they have real consequences; but learning about and reflecting on these constructs allows some limited freedom to resist the worst of these consequences. While it is not possible entirely to escape racism's grip, it is possible to lessen the injury given or endured, to be less white or to experience fewer of the slings and arrows of unexamined white privilege.

I think that white professors, me included, may not initially feel comfortable or competent to create classrooms where this kind of exploration goes on under the aegis of 'the Shakespeare survey'. But one can learn from what others have done, including how to deal with the resistance of white students and how to avoid tokenizing students of colour or making them 'represent' a particular social identity. We can learn strategies for overcoming the 'white fragility' that can make white people hang back from fully engaging with their own race or the race of others. This is hard work, but the classroom is where we live out most painfully, perhaps, but also most consequentially, what it means to redistribute racial authority in our daily practices.

WRITING

It is undoubtedly easier to rethink one's critical practice in the relatively controlled environment of the printed page than in the volatile and constantly changing environment of the classroom. That is probably why Shakespeare professors often stick to classroom scripts that entertain and challenge, certainly, but do so within the unspoken framework of a white epistemology. But the kind of critical writing I am attempting in this essay feels a little risky because it participates in none of the genres valorised in the elite academy. It is not a reading of an early modern text, not a theorization of racial formations or a report on archival findings concerning early modern racialized subjects. Instead, it tries to make practical suggestions about what an antiracist praxis could look like and suggests that this will be most consequential when it breaks the unwritten rule that real scholars, especially at elite institutions, never drop the pose that they and their students stand apart from their object of inquiry, endlessly performing what Donna Haraway provocatively called 'the God trick'.[23] This is the pretence of 'seeing everywhere from nowhere,' seeing as a disembodied subject looking from above, like God, while remaining unseen and unmarked. A ploy of domination, it silently makes a partial and interested perspective seem like a universal and total one, obliterating difference. While Haraway called this a patriarchal trick, it is also a white trick. In the classroom, never acknowledging my whiteness and the blindness it can induce silently delegitimizes any distinctive knowledges and perspectives my students of colour may bring to the study of

Shakespeare. I become the one who knows, and the students must try to mirror my knowledge.

I sometimes wonder if we don't perpetuate the god trick in our race-themed SAA activities when the difference between seminars and workshops instantiates an unproductive distinction between sessions in which tenured and tenure track faculty talk about discoveries in early modern race studies and forge new readings of familiar texts, while other Shakespeareans (often part-time faculty or those at teaching-intensive institutions) discuss their daily struggles with the embodied differences among their students and how to create less white and less injurious classrooms. To write about an anti-racist pedagogy is just, somehow, so 'ed school', so uncool to those in the serious scholarly business. But fuzzing up the line that separates the workshop and the seminar, moving back and forth across it, may be yet another way productively to change how a white discipline does its work. It is not only important to 'know stuff' about early modern race, but also to struggle with what engaging seriously with race means for how we interact with others in classrooms and department meetings.

HIRING

How might we make early modern studies less white? The go-to answer is to hire more early modern scholars of colour. But racism within higher education and the operation of institutional racism across generations of American social life mean that there are too few PhDs of colour to fill current demand in many fields. We have to go at least two steps back down the pipeline and think about how we interest undergrads of colour in investing in early modern studies. Exciting early modern classes are a good place to start, including teaching courses where race is foregrounded and anti-racist pedagogy is the norm. Also useful is asking students of colour what co-curricular activities would interest them and being willing to be surprised at the answers. It may be that they want to go to *American Moor* or host a conversation with Joyce Macdonald or Ian Smith about how they got interested in early modern studies and how they are making their way in the field. Or it may be that they will want to go see a traditional staging of *Macbeth* or invite Tiffany Stern to talk about early modern theatre culture. We can't predict the interests of any student, but we owe it to students of colour to engage them directly, opening ourselves to intellectual and social exchanges that may surprise and challenge us white Shakespeare scholars, revealing how our whiteness frames our expectations of our students as well as our other institutional practices. We will not, however, be truly welcoming to students of colour until we can recognize and engage with their individual intellectual commitments and interests, just as we do with our white students.

Departments offering the PhD have their own pipeline to build. They must affirmatively admit and vigorously recruit students of colour and provide them with classes and a graduate culture that welcomes them. Again, that can mean many things, but among those are: making certain that lecture series feature faculty of colour talking on many subjects and not just on race; allowing faculty of colour from other institutions to serve on dissertation committees when a student makes this request; and making sure that all department faculty understand and abide by prohibitions against harassment and discrimination in all its forms and are familiar with literature detailing the adverse effects of micro-aggressions and thoughtless speech acts. Those who lead departments, moreover, have to avoid presenting such information as a politically correct nod to the radical left rather than as a positive if small step toward less white and less injurious places of learning.

And yet, for many decades, even with strenuous pipeline building, there will be too few scholars of colour who can be hired for early modern tenure track jobs. At least for now reducing the whiteness of early modern studies can't have only a demographic solution. Instead, we must enlarge our understanding of progressive hiring so that we are not only seeking out candidates of colour but also hiring scholars of whatever race who make race an essential framework for their teaching and writing and who are willing to put themselves on the line to redistribute racial authority in their institutions and classrooms. One can easily see evidence of such commitments – less in the formal diversity statement that too often rehearses platitudes – but in the syllabi of courses applicants have taught, in the handling of the dissertation topic and the critical framework used to develop it, and in extra-institutional activities like prison teaching. We can't fetishize hiring faculty of colour, important as that is, if that offloads from the rest of us the responsibility for seeing that all of our hires – and we ourselves – are committed to the transformation of the field in a 'less white' direction.

SERVICE

I hope it is not news that the institutional work of making our places of work less white should not be primarily laid upon faculty of colour. Just as it is demeaning to assume that all faculty of colour will write about race, it is equally wrongheaded to make such faculty speak for diversity in every university forum and not to put white faculty on the frontlines of such transformative work. After all, a white academy was largely made by white people. Its transformation in a less-white direction should also be in large measure the responsibility of white people. Well-run diversity committees that require a lot of learning, as well as a lot of action, are great places to put powerful white faculty. There is other standard wisdom out there about how to staff faculty committees. For example: don't burden junior faculty with too much service or they won't get tenure; don't burden faculty of colour at any rank with too much service because they are already doing enormous amounts of invisible labour as mentors and advisors to students, to provosts, to foundation officers, etc. This is true, and yet, to be 'protected' is also sometimes experienced as disempowering.[24] One idea might be to ask every junior faculty and faculty of colour what one committee they want to lead or be part of and then try to honour their requests. It might shake up expectations about who fits where and wants to do what.

More ambitiously, if the department decides, as the result of an external review, student demands, self-reflection, or inspired leadership that it wants to become less white in all its practices, then an empowering exercise would be to charge every department committee with suggesting at least two policies or actions that would help realize that goal. Undergraduates and graduate students could also be asked for ideas. The results would be compiled and discussed at a town hall to decide on actions. Who knows what ideas would bubble up if constituencies were invited to undertake such an experiment.

CONCLUSION

I confess I have sometimes treated early modern race scholarship in the same way I have treated other forms of scholarship, as something I needed to know to stay abreast of my field both as a teacher and a scholar. But the transformative experience of the last couple of years has been recognizing that that is not enough, that being 'less white' in my teaching, scholarship and service is an important next step in an evolving praxis. I was pushed to this awareness by the Black Lives Matter Movement, certainly, but also by such intellectual experiences as the SAA workshop I have described, and also by teaching for the last several years in a medium-security women's correctional facility near New York City.

My classes there have given me very smart students whose circumstances and earlier educational experiences have not typically made them defer to professorial authority they feel is unearned and have not led them to separate their lived experience neatly from what they read in books. Every day they deal with the racial injustice at the heart of the US mass incarceration system.[25] Why should they assume that the prison classroom will be a respite from or challenge to that system rather than an extension of it? To earn trust I have to own my whiteness and the role that I play in racist systems; and I have to acknowledge and embrace the kinds of knowledge and expertise they bring to the classroom. I have been given a great gift by these students as we have worked together to make the classroom a site for their empowerment and the exercise of their critical intelligence on questions that matter to them. I have been taught ways to be somewhat 'less white,' but this is a process, not a done deal. The great lesson for me, which students and faculty of colour have long known, is that white ignorance and arrogance have no limits. I am grateful to the many people who have helped me push back those limits just a little.

NOTES

1. Robin DiAngelo in *White Fragility: Why It's So Hard For White People to Talk about Racism* (Boston: Beacon Press, 2018), 150, suggests that being 'less white' is an important goal for faculty and for institutions wishing to reduce racism in their activities, total elimination of racism being nearly impossible given our culture's saturation with racist attitudes and practices.
2. Ibid. DiAngelo's book attempts to define and explain the reluctance of white people to engage in direct public conversations about race or to have their world view challenged. She suggests a number of strategies for building the capacity to undertake such conversations. Other important studies of whiteness include Carol Anderson, *White Rage: The Unspoken Truth of Our Racial Divide* (New York: Bloomsbury, 2016); Richard Dyer, *White*, rev. edn (London: Routledge, 2017); Joe R. Feagin, *The White Racial Frame: Centuries of Racial Framing and Counter-Framing*, 2nd edn (New York: Routledge, 2013); Nell Painter, *The History of White People* (New York:

Norton, 2010); Paula S. Rothenberg, ed. *White Privilege: Essential Readings on the Other Side of Racism*, 4th edn (New York: Worth Publishers, 2012); and Shannon Sullivan, *Revealing Whiteness: The Unconscious Habits of Racial Privilege* (Bloomington: Indiana University Press, 2006).

3. On the quotidian as the sphere of daily racist practice see, among others, Imani Perry, 'Cultural Studies, Critical Race Theory and some Reflections on Methods', *Villanova Law Review* 50 (2005): 915–24, esp. 920.

4. Miles Grier, 'The Color of Professionalism: A Reply to Dennis Britton', in *Early Modern Black Diaspora Studies: A Critical Anthology*, ed. Cassander L. Smith, Nicholas R. Jones, and Miles P. Grier (New York: Palgrave Macmillan, 1918), 229–38, esp. 230.

5. See, for example, Ann Thompson, 'Feminist Theory and the Editing of Shakespeare: *The Taming of the Shrew* Revisited', in *Shakespeare, Feminism and Gender*, ed. Kate Chedgzoy (Basingstoke, UK: Palgrave, 2001): 49–69; Valerie Wayne, 'The Sexual Politics of Textual Transmission', in *Textual Formations and Reformations*, ed. Laurie E. Maguire and Thomas L. Berger (Newark: University of Delaware Press, 1998), 179–210; and, more recently, Valerie Wayne, 'Remaking the Texts: Women Editors of Shakespeare, Past and Present', in *Women Making Shakespeare: Text, Reception, Performance*, ed. Gordon McMullan, Lena Cowen Orlin, and Virginia Mason Vaughan (New York: Bloomsbury, 2014), 57–67.

6. Kim F. Hall, *Things of Darkness: Economies of Race and Gender in Early Modern England,* especially Chapter 2, 'Fair Texts/Dark Ladies: Renaissance Lyric and the Poetics of Color' (Ithaca, NY: Cornell University Press, 1995), 62–122.

7. For a useful resource dealing specifically with the language of race in the early modern period see the TIDE project, sponsored by the European Research Council, on *Keywords of Identity, Race, and Human Mobility in Early Modern England.* Available at https://library.oapen.org/handle/20.500.12657/50188.

8. Peter Erickson, 'Race Words in *Othello*', in *Shakespeare and Immigration*, ed. Ruben Espinosa and David Ruiter (New York: Routledge, 2014), 163.

9. Emily Weissbourd, '"Those in Their Possession": Race, Slavery, and Queen Elizabeth's "Edicts of Expulsion"', *Huntington Library Quarterly* 78 (2015): 1–19, also argues for interconnections among geographic sites, in this case the connection between the Iberian slave trade and the probable existence of Black slaves in early modern England. See esp. 13–17.

10. Toni Morrison, *Desdemona*, Lyrics by Rokia Traoré (London: Oberon Books, 2012). Erickson, in 'Race Words in *Othello*', suggests that Shakespeare's Barbary *could* be white, or perhaps Berber or Arab, but argues that the geographical referent and the association with the 'barbary horse' with which Iago associates Othello indicate her blackness.

11. Morrison, *Desdemona*, 45.

12. Early modern race studies goes back to pathbreaking work by such scholars as Eldred Jones, *Othello's Countrymen: The African in English Renaissance Drama* (London: Oxford University Press, 1965), Elliot H. Tokson, *The Popular Image of the Black*

Man in English Drama, 1550-1688 (Boston: G.K. Hall, 1982), Peter Hulme, *Colonial Encounters: Europe and the Native Caribbean, 1492-1797* (London: Routledge, 1986), Anthony Gerard Barthelemy, *Black Face, Maligned Race: The Representation of Blacks in English Drama from Shakespeare to Southerne* (Baton Rouge: Louisiana State University Press, 1987), and Ania Loomba, *Gender, Race, Renaissance Drama* (Manchester: Manchester University Press, 1989).

13. In '"A New Scholarly Song": Rereading Early Modern Race', *Shakespeare Quarterly* 67.1 (2016): 1–13, Peter Erickson and Kim F. Hall lodge a cogent critique of the claims that discussing race in the early modern period is anachronistic or that its specificity is subsumed by Shakespeare's supposed universality. See esp. 4–5.

14. Scholars have certainly begun to call attention to Shakespeare's 'other race plays', meaning all those lacking a Jew, Moor, New World person, or Egyptian. David Brown, for example, ran a seminar on this topic at the 2020 conference of the Shakespeare Association of America.

15. Imtiaz Habib, *Black Lives in the English Archives, 1500-1677: Imprints of the Invisible* (Aldershot, UK: Ashgate, 2008); Ania Loomba, *Shakespeare, Race, and Colonialism* (Oxford: Oxford University Press, 2002); Ania Loomba and Jonathan Burton, *Race in Early Modern England: A Documentary Companion* (New York: Palgrave, 2007); Dennis Britton, *Becoming Christian* (New York: Fordham University Press, 2014); M. Lindsay Kaplan, *Figuring Racism in Medieval Christianity* (New York: Oxford University Press, 2019); Mary Floyd-Wilson, *English Ethnicity and Race in Early Modern Drama* (Cambridge: Cambridge University Press, 2003); Francesca Royster, 'White-Limed Walls: Whiteness and Gothic Extremism in Shakespeare's *Titus Andronicus*', *Shakespeare Quarterly* 52.4 (2000): 432–55; Peter Erickson, 'Can We Talk About Race in *Hamlet*?', in *Hamlet: New Critical Essays*, ed. Arthur Kinney (New York: Routledge, 2002), 207–13; Benjamin Minor and Ayanna Thompson, '"Edgar I Nothing Am": Blackface in *King Lear*', in *Staged Transgression in Shakespeare's England*, ed. R. Loughnane and E. Semple (Basingstoke: Palgrave Macmillan, 2013), 153–64; Margo Hendricks, '"Obscured by Dreams": Race, Empire, and Shakespeare's *A Midsummer Night's Dream*', *Shakespeare Quarterly* 47 (1996): 37–60; Ian Smith, 'Othello's Black Handkerchief', *Shakespeare Quarterly* 64 (2013): 1–25.

16. For a stringent investigation of teaching intersectional courses on gender and race see Kim F. Hall's 'Beauty and the Beast of Whiteness: Teaching Race and Gender', *Shakespeare Quarterly* 47.4 (1996): 461–75.

17. For the SAA seminar we read Kyoko Kishimoto's 'Anti-racist Pedagogy: From Faculty's Self-reflection to Organizing Within and Beyond the Classroom', *Race, Ethnicity and Education* 21.4 (2018): 540–54. I found useful Kishimoto's exploration of how social positioning affects one's assumptions and beliefs and how good intentions can go astray as when 'in an effort to teach or research about racism, white faculty may tokenize the successes of people of colour, take on the "saviour's mentality", separate themselves from other white people and/or seek approval from people of colour so that they can be seen as the "good white person", but without constant self-reflection, these behaviours, despite good intentions, can actually promote racism and perpetuate power or dominant discourse'.

18. Charles Mills, 'White Ignorance', in *Race and Epistemologies of Ignorance*, ed. Shannon Sullivan and Nancy Tuana (Albany, NY: SUNY Press, 2007): 11–38.

19. Mills, 'White Ignorance', 35.

20. Ayanna Thompson in *Passing Strange: Shakespeare, Race, and Contemporary America* (Oxford: Oxford University Press, 2011) uses contemporary American film, performance, and video to query ideas such as the universality of Shakespeare or the possibility that using blackface in 'original practices' performance can escape reproducing exclusion and injury. See in particular Chapter 2, 'Universalism: Two Films that Brush with the Bard, *Suture* and *Bringing Down the House*', 21–43, and Chapter 5, 'Original(ity): *Othello and Blackface*', 96–117. Also pertinent is Arthur L. Little, Jr. essay, 'Re-Historicizing Race, White Melancholia, and the Shakespearean Property', *Shakespeare Quarterly* 67 (2016): 84–103. In this essay Little engages the question: 'Is Shakespeare or the Renaissance/early modern period white property?', ibid., 88.

21. Keith Hamilton Cobb, *American Moor*. Dir. Kim Weild. Cherry Lane Theatre, New York City, August–October 2019.

22. See also Barbara Applebaum, *Being White, Being Good: White complicity, White Moral Responsibility, and Social Justice Pedagogy* (Lanham, MD: Lexington Books, 2010).

23. Donna Haraway, 'Situated Knowledges: The Science Question in Feminism and the Privilege of Partial Perspective', *Feminist Studies* 14 (1988): 575–99, at 581.

24. For an interesting account of one African American faculty person's desire to be included in faculty governance and the barriers she faced, see Carmen Harris, 'Still Eating in the Kitchen: The Marginalization of African American Faculty in Majority White Governance', *Written/Unwritten: Diversity and the Hidden Truths of Tenure*, ed. Patricia A. Matthew (Chapel Hill: University of North Carolina Press, 2016), 165–77.

25. For a highly readable exploration of race and mass incarceration in this country see Michelle Alexander, *The New Jim Crow: Mass Incarceration in the Age of Colorblindness* (New York: The New Press, 2012).

CHAPTER NINETEEN

No Exeunt

The Urgent Work of Critical Whiteness

PETER ERICKSON

It's hard for me not to notice the fact that I'm not white. White people don't have to have a constant awareness of race. They can just walk around without people staring at them and feel comfortable in their own skin. *You only become aware of race when you feel threatened by a black guy.*

—Thomas Bradshaw[1]

No, Richard, I don't understand! Or at least that's what you keep telling me. Jean, you don't understand! Jean, you don't get it! Because you're white! Jean, you're white, white, white, white, white. WHAT, RICHARD?! WHEN DID I SUDDENLY BECOME THIS WHITE? I thought it didn't matter! I thought that was the whole point! I don't understand how suddenly this is a problem.

—Branden Jacobs-Jenkins[2]

I am a white person in Shakespeare. That is, I am a white scholar in the field of Shakespeare Studies. I have not always thought of myself as white. Consciousness of my white identity, and of the unearned white privilege that goes with it, has been a gradual development over the course of my life. I am now at the end of my career and you have reached the final chapter in this book. As the two come together, I am seizing this moment to tell you how I got here and what I think is the opportunity, indeed the necessity, for our field in close reading of Shakespeare through the lens of racial whiteness.

I was engaged in Civil Rights activism at Amherst College, supporting voter registration in Raleigh, North Carolina and assisting with the census in Greenville, Mississippi. After receiving my B.A. in 1967, I left immediately for Birmingham, UK, to study with the Jamaican-born British cultural theorist, Stuart Hall,[3] at the Center for Contemporary Cultural Studies, before being called up for the draft and having to postpone my graduate work.

The catalytic experience which would forever leave its mark on me, took place in 1969–70 during the Vietnam War when I performed two years of alternate service as a conscientious objector in Haiti. Serving as the pharmacy manager at the Hospital

Albert Schweitzer in Deschapelles, a town in the isolated Artibonite River Valley, I began to register the deep effects of what it meant to live as a white racial minority for a sustained period. Under the regime of dictator, Papa Doc Duvalier, aided by the terrifying paramilitary group, the Tonton Macoute, I was not protected by my whiteness.

Yet, when I resumed graduate school at the University of California, Santa Cruz immediately after leaving Haiti, the learning curve sparked by this formative experience effectively halted and went underground. I was not then able to apply it to my academic life. Not until I went head-to-head with senior faculty in the English Department at Williams College, my first academic appointment, was I able to begin merging my two years in Haiti with my teaching by purposefully disrupting the literary canon that formed the curriculum. Conversations with the now-deceased Black writer, Melvin Dixon, a colleague who became a close friend, were crucial to emboldening my rebellion. We discussed erasure in the academy – specifically the absence of women, Black and queer writers – and the lengths to which the establishment would go to protect the status quo. In so doing, these self-described 'humanists' perpetuated hundreds of years of injustice in the classroom, on tenure committees, and through the editorial boards of professional journals. As I have written elsewhere, my encounter with Alice Walker's work in the late 1970s, and the poetry and essays of Adrienne Rich, helped me to find my voice and sustained me during the Culture Wars of the 1980s.[4] My education continued through ongoing dialogues with writers including the Black poet, June Jordan and scholars such as Jean Howard, who introduced me to Kim F. Hall.[5] Because of their supportive companionship I found my way to others equally committed to literature and literary criticism as social justice activism.

Initially, my specific focus on white identity formation was part of a larger discussion about multiculturalism.[6] As my Shakespeare scholarship continued to evolve, I also expanded my study of contemporary Black and feminist writers, including poet Rita Dove and, later, Black visual artists such as Fred Wilson and Glenn Ligon, to cite two, and the images of Blacks in Western art.[7] Engaging with this broad range of creative production, I increasingly understood that I could not speak of racial whiteness unless I could speak with deeper awareness of my own ideological formation. In short, I could not separate myself as a white person from my work as a white scholar. My theoretical framework was built on the principle of transformation, fundamentally changing 'the conventions by which we understand and organize canons', requiring a willingness to shake the deepest foundations of my white identity.[8] Only then would I be able to access dimensions of Shakespeare's work that would otherwise have eluded me. More significantly is what this taught me about myself and about what it meant to be white as a way of being in the world: whiteness is a way of being from which I can never be distanced and cannot hide. Close reading is where the text and I, as a white person, intersect and create meaning with and for one another. They not only collide but also challenge and stimulate one another.

My goal in this essay, as it has been in much of my work for the past forty years, is to perform where this journey has taken me, and how these experiences intersect with close reading of Shakespeare's texts. How can I, as a white scholar, occupy a site in which this shared whiteness – of Shakespeare, his characters, and myself – be differentiated and how can these distinctions become a source of tension and insight? What does it mean to read Shakespeare through the lens of racial whiteness?

First, as a white scholar I must resist the reflex that causes me to automatically translate race as 'Black' or as 'of colour', meaning everything except 'white'. There must be a tacit acknowledgement of whiteness, including my own, as a distinct racial category.

Second, I am a white person in Shakespeare, but I am also a white person outside of Shakespeare, adopting a sharply critical, indeed, self-critical, stance. I must remain aware of negotiating and simultaneously pursuing both sides of this dual identity. My inside/outside position creates a productive *frisson*. My critical apparatus must be informed by an ethos of self-awareness.

Third, I accept the value and the validity of the cross-historical – that the past and the present intersect in literary criticism as they do in life. Sitting in a theatre watching one of Shakespeare's plays makes this abundantly clear. For the duration of a performance, I am conscious of living in two worlds. I puzzle over their divergencies and the impossibility of seamless continuity or neat synthesis, despite claims that Shakespeare represents timeless values. Having a much longer historical timeline for race studies does not mean collapsing and merging all the points along the line as though they are the same. Rather, it means connecting the dots, each of which simultaneously retains its own separate and distinct integrity. The fiction of Shakespeare's permanent, unvarying universality is contradicted by this condition of historical differentiation. Shakespeare is neither 'aesthetically autonomous' nor 'historically transcendent', nor fixed in time.[9] He is subject to the change in issues that concern me as a contemporary person and the values that guide my work.

Finally, my relationship with Shakespeare's whiteness is mediated by his characters. I must be open to the myriad and complex ways in which his characters express and reveal their whiteness. Shakespeare's characters do not articulate racial whiteness in the direct way that the characters speak in contemporary plays by the Black playwrights, Thomas Bradshaw and Branden Jacobs, quoted in my opening epigraphs. Some of the immediately recognizable eerie calling out and the uncomfortable feeling associated with a white person hearing them also resonates on the lower frequencies in Shakespeare's drama. In this realm, actions may sometimes speak louder than words. Portia doesn't have to say she's white; her good riddance to the Prince of Morocco – 'Let all of his complexion choose me so' (2.7.79)[10] – exhibits her whiteness without the word. White behaviour is never totally silent and nonverbal but rather indirect and thus potentially available for decoding. Even when the implied white entitlement is not spelled out, Shakespearean actions still speak loudly: whiteness is performed in behaviour and gestures. Although the discourse of racial difference is unquestionably present, it can be difficult to discern the precise nature of white characters' evasive attitudes toward that discourse. As in the contemporary world, we may encounter in individuals a complete lack of self-awareness or no explicit concept of racism or an absence of any fully articulated sense of shame or embarrassment. Instead we more often seem to face an elusive or subterranean entitlement whose implied presence permits and invites analyses. These strategies are particularly manifest across Shakespeare's dramatic engagements with cross-racial interactions. In close reading through the lens of racial whiteness we find abundant evidence in the voices of Shakespeare's characters to counter claims that we are imposing the present on Shakespeare in ways which are ahistorical or that 'race is not relevant'. Even a few, brief but detailed analyses of the relationship between Blackness and whiteness give the lie to such counter claims. We see it and hear it in Shakespeare's language: the dynamics of this relationship is enacted explicitly and, even more often, implicitly, hidden within his characters, defining how they see and experience one another and their world.

WHITE CHARACTERS NEGOTIATING BLACKNESS

In the final scene of *The Tempest* (1611) the ever-optimistic Gonzalo enumerates his inclusive account of what he sees as the play's happy ending with a troubling mention of Alonso's daughter: 'And set it down / With gold on lasting pillars: in one voyage / Did Claribel her husband find at Tunis' (5.1.208–10). With respect to Claribel, the prospect of 'gold on lasting pillars' sounds like the empty gesture of symbolic gold statues at the end of *Romeo and Juliet*. Gonzalo's glowing reference to Claribel, a character who never appears onstage has the unintended effect of reviving the unresolved issue concerning the problem of her marriage 'to an African' (2.1.126), the problem being the anticipated subordination of her whiteness to his Blackness. On this earlier occasion, even Gonzalo conceded that her father Alonso made a mistake in supporting a mixed-race marriage. Sebastian's accusation of Alonso: 'The fault's your own' (2.1.135) is explicitly acknowledged by Gonzalo as 'The truth' (138), albeit harshly stated. Nothing in Claribel's condition has changed since the initial expressions of regret about the circumstances of her marriage. Yet, for the happy ending to work, the truth must be left out of account, with the result that the troubled feeling circulating about the marriage remains unresolved.

In his original attempt to raise spirits by engaging in positive thinking about Claribel's wedding, Gonzalo instead clumsily raises a sore topic: 'Methinks our garments are now as fresh as when we put them on first in Africa, at the marriage of the King's fair daughter Claribel to the King of Tunis' (2.1.70–3). Implicitly taking responsibility, Alonso moans his unhappiness: 'Would I had never / Married my daughter there!' (2.1.108–9). Converting the language of Gonzalo's fantasy of a happy scene, Sebastian bluntly points to the dilemma created because Alonso 'would not bless our Europe with your daughter, / But rather loose her to an African' (2.1.125–6). Alonso's failure to advise his daughter appropriately amounted to her abandonment: 'You were kneeled to and importuned otherwise / By all of us, and the fair soul herself / Weighed between loathness and obedience at / Which end o'th'beam should bow' (2.1.130–3).

Since Claribel as an offstage character never speaks, her apparent discontent is not fully dramatized. Yet the questions persist, what does the 'loathness' attributed to her entail and how should we respond? In retrospect, Alonso worries: 'I ne'er again shall see her' (2.1.111), while for Antonio her remoteness presents an opportunity for dynastic plotting (2.1.242–4). But these issues seem insufficient to explain the principal undercurrent of loaded emotion associated with the distant marriage itself. Sebastian emphatically reiterates Gonzalo's terms 'Afric' and 'fair daughter Claribel' in his reformulations: 'loose her to an African' and 'the fair soul herself' convey a negative tonal resonance of racial difference. The use of 'fair' signifies her whiteness, which in turn is reinforced by the senses of clear, bright, shining and beautiful already contained in the meaning of her name. Although the King of Tunis's complexion is not specified and we cannot specifically identify him as Arabic, Berber, or Black African, the connotation of non-white is strongly present. By implication, the unseen King of Tunis is potentially another version of a dreaded 'thing of darkness' and, as such, a major source of the rhetorical uneasiness that underlies the contentious concern for the future of Claribel.

This racial dimension is magnified by the larger symbolic context of the play's racial geography when we imagine Prospero's island as having an in-between position in the Mediterranean similar to that of Sicily.[11] To the north are Naples and Milan, the 'rightful' political sites of King Alonso and Duke Prospero, respectively. To the south is the North African coast with the adjacent countries of Tunis and Algiers, which from the perspective of Sicily, are not distant but close. The proximity of Tunis from the standpoint of Sicily intensifies the threat presented by the foreign zone Claribel has entered. But the danger of Africa is doubled because Algiers, the country next door, is the place from which Sycorax, Caliban's mother, who is Black, and claimant of the island now displaced by Prospero, originates (1.2.263). This overall geographical network supports the dramatic structure of the play and, in particular, helps to explain the structural interaction between the African motif in the adjacent scenes, 1.2 and 2.1.

Though not exact parallels, the images of the Miranda-Caliban and the Claribel-King of Tunis pairs echo each other and reinforce the play's racial theme. The hypothetical danger to which Claribel is exposed may not be as serious as the nightmare version of the threat that Miranda confronts in the Black Caliban, yet their situations are similar and in both cases the solution requires a defence of racial whiteness. Alonso's failure to protect his daughter sharply contrasts with the fervent intervention that Prospero carries out with consistent success and with particular alertness to mixed-race reproduction: 'Thou didst prevent me; I had peopled else / This isle with Calibans' (1.2.350–1). Ultimately, Miranda is rescued from Claribel's fate because she is provided with a white male partner, who makes his appearance already at the end of act 1, scene 2 as the clear alternative to Caliban, who exits as Ferdinand enters. The marital dynamic highlights Ferdinand's whiteness as an officially approved alternative to the Black African portrayed as a source of grief. This tension produces an ongoing tonal ambivalence that decreases the surface comic effect and increases the underlying anxiety.

This early alignment of white characters in a prospective bond assures Miranda's safety and thus immediately quells the disquiet that causes Claribel's marriage to feel vaguely unsafe. Even before we have heard about Claribel's problem as the new Queen of Tunis, Ferdinand offers to make Miranda 'Queen of Naples' (1.2.449). This contrast provides the dramatic basis that highlights the racial point – the triumph of whiteness, which as enacted here achieves both white sexual purity and white political control. It is Shakespeare who articulates the happy ending proposed by Prospero's Epilogue: 'As you from crimes would pardoned be / Let your indulgence set me free' (19–20). Just as Prospero sets Ariel free, so Shakespeare sets Prospero free by granting his request for pardon without requiring any explanation of what the pardon is for and why it is needed. Both magician and author orchestrate a white story and ask that it remain unexamined.

The Tempest circumvents tragedy to achieve a romance of absolute whiteness through Prospero's magic power of supervision. Going beyond the abstract figure of the Ethiop, *The Tempest* offers the story of encounter with a specific individual, the African King of Tunis, when the white delegation voyages to North Africa to attend Claribel's wedding. However, this event is downplayed because it is not dramatized and we never see the wedded pair. The wedding is circumscribed as an isolated, one-time event. There is no suggestion that the King of Tunis will visit his new in-laws or ever venture to cross the boundary into white territory; it can be assumed that the African will stay in his own homeland and never be seen again. This separation is further emphasized by the departure of the white people from the island; their return to Naples and Milan increases their distance from the African coast. Prospero reaffirms an ongoing zone of white power and white security into the next generation overseen by Ferdinand and Miranda. The exception of Claribel's destiny outside of the charmed circle remains an unfortunate lost cause, which serves as a patent warning.

BLACK CHARACTERS NEGOTIATING WHITENESS

We do not need a character to proclaim a self-definition as white in order for us to identify the character as racially white. Whiteness declares itself in the course of cross-racial interactions with Black characters. Separated by a decade in Shakespeare's *oeuvre*, Aaron the Moor in *Titus Andronicus*, and Othello the Moor manifest two sharply different modes of Black identity. But these differences are decisively shaped in their responses to the respective contexts of white behaviour that surround them. Their Blackness cannot be approached as an isolated phenomenon but includes the larger picture of the particular white responses they faced and must decide how to engage. When the white Tamora orders the Black Aaron to kill their newborn baby, he refuses, protects the Black child, and disparages whiteness:

> Coal-black is better than another hue
> In that it scorns to bear another hue;
> For all the water in the ocean
> Can never turn the swan's black legs to white,
> Although she lave them hourly in the flood.
>
> —*Tit* 4.2.101–5

And in the case of Othello, when the Duke of Venice plays a key role in determining the racial dynamic of Othello's identity, the Duke does so as a white person.

In order better to highlight the contrast between Aaron and Othello, I shall reverse the chronological order of the plays and start with the latter figure. As the centre of bureaucratic power, the impersonally named Duke of Venice defines Othello's racial identity for him as 'far more fair than black' (1.3.291). In invoking the image of 'more fair' to authorize Othello's predominant whiteness, the Duke draws on two conventional motifs. The first alludes to the religious promise that Black Africans can legitimately gain access to whiteness through the process of Christian baptism that offers the prospect of making the soul white.[12] This outcome risks a potential split between exterior blackness and interior whiteness that erodes individual integrity because whiteness is achieved by circumventing and implicitly denigrating black skin.

The second source involves the power of political ritual. The Duke of Venice uses his authority to designate Othello as white in an act comparable to the display of King James's transcendent capacity to overcome the impossibility of washing the Ethiop white – 'Whose beams shine day and night, and are of force / To blanch an Ethiop, and revive a corse' – in Ben Jonson's *Masque of Blackness* (1605).[13] Yet there is a crucial difference between Shakespeare's and Jonson's versions. The miraculous aura of James's purported action is presented as having the literal efficacy to change reality, whereas Othello's whiteness is a fiction created by the Duke of Venice's verbal fiat and finesse. Moreover, the 'blanching' process is conspicuously incomplete because Othello's Blackness, though minimized by the Duke, remains in place. This Blackness is negatively tinged. Though Othello is accorded white status, he is not entitled to become completely white; when his provisional whiteness is cancelled, his residual blackness returns to the forefront as 'Haply for I am black' (3.3.267) announces. The terms set by the Duke to honour Othello's successful entry into Venetian society are hedged with limits and thus carry a long-term cost, which Othello eventually has to pay.

The decisive moment in act 1, scene 3 is a strategy constructed by a white character – not Iago but the Duke of Venice.[14] Iago wears his white racism on his sleeve, but the Duke's more subtle racial condescension is equally destructive. In pronouncing Othello white, the Duke deprives him of the blackness he needs to maintain a strong sense of self. The 'far more fair than black' formulation leaves no room for a viable black identity; the ultimate negation of Othello's identity has already occurred. As soon as his putative whiteness is called into question, Othello is vulnerable because he has no solid core of Blackness to which he can reliably return.

In the play's horrifying final scene, Othello works to preserve Desdemona's whiteness. Although he follows Iago's advice about the method of killing (4.1.206–7), the rhetorical emphasis on her whiteness is Othello's specific contribution (5.2.3–5). But Othello also struggles to preserve the vestiges of his own whiteness bestowed on him by the Duke of Venice, as well as to erase his own blackness. Othello's suicide enacts a drama in which he plays two roles that in effect show white Othello killing Black Othello. As the subject 'I', Othello attempts to stage one last time the heroic military figure whose 'virtue' has been endorsed by the Duke as 'far more fair than black'. The 'malignant and turbaned Turk' whom the first Othello imagines 'smot[ing]' is also an image of Othello – equivalent to his counter-status as a nonwhite foreigner, the Black 'element' that needs to be eliminated. Only when his self-presentation as a fictional white man is briefly restored can his life be rounded with a kiss.

The 'far more fair than black' description to which Othello acquiesces as a condition for belonging in Venetian society, Aaron vehemently refuses. His striking rejection of any whitening of the soul – 'Aaron will have his soul black as his face' (3.1.206) – may be heard as villain talk designed to prove that he is evil through and through. Yet this consistency of exterior and interior Blackness takes on another dimension when he is confronted with his baby in act 4, scene 2. Here he achieves a coherence of black identity not available in Othello's white/Black split in which white is featured and black is diminished. The precipitating cause is the instruction from Tamora, his white partner, to kill their mixed-race offspring: 'The Empress sends it thee, thy stamp, thy seal / And bids thee christen it with thy dagger's point' (4.2.71–2). Technically the baby is biracial but under the circumstances is treated by both parents as exclusively Black. For Tamora, the baby is all black because she acknowledges no part of herself in the baby; the idea of pure Blackness facilitates her unqualified rejection of the child. Black purity also serves Aaron's positive identification with the potential for black generational continuity that he sees in the child and wants to save. For Aaron, his Black stamp and seal are a source of immediate pride and long-term vision.

Aaron's defence of the integrity of Black identity is immediate and explicit: 'is black so base a hue?' (4.2.73). He quickly moves to answer his own rhetorical question:

> Coal-black is better than another hue
> In that it scorns to bear another hue;
> For all the water in the ocean
> Can never turn the swan's black legs to white,
> Although she lave them hourly in the flood.
> Tell the Empress from me I am of age
> To keep mine own, excuse it how she can.
>
> —*Tit* 4.2.98–104

The implied assumption behind the idea of washing the Ethiop white is that a Black person desires to be white. But Aaron defies this logic by declaring so clearly that he 'scorns to bear' the hue of whiteness; blackness for him is not a state of futility but rather a source of strength.

In this context, Aaron becomes a more complex character. Though he may still be a villain, he also becomes a man who articulates a strong black identity – exactly what Othello conspicuously lacks. The surprise of becoming a father affirms his black humanity against the background of his critique of whiteness. Once we have seen Aaron from a different perspective, we cannot go back and we cannot forget. Reverting to the designated villain role is motivated by Aaron's desire to protect his son. Yet Aaron stereotypes the stereotype with such an exaggerated, hyperbolic, over-the-top performance of the villain's melodrama that it comes across as deliberate caricature that is no longer plausible.

Both Aaron and Othello define themselves in relation to the pressures of whiteness that surround them. Aaron represents the voice that speaks for Blackness. Othello allows himself to be characterized as white. In either case, the Duke of Venice and Tamora, the power figures who shape these racial environments, enact identifiably white protocols.

NO EXEUNT

Let me now make the transition directly back to our own moment of racial reckoning. My project in performing these close readings has been to show the necessity of using critical race studies, and, in this essay in particular, critical white studies, as sharp scalpels for peeling back the layers of Shakespeare's whiteness and our own. I acknowledge that the approach I have taken – beginning with my formation as a white Shakespeare scholar and merging it with the act of dissecting Shakespeare's texts – risks the accusation of being personal but, perhaps, not personal enough. In 'Probing White Guilt, Pursuing White Redemption', I have critically questioned the self-pity demonstrated by white male characters, in some of the video works of William Kentridge, the white South African Artist, who are depicted as showing a nascent capacity for racial self-consciousness but who seem to expect credit merely for trying hard.[15] I hold myself to the same standard. I have no expectation of absolution by virtue of facing up to the problems of white identity. Rather, I choose to persist, as matter-of-factly as possible, in clarifying the critical perspective without lunging after a redemptive endpoint. Though I hope to open paths through which students might be inspired to pursue the analysis of racial whiteness, I do not want to engage in sentimental overreaching, wishful solutions and always premature celebration – distractions that obstruct the necessarily ongoing work.

I must take care not to embrace critical race studies and then delude myself that the work of dismantling white supremacy in our field is done. There is no 'exeunt' from the work of anti-racism. The antidote to self-satisfaction is to keep the dialogue going and to listen harder. As I take leave of this field, I implore my white colleagues to continue advancing racial equity by ensuring that critical whiteness studies are essential to early modern race studies. If they want to make a difference, I also ask those in positions of power to listen and learn especially from our younger colleagues of colour invested in this work and to be cognizant of how we hide behind our 'white fragility' as a tactic for avoiding change.[16] As public intellectuals and as educators we must write and teach and think with intention. Our intentionality provides our students with a model upon which they can reflect about what is at stake for them in their education and, also, what is at stake in their lives. Let us show them that there are no intellectual havens from the 'real world'. Our critical apparatus does not, cannot, stand apart.

Reading Shakespeare through the lens of racial whiteness has taught me so much about where we are now, how we got here and where we go next: to be anti-racist as a Shakespeare scholar is to be awake to the formation of discourses that have aided and abetted systemic racism, a system that suppresses diverse interpretation and, consequently, who we choose to see, who is heard, whose voices and perspectives are valued. It has determined what we teach, whose careers and ideas are advanced, how the Bard's plays are performed and by whom – in short, whose Shakespeare rules. We have an obligation to interrogate and to interrupt systemic racism in our field. The academy is called the ivory tower for a reason – it is white. If we are not to be a slave to our whiteness, we must start with an acknowledgement of how it shaped Shakespeare and how it shapes us.

NOTES

1. Thomas Bradshaw, *Intimacy, Intimacy and Other Plays* (New York: Theatre Communications Group, 2015), 118–19.

2. Branden Jacobs-Jenkins, *Neighbors, Reimagining A Raisin in the Sun: Four New Plays*, Rebecca Ann Rugg and Harvey Young, ed., (Evanston, IL: Northwestern University Press, 2012), Scene 18, 392. This epigraph is spoken by Jean, the only white character in the play.

3. See Stuart Hall with Bill Schwarz, *Familiar Stranger: A Life Between Two Islands* (Durham, NC: Duke University Press, 2017).

4. On this early engagement with Alice Walker, see Peter Erickson, 'Afterword', in *Rewriting Shakespeare, Rewriting Ourselves* (Berkeley: University of California Press, 1991), 170; and Peter Erickson, '"Cast Out Alone/To Heal/And Re-Create/Ourselves": Family-Based Identity in the Work of Alice Walker', *CLA Journal* 23 (1979): 71–94. On Adrienne Rich see, Peter Erickson *Rewriting Shakespeare, Rewriting Ourselves*, 146–66; and 'Singing America: From Walt Whitman to Adrienne Rich', *Kenyon Review* n.s. 17.1 (Winter 1995): 103–19. See also, 'On the Origins of American Feminist Shakespeare Criticism', *Women's Studies* 26.1 (1997): 27–37; 'Canon Revision Update: A 1992 Edition' [Thulani Davis, Rita Dove, Gloria Naylor, Alice Walker, and Toni Morrison], *Kenyon Review* n.s. (Summer 1993): 197–207; and Peter Erickson, *Patriarchal Structures in Shakespeare's Drama*, (Berkeley: University of California Press, 1985).

5. See my interviews with June Jordan in Peter Erickson, 'State of the Union', *Transition* 59 (1993):104–9; 'After Identity: A Conversation with June Jordan and Peter Erickson', *Transition* 63 (1994): 132–49.

6. My explicit focus on multiculturalism began in *Rewriting Shakespeare, Rewriting Ourselves* with 'Shakespeare, Angelou, Cheney: The Administration of the Humanities in the Reagan-Bush Era', 111–23; and 'Afterword: Identity Politics, Multicultural Society', 67–76. It continued in a series of writings on multicultural issues in the period of the early 1990s exemplified by 'Rather than Reject a Common Culture, Multiculturalism Advocates a More Complicated Route by Which to Achieve It', *Chronicle of Higher Education* 37, 41 (June 26, 1991): B1–B3; 'What Multiculturalism Means', *Transition* 55 (1992): 105–14; 'Multiculturalism and the Problem of Liberalism', *Reconstruction* [Cambridge, MA] 2.1 (1992): 97–101, followed by a brief exchange with Arthur Schlesinger, Jr. in 2.2 (1993): 10–11; 'The Question of the Canon: The Examples of Searle, Kimball, and Kernan', *Textual Practice* 6.3 (1992): 439–51; 'Profiles in Whiteness', *Stanford Humanities Review* 3.1 (Winter 1993): 98–111; and 'Seeing White', *Transition* 67 (1995): 166–85.

7. On Fred Wilson and Glenn Ligon see, Peter Erickson, 'Black Like Me: Reconfiguring Blackface in the Art of Glenn Ligon and Fred Wilson', *Nka: Journal of Contemporary African Art* 25 (Winter 2009): 30–47; and studies of Fred Wilson and Rita Dove in Peter Erickson, *Citing Shakespeare*, 22–39 and 119–50. Also, 'Rita Dove's Shakespeares', in *Transforming Shakespeare: Contemporary Women's Re-Visions in Literature and Performance*, ed. Marianne Novy (New York: St. Martin's Press, 1999), 87–101.

8. Erickson, *Rewriting Shakespeare, Rewriting Ourselves*, 6.
9. Ibid., 5.
10. The texts cited here are those of *The Arden Shakespeare Complete Works*, ed. Richard Proudfoot, Ann Thompson and David Scott Kastan (London: The Arden Shakespeare 2001).
11. Jonathan Bate calls attention to *The Tempest*'s relation to Sicily in 'Shakespeare's Islands', *Shakespeare and the Mediterranean*, ed. Tom Clayton et al. (Newark: University of Delaware Press, 2004), 289–307.
12. See Jean Michel Massing, *The Image of the Black in Western Art, Vol.3, From the 'Age of Discovery' to the Age of Abolition*, pt. 2 *Europe and the World Beyond* (Cambridge, MA: Harvard University Press, 2011), 292–4. The stress point is that symbolic whiteness of the soul cannot provide a complete white identity.
13. Ben Jonson, *The Complete Masques*, ed. Stephen Orgel (New Haven, CT: Yale University Press, 1969). For the presence of this emblem in English visual culture, see *Othello, the Moor of Venice: Texts and Contexts*, ed. Kim F. Hall (Boston: Bedford/St Martin's, 2007), 185, and *Race in Early Modern England: A Documentary Companion*, ed. Jonathan Burton and Annia Loomba (New York: Palgrave, 2007), 98–9 and 119–20.
14. In *A Fury in the Words: Love and Embarrassment in Shakespeare's Venice* (New York: Fordham University Press, 2013), Harry Berger, Jr. presents an extensive and persuasive argument that Iago's power as a mastermind is greatly overrated.
15. 'Probing White Guilt, Pursuing White Redemption: William Kentridge's *9 Drawings for Projection*', *Nka: Journal of Contemporary African Art* 28 (Spring 2011): 34–47. See also the analysis of John Howard Griffin's *Black Like Me* in 'Black Like Me: Reconfiguring Blackface in the Art of Glenn Ligon and Fred Wilson', *Nka: Journal of Contemporary African Art* 25 (Winter 2009): 30–47. For a literary example, see the discussion of Whitman's response as a white poet to Black figures in 'Singing America: From Walt Whitman to Adrienne Rich', *Kenyon Review* n.s. 17.1 (Winter 1995): 103–19.
16. 'White fragility', is a term used by Robin DiAngelo in her book, *White Fragility: Why It's So Hard for White People to Talk About Racism* (Boston: Beacon Press, 2018).

INDEX

Abercrombie & Fitch 85–6
academy 4, 11, 13, 86, 235, 241, 256, 261, 270, 272, 278, 285
acts of woman hatred 50
Adams, Joseph Quincy 4, 239
affective piety 65, 67
  see also *Measure for Measure* (Shakespeare)
affective whiteness 45
Africa 281
  see also Egypt
Ahmed, Sara 129
Akrigg, G. V. 32
Albanese, Denise 240
Aldridge, Ira *203*, 203, 204
Alexander, Michelle 85, 276 n.25
All for Love (Dryden) 177–87
  blank, fragile white becoming 178–9
  Caesar, power of 180–1
  Cleopatra, whitening of 180
  colonialism, resistance to 184
  disciplining power of whiteness 183, 184
  Egypt 185
  flight from whiteness 185–6
  loss and blankness 184–5
  perfect whiteness 177, 180, 181, 183
  political system, relevance to 181
  regularizing, effects of 182, 183
  Restoration Shakespeare 181–2
  revising Shakespeare 177
  scientific ideas about colour 177–8, 179–80, 183
  surveillance of Blackness and blankness 183
  white fragility 182, 183, 186
  'white rage' 186
American Moor (Cobb)
  black actors as white property 220–4
  black male voices 219
  discussion with Cobb 200, 201–2, 205

sound and listening 225–8, 229, 230
and white ignorance 269
anatomization of the female see blazon
Anderson, Carol 11, 151, 186, 254, 259, 261
anger 253–61
  see also white rage
  Boris Johnson 256–7, 259
  dangers to people of colour 254
  Merchant of Venice 254–6
  Stephen Bannon 258–60
  and white supremacy 253, 257, 258, 259
Anne of Denmark, Queen 143
Antony and Cleopatra (Sedley) 181
Antony and Cleopatra (Shakespeare) 105, 107–12, 180
Anzaldúa, Gloria 87
appropriation 220–1, 224, 229–30
Arendt, Hannah 173
Aristotle, *Politics* 153
art 10–11, 74–5 n.8
Arthur, King 139
As You Like It (Shakespeare) 106, 242, 250 n.35
asides 212–13
assassination of Lincoln 151
assemblage theory 6, 8, 16, 21 n.42
audiences, modern 201, 202, 204, 205, 216–17
auditions 220, 223, 224

Bacon's Rebellion (1676) 85
Baldwin, James 174, 247
Bannon, Stephen 258–60
  The Thing I Am 258
baptism 69
Baraka, Amiri 247
Bardolatry 199, 208
'beauty,' use of 7, 11, 31–37, 46–48, 51–57, 65, 67, 70–73, 80–82, 91, 94–95, 105–107, 109–112, 266

Bernard de Clairvaux, *Meditations* 65
Best, George 54, 135–6, 137
Bible, 1 Corinthians 3:16 6–7
Biblical origins of Britain 140
black holes 195
Black rage 258–9, 260
Black Shakespeare scholars 8–9, 166, 191, 192–3, 193–4, 230
Black voices 219, 221, 227
black woman sonnets 36–7
black women 47, 84, 194, 234 n.82, 259–60
blackface 6, 223
blackness
    blood and 54
    of Cleopatra 107, 108, 114 n.16, 115 n.26
    inferiority, equated with 53–4
    Ovidian discourse and 47
    of Romans/enemies 68–9
    of Saracens 53, 68
    sexuality and 36, 47
    and sodomy 84
    Sonnets and 36, 37
    'tainted,' associated with 84
    of torturers 67–8
    value for whiteness, creation of 57
    vice and 57
    whiteness, accentuation of 52
blankness 178–9, 183, 184–5
blazon
    conventions of 46
    mercantile tropes in Spenser 48
    parody of 49, 50
    Petrarchan 47
    theatrical representations of 46, 50, 55, 58–9
    in works of Shakespeare 48, 51–2
    see also white/red nexus
blood
    blackness and 54
    Christian 65, 66, 73
    in *Julius Caesar* 157–8
    race studies and 193
    and racial identity 69
    turned to milk 69
bloodlines 135–6, 138, 154
    see also genealogies
blushing 71
Boose, Lynda 96

Booth, John Wilkes 151, 161
borders and boundaries 124–5, 126–7, 130–1
Boyle, Robert 179, 180
Brexit 257, 259
British history 138–41, 143–4, 152
Britishness 137
Britton, Dennis 5, 158
Brooke, Arthur, *Tragical Historye of Romeus and Juliet* 96, 97, 99
Browne, Simone 183
Bulman, James 79
Butler, Judith 79

Callaghan, Dympna 128
Camden, William 139–40
Capitol, storming of (January 6, 2021) 2–4, 18 n.15, 18–19 n.19
Cary, Elizabeth, *The Tragedy of Mariam* 55, 56, 59
casting 95, 151–2
    see also auditions
category trading 85–6
Caviness, Madeline 24 n.75, 74 n.8
Cecilia, saint 70
Celtic myths 138–9
Chakravarty, Urvashi 152
Charnes, Linda 171
chastity 52, 142, 156
    see also female virgin martyrs
Chaucer, Geoffrey, *Second Nun's Tale* 70
Chorus, role of 95, 129, 130–1, 202
Christ
    blood/milk of 158
    whiteness of 65, 66, 67
Christian art 74–5 n.8
Christian whiteness 53, 68–9, 154, 157
    see also female virgin martyrs
Christian writers 53, 54, 65
citizenship in the US 3, 236, 237–9, 247 n.4, 248 n.7, 254
classical past 137–8, 152, 153
    see also Rome
classical texts 54
    Aeneid (Virgil) 138, 144, 145, 170
Cleopatra 107–12, 114 n.16, 115 n.26, 180
Coates, Ta-Nehisi 93, 98, 253
Cobb, Keith Hamilton *see American Moor* (Cobb)

college entrance exams 241
college students, engagement with 271
  colleges see academy
colonialism 153, 156, 159, 191, 199, 200, 204
colour, absence of 194–5
colour, scientific ideas about 177–8, 179–80, 183
comedy 50–1
commodities 48
'complexion,' use of 72–3, 81
complimentary poetry 30–1
Contarini, Gasparo, *The Commonwealth and Government of Venice* 79–80
control of Shakespeare 222–3
Coriolanus (Shakespeare) 5, 20 n.33, 258–9
corrective facilities, Shakespeare in 217, 273
Cosby, Bill 260
cosmetics 6, 10, 48, 61 n.14
court entertainments 139
Crane, Mary Thomas 167
critical race studies 8–9, 45
critical white studies 1–2, 9–11, 196
critical whiteness
  black characters negotiating whiteness in *Othello* and *Titus Andronicus* 282–4
  characters, whiteness of 279–80
  Peter Erickson, experiences of 277–9, 285
  white characters negotiating blackness in *The Tempest* 280–2
crusades 69
cultural capital
  of English 204
  Shakespeare as 11, 196, 200, 201, 204, 236, 256, 259
  of whiteness 35–6
cultural legacies 131, 132
curriculum 240–1
Cymbeline (Shakespeare) 51–2, 135–46
  blazon in 51–2
  British history 138–41, 143–4
  Britishness 137
  endings and collapse 144
  familial and racial integrity, treatment of 141–3
  headless corpse 144–5
  masculine bloodlines 135–6, 138
  masculine last stand 146
  succession crisis 135

Daileader, Celia 108
daily practice of scholarship 265–73
  editing Shakespeare 266–7
  faculty committees 272–3
  hiring of staff 271–2
  'less white,' becoming 265
  teaching Shakespeare 267–70
  writing about Shakespeare 270–1
Daniel, Samuel, *Tethys Festival* 139, 143
Demeter, Jason 151
deportation warrants 98, 102 n.36
  see also expulsion of blackamoors
Desdemona (Morrison and Traoré) 224–5, 225–6, 228–9, 230, 267
Devereaux, Robert, Earl of Essex 30
DiAngelo, Robin 11, 182, 183, 270
DiGangi, Mario 77
disfigurement 110–11
dishonesty 212, 215
dismemberment of women 50
  see also blazon
diversity in society 257
diversity in the arts 199, 200
divine whiteness 6–7, 65–7, 105
Dixon, Melvin 278
Douglass, Frederick 11
Dryden, John *see All for Love* (Dryden)
Du Bois, W. E. B. 225, 230
Dyer, Richard 9, 10, 244, 245

editing Shakespeare 266–7
education 167, 171–2
education and the Civil Rights Era 235–47
  citizenship in the US 237–9
  democracy and dictators, discussion of 242–4
  influence in US politics 247
  literary anthologies 241–2
  non-white representation 245–7
  schools 240–1
  Shakespeare in US education 240–1
  textbooks in the US 236–7
  White America 235–7
  white representation 244–5, 246, 251 n.56
Egypt 110, 182, 184, 185
Eichmann, Adolf 173
Elizabeth I, Queen 5, 30, 125, 129–30
Elyot, Sir Thomas, *The Governour* 82
Emerson, Ralph Waldo 4

enemies, blackening of 68–9
English, spoken 257
Englishness 121–2, 130, 256–7
Erasmus 167
Erickson, Peter 5, 9, 170, 229, 267, 277–9, 285
Eschenbach, Wolfram von, *Parzival* 53
ethnic minorities 238–9
Eulalia, saint 70
Euripides 54
Evil May Day Riot (1517) 98
exclusivity of whiteness 86, 222, 223, 232 n.23
expulsion of blackamoors 129–30
  see also deportation warrants
eyes, as window of the heart 46–7

faculty committees 272–3
'fair/fairness,' use of 7–8, 266
  Hamlet 172–3
  Henry IV, Part 1 124, 125
  Henry V 128
  Measure for Measure 72
  Merchant of Venice 80, 81, 82–3, 175 n.24
  Romeo and Juliet 91–2, 94, 95
  Sonnets 30, 31–2, 34–5
  Tempest 280–1
Fanon, Frantz
  Black Skin, White Masks 12, 220
  The Wretched of the Earth 112
female bodies 47, 52–3
  see also blazon; female virgin martyrs
female characters
  in comedies 50
  denigration of 46
  idealizing of 46
  in Jacobean tragedy 54–7
  Measure for Measure 70–4
  Romeo and Juliet 91–2, 94–5
  shame of 142, 145
  staging of 128
  white hands 106–7
  white racialization of 52, 59
  see also Cleopatra
female editors 266
female poets 50, 61 n.21
female subjectivity 55
female virgin martyrs 65–6, 67, 69–70, 73

femininity 56
Fineman, Joel 36
Florio, John 82
Folger, Henry Clay 4
Folger Shakespeare Memorial Library 4, 239
Ford, John, *'Tis Pity She's a Whore* 46, 58–9
forgetting 166
Foxe, John, *Acts and Monuments* 70
Friedman, Jamie 68
friendships, male 81–2, 83

Garber, Marjorie 11
gender formation 79
genealogies 122, 123–4, 125–6, 127, 128–9, 131–2
  see also masculine bloodlines
Geoffrey of Monmouth, *Historia regum Britanniae* 138–9
Gerzina, Gretchen 108
Gil, Daniel Juan 159
Girard, René 157, 161
Gleason, Elisabeth G. 79–80
global whiteness 1, 17 n.7
globalization of Shakespeare 204
glosses 266
'God trick' 270–1
Goddard, Harold 171
Graham, Lindsey 260
Greenblatt, Stephen 32, 173
Greene, Thomas 30
grief, racial (see melancholia/mourning)
Grier, Miles 265
Guiraut de Borneil 46

Hacker, Andrew 223
Hall, Kim F. 9, 92, 93, 108, 158, 179, 256, 266
Hamlet (Shakespeare) 165–74
  Achilles, pride of 171
  colour black, use of 169–70
  education 167, 171–2
  'fair,' use of 172–3
  forgetting 166
  Ghost (King Hamlet), immorality of 167–8
  monarchical legitimacy 169
  N-word, King Hamlet as 165, 166, 171–2, 173–4
  white melancholia 165–6
  white self of Hamlet 172–3

Hammonds, Evelynn 195
hands 80, 105–6
  see also white hands
Hannaford, Ivan 99
Haraway, Donna 270
Harris, Cheryl I. 5, 109, 160, 222, 223
Harris, John, *Mercurius Militaris* 121–2, 131–2
Harrison, William, *Description of England* 125
hatred of women 50
Hayakawa, S. I. 235
heart 46–7, 58, 59
Heng, Geraldine 69
Henriad (Shakespeare) 121–32
  borders and whiteness 124–5, 130–1
  boundaries, crossing of 126–7
  Chorus, role of 130–1
  cultural legacies and failure 131, 132
  Englishness 121–2, 130
  expulsion of blackamoors 129–30
  'fair/fairness,' use of 124, 125, 128
  genealogies 122, 123–4, 125–6, 127, 128–9, 131–2
  masculine descent 138
  monarchical legitimacy 169
  racial succession 128–9
  racial whiteness 122, 124, 125, 127, 130, 132
  rivers and maps 124, 125
  white hands 106
  wives 127–8
Henry Frederick, Prince of Wales 139, 143
Herbert, William, 3rd Earl of Pembroke 30, 31, 32
Hill, Edwin 221
Hillman, David 80
hiring of staff 271–2
historical sources 138–41
Hopkins, Lisa 125
Horsman, Reginald 238
humanism 4–5, 9, 10, 13–14, 82, 156, 161–2, 166–67, 167, 173, 196, 278
humanities 4, 11, 12

ideology 92
immigration 237–9, 257
Immigration (Johnson-Reed) Act, 1924 19 n.21, 238
incest 58

institutions, white supremacy and 4, 16, 78, 81, 82, 93, 192, 199, 206–207, 222, 230, 265–9, 270–72
insurrection, US Capitol 3–5 (see also riots
intersectional study of sexuality 77–8, 86–7
intimidation of whiteness 109, 116 n.39
intraracial riots 97–8
Isaac, Benjamin 153
Islamizing of Romans/enemies 68–9
ivory tower 285 (see also academy)
Iyengar, Sujata 71

Jacobean tragedy 54–7
Jacobson, Matthew Frye 238
James I, King 139
January 6, 2021 storming of the US Capitol 2–4, 18 n.15, 18–19 n.19
Jed, Stephanie 156
Jesus *see* Christ
Johnson, Ben, *The Speeches at Prince Henries Barriers* 139
Johnson, Boris 256–7, 259
Jones, Duncan 32
Jonson, Ben 7, 283
Julius Caesar (Shakespeare) 151–62, 236–7, 242–7
  in American education 236–7
  and America's Rome 2, 3
  blood imagery 157–8
  British history 152
  Brutus, liberality of 156–7
  Caesar, sacrifice of 157
  democracy and dictators, discussion of 242–4
  founding of Roman Republic 155–6
  influence in US politics 247
  in literary anthologies 242
  non-white representation 245–7
  racial purification 161–2
  racist uses of 151–2, 161
  Roman citizenship 154
  Roman racial formation 152, 161
  slavery 152–3
  tears 158–9
  through-lines of white supremacy 243
  tyranny 153, 154–5, 156
  white representation 244–5, 246, 251 n.56
  white subjectivity 156

whiteness and 153–4
whiteness as property 159–60

Kahn, Coppélia 18 n.17, 146, 152, 154
Karim-Cooper, Farah 80, 105, 108, 109
Kastan, David Scott 166
Katherine of Alexandria, saint 67, 68, 69, 70
Kavanaugh, Bret 260
Kendi, Ibram X. 85
'kind/kindness,' use of 83
King, Anchuli Felicia, *Keene* 201, 202, 203–5, 208
King of Tars, The (c. 1330) 53, 68
Knowles, Eric 86

language of race 266–7, 274 n.7
language of Shakespeare 200–1
LaPerle, Carol Mejia 185
Laurents, Arthur 95
less than human 212
'less white,' becoming 265
Leveaux, David 95
Levellers 121, 123
Liebler, Naomi Conn 92, 97, 157
lies/lying 212, 215
Life of St. Katherine 67, 68, 69, 70
Lincoln, Abraham 151
linguistic diversity 257
Lipsitz, George 255
listening 219–30
  American Moor 220–4
  Desdemona 224–5
  sound and listening 225–9
literary anthologies 241–2
Little, L. Arthur, Jr. 45, 73, 78, 98, 105, 153–4, 155–6, 165–6, 179, 183, 192, 196, 251 n.56
London 97–8
Loomba, Ania 53, 97
Lord Mayor's pageants 140–1
Lorde, Audre 87
love triangles 58, 63 n.54
Love's Labour's Lost (Shakespeare) 106

Macbeth (Shakespeare) 242
MacDonald, Joyce Green 77, 108, 181
male friendship 81–2, 83
maps 124
Margaret of Antioch, saint 70
Martin, Trayvon 226

martyrs 56, 57, 59, 67, 158
  see also female virgin martyrs
masculine bloodlines 135–6, 138
Masten, Jeffrey 82
Mazzio, Carla 80
McBride, Dwight A. 85, 86
McIntosh, Peggy 92
McNamer, Sarah 67
meanings 266–7
Measure for Measure (Shakespeare) 65–74
  affective piety 65, 67
  blackness of enemies 68–9
  blood and racial identity 69
  'complexion,' use of 72–3
  divine whiteness 65–7
  'fair,' use of 72
  female virgin martyrs 65–6, 67, 69–70, 73
  racial violence 67–8, 69, 70
  white skin in *Measure for Measure* 70–4
Meister, Tara N. 224–5
melancholia and mourning, white 11, 70, 165–6, 177–8
Merchant of Venice, The (Shakespeare) 77–87, 132 n.6, 254–6
  anger in 254–6
  category trading 85–6
  'fair,' use of 31–2, 80, 81, 82–3, 175 n.24
  gender formation 79
  hands in 80
  intersectional study of sexuality 77–8, 86–7
  male friendship 81–2, 83
  'a pound of flesh' 78–9, 82–3
  race trading 85
  sexuality and 79
  synecdoche 80–1
  'tainted,' use of 84
  Venice 79–80, 81, 83
  whiteness in 79, 80–1, 82–3, 83–4
Middleton, Thomas, *The Triumphs of Truth* 4
Milford Haven, Wales 143
milk, blood turned to 69
Mills, Charles W. 123, 181, 186, 269, 270
minstrelsy 223
miracles 69
misogyny 37, 50, 57, 109, 137
misogynoir 109
mixed parentage 135–6, 137
monarchy 121–2, 169
Montaigne, Michel de, 'Of Friendship' 82

INDEX

Moors 67–8
   see also Saracen blackness
Morison, Henry 30
Morrison, Toni 11, 267
Morrison, Toni and Rokia Traoré,
      Desdemona 219, 224–6, 228–30,
      267
Moss, Candida R. 66
mourning, black 54, 281
Much Ado about Nothing (Shakespeare) 5, 11
Munday, Anthony, *The Triumphs of
      Re-United Britania* 140–1
Munro, Ian 95

N-word, King Hamlet as 165, 166, 171–2,
      173–4
nationalistic rivalry 52
Newton, Isaac 177–8, 179, 183
nineteenth-century American Shakespeare
      theatre 214–15
   see also Aldridge, Ira
Noble, Graham 98
Nyquist, Mary 153, 180–1

Oluo, Ijeoma 110
Othello (Shakespeare)
   black characters negotiating whiteness
      282–3
   comparisons with 57
   language of race 267
   modern responses to 206 *see also
      American Moor* (Cobb)
   Ovidian discourse 46
   race studies and 219
   a white face version 194–5
Ovid, *Metamorphoses* 142
Ovidian discourse 46, 47

pageants 4, 140–1
Painter, Nell Irvin 93, 151
Paster, Gail Kern 158
Patterson, Steve 82, 84
Pembroke, Earl of 30, 31, 32
Peng, Kaiping 86
penis 83
'people'
   adjectives used with 5
   meaning of 4–5
   use of 5, 20 n.33, 211–12
perfect whiteness 177, 180, 181, 183

performativity, racial 79, 117 n.52
Petrarchan discourse 46–7, 48, 51, 55,
      56, 58
phenotypic whiteness 93–4, 95, 96,
      97–8, 245
Plutarch 155, 156
political theory 153
Pollack-Pelzner, Daniel 258, 260
positionality of students 269, 270
power of whiteness 86, 92–3, 107, 132,
      159, 179, 180–1, 183, 184, 222–3
   see also white supremacy
power, struggle for 52–3
presidential elections 191
   US 11, 18 n.15, 259
prisons, Shakespeare in 217, 273
property, black actors as white property
      220–4
property, whiteness as a 5, 109–10,
      159–60, 222
Prosser, Eleanor 168
purity, racial *see* genealogies; masculine
      bloodlines
purity, sexual 69, 71, 73

Quarshie, Hugh 220

race, history of 9–10, 53–4, 99
race studies *see* critical race studies;
      scholars/scholarship
race trading 85
'racial contract' 2, 18 n.11
racial difference 92, 94
racial exceptionalism 177
   see also white supremacy
racial exclusion 237
racial purification 161–2
racial purity *see* genealogies; masculine
      bloodlines
racial succession 128–9
   see also genealogies
racial terrorism 235
racial violence 67–8, 69, 70
racial whiteness
   Henriad 122, 124, 125, 127, 130, 132
   Merchant of Venice 80, 82
   staging of 128
racialized tension 95–6
rage *see* anger and also white rage
Rape of Lucrece (Shakespeare) 141–2, 156

Reames, Sherry 67, 69
red/white nexus *see* white/red nexus
redemption 73–4
representations of white people 10–11, 74–5 n.8
Restoration Shakespeare 181–2
riots and protests 2–3, 13, 15, 97–8, 121–3, 235, 254, 258
rivers 124, 125
romances 51, 53
romantic love 46–7
Rome
    America's Rome 2, 3, 18 n.14
    blackening of Romans 68–9
    citizenship 154
    founding of Roman Republic 155–6
    racial formation 152, 161
Romeo and Juliet (Shakespeare) 91–9
    ahistoricism of white 'normativity' 92–3
    casting of 95
    city riots 97–8
    'fair/fairness,' a descriptor of beauty 91–2, 94, 95
    lack of central problem 92
    phenotypic whiteness 93–4, 95, 96, 97–8
    'race,' use of 99
    racial difference 92, 94
    racialized tension 95–6
Rowe, Katherine 105
Royster, Francesca 5, 185
Ruether, Rosemary Radford 66

sacrifice 54, 130, 157–8, 161–2
saintly whiteness 67–8
Saracen blackness 53, 68
    see also Moors
scholars of colour 271–2
scholars/scholarship 191, 192–3, 193–4, 202, 205, 206–7
schools 240–1
    see also education and the Civil Rights Era
scientific ideas about colour 177–8, 179–80, 183
Sedley, Charles, *Antony and Cleopatra* 181
'see,' use of 33
self-fashioning 105–6
    see also Hamlet (Shakespeare)
Sellars, Peter 219, 228
Serres, Michel 130

sexual purity 69, 71, 73
sexuality
    blackness and 36, 47
    blood and 69
    gender and 79
    intersectional study of 77–8, 86–7
    Petrarchan discourse and 47
    whiteness and 47, 83
    whiteness as a 83–4
Shakespeare companies 213–14, 216
Shakespeare, William 7–8, 32–3
Shakespearean scholarship *see* scholars/scholarship
Shapiro, James 83
Shuger, Debora 153
Sidney, Sir Philip, *Astrophil and Stella* 47–8
Sinfield, Alan 92
slave trade, prefiguration of 98, 102 n.36
slavery 152–3
Smith, Bruce R. 225, 229
Smith, Ian 9, 93, 152, 186
Snook, Edith 31
Snyder, Susan 92
sodomy 83, 84
sonic colour line 225–8
Sonnets (Shakespeare) 29–38
    aristocracy, Shakespeare and 32–3
    'beauty,' use of 32
    black woman sonnets 36–7
    chronology 29–30
    complimentary poetry 30–1
    cultural capital of whiteness 35–6
    'fair,' use of 30, 31–2, 34–5
    No. 130 parodies of Petrarchan conventions 48
    patterns of ruination and triumph 33–5
    'see,' use of 33
    Sonnet 144 37–8
    white subjectivity, nature of 33
Sorel, Charles, *The Extravagant Shepherd* 49, 50
sound and listening 225–9
Southampton, Earl of 30–1, 32
speaking *see* Black voices; voices
Spenser, Edmund, *Amoretti* 48
Stein, Suzanne 167
Stern, Tiffany 181
Stoever, Jennifer Lynn 225, 230
storming of the Capitol (January 6, 2021) 2–4, 18 n.15, 18–19 n.19

Sullivan, Shannon 185
Sutphen, Joyce 32–3
'suturing' 182
synecdoche 80–1

'tainted,' use of 84
Taylor, Gary 6, 94
teaching Shakespeare 267–70
tears 152, 158–9, 161–2
Tempest, The (Shakespeare) 5, 280–2
textbooks 236
theatre
    Black actors in 223–4, 226, 229–30
    Englishness, mark of 121, 122
    female characters, representations of 128
    and racialized whiteness 6–7
    whiteness, discussion of 199–208, 213–14
theatrical subjectivity 46, 60 n.3
Thompson, Ayanna 67
Tillyard, E. M. W. 8
Titus Andronicus (Shakespeare)
    anger 253
    black characters negotiating whiteness 283–4
    blushing 71
    female shame 142, 145
    masculine bloodlines 136
    and whiteness 5
to-be-looked-at-ness 51
torture and torturers 67–8, 69, 70
tragedy *see* Jacobean tragedy
Tragedy of Mariam, The (Cary) 55, 56, 59
Tragical Historye of Romeus and Juliet (Brooke) 96, 97, 99
Troilus and Cressida (Shakespeare) 106, 171
troubadours 46
Trump, Donald J. 2, 259
Twelfth Night court entertainments 139
Twelfth Night (Shakespeare) 51, 107
tyranny 153, 154–5, 156

universality of Shakespeare 191–2, 195, 236, 269
universities see academy
us' and race 1, 7, 18 n.13, 66, 94–5

Vaughan, Virginia 6
Venice 79–80, 81, 83

Venus and Adonis (Shakespeare) 7–8, 31–2
Virgil, *Aeneid* 138, 144, 145, 170
virgin martyrs *see* female virgin martyrs
Visconsi, Elliott 186
voices 229
    see also Black voices

Wales 143
Watson, Robert N. 71
Wayne, Valerie 45
weaponizing Shakespeare 1, 12, 191, 195
Weheliye, Alexander G. 21 n.42, 153
Weil, Simone 212
Weimann, Robert 6
White, capitalisation of 66, 74 n.4
white face 194, *203*, 204
white fragility 26 n.93, 182, 183, 186, 273 n.1, 285
white hands 105–12, 180
    as weapons 111–2
    Cleopatra, white hand of 105, 107–9
    danger of 111–12
    hands 105–6
    ownership of Cleopatra 109–11
    white self-fashioning 105–6
white ignorance 269
white melancholia and mourning 11, 14, 21 n.46, 165–6, 184
white 'normativity' 92–3
'white people' 4–8, 21 n.42, 99, 194–5, 211
'white-people-making' 1, 7, 10–11, 17 n.5
white racial superiority 107, 109–10
white rage 151, 186, 196, 254, 257, 259, 260, 261
    Boris Johnson and 257
    Merchant of Venice 254, 255, 256
white/red nexus 46–53
    early modern self-dramatization 46–7
    mercantile tropes 48
    parodies of Petrarchan conventions 48, 49, 50
    Petrarchan discourse 46–7, 48, 51, 55, 56, 58
    power, struggle for 52–3
    theatrical representations of 50
    in works of Shakespeare 48, 51–2
    see also blazon
white self-fashioning 105–6
    see also Hamlet (Shakespeare)

white skin 1, 5–7, 9–13, 31, 46–47, 52, 55, 65–74, 80, 96, 108, 131, 156, 158, 179, 181, 183, 194, 244–5, 254
  see also white hands
white subjectivity 33, 36, 156
white supremacy
  see also academy
  and anger 253, 257, 258, 259
  of Antony 109, 110, 111
  Bardolatry and 208
  classical past, uses of 137–8
  education and 236, 243, 245
  institutions and 4, 230
  Julius Caesar and 151–2, 160–1
  medieval history of 66
  proof of 213–14
  racial exceptionalism 177
  and Shakespeare studies 191, 192, 194, 195–6
white-world-making 10–11
whiteness as miraculous 6, 7, 10, 69, 283
whiteness, failure of 14, 29 36. 86. 99, 122, 131, 132, 138, 144, 186, 213, 280–1
whiteness, introduction to 4, 5, 9–11
William of Newburgh 139
Winstead, Karen A. 67
Winter's Tale, The (Shakespeare) 106–7
wives 127–8
Wriothesley, Henry, 3rd Earl of Southampton 30–1, 32
writing about Shakespeare 270–1

Yancy, George 17 n.5, 182